Mr. Bob Leonard
2442 Sugarloaf Lane
Fort Lauderdale, FL 33312-4632

FLORIDA'S BIG DIG:

THE ATLANTIC INTRACOASTAL WATERWAY FROM JACKSONVILLE TO MIAMI
1881 to 1935

William G. Crawford, Jr.

FLORIDA'S BIG DIG: THE ATLANTIC INTRACOASTAL WATERWAY FROM JACKSONVILLE TO MIAMI, 1881 TO 1935.

Published by the Florida Historical Society Press

Paperback ISBN 10: 1-886104-26-3
Paperback ISBN 13: 978-1-886104-26-6

Hard Cover ISBN 10: 1-886104-29-9
Hard Cover ISBN 13: 978-1-886104-29-7

The Florida Historical Society Press
435 Brevard Avenue
Cocoa, FL 32922
www.fhspress.org

P•R•E•S•S

TO
CLAIRE

Early Florida canal company bucket, ladder-type dredge in the Matanzas-Halifax River Cut between Saint Augustine and Daytona Beach, early 1900s. (Courtesy, Saint Augustine Historical Society)

CONTENTS

ILLUSTRATIONS

PREFACE

America's modern-day Atlantic Intracoastal Waterway comprises a series of rivers, sounds and lagoons linked by artificially dredged canals, extending almost 1,400 miles inside America's east coast from Trenton to Miami. In 1935, the U. S. Army Corps of Engineers connected the last of what were once privately owned toll canals into a continuous waterway now under federal maintenance and toll-free. Florida's portion of the waterway — almost 400 miles long — connects Jacksonville in the northern part of the state with Miami at its southern tip.

Of the estimated 2,500 mega-yachts plying the waters worldwide, south Florida's east coast serves as home port to more than 500, in addition to thousands of smaller boats and watercraft such as the ubiquitous 'jet-ski'. While many boats use at least a portion of the Florida waterway each year, some travel the entire length of the Atlantic Intracoastal Waterway from as far north as Maine every winter. Along the south Florida coast between the Intracoastal Waterway and the Atlantic Ocean lie some of the most expensive homes in all of America. Of America's 250 richest towns by median home value, nine are located in southeast Florida along the Intracoastal Waterway. Among these well-to-do enclaves are Golden Beach and Key Biscayne in Miami-Dade County; Sea Ranch Lakes in Broward County; Gulf Stream, Highland Beach, Ocean Ridge, and Palm Beach in Palm Beach County; as well as Indian River Shores in Indian River County. Jupiter Island, in Palm Beach County, with a median home value of more than $3.9 million, holds the distinction of being the most expensive town in the entire country by median home value.[1]

The impact of the waterway on the Florida east coast economy is enormous by most estimates. The waterway adds an astonishing $38.4 billion to property values along the waterway. An estimated 203,519 jobs and 6,500 businesses depend on the waterway's existence. The waterway supports the annual passage of over 1.8 million tons of cargo and 300,000 registered vessels. Personal wages derived from the waterway's industries amount to more than $6 billion yearly.[2]

---

[1]Gossage, Bobbie, "America's Richest Towns," *Worth*, June, 2001.

[2]*Florida Inland Navigation District*, "Economic Analysis of the Atlantic Intracoastal Waterway in Florida," 2001; *Florida Department of Transportation*, "Florida Intracoastal and Inland Waterway Study, Final Report," May 2003, pp. 2-1 to 2-2."; Interview with David Roach, FIND, 29 May 2006.

Some years ago the author began a study of one of the waterway's so-called "spoil" islands. After a time it became apparent that no comprehensive history of the waterway had yet been written. Who financed and built the waterway, and why? Were tolls charged to pass through the waterway's several manmade canals? When did construction begin and end? How was it built? Which parts were naturally existing and which artificially dredged? These are just a few questions one encounters in attempting to piece together an understanding of Florida's longest continuous waterway. Although existing guide books for boat owners inform the traveler of the dozens of marinas, restaurants and tourist stops along the waterway, none examines the waterway's history in any great detail. No one book tells the all-encompassing story of the waterway's beginnings and the people who built it. This book attempts to fill that void by offering a look at how this once privately owned Florida tollway came to be built and how it became the federally maintained, free public highway known today as Florida's Atlantic Intracoastal Waterway.

The story of the waterway begins at the nation's founding with fierce debates over Congress's constitutional authority to fund waterway improvements at taxpayer expense. This contentious, continuing controversy eventually would result in a fascinating compromise: the forging of federal, state, and local partnerships in the development of the nation's transportation infrastructure and the formulation of a waterway policy that promoted America's navigable rivers and streams as toll-free public highways.

Florida's part of the story begins in 1824 when the U. S. Army Corps of Engineers performed a survey for a coastal road linking Saint Augustine and Biscayne Bay and later undertook dozens of surveys for future Florida waterway projects. Fifty-eight years later, in 1882, a private company, the Florida Coast Line Canal and Transportation Company, began dredging what would become known as the Florida East Coast Canal from Jacksonville to Miami. In 1929, the Corps of Engineers assumed control over the waterway. But well before the federal takeover, there were toll chains – as many as six of them—stretched taut across the old East Coast Canal from Jacksonville to Miami, requiring marine traffic to pay tolls to the privately owned canal company at each chain before passing through to the next.

While a great deal has been said and written about Henry Flagler's contribution to the development of Florida's east coast, almost nothing has been written about the Florida promoters who began the building of Florida's

Atlantic Intracoastal Waterway in 1881. Headed by Dr. John Westcott, a group of prominent Saint Augustine entrepreneurs formed the Florida Coast Line Canal and Transportation Company to dredge an inland waterway linking numerous east coast rivers, sounds and lagoons from Jacksonville to Biscayne Bay. For its efforts in dredging the waterway, the canal company collected tolls and received large tracts of land from the state's vast reserve of undeveloped public land lying along the Florida east coast. Although the toll collections never amounted to much, the land grants did. In fact, for dredging 268 miles of waterway, the canal company earned more than a million acres of Florida public land—only about three percent of the state's total land area—but valuable acreage, choice land lying east of the inhospitable Everglades along the high Atlantic coastal ridge extending south from Saint Augustine to Miami.

It was this Florida land that attracted a group of wealthy New Englanders to invest in the Saint Augustine canal company when local sources of capital ran dry. George Bradley of Pomfret, Conn., first treasurer of the Bell Telephone Company, led the group in financing the waterway's construction and even headed the company from 1899 until his tragic death in 1906. Bradley's estate would continue to finance construction until the waterway's completion and sale. With the proceeds of the sale, Bradley's estate would open in 1931 what would become the Emma Pendleton Bradley Hospital in East Providence, Rhode Island, the first hospital in the country devoted exclusively to treating children with mental illness, in memory of Bradley's only child. A colleague of Bradley, Albert Sawyer of Newburyport, Mass., also an early Bell Telephone promoter, formed the Boston and Florida Atlantic Coast Land Company—an enterprise associated with the Florida canal company—to buy 100,000 acres of the company's land grant for a dollar an acre, providing much-needed liquidity for dredging operations in the early years. Another early investor, one well hidden from the public, was Sir Sandford Fleming, formerly chief engineer of the Canadian Pacific Railway, designer of Canada's first adhesive postage stamp, and an early leader in the worldwide movement to adopt standard time zones.

For a brief time, a shortage of cash forced the New Englanders to turn to the man building Florida's first railway linking Jacksonville to Miami—Henry Flagler—as a new source of capital for dredging operations. After the Florida canal company agreed to share some of its south Florida land grant with the railroad magnate for the extension of the Florida East Coast Railway to Miami, Flagler headed the company for three years and contributed some cash. When the railway finally reached Miami in 1896, Flagler resigned as president and began to liquidate his small stake in the enterprise. The railroad magnate's real estate holdings remained, nonetheless, inextricably linked to the canal company's state-awarded land grant. For at least the next 30 years, Flagler and the Florida canal company jointly marketed — and in some cases, jointly developed — their immense south Florida land-grant holdings.

During the early 1900s, national attention focused on the possibility of connecting a half-dozen or so privately owned toll canals along the Atlantic Coast from Maine to Florida, including the Florida canal company's waterway, to create a toll-free, federally controlled, continuous intracoastal waterway. More than 35 citizens groups, including the Atlantic Deeper Waterways Association, lobbied Congress for inland waterway improvements throughout America. Something like a waterway renaissance occurred, spurring new waterway activity.

Very little has been written about this early twentieth-century national waterway phenomenon. Noteworthy are Harold G. Moulton's somewhat polemical study *Waterways Versus Railways* (Boston, 1912); William R. Willoughby's work on the St. Lawrence Waterway, *The St. Lawrence Waterway: A Study in Politics and Diplomacy* (Madison, 1961); and Ralph D. Gray's examination of the Chesapeake and Delaware Canal, *The National Waterway* (Chicago, 1989). Each work, to some extent, explores the importance of the waterway movement that prodded Congress into spending millions of dollars to improve the nation's inland waterways.

Joining the national movement, Florida groups along the Atlantic coast like the Florida East Coast Canal Association assembled as early as 1913 for waterway improvements and a federal takeover of the Florida canal company's waterway. Most important of these groups was the Association of Chambers of Commerce of the Florida East Coast headed by Charles Burgman of Daytona Beach. Here, too, little has been written about the people and events that shaped the Florida chamber movement to secure a federal takeover of the waterway. Spurred on by Burgman's chamber group, Florida legislators created the Florida Inland Navigation District in 1927 to purchase the privately owned toll way — the Florida East Coast Canal — for turnover to the U. S. Army Corps of Engineers for improvements and future maintenance. Many of the early chamber enthusiasts such as Fort Lauderdale's Commodore Avylen Brook, Vero Beach State Senator Anthony Young, and Stuart pioneer Stanley Kitching became members of the district's first board of commissioners, along with Burgman who presided over the group.

By 1935, with the Army engineers' completion of the last inland waterway improvements, the old privately owned Florida east coast toll way had become the southernmost link in the modern-day Atlantic Intracoastal Waterway, extending from Trenton to Miami.

This book is the story of people of vision and courage, of a small group of prominent Saint Augustine investors who conceived of the Florida waterway and began the first dredging work; of an obscure group of New England capitalists who provided significant financing and obtained a million acres of undeveloped Florida public land in pursuing what was, at best, a speculative enterprise; of innumerable citizen groups like the Florida east coast chamber associations and the larger Atlantic Deeper Waterways Association that demanded at the turn of the last century what they believed was the people's right—a public waterway, free of the burden of tolls; and finally, of the U. S. Army Corps of Engineers, who conducted all of the Florida waterway's early surveys and assumed the project's control in 1929 to convert what was once a private toll way into Florida's modern-day, toll-free Atlantic Intracoastal Waterway.

ACKNOWLEDGMENTS

A comprehensive study of the history of the waterway could not have been completed without the assistance of important repositories preserving a variety of papers and materials crucial to an understanding of how Florida's Big Dig came to be built. The author consulted three Florida manuscript collections, three collections outside of Florida, and one collection in Canada.

Important to this study was the collection of the Gilbert Youngberg papers at Rollins College, Winter Park, Fla. The Youngberg papers encompass myriad files maintained by Colonel Gilbert Youngberg, chief of the U. S. Army Corps of Engineers in Florida in 1922, and later chief engineer of the Florida Inland Navigation District from 1927 until his retirement in 1958. His papers illustrate the significant role played by the Army engineers in studying the private waterway before the federal takeover in 1927 and the later work of the waterway district in acquiring the waterway and the right-of-way for turnover to the federal government for conversion into Florida's modern Atlantic Intracoastal Waterway. Just as important was the collection of Albert P. Sawyer papers at the State Library of Florida. The Sawyer papers comprise correspondence from 1892 until 1912 between and among Sawyer, president of the Boston and Florida Atlantic Coast Land Company and trustee of three Florida land trusts, Sawyer's son, Hayden, and several investors and participants in the Florida waterway's construction, including George Bradley and George Miles of Pomfret, Conn., Boston investor Fred Amory, and the Florida canal company's Washington, D. C. lawyer, Sam Maddox.

A third collection—the A. M. Taylor Papers at the Library of Florida History in Cocoa, Florida—includes the correspondence and papers of Abram Morris Taylor, a Saint Augustine state senator and member of the first board of commissioners of the Florida Inland Navigation District from its inception in 1927 until his death in 1945. The Taylor papers include rare early documents providing details on the district's formation, including board minutes and appraisal studies of the Florida waterway as well as correspondence and documents illuminating the critical role played by the Association of Chambers of Commerce of the East Coast of Florida in the District's purchase of the waterway for turnover to the federal government for improvement and future maintenance.

Brown University's John Hay Library maintains the papers of Elmer Lawrence Corthell (1840-1916), the acclaimed Chicago railway and waterway engineer. In 1889, Corthell performed an important early survey for what would become Florida's Atlantic Intracoastal Waterway. The Hay Library houses the only known copy of this survey. The Tulane University Library maintains many important inland waterway association materials and publications of significant historical value and of regional and national importance from the first issue of the *Bulletin of the Mississippi to Atlantic Inland Waterway Association* (1911) to publications of the National Rivers and Harbors Congress.

Another important collection consulted was the Joseph Hampton Moore papers at the Historical Society of Pennsylvania. Moore, a Pennsylvania congressman, founded the Atlantic Deeper Waterways Association and headed the group from its birth in 1907 until 1948. Moore justifiably may be called the "father" of the modern-day Atlantic Intracoastal Waterway. Among the group's members were congressmen and senators representing 15 Atlantic coastal states from Maine to Florida as well as members of local boards of trade and chambers of commerce who united under Moore's leadership to lobby Congress to finance inland waterway improvements on a massive scale along the Atlantic coast, connecting what were once separately controlled and often privately owned canals into America's modern-day Atlantic Intracoastal Waterway from Trenton to Miami.

Housed at Trent University's Archives, Peterborough, Ontario, Canada, the Hall, the Gillespie Papers include correspondence between and among acclaimed Canadian railway engineer Sir Sandford Fleming, Sandford H. Fleming (Sandford's son), legal representatives for three Canadian contractors and engineers, and the New England group of investors who controlled the company that built the Florida waterway. In the early 1880s, Sandford H. Fleming and three Canadian entrepreneurs formed an early joint venture to build a portion of the Florida waterway and later became investors in the project. Correspondence from December 1911 until July 1920 document efforts by the Canadians to press the New England group controlling the waterway and the Boston & Florida land company for returns on their Florida investments made as early as 1892.

The author wishes to thank those who have been especially helpful in the research underlying the writing of this book: Dr. Joe Knetsch, one of Florida's foremost scholars on the history of Florida's public lands, who introduced the author to the Youngberg papers at Rollins College and the

Sawyer papers at the Florida State Archives, Tallahassee, Fla., and provided over the years a steady stream of relevant papers and primary materials of great aid and assistance; Mr. Rodney Dillon, who edited the author's first publication of a history of Florida's Atlantic Intracoastal Waterway in the Broward County Historical Commission's journal *Broward Legacy* (1997) and encouraged the writing of this book; Dr. Paul George, historian at the Historical Association of Southern Florida, whose *Tequesta* journal for which Dr. George also serves as editor, published the author's first article on the Sawyer papers (2002); Professor Kathleen J. Reich, Rollins College, Archives and Special Collections; Mr. David Roach, Executive Director of the Florida Inland Navigation District, for access to the District's archives on its early history, now on CD-ROM; Mr. Charles Tingley, of the Saint Augustine Historical Society, who guided the author through the Society's archives and often sent, without asking, both materials on and early photographs of the Florida waterway; and last but not least, the author's wife, Dr. Claire M. Crawford, without whose research assistance and support this book could not have been written.

CHRONOLOGY

1643 First Atlantic intracoastal canal dug from Ipswich Bay to Gloucester Bay, Massachusetts.

1787 Northwest Ordinance establishes America's free waterways policy.

1802 Congress enacts Military Peace Establishment Act, creating military academy at West Point, the nation's first engineering school.

1808 Albert Gallatin, Jefferson's Treasury Secretary, submits Report on Roads and Canals, recommending four Atlantic intracoastal canals along Atlantic Ocean from Massachusetts to Georgia.

1818 New York begins construction of Erie Canal; completed in 1825.

1824 Florida Territorial Council recommends building east coast canal.

1824 Congress passes General Survey Act authorizing military engineers to make surveys for roads and canals; army engineer James Gadsden recommends canal at Haulover in present-day Brevard County, linking the Mosquito Lagoon to the Indian River.

1844 Army engineer Blake surveys the route of the proposed Haulover canal.

1850 Congress passes Swamp and Overflowed Lands Act authorizing the granting of what would total 22 million acres of land to new State of Florida.

1854 Army engineer Wright builds Haulover canal at Titusville, linking the Mosquito Lagoon to the Indian River.

1855 Florida Legislature creates Internal Improvement Fund to hold federally patented lands in trust.

1879 Florida Legislature authorizes granting of swamp and overflowed lands to railroad and canal companies.

1881 Florida Legislature charters Florida Coast Line Canal & Transportation Co. ("Canal Company") to dredge canals between Matanzas and Halifax rivers and between Mosquito and Indian Rivers; John Westcott becomes president.

1882 Canal Company authorized to extend waterway to Lake Worth.

1885 Jay Cooke begins to invest in Canal Company; Canal Company authorized to extend waterway to Key West.

1886 Cooke enlists Bell Telephone treasurer George Bradley to invest in Canal Company.

1888 Bradley enlists Connecticut neighbor George Miles as engineer in the Florida waterway work. Westcott dies; John Denny of Boston becomes Canal Company president.

1890 State of Florida conveys more than 345,000 acres of state land to the Canal Company for dredging 134 miles of waterway.

1892 Haupt and others advocate Army engineers' building Atlantic Intracoastal Waterway from Cape Cod to Florida for military defense and commercial purposes.

Canal Company sells land to Boston & Florida Atlantic Coast Land Company and Bradley trusts to raise funds.

Canal Company agrees to share state land grant with Flagler; Flagler agrees to extend railway to Miami.

1893 Henry Flagler becomes president of Canal Company.

1896 Flagler resigns; Miles becomes Canal Company president. Flagler railway reaches Miami.

1897 Canal Company investors form Indian River & Bay Biscayne Inland Navigation Company to operate line of steamers on the waterway.

1898 Miles's Navigation Company steamer moves munitions for U. S. Army down the Florida East Coast Canal during the Spanish-American War.

1899 George Bradley succeeds George Miles as Canal Company president.

1903 Canal Company completes 300-mile waterway between Ormond Beach and Miami; Matanzas-Halifax canal still unfinished. A. P. Sawyer dies.

New York residents vote to spend $101 million to improve Erie Canal.

1904 State of Florida freezes land grants, orders Canal Company to return land. Flurry of litigation begins.

1906 George Bradley dies; Bradley's will assures Florida waterway's completion and establishes Emma Pendleton Bradley Hospital, the nation's first psychiatric hospital for children.

St. Louis Convention and National Rivers and Harbors Congress meetings at Washington, D.C., spur national movement for inland waterway improvement.

1907 Canal Company and State of Florida settle lawsuits.

Pennsylvania congressman J. Hampton Moore forms Atlantic Deeper Waterways Association to lobby Congress for Atlantic Intracoastal Waterway from Maine to Florida.

1908 Moore and Small introduce resolutions in U. S. House of Representatives for the first Atlantic Intracoastal Waterway survey from Boston to Key West.

1910 Flagler sues Canal Company for additional land grants.

1912 State makes last of land grants to Canal Company totaling 1,030,128 acres of public land for dredging 268 miles of waterway in November.

1913 Florida East Coast Canal Association formed to demand turnover of the Florida East Coast Canal to the federal government in November.

1922 U. S. Army Corps of Engineers holds four hearings in cities and towns along the Florida east coast to survey need for federal takeover of the privately owned East Coast Canal.

Daytona Beach real estate developer Charles Burgman revitalizes Florida east coast chamber association to press federal takeover efforts.

1925 Bradley estate sells Florida waterway to West Palm Beach real estate developer Harry S. Kelsey for $550,000.

1927 Congress appropriates funds for Florida East Coast Canal improvements and Cape Cod Canal purchase. Florida Legislature forms Florida Inland Navigation District to purchase waterway for turnover to federal government. A district bond issue finances the waterway's purchase for $725,000.

1929 Toll chains dropped. Old Florida East Coast Canal becomes toll-free federal Atlantic Intracoastal Waterway from Jacksonville to Miami.

1931 With the last proceeds of the Florida waterway's sale in hand, Bradley estate opens Emma Pendleton Bradley Hospital in East Providence, Rhode Island—the nation's first psychiatric hospital devoted exclusively to children.

1935 Atlantic Intracoastal Waterway from Trenton, N.J., to Miami, Fla., opened under Army Corps of Engineers' control.

INTRODUCTION

Public Highways, Forever Free

During America's Canal Era, between 1790 and 1860, privately owned canal companies built dozens of inland waterways as a cheap but slow means of carrying passengers and goods from town to town. All charged tolls for passage of marine traffic. Chief among them were New York's Erie Canal, the Chesapeake and Ohio Canal, and South Carolina's Santee Canal, as well as Atlantic coast inland waterways such as New Jersey's Delaware and Raritan and Virginia's Dismal Swamp canals.[1]

By 1814, the Dismal Canal Company, a privately owned venture, had already constructed a 22-mile Atlantic coast canal through the Dismal Swamp, connecting the Chesapeake Bay with Virginia's Albemarle Sound; 15 years later, Congress would pay $200,000 for some of the Dismal Swamp company's stock to aid further waterway improvements. In 1855, private efforts concentrated on the building of another waterway following a more easterly path known as the Albemarle and Chesapeake Canal, completed in 1859. The state of New York in 1817 began construction of the 363-mile Erie Canal from the Hudson River to Lake Erie, linking New York City with the Great Lakes and opening the Midwest for future development. Eight years later, the Empire State finished the waterway at a cost of $7 million, an enormous sum at the time.[2]

Even before America's independence, as early as 1643, waterway improvements had been made at private expense in digging an inland waterway from Ipswich Bay to Gloucester Bay, Mass. The cutting of a canal across Cape Cod, a link in today's Atlantic Intracoastal Waterway system, proposed as early as 1676, would not be completed until almost 250 years later in 1914 when a company headed by August Belmont built today's Cape Cod Canal. In 1755, George Washington conducted a survey for Virginia's Dismal Swamp Canal to connect the Chesapeake Bay with Albemarle Sound, another link in today's Atlantic Intracoastal Waterway

---

[1]Shallat, *Structures*, 26. See, also, Shaw, *Canals*, for an excellent comprehensive study of American canal history.

[2]U. S. Army Corps of Engineers, *Intracoastal Waterway*, Part I, 2. Ketcham, *James Madison*, 170-71, fn. 44.

system, but the canal would not be completed until 1820. Thirty years later, James Madison secured funds from the Virginia legislature to survey still another Atlantic Intracoastal Waterway link, a canal from Norfolk by way of the Elizabeth River through the Great Dismal Swamp to Albemarle Sound connecting cities and towns along the Virginia coast with those of neighboring North Carolina. In December 1813, Robert Fulton published a report on the practicality of steamboats navigating the Atlantic inland waters from Chesapeake Bay to the Saint Mary's River, near today's Jacksonville, Fla., in what was then East Florida, a distance of 1,500 miles. Fulton's report would surface time and time again in the coming decades, as advocates for a continuous inland waterway along the Atlantic coast lobbied Congress for taxpayer funds to construct what would become the Atlantic Intracoastal Waterway.[3]

Federalism

While America's earliest waterways had been built without federal aid, after a time, and only after considerable – seemingly endless – debate, persuasion, and compromise, Congress eventually injected itself into the business of building canals to move the nation's burgeoning commerce and connect a westward-expanding nation. At first, Federalists engaged in fierce battles with Republicans over the powers granted the new American government under the Constitution to improve inland waterways. As early as the 1790s, Alexander Hamilton and other Federalists argued that the new country's economic development depended on the federal government's improvement of inland waterways. The Constitution empowered Congress to finance such improvements. Congress had implied powers under the Constitution to create a national bank, a corps of civil engineers, a lighthouse board and other governmental agencies necessary to carry out the federal government's purposes. Moreover, a peacetime army possessed authority to survey inland waterways, dredge harbors for the navy, and use army experts to supervise construction of public works, as Shallat has observed.[4]

Vehemently opposed to Hamilton's expansive view of the federal government's powers, Thomas Jefferson argued that Congress had only limited

---

[3]Intracoastal Waterway: Part I, 2. Ketcham, *James Madison*, 170-71, fn. 44.
[4]Shallat, *Structures*, 118. Hull, *Origin*, 9, 119.

authority under the Constitution, lodging his famous objection to the federal government constructing even a postal road from Maine to Georgia. Jefferson viewed federally funded public transportation projects as "a source of boundless patronage." The building of public roads, the Virginian predicted, would become "a bottomless abyss of public money, a cash cow for the friends of Congress."[5]

The conflict arose out of the vigorous debates over the Constitution's adoption in 1787. Hamilton, James Madison, and John Jay wrote 85 position papers, popularly known as the Federalist Papers, exposing the inadequacies of the old Articles of Confederation and emphasizing the advantages of a new federal constitution. In Paper No. 42, Madison argued for the need to assist commerce among the states, pointing to Switzerland, Germany, and the Union of the Netherlands to illustrate what he foresaw as the "necessity of a superintending authority over the reciprocal trade of confederated States." Swiss law required each canton to "allow merchandise a passage through its jurisdiction into other cantons, without an augmentation of tolls," while German law prohibited "princes and states" from imposing "tolls or customs on bridges, rivers, or passages, without the consent of the emperor <u>and the diet</u>." Netherlands law, the Virginian added, restrained "members" from imposing tolls "disadvantageous to their neighbors, without the general permission." America's new Constitution would follow these traditions, vesting exclusive jurisdiction in Congress over the "power to regulate commerce among the several states," a principle soon to become a dominating force in the creation of a national free-waterways policy. The new Constitution would remedy a fundamental omission in the old Articles of Confederation that allowed the states to impose their own tolls and duties on the ever-increasing commerce among them.[6]

Three delegates attending the Constitutional Convention at Philadelphia in 1787 introduced a measure to authorize Congress to build waterways at taxpayer expense. Madison joined Benjamin Franklin and James Wilson in the proposal, but the motion was defeated. For the next several decades, this explicit rejection of express authority would profoundly affect proposed improvements in the nation's inland waterways, creating serious doubts over whether Congress possessed the power—even implicitly—to build waterways at public expense. True to his belief that the federal gov-

---

[5]Hull, *Origin*, 9, 119.

[6]Lodge, editor, *Federalist*.

ernment lacked the power to construct waterways, Madison would veto a bill to finance internal improvements, including inland waterways, almost 30 years later as his last act as president. Insisting that Congress lacked authority to fund such projects without a constitutional amendment, Madison formally advised legislators in his veto message that "such a power is not expressly given by the Constitution" and could not be "deduced from any part of it without an inadmissible latitude of construction and reliance on insufficient precedents."[7]

A Free Waterways Policy

Public support for building inland waterways at taxpayers' expense would eventually grow despite Anti-Federalist reservations. Congress began formulating a twofold waterways policy that at once declared the nation's inland waterways "public highways" and abolished tolls on federally controlled waterways. So deep had been the roots of these policies, they had taken hold even before the Constitution's ratification by the states. As far back as 1787, the Continental Congress passed the Northwest Ordinance governing the territory north of the Ohio River and east of the Mississippi River, comprising present-day Ohio, Indiana, Illinois, Michigan, Wisconsin and part of today's Minnesota. Article Four of the law mandated that "the navigable waters leading into the Mississippi and St. Lawrence" rivers and "the carrying places between them" were to be "common highways and forever free," without "any tax, impost or duty therefor." The measure gave birth to what justifiably may be called the nation's first "free waterways" policy. The scheme promoted both the public's unfettered right to use inland waterways and the elimination of tolls. The policy later led to the incorporation of free-waterways language in the constitutions of many states admitted into the Union after 1790 and the inclusion of similar provisions in federal enabling acts admitting several new states. In legislation regulating public lands in the newly acquired Territory of Florida, Congress declared as early as 1823 that "all the navigable rivers and waters in the districts of East and West Florida shall be, and forever remain, public highways." Today the public highways doctrine remains an integral part of federal law. By an act of Congress, all navigable rivers within the public lands of all states are to "remain and be deemed public highways." As

---

[7]Ketcham, *James Madison*, 226-27. *Compilation*, II, 569-70.

recently as 1981, the United States Supreme Court reaffirmed the principle in a dispute between the state of Montana and the Crow Tribe of Indians over certain rights to the bed of the Big Horn River.[8]

Early Florida

A few years after the creation of the Territory of Florida in 1821, the Florida territorial council, the domain's legislative body, began authorizing several private companies to construct inland waterway projects inside Florida's Atlantic coast. In 1828, council members incorporated the Indian River Navigation Company to open canals for steamboat navigation inside Florida's east coast from today's Jacksonville on the Saint Johns River south to Saint Augustine. Three years later, the council chartered the Planters and Citizens' Canal Company to construct a canal south of Saint Augustine to connect the Matanzas and the Halifax rivers. And in 1837, council members authorized the East and South Florida canal company to undertake another inland waterway project. To raise capital for inland waterway construction, council members even permitted companies to conduct lotteries. While many in number, these early Florida canal projects largely failed to produce lasting results.[9]

Opponents in Congress initially resistant to waterway construction at federal expense eventually saw wisdom in offering at least some assistance to canal building. Inside the Mid-Atlantic coast, a private company opened a toll canal in 1829 between the Chesapeake and Delaware bays, a link in the future Atlantic Intracoastal Waterway system. The federal government contributed $450,000 toward the total cost of $2,250,000. At the same time, while President Andrew Jackson espoused the benefits of federal aid to internal improvements in his first message to Congress, he nonetheless declined to use the power given him under the General Survey Act to order

---

[8]*United States Statutes at Large*, Vol. 1, Statute I, ch. VIII, August 7, 1789; and ch. 29, Sec. 9, I Stat 468, May 18, 1796; Hull, *Origin*, 1-8; *United States Statutes at Large*, ch. 29, Sec. 12, II Stat 754, March 3, 1823; Title 43, U.S.C.A. Sec. 931 and scores of annotated cases cited thereunder, including *Montana vs. United States*, 450 U.S. 544, 101 S.Ct. 1245 (1981).

[9]"An Act to open a Steam boat passage near to the Atlantic coast," *Acts of the Legislative Council of the Territory of Florida, 7th session, 1828.* "An Act to incorporate the Planters and Citizens' canal company, in the Eastern district of Florida," *Acts of the Legislative Council of the Territory of Florida, 8th session, 1831.* Blake, *Land into Water*, 31, citing Acts of 1837, 12 February 1837. Martin, *Florida*, 132-33, 136-37.

surveys of proposed roads and canals. Not even surveys before actual construction could be conducted at federal taxpayer expense.[10]

Although Congress refused to fund inland waterway projects directly with federal taxpayer money, between 1825 and 1830 legislators indirectly supported them by authorizing spending more than $1.5 million to purchase stock in several canal construction companies. In 1824, government officials began granting public lands to several states, including Alabama, Ohio, Indiana, Illinois, Michigan, and Wisconsin to aid waterway construction. Ultimately, Congress would grant more than 4.5 million acres of federal lands for the construction of inland waterways. These early land grants would establish the federal government's policy of granting alternate sections of land to encourage building both waterways and railways, making government a partner in private efforts to develop the nation's transportation infrastructure. Later, the newly born, cash-strapped state of Florida would adopt a similar policy of granting alternate sections of public land to encourage private development of the state's railroads and inland waterways.[11]

From 1823 until Congress stopped the practice in 1838 with the repeal of the General Survey Act, the U. S. Army even loaned engineers to both private and state-financed canal construction projects underway in several states, arguing that great benefits would accrue to the country in assisting such efforts. Congress also began pursuing a policy of providing large-scale government assistance to the nation's railroads, a movement that by the 1850s would seriously hamper the development of America's inland waterways. Some federal aid included purchasing railway company stock, although Congress largely supported railway expansion by making massive land grants for construction .[12]

The growing need for more means of transportation eventually led to the formation of citizen groups to lobby Congress to fund inland waterway construction. In 1846, the first of a series of national waterway conventions took place at Memphis. Presided over by South Carolina's Senator John Calhoun, the convocation supported federal public works designed to promote the shipping of western products through southern port cities. Legis-

---

[10]U. S. Army Corps of Engineers, *Intracoastal Waterway, Part I*, 2. Hull, Origin, 15.

[11]Thompson, "Ups and Downs of Waterways," 9; Association of American Railroads, *Economic Survey*, 33. See, also, Rae, "Federal Land Grants," 167-77. Hill, *Roads*, 30, 68, 87, 90; Parkman, *History*, 104.

[12]Hull, *Origin*, 18.

lation encouraging waterway improvements passed Congress, but President Polk vetoed it, again reflecting the reluctance of many to aid inland waterways at federal expense. The following year, scores of delegates from 19 states, including large delegations from the Midwest and Northeast, attended a second convention, this time at Chicago, with representatives from the northern states present to turn away the South's requests for southern port aid. Florida's lone delegate was John G. Camp, United States Marshal for Middle Florida. One of the adopted resolutions made the rather legalistic argument that because the federal government asserted jurisdiction over navigable rivers and lakes to collect taxes and regulate steamboats, it also had the power, by implication, to use public money to improve inland waterways, "If it [the federal government] has power to control and restrain," the resolution urged, "it must have the same power to protect, assist and facilitate." Writing delegates from his Marshfield farm that ill health prevented his attending the meeting, Massachusetts U. S. Sen. Daniel Webster contended that Congress had the power to improve inland waterways at taxpayer expense. "Of the power of the Government to make appropriations for erecting harbors and clearing rivers, I never entertained a particle of doubt," the great defender of the Constitution declared, adding that Congress's power in promoting such internal improvements was not "partial, limited, obscure, applicable to some uses and not applicable to others, to some States and not to others." In the coming decades, still more assemblies, with even larger delegations, would take over where these two waterway conventions left off, promoting scores of inland waterway improvements, ranging from projects in the Northwest's Columbia River to improvements in the Mississippi River to the creation of the Atlantic Intracoastal Waterway stretching from Maine to Florida. In the meantime, in the early years, new states like Florida would struggle to build a much-needed transportation network, with little or no cash to pay for the difficult and costly work that lay ahead.[13]

---

[13]Remini, *Daniel Webster*, 635; Rivers and Harbors, 41; Webster to Convention, 26 June 1847, Rivers and Harbors, 45-46.

Chapter 1

WESTCOTT'S DREAM

Three years after America's acquisition of the Florida territory from Spain, U. S. Army engineers still laboring under Congressional restraints against funding transportation projects surveyed a potential route for a coastal road along Florida's Atlantic coast, a project that would eventually lead to the Army's first inland waterway project on the east coast. In 1824, James Gadsden, the Army's first chief engineer in the territory, surveyed the coast to determine the possibility of building a military road south to the tip of the peninsula at Cape Florida. His report rejected a road but endorsed constructing a waterway at the Haulover—opposite what is now Titusville, near today's Kennedy Space Center—to connect the Mosquito Lagoon with the Indian River, an important link in Florida's modern Atlantic Intracoastal Waterway. Two years later, residents of St. Augustine, Matanzas, and Tomoka in the northeastern part of the Florida territory petitioned Congress to change the plan to make New Smyrna the southernmost end of the military road while also asking that remaining funds be used to build another waterway linking the Matanzas and Halifax rivers—a connection that in time would become another important link in Florida's Intracoastal Waterway. But Congress appropriated only enough money to dredge from Georgia's Cumberland Sound south to Florida's St. Johns River.[1]

Thirteen years after the Gadsden study, Congress authorized a survey of another link in today's Atlantic Intracoastal Waterway—the stretch between the southern end of the Dismal Swamp Canal, in North Carolina, and Winyah Bay, in South Carolina. During the two-year period ending in 1838, Congress appropriated funds for the removal of a shoal inside the Atlantic coast in the New River running through North Carolina. Some years later, in the Florida territory, a year after the Second Seminole War's end, Quartermaster General Thomas Jesup emphasized the importance of constructing an inland waterway along the east coast. "The difficulties which I

---

[1]Buker, *Sun*, 113.

experienced when directing the operations against the Seminoles in the campaign of 1837-8 in supplying the division of the Army operating south of the Haulover," he wrote, "enable me to speak with positive certainty as to the necessity of improving the inland communications from St. Augustine to Key Biscayne." A few months later in January 1844, Jesup repeated his plea for a waterway, urging that defense of Florida's Atlantic coast would be "greatly facilitated" and that navigation along that coast had been more dangerous than along any other portion of the Atlantic coast. A waterway connecting the Matanzas and Halifax rivers could be constructed at comparatively little cost, Jesup argued, adding that a short canal to the south connecting the Mosquito Lagoon and the Indian River could be opened with no more than two locks. South along the Indian River to Jupiter Inlet, no more than the removal of a few oyster shoals would be required to make that section of the waterway navigable. South of Jupiter Bay, through Boca Raton sound (lake), the Hillsboro Inlet, farther along to the New River Inlet, and then finally on to Biscayne Bay, the work would require only ten miles of dredging, an astounding underestimation of the work that lay ahead. Unfortunately, the Army failed to take action on any of Jesup's recommendations.[2]

Other engineers moved forward with plans for improvements even though no government money could be found to fund them. Former Army engineer First Lieutenant Jacob Edward Blake conducted another survey of the Haulover between the Mosquito Lagoon and the Indian River. Blake recommended the building of a canal 725 yards long to connect the two bodies of water. To construct the waterway, he specified that eight-inch-square, 12-foot-long poles be driven twelve feet apart and that two-inch planks be riveted to the poles to strengthen the structure. The canal bottom should be covered with two-inch planks to "render the whole free from liability to fill up & [make] the canal at all times passable." Although Congress appropriated $1,500 to cut the canal, the work would not begin until 10 years later.[3]

Horatio Governeur Wright

---

[2]*Ibid.*, 114-15; Carter, editor, *Territorial Papers* 26 (Florida), 830-33. ACE, *Intracoastal Waterway*, 8.

[3]Buker, *Sun*, 116-17. See, also, Knetsch, "Steps Toward the Intracoastal Waterway," 27; Worth to Aber, 10 November 1843, 780, and Blake to Worth, 11 December 1843, 803, in Carter, editor, *Territorial Papers* 26 (Florida).

Despite Congress's delay in funding inland waterway improvements, others outside the Army Corps of Engineers pushed for construction of an inland waterway from St. Augustine south to the tip of the Florida peninsula. In 1851, early Tampa Bay pioneer John Darling, a member of Florida's first Board of Internal Improvements, proposed not only the draining of the Everglades but also "the construction of a Canal, to connect the inland waters and form an Inland Water Communication from Cape Florida along the Atlantic Coast to St. Augustine." Three years later, just before the beginning of the Third Seminole War, the first real improvement in the inland waterways along the Florida coast materialized. Thirty-four-year-old Lieutenant Horatio Governeur Wright, chief engineer in Florida from 1852 until 1854, began constructing a waterway at the Haulover between the Mosquito Lagoon and the Indian River twelve feet wide and two feet deep. Wright possessed a sterling background for the task. He had graduated second in his class at West Point in 1841. The following year, he was made an assistant professor of French at the academy, and sometime later, a professor of engineering. In 1848, the Army promoted him to the rank of first lieutenant and placed him in charge of building forts and improvements in Florida. Following the construction of the Haulover Canal, Wright would later serve as a distinguished brevetted general on the Union side during the Civil War.[4]

The Civil War And Its Aftermath

The Civil War devastated Florida's economy, leaving the state nearly destitute and with little means of transportation. The Union blockade of the Florida coast stopped all efforts to construct a continuous waterway. And because of a lack of maintenance, Wright's Haulover Canal grew congested and nearly impassable. After the war, in 1867, to foster east coast development but without funds to provide incentives, Florida officials began granting public land to encourage private companies to build waterways and railways throughout the state, but these early efforts bore little if any fruit.

---

[4]Darling to Brown, 6 May 1851, Florida Department of State, Division of Archives and Records Service, Series 755, Carton 2, cited in Knetsch, "John Darling," 13. Buker, *Sun*, 116. For a biographical background on Wright, see, Wilson, editor, *Appleton's Cylopaedia*; Warner, *Generals in Blue*, 575-76; and U. S. Army Corps of Engineers, *Army Register for January, 1884*, 36.

State officials sold 250,000 acres of public land at five cents an acre to the Florida Canal and Inland Transportation Company to construct a waterway from the Amelia River south to Jupiter Inlet, using the St. Johns River and other natural streams wherever possible, but the company never finished the project. A year later, state legislators chartered five canal companies, including the Southern Inland Navigation Company headed by William Gleason, to create inland waterways. State officials deeded almost 1.4 million acres of public land to Gleason's company until a federal judge voided the transfer. By 1878, long neglected and with no maintenance funds available, Wright's Haulover canal admitted boats only as wide as 11 feet and drawing no more than a foot and a half of water.[5]

Federal officials soon began improving the nation's inland waterways, with the hope that waterway transportation, in competition with the railroad, might reduce already high railway rates. In December 1873, in his annual message to Congress, President Ulysses S. Grant expressed dissatisfaction with excessive rail rates and the "lack of cheap transportation," urging appropriations for river and harbor improvements. Less than three years later, Grant signed into law a rivers and harbors appropriations bill to finance waterway improvements, and, in 1882, Congress passed its first $10 million bill for river and harbor improvements.[6]

Meanwhile, in the 1870s, Florida legislators passed two laws to encourage the incorporation of private railroad and inland waterway companies and the creation of a transportation infrastructure. In 1874, Florida legislators authorized the incorporation of railroad and canal companies by private individuals. Five years later, state law makers changed the state's corporation act to authorize the state's conveyance of alternate sections of state lands to railroad and canal companies for constructing rail and water ways. The legislation permitted state officials to convey public land a distance of six miles on either side of a proposed railroad or waterway upon completing a six-mile section, a grant of roughly 3,840 acres for every mile of rail laid or waterway dredged. In Washington, Florida's first black congressman, Josiah Walls, promoted the construction of a continuous Florida east coast inland waterway in a speech on the floor of the House. Pushing first for the building of a cross-Florida canal, Walls also foresaw the need for an east coast inside passage extending from the St. Johns River south to Key

---

[5]Buker, *Sun*, 116-17. *MIIF*, 9 April 1867; also cited in Shofner, *Nor Is It Over*, 118. Blake, *Land*, 45, 47; Davis, *Civil War*, 671-72.

[6]Hull, *Origin*, 24, 25.

West by way of the Matanzas, Halifax and Indian Rivers, Lake Worth, to the New River, ending at Biscayne Bay. Federal officials paid some attention to Florida, starting construction of a channel eleven feet deep and eighty feet wide between the St. Johns River and the Nassau Inlet in the northern part of the Florida peninsula.[7]

By 1880, Florida's population had grown to 269,493 — a decidedly small figure by northern standards — but a substantial increase (43.5%) over the census a decade before. Comprising more than thirty-four million acres, Florida remained a vast, mostly undeveloped and largely unpopulated land. This was particularly true in the southern part, where no rail or inland waterway facilities existed at all. Even though the federal government had begun surveying the state in 1824, the Everglades below Lake Okeechobee would remain unsurveyed and a generally unknown region until the early 1900s brought state surveying crews to the "River of Grass" for the first time. The geographical limits of what was then Dade County in the southeastern part of the state encompassed 7,200 square miles, stretching from the Jupiter Inlet to the southern tip of the Florida peninsula. Including land now within present-day Palm Beach, Broward and Miami-Dade counties, Dade County was home to just 257 settlers despite its immense size. The federal Census of Agriculture described Dade County's uncertain geography as a "[w]oodland, a strip along the coast and in the northern part of the county, about 500 square miles; of the rest, everglades, marsh, prairie, savanna, and swamp, it is impossible to give a trustworthy estimate of the proportions." According to the census, not a single acre under cultivation was to be found anywhere in the area.[8]

Quincy Adams Gillmore

Even without long-needed improvements, three steamboats made the Indian River run from Titusville south to Jupiter while other vessels made local runs south through the Mosquito Lagoon and down the Halifax River to New Smyrna and Melbourne. Although these runs occurred with some regularity, these stretches proved practically impassable for most boat traf-

---

[7]Act of Legislature of Florida, February 19, 1874. *Speech of Hon. Josiah T. Walls, M. C. of Florida before the Transportation Committee of the United States Senate.* January 28, 1874. Advocating the Construction of a Ship Canal through the Peninsula of Florida. *Intracoastal Waterway, 1948,* 2. Act of Legislature of Florida, 12 March 1879.

[8]U. S. *Census of Agriculture* (1880), 62.

fic without further deepening. Lieutenant Colonel Quincy Adams Gillmore, chief Army engineer in Florida from 1869 to 1884, sent an assistant, J. Francis LeBaron, to survey and report on the condition of Wright's Haulover canal at Titusville. Born in Lorain County, Ohio, in 1825, Gillmore graduated at the top of West Point's Class of 1849 and served with distinction as a Union general during the Civil War. During his tenure as Florida's chief engineer, he supervised a wide array of important projects designed to enhance navigation, including the improving of the St. Johns River Bar, the Upper St. Johns River, and the Volusia Bar. Gillmore also conducted surveys of the St. Augustine Harbor, the Mosquito (now Ponce) Inlet, and studies of proposed inland waterways along the Atlantic coast from the St. Johns River to the Mosquito Lagoon, from the Indian River to Jupiter Inlet, and farther south to Lake Worth.[9]

In August 1881, Le Baron found that a private company some time before had re-dug Wright's old Haulover Canal at Titusville to accommodate boats with an 11-foot width and 16-to-18-inch drafts. Lined with treacherous coquina banks on both sides, the slender waterway provided a small passageway with an average width of only eight feet and a depth of just 24 inches. Le Baron recommended an enlarged canal with a bottom width of 60 feet and a depth of four and a half feet at an estimated cost of $66,000. Such a waterway, he believed, would benefit a 160-mile strip of Florida east coast land stretching from the Haulover Canal south to Lake Worth, supporting a growing population of 1,600 in the area. Agricultural production appeared impressive. There, 87,000 orange trees grew in 240 groves, along with 220,000 pineapples and 120,000 bananas. At Lake Worth, 12,000 coconut palm trees grew in twenty groves. Although some produce had been transported through the small channel, the overwhelming amount had been hauled over land from Titusville west to Salt Lake Landing or from Rockledge on the coast to Lake Poinsett Landing, and then by steamboat up the St. Johns River to Jacksonville, spending at least 50 hours in transit. Settlers expected to ship 75,000 pineapples from Lake Worth that year. Indian River boat traffic consisted largely of sailboats, sloops, and small schooners from

---

[9]Dovell, *Florida*, II, 612. Shallat, *Structures*, 102, Appendix A. For biographical background on Gillmore, see, Wilson, *Appleton's Cyclopaedia*; Warner, *Generals in Blue*, 176-77; and, *Army Register for January, 1884*, Corps of Engineers, 36. See Gillmore's report of November 3, 1884, in *Annual Report of Chief of Engineers, 1884*, 1291, for his preliminary examination of a proposed canal route from St. Johns River to Jupiter Inlet and Lake Worth, via the Mosquito Lagoon and the Indian River.

forty to forty-five feet long and ten to fourteen feet wide. Unable to pass through the old Haulover passage, a vessel loaded with freight made the trip outside the canal along the coast from Jacksonville to the old Indian River Inlet. While mail carried on sailboats from St. Augustine to Daytona made it through the old cut, the restricted passageway delayed delivery considerably. Gillmore recommended improvements to his superior, Horatio Wright, the builder of the first Haulover Canal and now a brigadier general and chief of Army engineers, but despite Gillmore's endorsement, improvements in the cut would have to wait a few more years.[10]

Swamp Lands Mean Transportation

Foremost among the factors that would affect Florida's future development was the federal government's possession of over twenty million acres of what was described as "swamp" land, nearly two-thirds of the state's land area. In the years following Spain's cession of the Floridas to the United States in 1821, the federal government held most of the land, including swamp land, in trust for the new Territory of Florida until its admission to statehood in 1845. In 1826, Congress began studying the wet, marshy, and inundated public lands within Missouri and Illinois. Members made several unsuccessful attempts to cede swamp lands to those states to encourage drainage and other improvements. Twenty-three years later, however, in 1849, Congress granted the State of Louisiana all swamp lands within its borders because of the state's efforts in draining the lands. Under an act of Congress approved the next year, the federal government began to grant the five-year-old state of Florida millions of acres of swamp lands to encourage internal improvements such as drainage and reclamation.[11]

Florida's Public Lands

In 1855, a year after Wright's construction of the first Haulover canal, Florida legislators created the Internal Improvement Fund to hold title to the state's federally granted swamp lands. Title to the land vested in the gover-

---

[10]Sen. Ex. Doc. No. 33, 47th Cong., 1st Session., Letter from the Secretary of War transmitting copy of report from Lieutenant Colonel Q. A. Gillmore, Corps of Engineers, upon a survey of Indian River, Florida, with a view to opening a passage to the Mosquito Lagoon, by way of the Haulover, January 4, 1882.

[11]Hibbard, *History*, 269-70. *U. S. Statutes at Large*, volume 9, 519.

nor and four other cabinet members as trustees of the Internal Improvement
Fund. The fund was to be used to encourage drainage and other internal
improvements and foster settlement and cultivation of state-owned lands.[12]

At the outset, Florida trustees reportedly made plans for private companies to build two railway lines and an inland waterway. The two rail lines
were to connect Jacksonville on the Atlantic Ocean with Pensacola on the
Gulf of Mexico and Amelia Island on the Atlantic with Tampa Bay on the
Gulf. Near the intersection of the two routes, the two lines were to connect
via a branch of the Savannah, Albany and Gulf Railroad to the major Atlantic seaboard lines heading north. A 14-mile-long waterway was to link centrally-located Lake Harney, which was connected to the St. Johns River, to
the Indian River, and then run south along the Atlantic coast, to provide
water transportation between Jacksonville via the St. Johns River and the
lower east coast. To aid the waterway project, trustees planned to provide
$4,000 in cash and 4,000 acres of land for every mile of waterway dredged.
To assist the two railway projects, state trustees intended to donate half the
public lands on either side of the railway lines for a distance of six miles in
alternate sections. The state also agreed to endorse railway company bonds
at the rate of $10,000 for each mile of railway bed constructed for the pur-
chase of rail iron and engines and to pay interest on the bonds until the new
companies operated profitably.[13]

Railway and inland waterway land grants eventually struck many as con-
trary to the federal government's purpose in making conveyances strictly
for drainage and reclamation purposes. But in a landmark decision handed
down in 1878, Florida Supreme Court justices unanimously decreed that
state law permitted improvement fund trustees to grant swamp lands to the
St. Johns Railway Company for construction of a railway between Toccoi
and St. Augustine. The chief justice of the court, James D. Westcott, Jr.,
withdrew from participating in the case because his uncle, John, was president of the railway seeking the grants. Just a few years later, John, as president of the Florida Coast Line Canal and Transportation Company, would
claim thousands of acres of coastal "swamp" land for the construction of
what would become Florida's Atlantic Intracoastal Waterway. The justice
substituting for James Westcott on the court—Pleasants W. White—who
wrote the court's opinion, would later become one of the Florida canal com-

---

[12]Acts of 1855, chapter 610, *General Statutes of Florida, 1906*, sections 616, 617, and 620.

[13]"Railroads and Railroad System of Florida," *DeBow's Review* 19 (September 1855): 316-
323.

pany's lawyers whose principal assignment was to secure land grants from state trustees as John Westcott's company became entitled to land for dredging work.[14]

In February 1880, a mere 35 years after statehood, the federal government granted Florida more than two million acres of swamp lands to encourage construction of internal improvements. Within the next few decades, the federal government would grant Florida additional tracts of swamp lands totaling, in all, almost 22 million acres—approximately 58 percent of the state's total land area. But there was one small hitch. The state's agreement to endorse the old railway bonds had thrown the state's Internal Improvement Fund into federal receivership and frozen the transfer of state lands because of railway bond defaults. In 1881, however, the state trustees' sale of four million acres of swamp land to Hamilton Disston, a wealthy Philadelphia saw manufacturer, for a million dollars resolved the federal litigation over the fund and freed up the state's lands. State trustees began to grant millions of acres of "swamp" land to railroad and canal companies to encourage development of Florida's transportation infrastructure. After the Disston sale, during the year 1882 alone, the trustees granted an additional 10.5 million acres to stimulate Florida's growth. As a consequence, within ten years' time, the number of miles of railroad in the state would grow fivefold, from 500 miles to 2,566 miles.[15]

On March 8, 1881, Florida legislators authorized the formation of the Atlantic and Gulf Coast Canal and Okeechobee Land Company of Florida to drain a large expanse of the Everglades and develop an Atlantic intracoastal waterway. Headed by William S. Stokley, recently defeated for re-election as mayor of Philadelphia, but controlled by Hamilton Disston, the company made plans to reclaim an area of more than eight million acres of swamp land (more than a thousand square miles) by dredging canals from Lake Okeechobee to the St. Lucie and Caloosahatchee rivers, with the company to receive half of the lands reclaimed. The enterprise also intended to construct an inland waterway along Florida's Atlantic coast "suitable for commodious light-draught steamboats," from the St. Johns River south to Lake Worth. Promoters expected the waterway to afford nearly 330 miles of navigable inland waters. Although Disston's company began dredging and actually reclaimed millions of acres of swamp land—ultimately earning two

---

[14]*TIIF vs. St. Johns Railway Co.*, 16 Fla. 531 (1878).

[15]Blake, *Land*, 43, 50. Skillman, editor, *Compiled General Laws of Florida*, 40; Cutler, *History*, I, 162; Dovell, *Florida*, II, 614; Akin, "Sly Foxes," 24.

million acres of state land, the firm never embarked on construction of the inland waterway. Four enterprising St. Augustine entrepreneurs, however, would take up the work the Disston company declined to pursue.[16]

An inland waterway inside Florida's Atlantic Coast had long been the dream of seventy-four-year-old Dr. John Diament Westcott, a former surveyor general of Florida and a pioneer St. Augustine resident. Along with Henry Gaillard (Westcott's son-in-law), James Hallowes, and James Colee, Westcott incorporated the Florida Coast Line Canal and Transportation Company, the first enterprise to construct what was to become Florida's Atlantic Intracoastal Waterway. Westcott became the Florida canal company's first president; James Colee, the company's longtime engineer. A two-year-old state law entitled Westcott's firm not only to collect tolls on the waterway but also to acquire 3,840 acres of state land for each mile of waterway dredged. The four incorporators, also the company's first directors, personally contributed $100,000 to the firm's coffers. Westcott pledged nearly half of the initial capital ($49,500), while Gaillard and Hallowes each subscribed $25,000, and Colee added another $500.[17]

Dr. John Westcott

The Florida canal company's directors were a uniformly distinguished lot and the venture's 74-year-old president proved no exception. Westcott was a member of the Sons of the American Revolution as a descendant of a soldier who had fought in the War for Independence. Born in Bridgeton, New Jersey, in 1807, Westcott had been educated briefly at West Point in 1824 before leaving for health reasons. He later studied medicine in Philadelphia. In 1831, young Westcott relocated to north Florida, first becoming a clerk to his older brother, James, who was then secretary of the Florida Territory. In the ensuing years, John pursued careers as a physician, surveyor,

---

[16]*Atlantic and Gulf Coast*, 3-4. "General Telegraph News—Draining Lake Okeechobee," *New York Times*, 4 June 1881. See, also, *MIIF*, 10 April 1895, pp. 309-311, for a brief history of the formation and operation of the company given by state improvement fund trustees in response to Florida House of Representatives' resolution no. 31 requesting a report on the company.

[17]Laws of Florida (1881), c. 3327; Articles of Association (Incorporation) for Florida Coast Line Canal and Transportation Company, dated May 7, 1881, Letters Patent issued May 23, 1881, recorded June 24, 1881, Book B, Pages 214-15, Secretary of State. Bathe, *St. Johns Railroad*, 13, 56. Poor, *Manual of Railroads 1881*, 418. Westcott, at least, continued to serve as a director of the Railway until at least 1883. *Poor's Manual of Railroads, 1885*, 254.

geologist, mineralogist, and chemist. He even delivered the mail in the primitive Florida wilderness. In 1845, John's older brother James represented Florida in the U. S. Senate upon the Florida territory's admission to statehood. A year later, John represented Madison County in the state House of Representatives. From 1853 until 1858, as surveyor general of Florida, Westcott supervised government surveyors mapping out the state's public lands. Short in stature—only five feet, four inches tall—he served during the Civil War on the side of the Confederacy as captain of the Florida Partisan Rangers Infantry, and later was promoted to the rank of major. In 1879, Westcott represented St. Johns County as a member of the Florida House of Representatives. In 1885, four years after the incorporation of the canal company, he would serve as the oldest delegate to the state's Constitutional Convention. In the years ahead, Westcott's longstanding political connections would prove invaluable to the fledgling Florida canal company in its quest to obtain the massive land grants promised for constructing the Florida waterway.[18]

Dr. John D. Westcott, first president of the Florida Coast Line Canal and Transportation Company from 1881 until his death in1889, shown in Confederate uniform as Captain, Company I, 10th Florida Infantry, CSA, from a carte-de-visite. (Courtesy, The Museum of the Confederacy, Richmond, Virginia)

Twenty-seven years younger than Westcott, James Louis Colee (pronounced *Cooly*), the company's engineer, was born in 1834, in St. Johns County, the son of George A. Colee, an early Florida settler. The town of Colee in St. Johns County was named for James's brother, George. Before the Civil War, James Colee owned a lumber mill and considerable land. During the conflict, Colee, like Westcott, served on the side of the Confederacy. A stockholder in the First National Bank of St. Augustine, Colee also operated the St. Augustine Transfer Company with his son, Louis. Colee would serve as St. Johns County's state representative for four years, and as a St. Johns County commissioner for the last 12 years of his life. This 47-year-old Colee would perform surveys and a variety of other work for the Florida

James Louis Colee, an original incorporator and director of the Florida Coast Line Canal and Transportation Company. The company's longest serving employee, Colee worked as an engineer from the company's inception in 1881 until his death at Saint Augustine in 1912. (Courtesy, Donn L. Colee, Colee family collection, West Palm Beach, Florida)

waterway work as an company engineer until his death in 1912.[19]

---

[18]Glick, *Waistcote*, 133-43; *Appleton's Cylopaedia*, VI, 442, states that James Westcott "occasionally" performed the duties of governor while serving as Secretary of the Florida Territory; James's biographical sketch at *Biographical Directory*, 2036. For John Westcott, see Hammond, *Medical Profession*, 673-74; Cutler, *History*, I, 160; Hartman, *Biographical Rosters*, III, 1164; Knetsch, "Finder," 81-104; Knetsch, "Inventive," 5-17; also U. S. Military Academy, Cadet Application Papers, John D. Westcott application and related letters. Rerick, *Memoirs*, II, 157-58.

[19]"J. L. Colee, Sr., Is Taken in Death," *St. Augustine Evening Record*, 8 January 1912; Hartman, *Biographical Rosters*, II, 810; Cutler, *History of Florida*, II, 97 [listing for Louis Albert Colee]; Cutler, *History of Florida*, III, 67 [listing for Harold Wilfred Colee].

Thirty-year-old Henry Frierson Gaillard, the canal company's treasurer, was a member of a distinguished French Huguenot family whose first American ancestor, Joachim Gaillard, settled in South Carolina almost 200 years before in 1685. Of all the company's initial directors, Henry Gaillard remained an officer and director longer than any other. Born in Eutawville, South Carolina, Gaillard came to Florida as a young man, making his home at St. Augustine. In 1885, he served as both secretary and treasurer of Westcott's canal company. Eleven years later, Gaillard would serve as mayor of the town of St. Augustine. He also served as St. Augustine's postmaster and as cashier of the First National Bank. A member of the Florida senate during the 1897 and 1899 sessions, Gaillard later moved to Jacksonville where he worked as a cashier of the Commercial Bank, president of the Florida Fire and Casualty Company and served as a member of the city's board of bond trustees. Considered a man of integrity, he was once described as "slow to adopt new views, but steadfast after they are adopted." Gaillard's many political connections, like Westcott's, would serve the Florida canal company well as the enterprise sought to claim hundreds of thousands of acres of state land for its dredging work [20]

Youngest of the directors, James Mongin Hallowes possessed the longest Florida lineage. A descendant of early British East Florida pioneer Francois Philippe Fatio, the 22-year-old Hallowes was an heir to his father's interest in the New Switzerland plantation in St. Johns County, established in 1771. Born at Bolingbroke, Georgia, James was the son of Miller Hallowes, a mercenary soldier who fought with Simon Bolivar. In the 1920s, James's son, also named Miller Hallowes, became an agent for Henry Flagler's Model Land Company and the Florida canal company at Fort Pierce, managing the sale of thousands of acres of state land acquired by Flagler for building the first continuous railway and the Florida canal company for constructing what would become Florida's Atlantic Intracoastal Waterway.[21]

At first, the Florida Legislature authorized the St. Augustine canal company to dredge waterways only between the Matanzas and Halifax rivers and farther south between the Mosquito and Indian rivers for the passage of

---

[20]Gaillard, "Brief Outline"; *St. Augustine City Directory* (1885); Elliott, *Florida Encyclopedia*; St. Augustine *Tatler*, 23 January 1892, 18 January 1896; Florida House, Clerk, *People of Lawmaking*; "Henry F. Gaillard Died Yesterday in Jacksonville," *St. Augustine Evening Record*, 16 December 1922; Chapin, *Florida*, 244, 247; Goreville, *St. Johns Railroad*, 13, 56.

[21]Armstrong, *Hallowes*; Davis, "Notes on Miller Hallowes," 405-07; *Fort Pierce City Directory, 1927-1928*, ad for Fort Pierce Bank and Trust Company: Brown, "Henry Flagler," 52.

steamers and other water craft drawing three feet of water or less. In July 1881, canal directors amended the firm's articles of incorporation to authorize the waterway's extension to Lake Worth. Less than a year later, directors voted to extend the waterway all the way to Biscayne Bay. While the company began operations with only $100,000 in capital, directors later added personal funds to finance surveying and other work before the start of dredging. Meanwhile, state trustees reserved from sale approximately two square miles of public land near St. Augustine for transfer to the canal company for future dredging work. Company directors borrowed $75,000 to build a dredge and two steamers and begin dredging work. The loan, the first of many to follow, was secured by a mortgage on all of the company's assets, including public lands to be conveyed to the company. Daniel G. Ambler of Jacksonville, one of Florida's earliest private bankers, arranged the financing. An early investor in the Ambler financing was famed Civil War financier Jay Cooke, who within a few months' time would become one of the company's leading promoters outside Florida.[22]

Of the importance of the inland waterway in aiding commerce along Florida's lower east coast, John Westcott wrote, "The Canal is an immediate necessity. All the Settlers South of here on the Coast, are clamorous for the work to be commenced at once. The Halifax country is now an important point to Secure, or other improvements may be made. So it is with the Indian River Country." He had already loaned the company $2,986 for the project; the other stockholders together contributed $350. He estimated the initial construction cost at $60,000 for a small waterway 30 feet wide to

---

[22]*Laws of Florida* (1881), c. 3327; Articles of Association (Incorporation) for Florida Coast Line Canal and Transportation Company dated May 7, 1881, Letters Patent issued May 23, 1881, recorded June 24, 1881, Book B, Pages 214-15, Office of Secretary of State. Articles of Association for Florida Coast Line Canal and Transportation Company dated July 16, 1881, Letters Patent issued August 3, 1881, recorded in Book B, Pages 254-55, Office of Secretary of State. Additional Articles of Association for Florida Coast Line Canal and Transportation Company dated June 24, 1882, filed June 27, 1882, recorded August 10, 1883, in Book B, Page 440, Office of Secretary of State. *MIIF*, 8 August 1881, 29; Mortgage executed by Canal Company to D. G. Ambler, Trustee, dated August 8, 1881, recorded in the Office of the Secretary of State in unnumbered book of record covering that period of time from January 19, 1866 to March 4, 1891, at page 458 thereof, to secure a bond issue of $75,000, referred to in satisfaction or release of Mortgage entitled, "Indenture," executed by Daniel G. Ambler, Trustee, in favor of Florida Coast Line Canal and Transportation Company, on May 21, 1888, St. Augustine Historical Society, St. Johns County Court records, Civil Cases, Box 298, Folder 155. For biographical material on Ambler, see, Dovell, *History of Banking*, 61-62, 67-68; Gold, *History of Duval County*, 365-67; and Davis, *History of Jacksonville*, 478-79. Affidavit of Frank H. Swan attached to Winters to Green, 22 October 1929, FIND ADM Box 70.01.

allow passage of small steamers drawing three feet, much like those already plying the Ocklawaha and St. Johns rivers above Lake Monroe in central Florida. To improve the Indian River, Mosquito Lagoon, and Halifax River to a depth of six feet, he projected the extension of initial dredging over a distance of at least 50 miles.[23]

Apart from investing his own money in the project, the 75-year-old Westcott undertook the initial surveying work at no cost to the company. Describing the difficult conditions under which he worked, the former surveyor general of Florida observed, "I performed the work myself, and by working early & late, I have always been able to perform more work, than the generality of Surveyors or Engineers." "To get at the proper line [for the dredging of the cut]," he went on, "between Halifax & Matanzas I traversed the whole country making no less than Seven distinct levels from East to West & from N. to S. to get at the Shortest line, with the least excavation, as described to you in the Several profiles of the work done, and line adopted." With the opening of the waterway, he predicted significant transportation savings, "This coast line perfected, fruit & vegetables could be delivered from Biscayne Bay to Jacksonville in 24 hours, in Savannah 8 hours more, there to be distributed to every part of the U. S." and, perhaps foreseeing Miami's founding, thought "[a] new City will soon develop at Biscayne Bay or Barnes Sound, Larger & better than Key West, and open a New line of Commerce for our western products."[24]

In July 1882, Jay Cooke of Washington joined in the Florida waterway project, bringing the work of the canal company to the attention of potential investors outside the state. He published a prospectus announcing that the company had been organized with a capital of $500,000, offering for sale seven percent, 20-year bonds. His plan promised investors a first mortgage on the company's property, including "the large grant of land to which the Company will be entitled under the law of the State, when the necessary cuttings and improvements of the canal shall have been made." The circular limited the work ahead to only a portion of the entire waterway, but a substantial one, and one which would prove extremely difficult to complete. Only the section from St. Augustine south to Jupiter Inlet, a distance of about 240 miles, which had already been surveyed, was to be opened for

---

[23]Westcott to Coryell, 14 January 1882. Transcribed by Joe Knetsch, Florida Division of State Lands, 28 July 1992. Photocopy of the original letter is located in the Florida Collection, Florida Department of State, Tallahassee, Florida. *See*, Florida canal company minutes, 7 June 1882, FIND ADM Box 70.01, for Coryell as general manager and director.

[24]*Ibid.*

navigation. The financing was to pay not only for dredging but also for two steamboats to run on the completed waterway. With the waterway's opening, Cooke anticipated "a large emigration" flowing into Florida east coast, taking advantage of "the equable climate, and the fertile lands with a view of producing oranges, lemons, pine-apples, cocoa-nuts, and other tropical fruits, together with strawberries, vegetables and fruits for the winter or early spring markets of the north." He assured investors that he had "thoroughly examined" the formation of the canal company and the state's legislation governing the waterway, as well as the mortgage, "which has been executed and recorded." While it appears that Cooke failed to raise the funds sought in his prospectus, his nephew Henry would become in a few years' time an important backer of the Florida waterway.[25]

The first evidence of the company's work appeared in November 1882 (a year and a half after incorporation) when the company's directors began construction of a primitive ladder or bucket-type dredge for work south of St. Augustine in the Matanzas River. The next month, the company began deepening the Matanzas in Mala Compra Creek to reach the divide separating the Matanzas and Halifax rivers. By January 1883, the firm had dredged a four-mile-long canal, 36 feet wide by six feet deep, from the south end of the Matanzas River to the mouth of the Mala Compra. In his annual message to Florida legislators, Governor William Bloxham hailed the achievement of the canal company, calling the venture "not second in importance to any public improvement in the State." Jacksonville's *Florida Times Union* predicted the waterway would be "one of the most popular tourist routes, in addition to the immense freights to and from this heretofore pent up region [the Halifax River area], which, by many is considered the garden spot in Florida." Ingham Coryell, the canal company's first general manager, spoke encouragingly about the prospects of an early opening of the waterway, noting that a steamboat en route to the area would be put into service as a supply and passenger vessel over the thirty miles now open to navigation.[26]

---

[25]Florida Coast Line Canal and Transp. Co., *Prospectus*. Subscribers to the text of the offering are Jay Cooke and J. K. Upton as financial agents of the company. Two maps are appended to the text. For biographical information on Cooke, see, Oberholtzer, *Jay Cooke*, I and II, and Larson, *Jay Cooke*, generally, and for information on Henry D. Cooke (son of Henry D. Cooke), see, Oberholtzer, *Jay Cooke*, II, 18 and following pages. For detailed information on Cooke's purchase of Ambler bonds, see Affidavit of Frank H. Swan, attached to Winters to Green, 22 October 1929, FIND ADM Box 70.01.

[26]"Governor Bloxham's Message [East Coast Canal]," *Florida Star* (Titusville), 11 January 1883; O'Brien, Florida, 15; "Cutting the Canal," *Florida Times Union*, 23 February 1883.

Coryell confidently announced that a waterway would be cut to the Halifax River by June 1883, expecting no extraordinary difficulty. The company disclosed plans for a 135-foot steamer docked at St. Augustine for daily trips to the company's dredge boat, ferrying not only supplies for dredging but also tourists interested in visiting the project. At the beginning, the canal company employed "endless chain" or ladder-type dredges, which inevitably experienced breaks in the chains connecting the buckets that scooped up the dredged material. At the forward end of these early dredge machines, twenty large steel buckets attached to chains running at an angle of 40 degrees over two drums scooped up mud and sand from the canal bottom and deposited the spoil on slides forty feet long along both sides of the cut. But because of persistent maintenance problems, these bucket dredges eventually gave way to a variety of other and more dependable dredges, including the clamshell, the dipper, and the suction dredge, which proved to be more suitable for the variety of soil, rock, and mud the Florida canal company was to encounter during the next thirty years. Built at St. Augustine, the first ladder-type dredge housed a water tank and a repair shop on the lower deck; on the upper deck, a kitchen, a store room, a dining room, and sleeping quarters. The first stretch of waterway was just thirty feet wide and four-and-half feet deep. No trouble with quicksand had been encountered and none was expected in the stretches ahead.[27]

By March 15, the company's 102-foot-long, twenty-foot-wide dredge faced an expanse of savanna three-quarters of a mile long, followed by a half-mile of hammock and two miles of sand flats, coquina rock, cabbage palms, and palmettos before reaching the marshes of Smith's Creek. Canal officials planned the dredge to make from 500 to a thousand feet a day. A stern-wheel steamer, 101 feet long and 19-feet wide, was to be placed on the Halifax River to help with the work. Now cutting in the sixth mile, the canal company had been spending an astonishing $1,000 a day in the operation. The Titusville-based *Florida Star* conceded that earlier predictions of a rapid completion of the waterway had been too ambitious, but nonetheless concluded that if the company's dredge was working in the old Haulover Canal by the close of 1883, the enterprise would be "a great success" and an "honor to the men who conceived the plan and are executing the work."[28]

---

[27][Special Correspondent of the *Star*, T. P. W. Jacksonville, Fla., February 23, 1883], *Florida Star* (Titusville), 1 March 1883; "The Dredge Boat," *Florida Star* (Titusville), 15 March 1883; Miles, "Waterway of the Florida Coast Line Canal," 164.

[28]"The Coast Canal," *Florida Star* (Titusville), 22 March 1883.

The state's engineer, H. S. Duval, reported the results of his inspection of the company's first work in May. Westcott's map of the dredging, Duval complained, failed to show the actual profile of the waterway and the waterway's depths at periodic intervals. At best, the map presented little more than a crude depiction of the waterway's intended route. In truth, the map represented little more than a duplicate of the map used to promote Disston's Atlantic Coast Steamboat Canal and Improvement Company, with the new Florida canal company's route merely delineated in red ink. Despite its deficiencies, Duval approved the map. The company's dredge had cut a waterway thirty feet wide and more than six miles long south of the mouth of the South Matanzas River, working its way through marsh and heading for Smith's Creek, tributary to the Halifax River.[29]

In June, recognizing "the great importance" of the waterway, state trustees voted to transfer to the company both the odd *and* even sections of public land for six miles on either side of the line of waterway for each mile of canal constructed, the first of thirteen deeds to be delivered to the canal company over the next thirty years. Two of the five trustees—Henry L'Engle, state treasurer, and the state's attorney general, George Raney— voted against the conveyance. One trustee who voted for it, Pleasants White, a former Florida Supreme Court justice and now commissioner of lands and immigration, would a few years later become the canal company's lawyer, hired to obtain hundreds of thousands of acres of public land grants from the same Internal Improvement Fund he once helped oversee. In exchange for liberalizing the grant, Florida canal company officials agreed to give up the right to select lands up to twenty miles from the waterway to make up any deficiency in lands within six miles of the waterway. The trustees conditioned the new grant on the assurance that the company would prosecute the work to completion "with reasonable diligence," a requirement that would surface time and time again in the coming decades as disputes arose over whether or not the company had finished dredging portions of the waterway with sufficient speed.[30]

---

[29]*MIIF*, 2 June 1883, 233-37; Profile of route of the "Florida Coast Line Canal & Transportation Company, filed at State Land Office on December 29, 1882, and at the Office of the Secretary of State on April 22, 1885, Florida, Office of Secretary of State, Railroad Maps, Map No. 76, Florida State Archives.

[30]Westcott to TIIF, 2 June 1883, "Old Railroad Bonds, etc," Drawer 3, Land Records and Title Section, Division of State Lands, Florida Department of Environmental Protection, Tallahassee, FL; *MIIF*, 4 June 1883, 238-39.

Echoing the trustees' assessment of the waterway's importance, *The Florida Star* called the canal company's work "[t]he greatest enterprise of the day, to East Florida." Doubting that railroads would ever reach as far south as the Indian River area, the paper claimed that the "opening up of this [Indian River] country to travel and settlement largely depends on a ready, cheap and convenient mode of transportation. Honest railroads, if ever built will do much, but the canal more to hasten so desirable an object." The newspaper went on to argue that, if built, no railroad could reach so many "flourishing settlements, promising villages and towns as the Coast Canal." Of those who suggested the impossibility of the canal company's task in cutting through "granite," rock and sand, the editor painted them as "interested parties laboring for some pet or paper railroad scheme into which they seek to draw capitalists," adding, "[r]ailroads that cannot live with the canal are little needed, those that can are wanted." However sanguine the newspaper may have been about the waterway's prospects, in the next decade Henry Flagler would prove the paper dead wrong in its assessment of the demand or desire for a railway.[31]

By the summer of 1883, sixteen miles south of St. Augustine, one canal company dredge pushed south while another dredge worked north. Forty-five miles south of St. Augustine, dredging at Smith's Creek began in September 1884, with the second dredge cutting north through the marsh. By the end of 1884, the canal company had completed twenty miles of waterway—six miles of waterway working north and fourteen miles cutting south. On all of its dredging projects, the Florida canal company had spent an astounding $130,000. Although a small amount by today's standards, the company's expenditures nearly equaled the state government's budget of $196,000 for the entire year. Payments for dredging work had utterly exhausted the firm's slender financial resources.

The completion of the Florida waterway would now depend on attracting new investors not only possessing vast amounts of capital but willing to assume the substantial risks of a speculative and thoroughly unproven venture.[32]

---

[31]"A Visit to the Dredge and Coast Canal, Its Importance," *Florida Star* (Titusville), 21 June 1883.

[32]O'Brien, *Florida*, 15; "Gov. Bloxham's Message," *Florida Times Union*, 7 January 1885.

Chapter 2

New England Money

Just three years into the dredging, the drying up of local sources of capital forced Westcott and the other canal company directors to look for additional funds outside Florida. While Dan Ambler's early financing enabled some work on the construction of the channel between the Matanzas and Halifax rivers — the most difficult of all the sections — and the cut that would consume another twenty-five years to complete, Florida canal officials needed considerably more money for construction.

To attract new investors, company directors hired Robert O'Brien, a St. Augustine civil engineer, to prepare a report on the prospects of the proposed Florida waterway and its projected completion cost. O'Brien issued a glowing report on February 9, 1885, predicting that with "the utmost energy" it was possible to open the waterway for navigation from St. Augustine to Jupiter Inlet by the end of that year and to Biscayne Bay by the end of the next year for only $243,000.[1]

Along with Westcott as president, directors now included Jay Cooke's nephew, Henry D. Cooke, as vice president, Samuel Maddox, a prominent Washington lawyer, as secretary, and John W. Denny, a Boston investor who would later head the company. No longer directors were young James Hallowes and James Colee, although Colee remained connected to the enterprise as an engineer. On February 24, 1885, the new board agreed to extend the waterway south all the way to Key West. That same month, Florida legislators voted to allow the waterway's extension to Key West and to set aside additional land grants for the work. And to finance canal improve-

---

[1]O'Brien, *Florida*, 7-8.

ments, directors pledged all of the company's promised state land grant as security for a $400,000 bond issue.[2]

Samuel Maddox

A member of the American aristocracy like Westcott, the Florida canal company's 35-year-old secretary, Sam Maddox, descended from another Samuel Maddox who emigrated to Maryland with his uncle, Thomas Notley, around 1646. Notley later became proprietary governor of the Chesapeake Bay colony. Born in the small country town of Breathedsville, in northwest Maryland, on August 28,1850, Sam Maddox graduated from St. John's College at Annapolis and early on pursued a career in civil engineering, building railroads and bridges before embarking upon the practice of law in Washington at age twenty-five. A lifelong bachelor, Maddox belonged to the prestigious Metropolitan Club, whose original members included one of the Florida canal company's first major investors, Jay Cooke, and Cooke's brother, Henry D. Cooke, father of the company's vice president. A distinguished member of the Washington bar, Maddox headed the prestigious Bar Association of the District of Columbia from 1898 until 1900.[3]

On May 13, 1885, for completing a 26-mile stretch of waterway southeast of St. Augustine, state trustees deeded 87,670 acres of public land to the canal company in addition to a small tract comprised of 4,489 acres initially granted in the early stages of construction. Florida's Attorney General, Charles M. Cooper, one of the five signers on the state trustees' deed, advised — and the trustees agreed — that state law did not entitle Westcott's firm to public land along the waterway route where there had been no cutting though dry land and only improvements in existing rivers, streams and sounds had been made. Despite the initial reluctance of trustees to grant

---

[2]Deed of Trust executed by Florida Coast Line Canal and Transportation Company (hereinafter "Canal Company") in favor of the American Loan and Trust Company of New York, Trustee, on February 23, 1885, and recorded on April 22, 1885, in Mortgage Book "D," at page 114, of the Public Records of St. Johns County. Additional Articles of Association for Canal Company dated February 24, 1885, filed March 18, 1885, recorded November 11, 1885, in Book B, Page 562, Office of Secretary of State. These articles were authorized by *Laws of Florida* (1885), c. 1987, § 12. The waterway's extension was authorized by *Laws of Florida* (1885), c. 3641, approved February 6, 1885.

[3]"Samuel Maddox's Rites Tomorrow," *Washington Times*, 2 April 1919. Metropolitan Club, 3; Charlick, *Brief History*, 65, 103, 104, 105; Crawford, "Sam Maddox."

land and the limited capitalization available, Westcott's company managed nonetheless to open a new Haulover cut between the Mosquito Lagoon and the Indian River, a waterway much larger than the small and practically unusable canal Lieutenant Wright had built more than 30 years before.[4]

George Lothrop Bradley

Sometime in 1886, Jay Cooke persuaded 40-year-old George Lothrop Bradley, a director and first treasurer of the American Bell Telephone Company, to invest in the Florida canal company. In just a few short years, Bradley would become the company's largest stockholder, soon replacing Westcott as the leading figure in the Florida waterway's construction, even heading the enterprise for seven years from 1899 until his death in 1906.[5]

Born in 1846 at Providence, Rhode Island, a descendant of the Reverend Hezekiah Smith, a renowned Massachusetts chaplain during the Revolutionary War and for forty years a member of the Board of Fellows of Brown University, Bradley was another stalwart member of the American elite like Westcott and Maddox. Bradley's father, Charles Smith Bradley, also an early Bell Telephone director, was born at Newburyport, Massachusetts, in 1819; he entered Brown University at the age of fifteen and graduated in 1838 with highest honors as class valedictorian. After studying law at Harvard Law School, Charles began a long and distinguished career as a lawyer at Providence, in partnership with Charles Tillinghast. In 1854, the township of North Providence elected the senior Bradley to the state senate. In 1863, as the Democratic Party's nominee, Charles vied for a seat in Congress but failed in the effort. Despite his defeat, in 1866 Rhode Island state legislators elected the senior Bradley to serve as chief justice of the Rhode Island Supreme Court, a post he would hold for three years. From 1876 until 1879, he served as professor at Harvard Law School, gaining wide acclaim for outstanding public oratory. Charles Bradley traveled extensively and acquired along the way a love for books, sculpture and painting his son George would soon share.[6]

---

[4]Deed No. 13,089 executed by TIIF in favor of Canal Company on May 13, 1885, and recorded May 22, 1885, in Deed Book "EE," Page 76, of the Public Records of St. Johns County, Florida; for state engineer H. S. Duval's report on the completion of the distance, see, *MIIF*, 20 April 1885, 357.

[5]Miles, "History," 2.

[6]Bayles, editor, *History of Providence County*, I, 41-44; Peters, compiler, *Bradley of Essex County*, 118-122; Smith, E. V., *Souvenir Edition*.

George Lothrop Bradley (1846-1906), president of the Florida Coast Line Canal and Transportation Company from 1899 until his death in 1906 at age 59, and the firm's largest investor. His will directed his estate to complete the Florida waterway and to later found, in 1931, what would become the Emma Pendleton Bradley Hospital, the nation's first hospital devoted exclusively to the treatment of children with psychiatric illness. (Courtesy, Emma Pendleton Bradley Hospital, East Providence, Rhode Island)

When he was just thirty years old, young George Bradley helped organize the first of the Bell Telephone companies, joining one of Alexander Graham Bell's chief backers, Thomas Sanders, a Bradley family relative, along with the Saltonstalls, also family relatives, and later, Colonel William H. Forbes in providing much-needed financing. Bradley and his father not only contributed capital but also furnished expertise in creating the management structure to oversee the company. Educated in mining engineering at the renowned academy at Freiberg, Germany, from 1864 until 1866, young Bradley returned to America to develop a Colorado mine but was unsuccessful. At Providence once again, Bradley met Alexander Graham Bell. Introducing Bell's telephone invention to friends in Boston, Bradley helped to organize the New England Telephone Company in 1878. In New York City, he again promoted the telephone, assisting in the formation of the National Bell Telephone Company. Both Bradley and his father became directors of the new company, with board members electing George Bradley to the posts of vice-president and treasurer. Bradley's telephone stock soon skyrocketed in price from $50 to $800 a share, earning him a fortune of over a million dollars. Later settling in Washington, D.C., in 1883, Bradley joined William C. Whitney in making another fortune investing in the Mergenthaler Linotype Company, a firm revolutionizing the printing business with the introduction of the linotype press. Now quite wealthy, Bradley would routinely occupy three different permanent residences for the rest of his life: his father's mansion at Providence; his home at Washington, D.C.; and a summer residence, "Rathlin,"at Pomfret, Connecticut; in addition to regular summer stays with friends and acquaintances at Newport, Rhode Island and Bar Harbor, Maine. Joined by colleagues who also were early investors in the telephone and linotype machine ventures, Bradley began investing large sums of money in the Florida canal company.[7]

George Miles

With both Cooke and Bradley backing the enterprise, in 1887, company directors began spending money and energy on improving the easier cuts south of the difficult Matanzas-Halifax canal to gain state land grants quickly to finance dredging in the southern portions of the state. Dredging work ultimately costing the canal company more than a quarter of a million dollars—largely at Bradley's expense—lumbered on until 1888. Bradley pitched the Florida project to his young Pomfret neighbor, George Francis Miles, an Irish-born engineer. For years Miles and his wife Helen had spent their summers at their home "Gladwyn" as neighbors of the Bradleys, who resided at "Rathlin." Correct in posture and fastidious in dress, the 25-year-old engineer was tall, fair-skinned and had blond hair. Miles reputedly pos-

---

[7]*National Cyclopaedia* 14:440-41. Mooney, "Robert Devonshire's Letterbook," 118. For information on Bradley's mining education in Germany, see, Volkmer to author (in German), 22 June 2000; Bicknell, *History*, 6-10; see, Bayles, editor, *History of Windham County*, Pt. II, 704 (opp.) for a sketch of "Rathlin" in this 1889 edition. For a printed circular of the National Bell Telephone Company dated April 26, 1879, showing a list of company directors, see, Circular, April 26, 1879, AGBP, Folder: The Telephone, American Bell Telephone Company, 1877-1880). In an early biography of Theodore N. Vail, Paine describes Bradley as a relative of Sanders. Paine, *In One Man's Life*, 111, 123, 140. See also, State Street, 52, Casson, *History of the Telephone*, 60-61; Walsh, *Connecticut Pioneers*, 57, 84-85, 331; Brooks, *Telephone*, 40-41, 66-67. See, Fagen, editor, *History of Engineering and Science in the Bell System*, 25-33, for early corporate history and a historical chart of the parent organizations of the Bell System. For Bell correspondence on the relationship between Bell and the Bradleys, see Mabel Hubbard (Bell) to AGB, 3 December 1876; Mabel Hubbard Bell to AGB, 17 May 1877; G. G. Hubbard, 13 March 1878; AGB to Mabel Hubbard Bell, 14 November 1878; G. G. Hubbard to AGB, 1 December 1878; G. G. Hubbard to AGB, 4 December 1878; G. G. Hubbard to AGB, 11 December 1878; G. G. Hubbard to AGB, 26 January 1879; AGB to G. G. Hubbard, 25 February 1879; AGB to G. G. Hubbard, 28 July 1880; all in AGBP, Folder: The Telephone, American Bell Telephone Company, 1877-1880.

sessed a photographic memory. Born in Cork, Ireland, the son of a prominent family, Miles graduated from Queen's College with a bachelor's degree in engineering. He studied for a year under William Barrington of Limerick before becoming resident engineer on the Limerick and Kerry Railway. By 1883, Miles had traveled to Canada to work on what would become the Canadian Pacific Railway. Heading up the Nepigon Bay section, the young Irish engineer, then only twenty years old, led the dangerous and complex work of constructing a massive 10-story-high bridge 1,200 feet long. Sometime later, Miles moved to the United States. After finishing several projects, Miles turned his attention to the development of what would become Florida's Atlantic Intracoastal Waterway. In the years to follow, Miles would serve as general manager and later head the Florida canal company.[8]

As early as 1886, Miles led a group of four Canadian contractors and engineers, including Sandford H. Fleming, son of acclaimed Canadian railway engineer Sir Sandford Fleming, in assessing the route of the proposed Florida waterway as far south as Palm Beach. The group realized that the southern part of the state needed development but lacked practical means of transportation. The four then formed a construction company to do some of the Florida canal company's early dredging, getting paid with securities instead of cash. Each invested about $15,000 in the venture, but these amounts were not nearly enough to complete the work. Each also pledged canal securities earned in the work as collateral for a loan from a St. Augustine bank to complete the contract. But in the end, Miles's group failed to finish the work, leaving the Canadian group with a debt that would remain unpaid for decades.[9]

In March 1888, after talks with a number of potential investors in Boston and Montreal, Miles met with Donald MacMaster, a 41-year-old Montreal barrister, to consider the amount of state land available for the dredging

[8]Miles, "History," 3. "George Miles Retired Civil Engineer Dies." *Putnam* (Conn.) *Patriot*, 19 December 1940. Author's copy transcribed from an article on microfiche at the Putnam Public Library by Mary G. Page, Pomfret (ConnecticutSt.) Historical Society. "Cutting the Big Canal," *Florida Times-Union*, 18 August 1895. Personal correspondence from Ann Martha Rowan to Siobhan de h'Oir, 11 October 2002, in author's collection; also Rowan to author, 6 November 2002, and Irish Architectural Archive, *Biographical Index of Irish Architects*, extracted from Membership Applications, Vol. IV, at page 8, Institution of Civil Engineers of Ireland, Dublin, Ireland (National Library of Ireland, Microfilm Reference No. Pos. 9386. [Lula?], Evergreen Manor, South Woodstock, Connecticut, to Fred and Kay [Alfred and Kay Hanna], 4 December 1949, YP Box 5, File 18, provides first-hand impressions of Bradley and Miles.

[9]S. H. Fleming to Hall, 23 January 1912, HGP.

work that lay ahead. Because of the 1885 controversy over whether dredging in existing rivers, sounds, and lagoons entitled the company to the land
grants Florida trustees had set aside, doubt remained over whether the firm
would receive all of the reserved lands. MacMaster advised Westcott that
the enterprise might encounter "great difficulty" in floating a proposed new
bond issue, noting that a prospectus promoting the bonds claimed "a
reserve of 1,000,000 acres of land" for the waterway project, without disclos-
ing that Florida trustees had ruled three years before that public land along
the waterway route couldn't be granted where there had been no actual cutting through dry land. Appreciating that the "big cut" between the Matanzas and Halifax rivers and another between the Indian River and Lake
Worth "a very formidable undertaking," the Montreal lawyer recommended that Florida legislators pass a law making it clear that the Florida
canal company would receive outright all the land to which it was entitled,
whether the dredging was done on dry land or in existing waterways.

Elaborating on his view that Westcott's company ought to be entitled to
the land grants whether the dredging occurred on land or in water, Mac-
Master forwarded to Westcott a legal opinion addressed to Charles Cooper,
Florida's attorney general, which Westcott passed along to Cooper for
review. Perhaps prompted by MacMaster's memorandum, during the next
session Florida legislators passed legislation granting the canal company
3,840 acres for every mile of waterway constructed from St. Augustine to
Biscayne Bay, whether the company cut through dry land or not.[10]

Despite the prickly legal issues raised in Montreal, Florida canal directors
forged ahead on May 1, 1888, with a $1.4 million bond issue to finance
waterway construction A few weeks later, the company paid off Ambler's
$75,000 bond issue, the firm's first outside financing. But while dredging
operations moved ahead, the canal company lost the heart and soul of the
waterway project a few months later. On January 2, 1889, Dr. John Westcott, the firm's founder, passed away at the age of eighty-one.[11]

---

[10]MacMaster to Westcott, 31 March 1888; MacMaster to Cooper, 31 March 1888; both in
"Old Railroad Bonds, etc." "Drawer 3," Land Records and Title Section, Division of State
Lands, Florida Department of Environmental Protection, Tallahassee, Fla. "MacMaster,
Donald," et al., ed., *Appleton's*, vol. 4, p. 148.

[11]Deed of Trust executed by Canal Company in favor of the American Loan and Trust
Company of New York, Trustee, on May 1, 1888, and recorded on May 1, 1889, in Mortgage
Book "G," at page 326, of the Public Records of St. Johns County. Satisfaction or release of
Mortgage entitled "Indenture," executed by Daniel G. Ambler, of the City of Jacksonville,
State of Florida, Trustee in favor of Canal Company, on May 21, 1888, St. Augustine Histori-
cal Society, St. Johns County Court records, Civil Cases, Box 298, Folder 155. Miles, "His-
tory," 5.

Some months before Westcott's death, Miles had engaged 48-year-old Elmer L. Corthell, a world-renowned inland waterway and railway engineer based in Chicago, to perform a comprehensive survey of the proposed Florida waterway route and provide estimates of the construction cost. Among many routes across Central America that had been considered, Corthell had been an early promoter of a scheme to construct a ship-railway across Mexico's Isthmus of Tehuantepec before the construction of the Panama Canal. Corthell also organized the Massachusetts Maritime Canal Company to construct a canal across Cape Cod but was not successful.[12]

Miles chose Corthell principally because of his association with Captain James Eads in the latter's widely-publicized construction of the Mississippi River jetties. He also relied on an unnamed American western railroad president's assurance that Corthell stood as the leading authority on "all Engineering questions relating to the improvement of Rivers and Harbors." Corthell began the Florida waterway project by enlisting another engineer, Col. A. F. Wrotnowski, to perform a detailed survey of the proposed east coast route from St. Augustine to Biscayne Bay. Corthell later personally inspected the line of the planned waterway, confirming that to make navigation practicable, the waterway would have to be enlarged to a width of not less than fifty feet and a depth of not less than five feet, considerably larger than what initially had been required by state law in 1881.[13]

Born in Clermont, France, 49-year-old Arthur Fancis Wrotnowski was actually a year older than his employer. A veteran of the Civil War like Corthell, Wrotnowski had been trained early on as a civil engineer, helping to draw for the Union army an important map of Vicksburg, Miss., indicating fortifications as well as the names, types, and locations of boats, roads, and railroads. Later, as an assistant engineer serving the United States Levee Commission, Wrotnowski contributed information on levee conditions along the Mississippi River for an important report to Congress on a plan to reclaim the surrounding basin. Just five years before the start of the Florida waterway survey, Wrotnowski helped form the Clermont Improvement Company, eventually surveying and laying out some 15,000 acres of

---

[12]Farson, *Cape Cod Canal*, 26-27; Wallace, *MacMillan Dictionary*, 236 (Fleming); Eads Concession; Wallace, "Elmer Lawrence Corthell;" "E. L. Corthell Dies; Noted Engineer," *New York Times*, 17 May 1916.

[13]Miles, "History," 4.

central Florida land for a town to be known as Clermont, named after his birthplace.[14]

Corthell's 1889 Report

Wrotnowski's study of the Florida east coast began on August 27, 1888, and concluded with a report to Corthell almost nine months later. The study summarized findings following a careful examination of the 326-mile route between St. Augustine and Biscayne Bay. Corthell's assistant found that already existing waterways, "consisting of Creeks, Bayous, Lagoons — Lakes, Sounds and Rivers," comprised nearly 87 percent of the entire route. Only about fifteen percent of the waterways needed dredging to a six-foot depth, just eleven percent required deepening to five feet. In his estimation, a mere thirteen percent of the work or forty miles of the entire route from St. Augustine to Biscayne Bay consisted of solid divides requiring cutting through dry land.[15]

Of the work already completed south of St. Augustine to the Jupiter Inlet, Wrotnowski found that in most instances the dredging work in natural waterways had not been well done or had been improperly located, causing the cuts to become obliterated or obstructed. Where the canal company had dredged in solid marsh or high lands, the canal cuts retained their dimensions. The natural differences in tide levels, such as those existing between the Matanzas Inlet and the Mosquito (now Ponce) Inlet, fifty-one miles south, actually benefited maintenance of the waterway by creating "sufficient scouring power to clear out all attempts at deposit of sand or sediment." He described the land below Lake Worth "the undeveloped country — with absolutely no settlers except two houses of Refuge twenty-five miles apart and a number of Indians living generally on the borders of the Everglades — ten or twelve miles west of the line of the canal." Observing the lack of transportation facilities in that section, the French-born engi-

---

[14]Johnson, Clermont, *Ancestry World Tree*, ancestry.com, "Arthur Fancis Wrotnowski," also noting that Wrotnowski named his son, Arthur Corthell Wrotnowski. Map, "View of Vicksburg and plan of the canal, fortifications and vicinity," Surveyed by Lieutenant L. A. Wrotnowski, Top: Engineer Drawn by A. F. Wrotnowski, C.E., Library of Congress, Washington, D. C. Wrotnowski, A. F., "Map of the town site of Clermont, Sumter County, Florida: the property of the Clermont Improvement Company," Florida State Library, Tallahassee.

[15]Wrotnowski, A. F., "Report upon the Examination of the Inside Waterways, East Coast of Florida, to E. L. Corthell, C. E." (Report of E. L. Corthell upon the Inside Waterway, East Coast of Florida, 1889), ELCP.

neer wrote, "There are absolutely no means of communication whatever—
except on foot from L[ake] Worth south to Biscayne Bay a distance of sixty-
six miles—which distance is traversed once a week by the mail carrier who
trudges along sore footed to make the connecting link to civilization with
the settlers of Beautiful Biscayne Bay."[16]

By March 15, 1889, the canal company had excavated nearly a million
(917,867) cubic yards of rock, marsh, mud, sand, and shell in dredging from
the Matanzas River at St. Augustine south to Jupiter Inlet since the start of
operations, Wrotnowski estimated. Canal dimensions ranged from cuts as
small as 33 feet wide by three feet deep through rock and other solid materials near St. Augustine to an open-water channel as large as eighty feet wide
but only a foot-and-a-half deep in one section of the Indian River.[17]

He recommended two different kinds of machinery to perform the dredging work. First, the company should build four Osgood dipper dredges
with ample power and steam generation and hulls 26 feet wide and 90 feet
long. Each dipper should be at least 38 inches by 70 inches in size. The company ought also to secure a dredge with the largest-size buckets of the
Menge or Allen ladder continuous bucket type to work in marshes, particularly below Lake Worth, believing a properly fitted Menge dredge superior
to the Osgood for work in that kind of material. In addition to the dredging
machinery, Wrotnowski recommended employing a snag boat fitted with a
derrick and capstan and propelled by at least a six-horsepower motor to
remove branches and other snags such as mangroves choking the waterway
and the building of eight hopper barges to carry away spoil material. With
some sense of satisfaction, Wrotnowski observed that the canal company
had already implemented a suggestion he had made in October 1888 to
mark the channel between the head of the Halifax River to the Jupiter River
by setting out 192 beacons and guide piles.[18]

In his final report to Miles on June 5, 1889, Corthell approved his assistant's report almost in its entirety, suggesting that the Florida canal company implement the bulk of the recommendations immediately. Of the
importance of the Florida project, he knew of "no coast in the world where
with so little artificial work there can be opened a navigable channel for
good-sized steam vessels for a distance of nearly 500 miles entirely removed
from the dangers of the sea and traversing in large measure natural lakes,

---

[16]*Ibid.*
[17]*Ibid.*, "Summary of Works Excavated to March 15, 1889."
[18]*Ibid.*

sounds and inland rivers of very considerable magnitude bordered on either side by fertile lands capable of producing a great variety of productions." There existed but "three barriers" to a continuous Florida inland waterway. The first was the divide between the waters flowing north into the Matanzas Inlet and the waters flowing south into the Halifax River between St. Augustine and today's Daytona Beach. The second was "the compact ridge" formed partly of sand and partly of coquina between the Mosquito Lagoon and the Indian River at Titusville, known then as now as the Haulover. The final separation was the divide between the Indian River and Lake Worth. Although he didn't consider the low-lying marshes between Lake Worth and Biscayne Bay a fourth barrier to free navigation, he did believe that the ocean inlets flowing into the planned waterway allowing an influx of salt water created a beneficial effect in maintaining the waterway, keeping channels free where they were almost completely filled with "rank vegetation, grasses and other fresh water plants." Recognizing that the canal company had spent about $400,000 in dredging the waterway and that the Florida legislature had extended the firm's charter and increased the land grants, Corthell also noted that state trustees had already deeded 92,147 acres of public land for the work performed and that 1.3 million acres had been set aside in reserve for the remaining work.[19]

Corthell endorsed raising the embankments on both sides of the canal "in exposed places sufficiently high to prevent the waves washing over them." For the overall dimensions of the waterway, he recommended an optimum width of 80 feet in marshy cuttings and open water and 60 feet in rock cuttings, with a standard depth of six feet to provide an adequate channel for "good-sized steamboats" even though state requirements called for a waterway only fifty feet wide and five feet deep.[20]

To overcome the difficult divide between the waters flowing north into the Matanzas Inlet and those flowing south into Smith's Creek, Corthell recommended a tide-level cut rather than the construction of a lock system principally because he doubted the authority of the canal company to overflow adjacent lands with water backed up by a dam to operate a lock. At the Haulover Canal between the Mosquito Lagoon and the Indian River, he strongly advised the construction of a lock system because of the wide expanse of water both north and south of the section and the tendency of

---

[19]Corthell to Miles, 5 June 1889 (Report of E. L. Corthell upon the Inside Waterway East Coast of Florida, 1889), ELCP.

[20]*Ibid.*

winds to both lower and raise water levels on either side, depending on their direction. He also believed that the lock would reduce the "continual wearing away of the channel" and the need for excessive dredging maintenance in the cut. The last point at which Corthell recommended special construction was the divide between Lake Worth Creek and Lake Worth, suggesting the building of two locks because of "the peculiar and extraordinary rapids" existing there during certain seasons of the year.[21]

To complete the Florida waterway to "Cocoa Nut" (present-day Cocoanut Grove) on Biscayne Bay — a distance of 326 miles, Corthell estimated the work's completion cost at $1,080,671 for a section of optimum dimensions — 80 feet wide in earth, sixty feet wide in rock, and six feet deep. To finish the waterway to the southern end of Lake Worth, Corthell projected construction expenses at just under a million dollars — $939,510. The amount of excavation for the entire length of the project was expected to total over 4.5 million cubic yards, with the route consisting of highlands, coquina rock, and marshes, except where open water existed. He estimated the cost of maintaining the entire waterway at $25,000 per year.[22]

Also investigated was the possibility of constructing either a three-and-a-half-mile waterway or a boat-railway between the Indian River near Rockledge and Lake Poinsett to connect with the St. Johns River and points north to Jacksonville. Corthell thought undertaking either project feasible. But he increased Wrotnowski's estimate for the cost of the boat railway from $111,811 to $130,000. For the projected cost of the canal and one lock with an 18-foot lift, Corthell bumped his assistant's estimate from $152,452 to $175,000. Comparing the two projects, he preferred the waterway because of the railway's greater operating expense, unless further examination showed more rock along the route of the waterway than anticipated.[23]

Twenty days after the first report, Corthell added to his recommendations and urged that the canal company initially dredge the waterway only to the minimum dimensions required by the state. Later, as the company collected tolls and sold off its land grants, the waterway could be enlarged to optimum dimensions. To build a waterway only fifty feet wide and five feet

---

[21]*Ibid.*

[22]Corthell to Miles, 5 June 1889; Wrotnowski, "Total Estimated Cost of Complete Canal from St. Augustine to Cocoa Nut, Biscayne Bay" (Report of E. L. Corthell upon the Inside Waterway East Coast of Florida, 1889), ELCP.

[23]Corthell to Miles, 5 June 1889 (Report of E. L. Corthell upon the Inside Waterway East Coast of Florida, 1889), ELCP.

deep from St. Augustine to Biscayne Bay, Corthell estimated total costs at only $842,825. For a waterway to the south end of Lake Worth, he projected expenses amounting to $624,080.[24]

Encouraging canal directors to go forward with the project, Corthell pointed to the burgeoning economy along the east coast as justification for completing the waterway. Production of oranges in the Halifax River area had reached 50,000 boxes annually. At Titusville, two years before, orange shipments amounted to 60,000 boxes; the current season's shipments were likely to exceed 100,000 boxes. Pineapple shipments remained strong at 150,000 boxes annually, increasing at the astounding rate of fifty percent each year. Carriers shipped 9,000 crates of cabbages, beans, tomatoes, egg-plant, Irish potatoes and other vegetables. Two steamboats working the Indian River the year before had carried 8,455 passengers, mostly tourists, and for the past twelve months, transported 12,000 passengers. All things considered, a completed channel between St. Augustine and Lake Worth would increase the number of passengers on boats using the company's waterway to between 75,000 and 100,000.[25]

A traveler down Florida's east coast, William Drysdale, described for the *New York Times* an all-day and all-night trip down the Indian River from Titusville to Jupiter aboard the steamer *St. Lucie* with intermediate stops at Rockledge, Tropic and Waveland. Stopping at the tiny settlement of Tropic, Drysdale found rich farm land yielding large quantities of pineapples, beans and tomatoes, selling for as much as $1,000 an acre. Growers shipped produce by steamer to Titusville and then by rail to northern markets, a trip requiring as much as a week to bring fruits and vegetables to New York, which Drysdale thought at least three days longer than necessary. Fully half the oranges that found their way to New York were Indian River-grown fruit. Approaching the Jupiter Narrows, the river narrowed from as much as six miles wide to 600 yards, to an even more slender waterway with barely enough room for the 40-foot-wide *St. Lucie* to make her way through overgrown brush and hanging tree branches. Deck hands with poles pushed the boat through while her engine intermittently stopped and started in passing through the treacherous vegetation. On a high bluff at the end of the journey stood the Jupiter Inlet Lighthouse, constructed in 1860.[26]

---

[24]Corthell to Miles, 25 June 1889 (Report of E. L. Corthell upon the Inside Waterway East Coast of Florida, 1889), ELCP.

[25]*Ibid.*

[26]"Down the Indian River," *New York Times*, 9 June 1889.

Drysdale gave up trying to find out the name of the company building the east coast canal, "for if a man once begins to get on the track of the endless Florida improvement companies he is forever lost and mixed up." He thought the company had "a large subsidy in Florida lands, or is trying to get one — I forget which." But in the end, Drysdale believed the company wouldn't be able to complete the project without large federal subsidies.[27]

Canal Reserve Lands

To back up promises to deed large tracts of public land for dredging the Florida waterway all the way to Key West, Florida trustees had set aside by 1885 nearly a million acres of public land on both sides of the proposed Florida waterway as "canal reserve" lands. For work between St. Augustine and Jacksonville (the Northern Division), trustees reserved approximately 153,000 acres for the canal company. For dredging the waterways between St. Augustine and Biscayne Bay (the Middle Division), trustees set aside 500,000 acres; for work south of Biscayne Bay along the Florida straits to Key West (the Southern Division), trustees segregated more than 300,000 acres, although the company later abandoned work on that section.[28]

John W. Denny

In February 1890, John Denny, Westcott's successor as Florida canal company president, began corresponding with Lucius Wombwell, Florida's first commissioner of agriculture (1888-1901) and a trustee of the state's Internal Improvement Fund, about the vast expanse of "Reserve Lands" set aside for the canal company. So anxious was Denny to sell these lands to finance dredging operations, he even asked Wombwell about selling the lands *before* the company actually received the deeds to the property. To speed up sales, he suggested that a state-designated representative and James Colee, the company's agent (and one of the company's original directors), travel to the southern part of the Florida peninsula to inspect the firm's reserved lands. He had also asked Judge Pleasants White, a former circuit judge, a former state land commissioner, and now the canal company's wise selection as lawyer in state land transactions, to make up a list of the reserve lands in

---

[27]*Ibid.*

[28]O'Brien, *Florida*, 2, 3, 8.

present-day Miami-Dade County. Denny complained that state trustees had sold a tract of the company's reserved land to Sylvanus Kitching, an early Sebastian settler, for a dollar an acre. The canal company would later engage the British-born Kitching to supply 200 cords of wood a week to stoke the fires of the company's dredge boilers. Thirty-seven years later, in 1927, Sylvanus's son, Stanley Kitching, would become Martin County's first representative on the Board of Commissioners of the Florida Inland Navigation District, a special taxing district formed to hand over the canal company's Florida waterway to the federal government for conversion into today's Atlantic Intracoastal Waterway.[29]

Denny complained again that the state had sold some of the company's reserved land to a Julius Tyler and a Mary Hendry, two who had applied to the company to buy reserve lands as early as the spring of 1888. And in May, Denny protested that Florida trustees had sold twenty lots from reserve lands at a dollar an acre since April 1, 1888, without the canal company's permission. To facilitate sales, writing from Hyde Park, Massachusetts, Denny asked trustees to remove restrictions against selling reserve land to single men if they actually resided on the property, as opposed to those who were heads of a household as state law then required. Awaiting the state's delivery of deeds to the company's land grant, Denny agreed to escrow the proceeds of the sale of reserve lands with the state's Internal Improvement Fund, with payment to be made when the company completed a portion of the waterway. A year letter, state trustees voted to approve the canal company's plan.[30]

Meanwhile, Florida canal officials made increasing progress in constructing the waterway. Writer Robert Ranson accompanied state engineer John Bradford on the steamer *St. Lucie* traveling south for an official examination of the Indian River route between Titusville and Jupiter, returning north on the *S.S. Denny*, which drew only four feet of water. Along the way Bradford made measurements and soundings at every place where government charts showed a channel less than fifty feet wide and five feet deep. Begin-

---

[29]Denny to Wombwell, 19 February 1890, Florida, Department of State, Archives, Series 914, Carton 47. "Kitching Speaks on Water Ways," dated by Youngberg as February 10, 1933, YP Box 2, File 4; GAY, "Florida Inland Navigation District," 27 May 1935 [Remarks at luncheon honoring Colonels Hannum and Dunn], YP Box 2, File 10. For biographical material on White, see Rerick, *Memoirs*, I, 722-24.

[30]Denny to Wombwell, 19 February 1890; Denny to Wombwell, 15 May 1890; Denny to Wombwell, 24 May 1890; all in Florida, Department of State, Archives, Series 914, Carton 47. *MIIF*, 22 June 1891, 151-53.

ning at Jupiter, Ranson found that the canal company's work consisted of twenty-three canals, including the Haulover, with some cuts no longer than a hundred feet; others, over a mile long. In every case, the state's engineer found that the waterway had complied with state specifications. At the south end of the Indian River Narrows, entering St. Lucie Sound, a one-mile long canal there measured seven feet deep and ninety wide. The company marked the Indian River channel with red-and-white beacons rising ten feet above the water, with the white half of the marker showing the clear channel. Fulfilling one of Corthell's predictions, Ranson found that the currents had not only scoured out shoaling in several places but had actually deepened the cuts. Commending the work of "the persistent efforts of a handful of far-seeing men," Ranson informed his readers that the canal company had spent at least $80,000 for engineering and surveys alone in prosecuting the work.[31]

With a favorable report from Bradford, in September 1890, Florida trustees deeded 345,972 acres of state-owned lands lying along the Atlantic coast to the Florida canal company for dredging 134 miles of waterway from the west end of Brevard County's Haulover Cut to Jupiter in today's Palm Beach County. The grant consisted of a string of parcels extending altogether more than a hundred miles along the Atlantic coast south from present-day Stuart, in Martin County, to the tip of the Florida peninsula.[32]

Wasting no time in selling some of the land, the canal company sold 1,310 acres along the Middle River in today's Fort Lauderdale to Jacksonville attorney Duncan Fletcher for $2,293 or $1.75 an acre. Fletcher then deeded the tract to the Florida Fiber Company, a Duval County firm organized by Fletcher and others to grow sisal hemp. The fiber venture proved only partially successful and later went out of business. Almost forty years later, however, as a United States Senator, Fletcher would play a pivotal role in expediting turnover of what had become the privately-owned Florida East

[31]Ranson, "Improved Navigation of Indian River" [August 11, 1890], East Coast Advocate, 15 August 1890.

[32]TIIF Deed executed in favor of the Canal Company on September 24, 1890, and recorded on December 2, 1890, in Deed Book "D," at page 362, of the Public Records of Dade County, Florida.

Coast Canal to the United States Army Corps of Engineers for improvement and future maintenance as Florida's Atlantic Intracoastal Waterway.[33]

The East Coast Transportation Company

While Fletcher began developing his Florida Fiber tract, two steamboat companies vying for business on the Indian River portion of the Florida waterway at Titusville became embroiled in a lawsuit over the use of railway docks on the river. Controlled by the Jacksonville, Tampa & Key West Railway, the older and larger Indian River Steamboat Company sued the smaller East Coast Transportation Company, just two days after the East Coast company's incorporation, for challenging the larger steamboat company's monopoly of the Titusville docks in shipping Indian River citrus to northern markets. In an editorial appearing in the Titusville-based *East Coast Advocate*, Dr. Walter S. Graham, also a principal in the new East Coast company (and later, the founder and editor of the Miami *Metropolis*), considered the future of the smaller company a sure one, "It has the guaranteed and written support of many large shippers, and the moral support and sympathy of almost the entire river. It has been in existence for over six months; has run its steamer [the *Sweeney*] regularly for three months, and its business is at present more than paying expenses, in spite of the unjust discrimination by which it is handicapped, but which, we are confident, will soon be discontinued, if not voluntarily, by the strong arm of the law." Another Titusville newspaper, the *Florida Star*, confirmed the presence of John Denny, the Florida canal company's president, in the Lake Worth area, commenting that everyone seemed to "like the gentleman very much but they don't seem to extend the liking to the canal company of which he is the

---

[33]Warranty Deed executed by Canal Company in favor of Duncan U. Fletcher, Jacksonville, Florida, on November 22, 1890, and recorded in Deed Book "D," at page 402, of the Public Records of Dade County, Florida. From May through July, 1890, E. C. Patterson, Secretary of the Florida Fiber Company, wrote agriculture commissioner L. B. Wombwell to indicate the firm's interest in buying state lands reserved for the canal company below Lake Worth, especially land along the New River in what is now Broward County. Letters of E. C. Patterson to State Land Office, 23 May 1890, and to E. B. Wombwell, 2, 9, 21, 31 July 1890. Florida State Archives, Series 914, Carton 47. Warranty Deed executed by Duncan U. Fletcher and Anna Louise Fletcher, his wife, in favor of The Florida Fiber Company on January 13, 1891, and recorded in Deed Book "D," at page 402, of the Public Records of Dade County, Florida. *Tropical Sun* (Juno), 21 April 1892. For an autobiographical account of the venture, see Munroe, *Commodore's Story*, 215-17, 219. Dillon and Knetsch, "Florida Fiber Company" is an excellent account of this ill-fated enterprise.

head." The Brevard County paper questioned rather curiously whether Denny had "found out all he wanted to while here," implying that Denny's activities had been somewhat suspicious.[34]

Work on the Florida East Coast Canal proceeded so slowly in the southern part of the Florida peninsula that Judge John Broome couldn't preside over the Dade County Circuit Court at Juno during the first three days of the fall term in December 1890 because of delays in traveling by steamboat on the Indian River. So intolerable were the conditions that while the Dade County grand jury appeared satisfied with "so little crime in our County," jurors expressed disappointment over the "delay of the East Coast Canal Company in giving us a waterway by which vegetables from one end of the County to the other can be transported to market." "[F]eeling the necessity of this way," the panel urged that "the [Florida Canal] company put this enterprise into operation as speedy [sic] as possible."[35]

With both Indian River steamboat companies still tied up in litigation, Titusville's town council considered ways to open up the Indian River docks to the smaller East Coast Transportation Company. On February 26, 1891, council members passed an ordinance, popularly known as the Titusville Force Ordinance, which made it a criminal offense for anyone to exclude the public by charging fees for the use of the docks on the Indian River. Modeled on a similar ordinance passed in July 1890, but rescinded following a public outcry, the new law sought to prohibit the larger Indian River company from charging the smaller company's *Sweeney* fees for tying up at the Titusville docks. In an editorial, the *Florida Star* condemned the town council for enacting the new ordinance. While the best policy was to protect the public's free use of the docks, the paper urged the council to await a Florida Supreme Court decision, adding that "a small town cannot dictate to or manage a great corporation." While Titusville council members worked to resolve the dock litigation, the Florida canal company man-

---

[34]*Indian River Steam-Boat Co. v. East Coast Transp. Co.*, 10 So. 480 (Fla. 1891). "Future of the E. C. T. Co.," *East Coast Advocate* (Titusville), 30 January 1891. Advertisements for both Flagler's steamboat company and its competitor, the smaller East Coast company, appear adjacent to each other to the right of the editorial in this and many other issues of the paper. Walter S. Graham is named as editor in the paper's masthead. *Florida Star* (Titusville), "Lake Worth" [regular column], 19 February 1891.

[35]Minutes of the Circuit Court, Book 1, pp. 15, 20-21, Public Records of Dade County, Florida.

aged to pay off its six-year-old $400,000 bond issue—fourteen years early. The payment left only the $1.4 million bond issue of 1888 outstanding.[36]

However miserable the conditions might have been in the southern sections of the waterway, in March 1891, the Florida canal company completed both the cutting of the Oak Hill canal and a newer and enlarged Haulover canal in present-day Volusia and Brevard counties, making possible for the first time the easy and cheap shipment of fresh produce between the Halifax and Indian rivers. Company officials also began the first work to the south on the reach between Jupiter Inlet and Lake Worth. The private waterway's development had already improved shipping Indian River citrus north from Rockledge. The East Coast Transportation Company's elegant new steamer *Sweeney* arrived in Titusville every other day from New Smyrna to ship Indian River oranges from Rockledge and Titusville north to New Smyrna where connections could be made to Henry Flagler's railroad and the St. Johns River steamers.[37]

Jacksonville's *Florida Times-Union* praised the Florida canal company's general manager, George Miles, for the success of the firm's dredging work, "Too much credit cannot be given this canal company, and especially to Mr. George E. [sic] Miles, the contractor, for the benefits bestowed on commerce and travel by this work." Emphasizing the importance of the dredging to the north between the Matanzas and Halifax rivers, the newspaper urged, "God speed the day when they [the canal company] will finish the work from this point to St. Augustine, which will open up the finest tourist route in the State—from St. Augustine to Lake Worth—and open up the whole East Coast to St. Augustine, giving us an outlet at that place both by water and rail." As a consequence of the waterway, the paper concluded, "Then will spring up an immense orange, pine-apple and vegetable trade that has been kept down for the want of good transportation facilities." But in April 1891, state trustees openly voiced their reservations against granting more public land until canal officials opened the divide between the Matanzas and Halifax rivers—the most difficult dredging of all the waterway work.[38]

---

[36]*Florida Star* (Titusville), "The Titusville Force Ordinance," 5 March 1891. Satisfaction of Mortgage executed by American Loan and Trust Company of New York, Trustee, in favor of Canal Company on February 20, 1891, and recorded on March 16, 1891, in Mortgage Book "I," at page 516, of the Public Records of St. Johns County.

[37]"Results of the East Coast Canal," 3 March 1891, *Florida Times-Union*, reprinted in *Tropical Sun* (Juno), 25 March 1891.

[38]*Ibid.*, MIIF, 26 April 1891, 146-47. *Tropical Sun* (Juno), 6 May 1891 [no title], p. 4.

Seven months later, on December 21, 1891, thirteen months after the Titusville wharf litigation began, the "strong arm of the law" finally sided with the smaller East Coast Transportation Company's right to use the town's docks. Denying the older company a monopoly over the use of the wharf, the Florida Supreme Court held that the Indian River Steamboat Company couldn't keep the rival company from using the docks to transfer freight to and from the railway.[39]

With a court victory in hand, in May 1892, East Coast Transportation Company officials announced that the *Sweeney* would now be making regular trips between Daytona and the St. Lucie River, at Stuart, especially for the pineapple business. The company had made a connection with Flagler's railroad, the Jacksonville, St. Augustine & Halifax Railway, giving the steamboat company a direct line in shipping fruit all the way to Jacksonville without changing cars. At the same time, a Florida canal company dredge worked in re-dredging the Haulover canal between the Mosquito Lagoon and the Indian River. The dredge was also expected to clean out the Oak Hill Canal between New Smyrna and Titusville. East Coast officials anticipated that the work would eliminate the too-often-encountered occurrence of steamers running aground in the waterways between Daytona and Titusville.[40]

A month later, the East Coast officials announced that Boston investor John Denny, the Florida canal company's president, had purchased eighty shares of stock in the small steamboat firm. The acquisition made Denny one of the largest stockholders, leading to speculation that the Flagler railway and the Florida canal company had pooled their interests to monopolize transportation along the coast. Accepting that Flagler had *already* been aiding the canal company financially, a Titusville paper discounted accounts of those who believed that the railway magnate had been making plans to extend the railway to Lake Worth. "In this we think they are mistaken, as the most reliable information we can get indicates that for this year, Mr. Flagler only contemplates the establishment of a complete, rapid and comfortable service right down the coast from St. Augustine to Rockledge," the paper editorialized in June 1892.[41]

---

[39]*Florida Star* (Titusville), [no title], 13 August 1891. *Indian River Steam-Boat Co. v. East Coast Transp. Co.*, 10 So. 480 (Fla. 1891)

[40]*Florida Star* (Titusville), "Notice [East Coast Transportation Co.] ," 26 May 1892.

[41]"Glorious Railroad News," *Tropical Sun* (Juno), 23 June 1892.

The Celestial Railroad: Jupiter, Mars, Venus and Juno

While the Florida canal company struggled to complete a waterway south of Jupiter at the southern end of the Indian River, a small railway — part of the Jacksonville, Tampa and Key West railway system — had already begun transporting passengers south from Jupiter at the south end of the Indian River overland to Juno on Lake Worth, beginning in 1888. At the northern end of Lake Worth, southbound passengers boarded a steamer owned by a Jacksonville, Tampa railway subsidiary — the Indian River Steamboat Company — bound for Palm Beach. Popularly known as the "Celestial Railroad," the three-foot wide narrow gauge railroad became the southernmost railroad in the United States, operating a seven-and-a half-mile-long line along a strip of land between Jupiter and Juno. Formally known as the Jupiter & Lake Worth Railroad, the railway began at Jupiter, the northern terminus, with intermediate stations at Mars, Venus, and Juno. Reaching the southern station at Juno on Lake Worth, another steamboat, the *Lake Worth*, a 21-ton sternwheeler, carried railway passengers south to Palm Beach. To travel farther south to Fort Lauderdale, Miami and the southern tip of the Florida peninsula, every Monday, Wednesday, and Friday at seven o'clock in the morning passengers boarded a stage coach at Lantana and traveled to the New River where they spent the night on the river bank at Fort Lauderdale, ending the trip the next day at Lemon City at the head of Biscayne Bay, all for a round-trip fare of sixteen dollars. Boarding and lodging at the New River camp cost just $2 a day.[42]

Several years later in May 1894, railway magnate Henry Flagler commissioned the Celestial Railway to transport building materials south for the construction of the new great hotel he was building at Palm Beach — the Royal Poinciana. So lucrative was the contract that the tiny railway reaped between $60,000 and $90,000 in freight income during the hotel's period of construction. Income during one 14-month period alone exceeded not only the total cost of the railway but also all revenues earned up until that time. Flagler tried to buy the tiny railway but the asking price was so high the railway magnate paid the exorbitant freight rates instead. He had his

---

[42]Shappee, "Celestial Railroad"; Prince, *Atlantic Coast Line*, 33, 55; Plat of "Map of Venus, Dade County, Florida," as recorded in Plat Book A, at page 14, of the Public Records of Dade County, Florida. "Go To Bay Biscayne Via The New Stage Line," advertisement, *Tropical Sun* (Juno), 30 March 1893.

revenge when he veered his railway line to the east of Juno and Jupiter, thereby rendering the little Jupiter and Lake Worth Railway unprofitable and making both Juno and Jupiter impractical destinations for business and tourism. The Jacksonville, Tampa railway, the Indian River Steamboat company and the little Celestial Railroad went into bankruptcy in 1896 while Flagler pushed his railway south like a juggernaut to Miami.[43]

Meanwhile, the Florida canal company struggled to finance enormously expensive dredging as operations pushed into south Florida. It was a "land poor" operation to be sure—thousands of acres of promised land grants, but little ready cash to pay for the difficult work that lay ahead.

---

[43]Shappee, "Celestial Railroad," 344-47.

Chapter 3

Beginnings

While Florida canal directors pushed to finish the waterway, the U. S. Navy began addressing the growing military need to bolster the country's Atlantic coast defenses. Surveys of the problem in the early 1890s prodded officials to formulate plans for constructing what would become the modern-day Atlantic Intracoastal Waterway. In October 1891, the Baltimore trade-paper *Manufacturers' Record* published the results of a naval study of coastal defenses, recommending constructing a series of Atlantic coastal waterways eight feet deep to enable American torpedo boats to seek safe harbor in time of war. The proposed route of the inland waterway extended from Cape Cod through Massachusetts and Rhode Island, opening into Long Island Sound, down through New Jersey's Delaware and Raritan Canal, then through the Delaware and Chesapeake Canal into Maryland's Chesapeake Bay. In the southern states, the course was to connect channels through Albemarle Sound and other waters in the Carolinas and in Georgia. Praising the scheme, the Baltimore paper pointed out not only the proposed waterway's use in military preparedness but that it would "facilitate greatly the trade of large areas of fertile tidewater country extending from Norfolk to Florida." Observing that "heavy traffic" already had been passing through the Albemarle and Chesapeake Canal connecting Norfolk to North Carolina's coastal towns, the paper waxed enthusiastic in assuring that the "same results would follow the construction of an equally good artificial waterway further down the Southern coast."[1]

Adding to the federal government's efforts, in January 1892, the New York Board of Trade adopted a resolution urging Congress to appropriate

---

[1]"An Inner Waterway Along the Atlantic," *Manufacturers' Record*, 17 October 1891. For decades to follow, the usefulness of the nation's inland waterways in national defense would remain an important concern of the federal government. See, also, "Interior Coastwise Routes," *New York Times*, 3 December 1891 for a skeptical examination of the cost of Atlantic coast inland improvements versus the defense benefits to be obtained and Buckman, "Defense Coordination," a 1940 study of the usefulness of the Panama and Florida canals during wartime.

$25,000 for a study of a proposed ship canal between New York Harbor and the Delaware and Chesapeake Bays. The proposal was touted as the first step in bringing to fruition Robert Fulton's century-old idea of creating a continuous inland waterway from New York to Florida. At the same time, the *Manufacturers' Record* published a series of articles written by acclaimed maritime engineer Lewis M. Haupt, all entitled, "The Intercoastal Waterway." The series supported a bill filed in Congress by Pennsylvania's Senator Matthew Quay to authorize the War Department to develop a plan for constructing an inland waterway from Philadelphia across New Jersey to New York Bay and prepare a cost estimate. Haupt advocated an "intercoastal waterway" to "develop and protect the traffic which is now subject to the risks and delays of a dangerous coast reaching from Florida to Cape Cod." Urging that the waterway would also "furnish in time of war a strategic line of defense," Haupt argued that its worth would "far exceed in value any sum which may be expended on its construction."

Describing proposed waterways along the Atlantic coast as far south as Florida, he outlined a plan for a Florida inland waterway *across* the northern part of the Florida peninsula that would link the Atlantic coast with the Mississippi River; but he neglected even to mention the struggling Florida canal company's project then underway along the east coast.[2]

The Boston and Florida land company

Meanwhile, to raise more cash for dredging the Florida waterway, directors sold 100,000 acres of the company's land grant for $1 an acre to the newly organized Boston and Florida Atlantic Coast Land Company. The sale comprised a string of parcels lying along the Florida east coast extending south from St. Augustine to Miami. Headed by 49-year-old Albert Page Sawyer of Newburyport, Massachusetts, another canal company investor, the Boston & Florida land company had been organized in Portland, Maine, only a few months before the sale to develop real estate in Florida. Sawyer and his business partner, George W. Piper, the land company's treasurer, Thomas B. Bailey of Cambridge, and Florida canal company engineer George Miles, then officially residing in Montreal, formed the company.

---

[2]"An Inner Waterway from New York to Florida," *Manufacturers Record*, 23 January 1892. Haupt, "The Intercoastal Waterway."

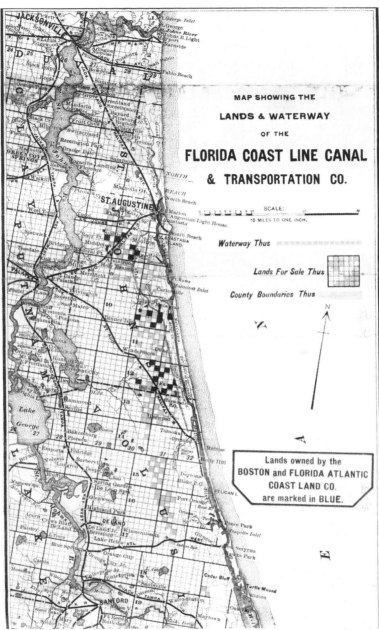

Map (partial) of the Florida east coast showing the northern section of lands owned by the Florida Coast Line Canal and Transportation Company and a related company, the Boston and Florida Atlantic Coast Land Company, which purchased 100,000 acres of the Florida canal company's land grant in 1892, from St. Augustine south to New Smyrna (today, New Smyrna Beach). Florida canal company lands are shown in lighter shading; Boston and Florida land company acreage, darker. (Courtesy, Trent University Archives, Trent University, Peterborough, Ontario, Canada)

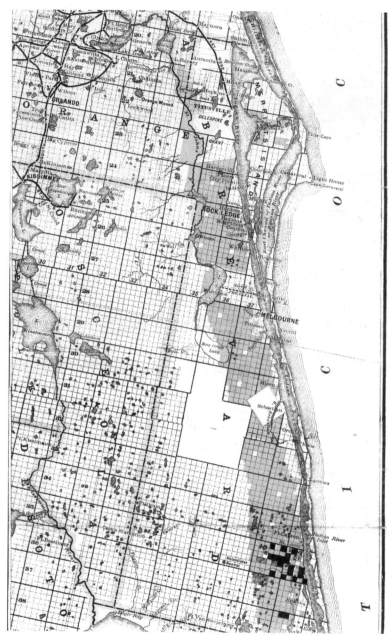

Map (partial) of the Florida east coast showing the Florida canal and Boston & Florida land companies' centrally located lands from Titusville south to Fort Pierce at Indian River Inlet, now Fort Pierce Inlet (1892). (Courtesy, Trent University Archives, Trent University, Peterborough, Ontario, Canada)

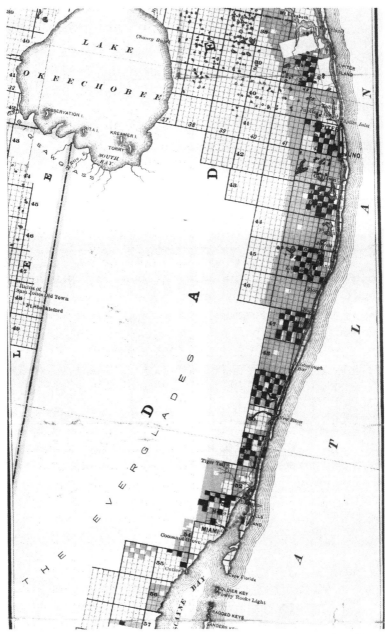

Map (partial) of the Florida east coast showing the Florida canal and Boston & Florida land companies' southern section of lands from Jupiter south to Miami (1892). (Courtesy, Trent University Archives, Trent University, Peterborough, Ontario, Canada)

Along with George L. Bradley, these four comprised the land company's board of directors.[3]

Sawyer, Piper, and Bailey, like Bradley, had been early investors in the first Bell Telephone companies and the Mergenthaler Linotype Company. Bailey had not only been an early stockholder in the Bell Telephone companies, but like Bradley, he also served as a director of the larger American Bell Telephone Company when the New England and Bell Telephone companies merged into one Massachusetts company in 1880.[4]

At first, Sawyer and his colleagues secured subscriptions for only half of the Boston & Florida land company's $100,000 preferred stock issue. To sweeten sales, Sawyer's group promised a share of "deferred" or common stock for the purchase of every two preferred shares. One of Sawyer's fellow Bell Telephone investors, W. W. Juergens, considered buying stock but declined in June 1892. Juergens found the Florida investment "safe enough and possibly a moderately profitable one," but in the end, the venture would "lock up money for a long time." In fact, the investment would "lock up" investors' money for decades until the land could be sold profitably. Nevertheless Miles persuaded one of his old associates, Sir Sandford Fleming, chief engineer of the Canadian Pacific Railway and an early promoter of Standard Time, to purchase $5,000 worth of Boston & Florida company stock. In time, Fleming would invest a total of $20,000 in the land company, in addition to his holdings in the Florida canal company. In March 1893, Miles reported back to Fleming, in Ottawa, that Henry Flagler had begun constructing a hotel on Lake Worth and purchased approximately 50 acres there for the staggering sum of $103,000. Two months later, Miles confirmed his appointment as general manager of the Florida canal company

---

[3]Warranty Deed executed by Canal Company in favor of Boston & Florida Atlantic Coast Land Company on January 4, 1892, and recorded in Deed Book "E," at page 343, of the Public Records of Dade County, Florida. Seth Perkins, general manager of the Canal Company, characterized the land company as an "allied company as to the Canal co." Perkins to Youngberg, May 4, 1928, YP Box 4, File 9. See, also, Akin, *Flagler*, 174-77. *Boston Directory*, 1143, listing for Albert P. Sawyer. For information on the revolutionary Gamewell Auxiliary system, see Gamewell, *Emergency Signaling* and Maver, *American Telegraphy*, 462-65. Certificate of Organization, Boston & Florida Atlantic Coast Land Company, filed for record on May 7, 1917, and recorded in Book 1 of Corporations, at page 29, of the Public Records of Broward County, Florida.

[4]Coon, *American Tel & Tel*, 79.

and optimistically predicted the completion of the waterway to Biscayne Bay by "the early part of next season."[5]

Albert P. Sawyer

Some years before forming the Boston & Florida land company, Albert Sawyer organized a real estate and insurance business with George Piper at Newburyport. Sawyer also served as a director of the Ocean National Bank and as trustee of the Five Cents Savings Bank, both of Newburyport. Piper initially served as auditor and later became a director of Newburyport's Institution for Savings, one of the oldest saving banks in the country, founded in 1820. Piper would also become a director of the First National Bank of Newburyport. After Piper's retirement from the partnership, Sawyer opened an office in Boston, engaging in numerous and diverse business activities, including heading up the Gamewell Auxiliary Fire Alarm Company, a firm capitalizing on the invention of new improvements in fire alarm telegraphy.[6]

To raise more cash, in May 1892, just four months after selling land to the Boston & Florida company, Florida canal officials sold additional large tracts to Sawyer as trustee of the Lake Worth and New River Land Trusts, two entities formed for the benefit of Bradley and his business associates and friends. The first of the Bradley trusts, the Lake Worth Land Trust, was formed on May 27 for Bradley who held twenty-nine of the forty authorized shares; Boston textile and insurance company director Frederic Amory —

---

[5]*Prospectus*, Boston & Florida Atlantic Coast Land Company, Boston, November 24, 1891. GFM to APS, 24 October 1892; GFM to APS, 29 October 1892; SM to Harris, 21 November 1892; all in SP Folder 1. SM to APS, 12 August 1893, SP Folder 2. Juergens to APS, 6 June 1893, SP Folder 2. For Fleming's own account of the Canadian railway, see Fleming, *Intercolonial*. For biographical information on Fleming as well as narrative of Fleming's role in the railway, see, generally, Berton's *Impossible Railway and National Dream*; Green, *Chief Engineer*; Maclean, *Man of Steel*. Miles to Fleming, 21 March and 1 May 1893, Flagler Enterprises Letters, MSS 0:107, Box 146, Special Collections, Robert Manning Strozier Library, Florida State University, Tallahassee, Florida For Fleming's early contribution to the development of Standard Time, see Grant, "Time-Reckoning." For information on the revolutionary Gamewell Auxiliary system, see Gamewell, *Emergency Signaling* and Maver, *American Telegraphy*, 462-65.

[6]Death of Albert P. Sawyer, "Death List of a Day — Albert P. Sawyer," *New York Times*, 22 November 1903, p. 7, col. 5; Sawyer, *Sawyer Families*, 95,134; Parsons, *Newburyport*, 83, 88; *Newburyport and Amesbury Directory* (1891), 351, 352; *Ibid.*, (1892-3), 351-52; *Official Program*, 68, 71, 91, 94; *Massachusetts Soldiers*, Record 446241 (Civil War service listing for Albert P. Sawyer).

later the canal company's president—owned two shares; Washington lawyer Samuel Maddox, the canal company's secretary, three shares; and Sawyer, six shares. The Lake Worth Trust bought 2,200 acres of canal company land. Ten years later, this trust would develop a tract of land aptly named, "Sawyer's Addition to the Town of Boynton," west of the original Town of Boynton's (today's Boynton Beach) limits. In 1913, Albert Hayden Sawyer, Sawyer's son, as successor trustee, would subdivide portions of three square miles of another tract of trust land near Lake Worth in present-day Palm Beach County. The New River Land Trust, the second Bradley trust, was created the day after the Lake Worth Trust to benefit Bradley alone. Initially, this trust bought 1,831 acres of canal company land in present-day Fort Lauderdale for $10,016. A few months later, the Florida canal company, the Boston & Florida land company and the two Bradley trusts jointly employed West Palm Beach real estate agent Albert W. Robert to market their immense holdings in what was then Dade County, stretching from Jupiter to the end of the Florida peninsula. By June 24, Robert had begun transforming a tract of land owned by the Lake Worth Trust into a large experimental farm known as the Belleville Plantation to grow fruits and vegetables and thereby entice prospective settlers to buy land for farming.[7]

The Amorys

Important investors in the Florida waterway venture, Frederic Amory and his brother, Harcourt, figured prominently in New England's textile, banking and insurance industries. The Amorys descended from Thomas Amory,

---

[7]Warranty Deed executed by the Canal Company in favor of Albert Sawyer, Trustee, on May 26, 1892, and recorded in Deed Book "E," at page 343, of the Public Records of Dade County, Florida; Lake Worth Land Trust, May 27, 1892, recorded in Miscellaneous Book 1, at Page 212, of the Public Records of Palm Beach County, Florida. New River Land Trust Declaration, May 28, 1892, Miscellaneous Book 1, at Page 218, of the Public Records of Palm Beach County, Florida; Warranty Deed executed by the Canal Company in favor of Albert P. Sawyer, Trustee, on May 26, 1892, and recorded in Deed Book "E," at Page 494, of the Public Records of Dade County, Florida. Plat of Sawyer's Addition to the Town of Boynton, recorded December 11, 1902, in Plat Book "B," at Page 68, of the Public Records of Dade County, Florida. Plat of E ½ of W ½ of Sec. 33, T. 44 , R. 43; West Half of Sec. 28, Tp. 44, R. 43; and West Half, Sec. 21, Tp 44, R. 43, recorded on September 2, 1913, in Plat Book 5, at Page 12 of the Public Records of Palm Beach County, Florida. Albert W. Robert to Albert P. Sawyer, June 13, 24, and July 19,1892, SP Folder 1. Albert W. Robert to APS, 13 and 24 June and 19 July 1892, SP Folder 1. Compare advertisements for "Albert W. Robert," Juno *Tropical Sun*, 16 June 1892, showing Robert as agent for the canal and Boston companies as early as June 1892.

an early merchant who settled in Boston in 1720, and James Amory, governor of Massachusetts from 1807 until his death in 1808. In 1793, James, a wealthy and prominent lawyer, was chosen to serve as the first president of one of America's earliest privately-owned canals — the Middlesex Canal — by the waterway's thirteen directors. An investor with Maddox and Bradley in the Lake Worth Trust, the 48-year-old Frederic Amory resided at Bar Harbor, Maine, kept a Boston office address and served as treasurer of both the Nashua Manufacturing and Jackson companies, two leading New England textile firms.[8]

The Amory brothers' father was James Sullivan Amory, a member of the first board of directors of the Boston Manufacturers Mutual Fire Insurance Company. Founded in 1850 by several textile manufacturers, the Boston insurance company was among the first to offer fire insurance for textile mills when traditional firms declined to cover the risk. James's cousin, William Amory, helped found the company, heading the firm from 1851 to 1865. After his father's retirement from the board of directors in 1876 after twenty-six years' service, Fred began serving as a director in 1877 and remained in office for another fifty-one years. From 1907 until 1923, Fred served as president of the Florida canal company, heading up the firm's work in completing the waterway begun in 1882.[9]

Eleven years younger than his brother Fred, 37-year-old Harcourt Amory served as treasurer of the Lancaster Mills and the Indian Head Mills of Alabama and as a director of the American Mutual Liability Insurance Company (the nation's first liability insurance company), the Mutual Boiler Insurance Company, the Saco-Lowell Shops, and the Textile Securities Company. Harcourt also served as a director of Boston's State Street Trust Company, maintaining the same Boston office address as Frederic.[10]

Today, Harcourt Amory is recognized as one of the nation's most important antiquarian book collectors. An 1876 graduate of Harvard University (and a roommate of Percival Lowell, his cousin and later founder of the

---

[8]Marquis, editor, *Who's Who in New England*, 36. Miles, "History," 8. Meredith, *Descendants of Hugh Amory*, page i and separate pedigree entitled, "The Amory Family of Boston," by George Tickner Dexter, folded within back cover and dated January 1, 1897, with some additional notes, November 1900. See, also, MacKenzie, editor, *Colonial Families*, volume 5, 3-7; Clarke, *Old Middlesex*, 17-18.

[9]Yorke, *Able Men of Boston*, 49-50, 247; *New England Historical*, 39: 89; State Street Trust, 5-7.

[10]"Harcourt Amory Dead," *New York Times*, 28 November 1925; *National Cyclopaedia*, volume J, 373; Hodges, *First American Liability*; Garvey, *Tenniel's Alice*, 9-10. See, State Street, for a listing of directors, including Harcourt Amory, at the end of this booklet published in 1923.

Lowell Observatory), Harcourt possessed a keen interest in collecting the works of the English satirist and mathematician Charles Lutwidge Dodgson, who often wrote under the pseudonym Lewis Carroll. At first, Harcourt bought editions of Carroll's *Alice in Wonderland* to study illustrations for figures he planned to carve for a children's toy theater. Although he never finished the theater, Harcourt continued to collect Carroll's books and drawings illustrating the satirist's works, as well as his manuscripts, letters and memorabilia. Later, the younger Amory acquired all of Dodgson's scientific papers and books. In 1898, he bought the only known copy of an 1865 edition of *Alice in Wonderland* in a special white vellum presentation binding. Two years after his death in 1925, Harcourt's widow donated his collection of Carrolliana, including Carroll's books and the drawings of Sir John Tenniel, an illustrator of the Carroll books, to Harcourt's *alma mater*, Harvard University. The Amory collection is widely regarded as one of the finest Carroll collections in the United States.[11]

Over the next three decades, these New England investors in the Florida waterway, particularly Bradley, Sawyer and Fred Amory, would remain close friends and invest in a wide variety of businesses, schemes and ventures throughout Florida and the United States. Their ventures would include such diverse endeavors as real estate development, fruit, vegetable and hemp growing, and the construction of a plant to manufacture a paint removal product, all in Florida; a scheme to convert sea water into gold in Maine; gold, silver and copper mining in the Southwest; and a chewing gum vending machine manufacturing concern located in New Jersey.

Tuttle and Cummings

While Bradley and his friends held on to their Florida waterway investments for decades, two early canal bond investors, Miami pioneer Julia Tuttle and prominent Washington attorney Horace Cummings, exchanged their holdings for substantial tracts of south Florida land. Born in Cleveland, Ohio, in 1849, 38-year-old Julia Tuttle decided after the death of her husband to return permanently in 1887 to the place she had only visited before—Dade County, Florida—where she purchased a square mile of prime real estate along Biscayne Bay and the north bank of the Miami River in present-day downtown Miami. Later, Tuttle became a prominent south Florida developer, famous for persuading Flagler to extend his railway

---

[11]Garvey, *Tenniel's Alice*, 9-10; Dickinson, *Dictionary*, 15.

south to Miami for a share of her Miami properties just before her death in September 1898 at the age of fifty-nine.[12]

Tuttle's partner in the Florida waterway investment, 50-year-old Horace Stuart Cummings maintained a legal residence in New Hampshire while practicing law in Washington. Born in Southborough, Massachusetts, Cummings was a grandson of John Sargent Tewksbury, a *Mayflower* descendant. After graduating from Phillips Exeter Academy and Dartmouth College, he studied law at Albany law school in New York and later was admitted to the Bar of New York City, where he practiced for a number of years before relocating to Washington. At the nation's capital, Cummings became famous arguing federal court cases during a career spanning forty years. Dartmouth College's Horace Cummings Memorial Hall, housing part of the engineering school, was named in honor of this distinguished lawyer in September 1929 as a result of a $200,000 gift made by Cummings' widow, Jeannette. Gracious and unpretentious, friends and acquaintances alike considered him a gentle and honest man. An organizer of the District's University Club, Cummings was, like fellow Florida canal company investor George Bradley, a member of both the Sons of the American Revolution and the Geographical Society. From 1876 until 1877, he served as a member of New Hampshire's House of Representatives.[13]

In June 1881, when John Westcott began organizing the Florida canal company, Cummings helped to create Washington's first telephone system — the National Capital Telephone Company — and served as the firm's first president. Henry D. Cooke, one of the Florida canal company's directors, served as the telephone company's vice president. Cummings also headed the Equitable Industrial Life Insurance Company, served as vice president of the Washington Loan and Trust Company, and invested in street railway construction and land development at the nation's capital. An old-family scion like the Amory brothers, Cummings joined James Sullivan Amory, Frederic's and Harcourt's father, as a resident member of the New England Historic Genealogical Society. In 1909, only two years before his death, Cummings published his experiences as a member of Dartmouth College's Class of 1862, updating the historical account the New Hampshire native wrote twenty-five years before.[14]

---

[12]Chapin, *Florida*, 122-25; Chandler, *Flagler*, 158-61.

[13]"H. S. Cummings, Old Lawyer Here, Called to Death," *Washington Times*, 7 December 1911; *National Cyclopaedia*, volume 12, 7-8; Corning, *Horace S. Cummings*.

[14]Van Orsdel, "History of the Telephone System in the District of Columbia," 175; *New England Historical* 66: 83; *New England Historical* 64: 98; Cummings, *Dartmouth*; *New England Historical* 45: 67-68.

Beginning with one conveyance on February 16, 1892, followed by three more transfers a year later, the Florida canal company redeemed nearly $30,000 worth of bonds owned jointly by Tuttle and Cummings by deeding to Tuttle alone almost 7,000 acres of valuable south Florida land. In legal proceedings brought by Cummings four years after Tuttle's death, a Dade County judge established his right to half of the immense tract of south Florida acreage.[15]

An almost unnoticed and seemingly inconsequential occurrence was the sale of a relatively small amount of Florida canal company land to insiders Henry Gaillard and James Colee, two of the enterprise's initial directors. In June 1891, the firm sold 594 acres to Colee for $1,308, representing a string of parcels stretching from present-day Martin County south along the Florida east coast to today's Fort Lauderdale in Broward County. In just two years, Colee's investment reaped handsome profits. In December 1893, Colee sold a forty-acre tract in present-day Fort Lauderdale for $400, a rise in value from an average price paid of $2.20 an acre to $10 an acre. A year after Colee's purchase, in July 1892, the canal company sold 320 acres in Dade and Broward counties to Henry Gaillard, the firm's treasurer, at $3 an acre for $960.[16]

Henry Flagler

Despite the substantial wealth possessed by Bradley and his associates, the New England group soon ran out of ready cash for dredging operations, holding hundreds of thousands of acres of Florida land, particularly in the

---

[15]Transcription of letter of Julia D. Tuttle dated March 20, 1893, Affidavit of Horace S. Cummings dated March 31, 1899, and list of lands of the Florida Coast Line Canal and Transportation Company dated March 31, 1899, filed on April 4, 1899, in Deed Book "U," page 301, of the Public Records of Dade County, Florida. Decree, *Horace S. Cummings vs. Henry E. Tuttle, et al.*, December 6, 1902, Minutes of the Circuit Court, Book 2, pages 296-302, Public Records of Dade County, Florida. In 1885, the Canal Company transferred 160 acres of its land grant in St. Johns County to Cummings, according to *Mitchell v. Furman*, 180 U. S. 402 (1901).

[16]Warranty Deed executed by the Canal Company in favor of James L. Colee on June 20, 1891, and recorded in Deed Book "E," page 150, of the Public Records of Dade County, Florida. Warranty Deed executed by James L. Colee and Mary P. Colee, his wife, in favor of Charles G. Bostrom on December 1, 1893, and recorded in Deed Book "K," page 82, of the Public Records of Dade County, Florida. Warranty Deed executed by the Canal Company in favor of Henry Gaillard on July 8, 1892, and recorded in Deed Book "G," page 68, of the Public Records of Dade County, Florida.

southern part, but of little value without better transportation and development. Henry Flagler, the man building the Florida East Coast Railway south from St. Augustine, soon furnished the transportation and helped develop the Florida canal company's land grant. He also became president of the Florida canal company for the next three years.

By the fall of 1892, Flagler had built a continuous east coast railway from St. Augustine south to New Smyrna. He considered extending the railway farther south to the end of the Florida peninsula. But what stopped Flagler literally "in his tracks," with no pun intended, was the lack of available state lands in the southern peninsula for the railway's extension. The State of Florida had reserved most, if not all, of the remaining available land along the coast exclusively for the Florida canal company. In obtaining its charter in 1881 and beginning dredging years before Flagler started building the railway, canal company promoters had beaten the Standard Oil tycoon to the punch. Flagler proposed a solution, a plan that would dramatically alter the canal company's land holdings and result in a decades-long *de facto* partnership between the two enterprises. Writing to Sam Maddox, the canal company's secretary, on November 4, 1892, Flagler offered to extend the railway south of Rockledge for what would ultimately amount to a quarter of the canal company's land grant:

"Other roads constructed in Florida have received from 6,000 to 20,000 acres of land for each mile of road constructed. These grants have nearly, if not quite, exhausted the lands at the disposal of the state for such purposes. Your own canal has received from the state a grant of alternate sections within the six-mile limit along its route. Our railroad will practically follow the same course, and for this reason we are shut off from any possible subsidy at the hands of the state. We believe therefore that you can well afford to aid us in this undertaking by dividing with us your land grant. If you cannot do this we should receive at the least 1,500 acres for each mile of road which we shall construct south of Rockledge, not, however, to exceed 104 miles."[17]

George Miles, the Florida canal company's general manager, urged the board to accept Flagler's proposal, pointing out the obvious benefit of the railway's extension to the firm's as-yet undeveloped south Florida land

---

[17]Exhibit "A" to Bill of Complaint, *Florida East Coast Railway Co. v. Canal Company, et al.,* St. Johns County Circuit Court, Chancery Case No. 1162. Case later transferred to Putnam County because of Judge Gibbs's recusal. See, also, Youngberg, "East Coast Canal," 24.

grant. The canal company's directors agreed to the plan but over strong opposition from a few of Miles's associates.[18]

As early as August 1892, Miles had been negotiating with Flagler to invest in the Florida canal company. At the same time, George Bradley pitched two Boston & Florida land company investors — Albert Sawyer and his business partner, George Piper — to become stockholders in the soon-to-be reorganized company. He contended that the two "would find a large profit" in the purchase. On October 14, with Maddox in New York completing arrangements with Flagler's lawyers, Bradley remarked that Flagler's involvement would make it "easier to sell our lands." But by the end of the year, Boston & Florida directors still hadn't sold all of the company's stock. Looking for ways to increase investor interest, Miles promoted making the preferred stock convertible into Florida land.[19]

The looming reorganization of the canal company strained relations between Bradley and Sawyer. In January 1893, Bradley complained to Sawyer that he and Piper had not satisfied their pledge to buy $15,000 of the Boston & Florida stock. He had relied on their pledge when he agreed to loan more money to the canal company for dredging work. Bradley also reminded Sawyer that he had entered into an agreement to pay as needed for the work in the south between Jupiter and Lake Worth up to $20,000, with Miles agreeing to pay the same amount. "I had your promise and Mr. Piper's to pay $15,000 of this sum & the remaining $5,000 I was to put elsewhere," Bradley fumed. In the reorganization, Bradley purchased $20,000 of the new stock and bonds, with the newly capitalized company assuming the obligations of the Jupiter and Lake Worth contract with its dredging contractor, Rittenhouse Moore. As a result of what he regarded as promises, Bradley thought he had the right to call on Sawyer to pay the rest of his $15,000 pledge. But Sawyer believed that his offer to pay for the stock had been "conditional." Bradley, as always, remained diplomatic, if still somewhat miffed, "I don't think that it is worth while for us to pursue the controversy on paper. I have every confidence in your honorable intention in the matter and only report that we view the matter differently." If Sawyer couldn't make cash investments, Bradley sought Sawyer's banking help, if the need should arise, in arranging temporary loans to tide him over."[20]

---

[18]Miles, "History," 7; Dau, *Florida*, 255.

[19]GLB to APS, 12 August and 14 October 1892; GFM to APS, 15 October 1892; GLB to APS, 21, 24 December 1892; all in SP Folder 1.

[20]GLB to APS, 18, 23 January 1893, SP Folder 2.

Meanwhile, Henry Flagler made his first cash payment to the Florida canal company in January 1893. The next month, Boston & Florida directors set in motion a plan to allow stockholders to exchange shares for land to encourage investment in the company. On March 16, at the annual meeting held at St. Augustine, Florida canal company stockholders elected Flagler a director. Company directors, in turn, chose Flagler to succeed John Denny of Boston as president. In addition to George Bradley and Fred Amory, other canal company directors selected were long-time Flagler associate Joseph Parrott, also chosen as vice president; Henry Gaillard (the only canal company original director still serving), treasurer; George Miles, general manager; and Sam Maddox, secretary. The following month, Flagler assured Miami pioneer Julia Tuttle, an early investor in the canal project, that the canal company expected to complete the canal from Lake Worth to Biscayne Bay within two years.[21]

Lake Worth settlers met at the Palm Beach Yacht Club on March 10 to consider Flagler's request (some might say, *demand*) for a donation of land or money amounting to $30,000 in exchange for the extension of the railway to Lake Worth. The meeting adjourned after the gathering agreed to the composition of a committee to secure pledges from land owners along Lake Worth. Reacting to Flagler plans for the railway's extension, the Titusville *Advocate* touted the likely increase in value of the Florida canal company's acreage in today's Broward County, "The land along New River and both forks of Middle River are either government or canal company lands. The latter may be had at reasonable prices, ranging from $2.50 to $10 per acre." "Of course the fronts on New River Sound," the paper went on, "are held at much higher figures; but if our judgment is worth anything as to the future of this locality high prices are well warranted, and present figures will double or treble within the next few years—for whatever settlement is made in the extensive territory traversed by New River and Middle River with its two forks, must do its trading at some point at or near the mouth of New River."[22]

---

[21]GLB to APS, 31 January 1893, APS to George T. Manson, 13 February 1893, SP Folder 1. Seth Perkins (Florida Canal and Transportation Company) to GAY, 4 May 1928, and Swan to GAY, 4 September 1928; both in YP Box 4, File 29. Akin, "Sly Foxes," 29. See, also, Akin, *Flagler*, 177-80, for a discussion of Flagler's investment and subsequent disinvestment in the canal company. Swan to GAY, 4 September 1928, YP Box 4, File 29. [No title], Tropical Sun (Juno), 30 March 1893. Typewritten notes of Youngberg on Flagler to Tuttle, 27 April 1893, Tuttle Collection, State Library of Florida, in YP Box 4, File 9.

[22]"Railroad Meeting," *Tropical Sun* (Juno), 16 March 1893. "Stagecoach Visits Fort Lauderdale in 1893," Titusville *Advocate*, reprinted in *Tropical Sun* (Juno), 9 March 1893.

During the same year, federal and state legislation authorized the federal government to take over maintenance of the 138-mile Indian River channel between Goat Creek and Jupiter Inlet. In exchange for the federal government's assumption of maintenance, the Florida canal company waived the right to collect tolls in that stretch, despite the company's substantial investment in making improvements there.[23]

By the end of April 1893, the influx of Flagler money enabled the canal company to begin construction at New Smyrna of two immense dipper dredges by the Albany-based Osgood Dredge Company. Each dredge was to be 90 feet long, thirty-five feet wide and nine feet deep and built out of native Florida wood, with eight cypress wood corner posts on the superstructure, each two feet square. The machinery housed on each dredge weighed over a hundred tons, including two locomotive boilers, each generating 130 horsepower. A 50-foot-long boom on each boat supported a 280-foot-long hoisting chain. A pressure of 75 tons could be exerted on each dipper handle, sufficient to cut readily through gravel, coquina, and sandstone, with each dipper handling two and a half cubic yards of material at a time. Each twelve-hour day, one dredge could excavate 2,000 cubic yards of earth. Canal officials planned the dredges to be ready within two months, expecting to pay between $65,000 and $75,000 for the completed work. The completed dredges were to be brought south through the inland waterway route, then only three feet deep, widening and deepening the channel along the way to Jupiter and then further on to Biscayne Bay. A single man would be able to handle the nine levers needed to operate the machinery. Only three men were needed for each dredge. The canal company scheduled two 12-hour shifts of three men each to operate the dredge day and night. The *Advocate* exuded considerable elation over a completed east coast waterway, "Think of it! A water route from St. Augustine to Biscayne Bay, paralleled by a superbly equipped railroad." "Immigrants," the paper confidently predicted, "will flock to these shores by the hundreds and pleasure seekers will tax the capacity of all the hotels that can be built for seasons to come. If there be an East Floridian sleeping a Van Winkle sleep, it is high time he

---

[23]Miles, "History," 6, 11-12. See, "Government Aid For The Indian River," Titusville *East Coast Advocate*, 30 January 1891, for a narrative of the U. S. Army Corps of Engineers' report recommending canal company relinquishment and federal takeover of the stretch of Indian River between Titusville and Jupiter. "East Coast Canal To Be Bought by Government For Much Less Than It has Cost to Build," *Miami Metropolis*, 27 November 1914. The Florida legislature authorized relinquishment of this stretch of the waterway by *Laws of Florida* (1893), c. 4283, approved June 2, 1893.

were aroused to the situation." Using an especially bad metaphor and even worse grammar, the paper concluded, "'The world do move' and East Florida is in the van."[24]

Canal company officials encouraged east coast residents to sign petitions asking the Florida legislators to extend the firm's charter for the waterway's completion. Looking with favor upon Flagler's election to the canal company's presidency, the editor of the Juno-based *Tropical Sun* recommended that its readers sign the petitions. "That the result of the consummation of the proposed canal be other than of the greatest importance and advantage to the entire East Coast Country is an idea not to be entertained," the paper exhorted. The waterway's completion would not only create a "steamer course that will attract countless visitors from all over the world" but also bring to Dade County the possibility of drainage and the reclamation of thousands of acres of rich vegetable lands now under water. The Florida canal company, the paper argued, ought to be permitted "not to rob the State or seize her lands," but a "reasonable time" to complete the project. Florida legislators finally agreed on "a reasonable time." Lawmakers authorized an extension of the canal company's charter to allow the completion of the waterway from St. Augustine to Biscayne Bay but permitted land grants to the firm only for portions of the waterway actually completed by June 1, 1897.[25]

Meanwhile James Colee, one of the company's engineers, built a wood station at the south end of Lake Worth to fuel dredge boilers. Company officials expected by the end of the month one of the larger Osgood dredges to be in the lake working south and the arrival any day of a second dredge, the *Alabama*, to relieve two others, the *Chester* and the *Urie*, on the work between the Indian River and Lake Worth. Rumors flew up and down the coast that Flagler planned to extend his railroad into the southern part of the Florida peninsula. Residents speculated that real estate prices might rise to as much as $1,000 an acre on land that had sold for as little as $1 an acre a few years before. Land sales boomed along the east coast. Prices were so good George Miles advised fellow Boston & Florida land company directors to consider raising land prices. But on a sour note, by what Bradley called "a possible error" of New River Land Trust agent Al Roberts, Fort Lauderdale-

[24]"New Canal Dredges," *Tropical Sun* (Juno), 27 April 1893, reporting news from the Indian River Advocate; "The East Coast Canal," *Tropical Sun* (Juno), 18 May 1893, reporting news from recent article in the *Manufacturer's Record*.

[25]"Sign the Petition," *Tropical Sun* (Juno), 6 April 1893. *Laws of Florida* (1893), c. 4284, approved May 27, 1893.

area sales totaled $1,000 less than anticipated. Facing additional calls for more capital, Bradley bemoaned Roberts' shortfall. Yet two months later, the struggling Florida canal company managed to redeem the $1.4 million bond issue of 1888, a surprising fifteen years before maturity. By July, the canal company's dredging contractor, Rittenhouse Moore, had put another dredge—a large clam-shell rig—on the Jupiter-to-Lake Worth cut, but the machine had not been making good progress.[26]

By August, the Florida canal company had put one dredge at Juno below Lake Worth working south and a second at Fort Lauderdale pushing north. By the end of October, despite the efforts of Judge White on the company's behalf, state trustees refused to turn over money owed the company on the sale of the canal company's reserve lands made in the 1880s. Characterizing Florida Governor Henry Mitchell as "more like an overgrown child than a man," Miles related that during the trustees' meeting in Tallahassee the governor turned his back on Judge White and refused to speak to him. Miles now headed south to canal properties near Fort Pierce on the St. Lucie River to build a large house for the first group of Scandinavian settlers arriving on the site of what would become an important joint development of the Flagler, Florida Canal and Boston & Florida land company interests – White City.[27]

Louis Pio Founds White City

Late September 1893, Miles learned of the possibility of attracting a large number of Scandinavian settlers through a 51-year-old Danish Socialist named Louis Albert Francois Pio. A graduate of the University of Copenhagen, Pio had been the leader of the Social Democrats Party in Denmark in 1871. A year later, Pio organized a Danish International, rallying 700 union members. When Pio refused to call off a mass meeting following a bricklayers' strike, he was arrested and imprisoned for three years by the Danish government. He survived a prison diet consisting of smoked and salted

---

[26][No title], *Tropical Sun* (Juno), 20 April 1893. *Business Directory*, 54. GLB to APS, 3 April 1893; GFM to APS, 8 April 1893; GLB to APS, 20 April 1893, J. A. Henderson to SFM, 4 May 1893; SP Folder 1. Satisfaction of Mortgage executed by Edward M. Cleary, as Substituted Trustee, in favor of Canal Company on June 13, 1893, and recorded on June 21, 1893, in Satisfaction of Mortgages Book 1, at page 119, of the Public Records of St. Johns County. Morris, *Encyclopedia of American History*, 263. GFM to APS, 8 July 1893, SP Folder 1.

[27]GFM to APS, 16 August 1893; GFM to APS, 28 September 1893; GFM to APS, 30 October 1893; GFM to APS, 2 November 1893; SP Folder 1.

horsemeat, bread, and thin beer, but developed ulcers and lost ten teeth. After his release from prison, Pio left Denmark for the United States. In Chicago, Pio lectured to Danish settlers about communism and socialism, promoting development of a utopian Danish colony in Kansas. In May 1877, Pio left Chicago with fifteen Danes to establish a settlement near Hays, Kansas, but later returned when the settlement failed to take hold. Eventually Pio entered the real estate business and in 1893 secured employment with the Flagler railway to promote a settlement in south Florida called White City, near Fort Pierce, after the so-called "White City" at the Columbian Exposition of 1893, which lasted from May 1 until October 30, 1893.[28]

When George Miles was first introduced to him, Pio had been working at the Chicago Fair's Florida State Building, whose construction Flagler financed, distributing a booklet he had written about Danes who had been successfully raising fruit trees and pineapples in Florida. But after only a few months' work in establishing the colony near Fort Pierce, Pio died tragically in June 1894 of typhus, apparently contracted while working in the Florida swamps, at the age of fifty-two. The rustic Midway Road running from west to east through the middle of Pio's White City settlement would recall, in name only, the famous Midway at the Chicago fair. Both the now nearly rural White City and the Midway Road running through it survive to this day, but only as mere vestiges of the great plans Pio had in store for his utopian community.[29]

Meanwhile, Flagler's railway had reached Fort Pierce over 200 miles south of St. Augustine by January 1894. Just five months later, work on the Florida waterway between Lake Worth and the New River at Fort Lauderdale progressed so quickly that the dredge working north from the New River almost reached the Hillsboro River at Deerfield, today's Deerfield Beach. The machine cutting south from Lake Worth pushed fairly easily along a route connecting a series of small lakes, ponds, and lagoons. But north of the Hillsboro Inlet, canal officials expected to encounter higher, more difficult land. A second dredge working south from Lake Worth averaged 200 feet every twenty-four hours, cutting a waterway twelve feet deep and 60 feet wide.[30]

---

[28]GFM to APS, 28 September 1893. Nielsen, *The Danish Americans*, 30, 184-89.

[29]*Ibid.* For general information on the Florida State Building at the Chicago exposition, see, Kerber, "Florida." See, also, Pozzetta, "Foreign Colonies," for a general discussion of early foreign settlements along the east coast, including White City and Pio's involvement.

[30]"The East Coast Canal," *Daily Florida Citizen*, 6 June 1894. GLB to APS, 24 January 1894, SP Folder 3. GLB to APS, 16 March 1894, SP Folder 3.

Toward the end of January, Bradley received something of a scare, learning that a fire had broken out at Sawyer's Boston offices at 19 Pearl Street. Fortunately the fire did not damage the books and records of the Florida enterprises. Still, examining a December 1893 financial statement on the Florida canal company, Bradley simply couldn't understand why its land sales department consumed so much cash to operate, a condition that would last for years until land sales turned profitable.[31]

Work along the six-mile-long waterway between the Jupiter Lighthouse and Lake Worth suddenly halted when the Florida canal company's contract with its Mobile, Alabama-based dredging contractor, Rittenhouse Moore, ended. Moore had been in St. Augustine in June to negotiate a new contract, expecting to resume work in a few days, but unfortunately he experienced such dire financial distress that creditors soon seized the company's dredges near Juno to satisfy company debts.[32]

South of Lake Worth, dredging a series of canals to Biscayne Bay together more than forty miles long progressed rapidly. By September 1894, the dredge *Biscayne* cut a canal south of the Hillsboro River near present-day Deerfield Beach at a rate of 450 feet a day. A month later, the canal company completed the waterway between the New and Hillsboro rivers. On the New River, it was said, sail craft easily ascended the waters, bringing supplies to the canal company's camp at Fort Lauderdale or to the dredge cutting north from the New River Inlet. An account of a hunting trip though present-day Broward County described an encounter with the Florida canal company's dredge about three miles north of the Hillsboro Inlet where everything the crew needed including fresh Chicago beef was on the vessel and the men stayed aboard for several days at a stretch. The dredge employed a dipper that scooped three-and-a-half cubic yards of earth each time, working day and night, seven days a week.[33]

Fulfilling a promise made three years earlier, Florida canal directors transferred 102,917 acres of the company's land grant to the Flagler railway for the railroad's extension from Fort Pierce to West Palm Beach. In January 1895, the Flagler railway and the canal company jointly developed the fledgling White City and Santa Lucia settlements near Fort Pierce in today's

---

[31]*Ibid.*

[32]"Juno on Lake Worth," *Daily Florida Citizen*, 7 June 1894; *Business Directory*, 14.

[33]*Business Directory*, 20, 22, 72. Scott, editor, "The Hunt," 12, 14. "The Hunt," a letter handwritten by Senie Douthit in January 1895 at Lemon City, is in the private collection of Patrick Scott, of Fort Lauderdale, Florida, editor of the Douthit letter. GLB to APS, 20 December 1894, SP Folder 3.

St. Lucie County. The enterprises appointed Iowa native Charles Tobin McCarty, the owner of a large lemon, orange, and vegetable growing operation at Ankona, to manage their colonies. The firms expected McCarty to advise settlers on climate and soil conditions and help supervise their farming operations. McCarty replaced Louis Bauch, a Danish settler who returned to Denmark to bring back still more Danish settlers to the Florida east coast. An Iowa lawyer, McCarty later served as attorney for the local school board, the town of Fort Pierce and the Flagler railway. Fifty-eight years later, in 1953, McCarty's grandson, Dan McCarty, Jr., would become governor of Florida at the youthful age of forty, the youngest ever to serve as governor in the Sunshine State's history.[34]

An important transportation enterprise, the Indian River Steamboat Company opened an office on the Palm Beach side of Lake Worth, but by April the firm would lay up its boats indefinitely, teetering on the edge of bankruptcy. Still, the steamer *Lake Worth* advertised excursions on Tuesdays, Thursdays, and Saturdays from Henry Flagler's year-old Royal Poinciana Hotel at Palm Beach to the southern end of Lake Worth to view the Florida canal company's dredges at work. Learning of the New England group's recent land sales, Bradley expressed great faith in the success of the Florida canal company, expecting the inland waterway to be open to the New River by fall of the next year. For their part, Miles and Sam Maddox urged fellow investors to raise sufficient funds to buy out Flagler's interest in the canal company, fearing that Flagler might purchase the waterway simply to eliminate competition.[35]

Florida canal company officials announced the imminent completion of the six-mile-long Jupiter-to-Lake Worth cut. The canal's completion would connect the Indian River, Lake Worth and Biscayne Bay, making possible a continuous inside passage from Titusville to Key West. But even though the canal company's dredge would steam south within just an eighth of a mile of Juno by April 1896, the dredge *Matanzas* would not make the final cut south into Lake Worth until two years later on May 5, 1898.[36]

---

[34]Youngberg, "East Coast Canal," 24, 28. "A Great Strip of Land," *Tropical Sun* (West Palm Beach), 31 January 1895; McGoun, *Southeast Florida Pioneers*, 148-50.

[35]*Business Directory*, 28, 30, 31, 46. GLB to APS, 8, 11, 20 February 1895, SP Folder 4. GLB to APS, 6 April 1895, SP Folder 4. "Daily Excursions on the Steamer 'Lake Worth'," advertisement., *Tropical Sun*(West Palm Beach), 14 February 1895.

[36]DuBois, *History of Juno*, 9.

In April 1895, Bradley learned that a firm in which both he and Sawyer held large investments, the Mergenthaler Linotype Company, planned to declare a whopping ten percent dividend on its stock. But on the Florida waterway, Bradley found out that Sawyer did not share in Maddox's view that "Mr. Flagler must control the waterway." Still, Bradley found himself "immensely interested" in the waterway's prospects for success. Like Maddox, Bradley remained thoroughly convinced that "Flagler must have the waterway and that he is still trying to get it in the most economical way."[37]

To fend off a possible takeover of the canal company by Flagler, Bradley began circulating a plan to pool at least $380,000 of canal company stock with Sawyer and Maddox as trustees. The proposal called for Bradley, Bradley's brother Charles, and the Amory brothers to pool together $260,000 worth of stock, with the balance to be contributed by the remaining smaller investors. Bradley further agreed to buy $200,000 worth of unsecured bonds from the canal company for a bonus of $200,000 worth of stock; he then planned to sell $200,000 worth of what he called "gilt-edged" bonds entitling investors to $100,000 worth of stock. As a result, Bradley expected to earn a profit of $100,000 in "bonus" stock if the stock increased to par value in a year's time. To provide security for the other investors, Bradley agreed to place $100,000 of his own bonds in the hands of Sawyer and Maddox, as trustees, with authority to sell the securities for the benefit of the series "A" unsecured bond investors if, at the end of three years, they were not able to dispose of their securities at par with interest, but without a stock bonus. The end game, Bradley thought, was the sale of all of the canal company securities to Flagler within a year's time, believing the outlook especially bright for Florida's east coast. The dredges in Florida had been doing excellent work, with canal officials expecting dredges working between Lake Worth and the New River to meet within two or three weeks and the waterway to Biscayne Bay completed by October or November.[38]

Florida Legislative Report of 1895

In May, a special joint committee of the Florida house and senate brought the New England group encouraging news, reporting back to the legislature

---

[37]GLB to APS, 17,19, 21, 22 April 1895, SP Folder 4.
[38]*Ibid.*

its investigation of the extent and quality of the waterway's construction. Committee members recalled that by 1890 the deepening of the Indian River had been completed to state specifications. Within the next three years, about forty miles of canals had been cut between Lake Worth and Biscayne Bay. At Sewall's Point in Martin County, though, there existed a quarter of a mile of shallow water averaging about four feet, said to be caused by shoaling from the ocean inlet. At Juno, farther south, committee members found about a mile of work unfinished, which when completed would open a canal into Lake Worth. There the canal company deployed a dredge, with seventy-five men shoveling the earth away in front of the dredge. With the waterway completed to Miami, the canal company was to have open for navigation about 300 miles of waterway, leaving only one small section to be completed—the nearly incorrigible Matanzas-Halifax cut between Ormond and St. Augustine. The committee found the work south of Lake Worth quite thorough. The canal company had cut at least thirty miles of canals through solid rock and muck. Despite these accomplishments, legislators observed a number of deficiencies and recommended that no further state land grants be made for construction of 102 miles of waterway from mile marker 24 to mile marker 126 until the canal company had dredged the cut through the difficult divide separating the Matanzas and the Halifax rivers. In the end, though, the committee endorsed an extension of time for completing the Florida waterway and an award of some land grants.[39]

At the national level, five years after the first serious planning for the construction of a continuous inland waterway route inside the Atlantic coast, the U. S. Navy conducted an experiment. To test the advantages of using such a route between Newport, Rhode Island, and Key West, at time of war, on March 15, 1895, the U. S. Navy dispatched a torpedo boat, the *Cushing*, south from the Washington Navy Yard, down the Potomac River to Norfolk, then by waterway to the chain of North Carolina canals, the Currituck, Pamlico Cove, and the Bogue, past Beaufort, expecting to go outside from Cape Fear for a few miles to Winyah Bay, South Carolina. Reaching the Florida inland waterway via inside the Georgia coast, Navy officials planned on the *Cushing* using a protected route from Jacksonville until forced outside once again at Jupiter, on the way to Miami, and then finally to Key West.[40]

---

[39]"The East Coast Canal: Extension of Time for Construction–The Investigation Report," (West Palm Beach) *Tropical Sun*, 20 May 1897, quoting article that appeared in 16 May 1897 issue of *Daily Florida Citizen*.

The Florida canal company, meanwhile, completed the stretch of waterway between Lake Worth and the New River when dredges operating from both ends of the section met. In April, while Flagler's engineers began surveying for the railway's extension to Miami, the Boston and Florida land and Florida canal companies joined Flagler in appointing William S. Linton of Saginaw, Michigan, as an agent in the sale and colonizing of lands south of Fort Pierce and north of the Miami River for a three-year period. But Flagler's interest in the canal company suddenly began to wane. The railway magnate agreed to take canal company land in exchange for financing dredging operations to Biscayne Bay at the rate of $7.50 per acre — a bargain for the canal company given the low land prices prevailing at the time.[41]

In July 1895, West Palm Beach resident A. L. Knowlton resigned his commission as justice of the peace to go to New River to survey the site for the new town of Fort Lauderdale, comprised of land owned by William and Mary Brickell and later shared with Flagler for laying out the town site. Knowlton completed the project just five months later in January 1896. In August 1895, the Florida waterway became navigable between West Palm Beach and Fort Lauderdale. The canal company placed one of its boats — the *Hittie* — on the waterway, scheduling a run between the two settlements every three weeks, while Flagler railway contractors began constructing a bridge to Palm Beach across Lake Worth at West Palm Beach. For the last thirty months, the waterway's cost had been staggering. Canal company officials reportedly spent a sobering $7,500 a month to dredge the Florida waterway. Bradley nevertheless remained confident that canal directors could attract more capital needed to finish the waterway. Canal investors might be able to sell a block of company stock to Springfield, Massachusetts investors, Bradley learned, a harbinger of the joining of Edward Walker, a building products manufacturer, in the work of the canal company within the next few months.[42]

---

[40]"The Cushing Will Cruise to Key West," *New York Times,* 16 May 1895.

[41]*Business Directory,* 32. Linton (Southern Florida Land Company) to Sawyer, 19 June 1895; Agreement between Jacksonville, St. Augustine & Indian River Railway Co. and Florida Coast Line Canal & Transp. Co., first parties and William S. Linton, second party, 21 May 1895; both in SP Folder 4; GLB to APS, 25, 27 July 1895, SP Folder 5.

[42]*Business Directory,* 33, 36. Wiggins, "Birth of the City of Miami"; See, also, "East Coast Line Canal and Transportation Company," (Titusville) *Indian River Advocate,* 23 August 1895. "Building the Big Bridge," *Florida Times-Union,* 17 August 1895. "Cutting the Big Canal," *Florida Times-Union,* 18 August 1895. GLB to APS, 18 August 1895, SP Folder 5.

James Colee, one of the four original directors of the enterprise but no longer serving on the board, worked hard as a waterway engineer and surveyor, leading a team of twenty men chopping wood in the wilderness on both sides of the canal to stoke the dredges' boilers. In September, canal company directors accepted Flagler's proposal to extend the railway beyond Palm Beach to Biscayne Bay for an additional 1,500 acres of the company's lands for every mile of railway constructed.[43]

Bradley announced the appointment of Henry Gaillard, the only original director still serving on the board, as assistant general manager, to assist Miles as general manager. The New England group also agreed to pay Miles a fifteen percent commission on all lands sold for their various land enterprises, with the understanding that Miles's agents were to be paid out of Miles's commission and that Miles's agency was not to be exclusive. The company continued to employ other real estate agents like Miami-based Fred Morse. But Morse also served as Flagler railway's right-of-way agent on the proposed line from the New River south to Biscayne Bay and, thus, urged cooperation between the canal company and the railway. Michigan investor William Linton, the New England group's real estate agent for land south of Fort Pierce and north of the Miami River, purchased an option to buy eighty acres of Lake Worth Land Trust muck land in south Palm Beach County for $4,000. Linton was to make a down payment of $400 with installments to be paid beginning in January 1896 and each month thereafter until June 1899. But by December 17, Linton had yet to make the initial payment, a harbinger of the bad news to come. In fact, it would not be until April 1896 before Linton finally came through with the purchase, signing the mortgage and notes to finance the transaction.[44]

In December 1895 something very strange occurred. Flagler began making plans to form the Model Land Company to hold the hundreds of thousands of acres the State of Florida and others, including the Florida canal company and the Boston & Florida, agreed to grant Flagler for extending the railway to Miami. The company's original incorporators included not only Flagler, as president, and associates J. R. Parrott and James E. Ingra-

---

[43]"Cutting the Big Canal," *Florida Times-Union*, 18 August 1895. Bill of Complaint, *Florida East Coast Railway Co. v. Canal Company, et al.*, St. Johns County Circuit Court, Chancery Case No. 1162, pp. 4-5. Case later transferred to Putnam County because of Judge Gibbs's recusal. Parrot to Sawyer, 9 November 1895, SP Folder 5.

[44]GLB to APS, 24 November 1895; Robert to APS, 26, 30 November and 17 December 1895; all in SP Folder 5; Robert to APS, 14 April 1896, SP Folder 6.

ham, but also the Florida canal company's general manager, George Francis Miles, who initially served as secretary and director of the Flagler company. Why Flagler chose to place on his board the canal company's general manager remains a mystery. Perhaps the decision was based on the already close relationship between the two companies. Perhaps the end game was for Flagler and the New England group of investors to develop and market all of their properties together under the Model Land Company name.[45]

---

[45]Certified copy of Articles of Incorporation of the Model Land Company, 4 December 1895, recorded in Corporations Book 3, Page 193, of the Public Records of Dade County, Florida.

Chapter 4

Developing the Land

As the Florida waterway neared completion, an 1896 West Palm Beach publication heralded the agricultural benefits of the Florida canal company's dredging activities to the south Florida area. Its author seemed to almost promise farmers "[a] large amount of additional muck will be reclaimed when the canal has finally been cut through into Lake Worth," as if an agricultural "gold rush" was about to take place. The *New York Times* joined the chorus of boosters, reporting that two dredges at work on the Florida waterway met at Fort Lauderdale on January 1, 1896. Known then as the Florida Coast Line Canal, the waterway had been substantially completed to Biscayne Bay, with only a six-mile divide between Jupiter and Lake Worth and a short distance between the Matanzas and Halifax Rivers remaining to be cut. As president of the company, Henry Flagler took the first trip down the waterway from Lake Worth to Biscayne Bay aboard the old Indian River steamboat *Sweeney*. Flagler would take a second trip down Florida's east coast, but this time as a passenger in one of his railroad cars traveling south on the completed Florida East Coast Railway, arriving on the first train to Miami on April 13, 1896.[1]

By the middle of February, the Boston & Florida land company had begun an important partnership with Flagler when Albert Sawyer agreed to grant Flagler a half interest in the Boston & Florida firm's properties in south Florida as part of the firm's 10,000-acre donation for the extension of the railway to Miami. James Ingraham, Flagler's land development head, brought news of an opportunity to locate a colony of four hundred Danish settlers at present-day Dania Beach. Flagler set the prices of land there, with pine land at $17 an acre and rich, agricultural muck land more than five times as expensive at $100 an acre. With the Boston & Florida company's consent,

---

[1]*Business Directory*, 47. "Florida Interior Water Ways," *New York Times*, 7 January 1896; Wiggins, "Birth of Miami."

Flagler subdivided their land at Modelo (so named for Flagler's Model Land Company), laying out lots for sale in the future city of Dania Beach.[2]

Two years later, the companies solidified the partnership by jointly developing land holdings at the burgeoning Halland settlement south of Modelo, naming the new community, "Town of Hallandale Beach." Flagler's land company also joined the Florida canal company, the Bradley trusts and the Boston & Florida land company in employing the same real estate agents to sell Florida land holdings at White City in present-day St. Lucie County, at Linton (now Delray Beach) and at Boynton (now Boynton Beach) in today's Palm Beach County and at Modelo and Halland in today's Broward County.[3]

The beginning of March 1896, canal directors authorized Miles "to make the terms he desired" for the sale of Florida land. Springfield building products manufacturer Edward Walker contributed $10,800 to the Florida canal company for twelve unsecured bonds, 120 shares of stock and 5,000 acres of land. It looked to be an astute investment on Walker's part for comparatively little cash given prevailing land values. Bradley now asked Sawyer to form a third trust like the Lake Worth and New River trusts, with a half interest to be owned by Walker and the other half titled in Bradley's name. Once again Bradley exuded confidence in the canal company's securities, wondering what better business he, Sawyer, and Albert Hayden (Sawyer's son) could engage in than to find purchasers for the company's unsecured bonds which were discounted by ten percent, and which carried stock certificates and 500 acres of land for each bond. That the waterway might be extended farther north to Jacksonville on the St. Johns River gave Bradley cause to believe the group might reap great profits in the end. With land prices rising to only $4 an acre, Florida canal company stock could be worth as much as $300 a share without a sale of the waterway.[4]

---

[2]GFM to ASP, 15 February 1896; Ingraham to GFM (copy of telegram), 15 February 1896; Ingraham to GFM (copy), 15 February 1896; Ingraham to APS/GFM, 23 March 1896; APS to Ingraham (copy), 24 March 1896; all in SP Folder 6. Akin, "Sly Foxes," 31.

[3]"Map of the Town of Hallandale beach, Dade Co., Fla.," prepared by W. C. Valentine on January 27, 1898, and recorded in Plat Book B, Page 13, of the Public Records of Dade County, Florida on September 1, 1911. See, e.g., MLC, Box 13, File 361 (Special File 439), numerous letters written in 1916 between A. H. Sawyer, representing the Boston company and the New River Land Trust, Frederick Morse, a Miami real estate agent, and James E. Ingraham, representing the Model Land Company.

[4]GLB to APS, 2, 8 March 1896, SP Folder 6.

A Springfield, Illinois investor, a Colonel Johnson, showed considerable interest in buying an immense tract of south Florida land jointly owned by Flagler, the Boston & Florida company, the Florida canal company and the New River Land Trust. This large expanse of property, which amounted to more than 22,000 acres, lay in the northern part of present-day Fort Lauderdale and the southern portion of today's Pompano Beach. Through Flagler's James Ingraham, the four enterprises offered to sell Johnson the tract (half of which was Boston & Florida company land). But Johnson never accepted the offer.[5]

With real estate sales apparently quickening, Florida canal company officials, including Miles, Sawyer and Bradley, along with Flagler associate Joseph Parrott and Boston & Florida land company investor Thomas Bailey along with Flagler associate Joseph Parrott and Boston & Florida land company investor Thomas Bailey, began organizing another Florida enterprise—the United States Paintoff Company—to manufacture "Paintoff," a newly-patented product for removing paint and rust from metal. In April, while Miles confirmed from St. Augustine on Florida canal company stationery "a good many orders" for the product, Bradley went along with building a plant in St. Augustine, relying on Miles to sell bonds to finance the project. Parrott became increasingly engrossed in the business, reporting good results after ordering part of a Jacksonville bridge cleaned with the new product. Both Bradley and Sawyer remained interested in buying more stock in the Mergenthaler Linotype Company, on whose board Bradley sat as a director. Sawyer's son, Albert Hayden, who would later inherit his father's interests in the Florida canal and Boston & Florida land companies as well as in the Lake Worth and New River trusts, busied himself earning commissions on the sale of Mergenthaler stock, while Bradley attempted to increase his stake in the company.[6]

Just as organizers completed the Paintoff company's organization, a new Florida canal company investor came fully into the picture. Edward M. Walker, a wealthy Springfield, Massachusetts, building products manufacturer, began contributing sizeable sums of capital to the waterway project. A lifelong bachelor like Maddox and head of T. M. Walker & Company,

---

[5]Ingraham to C. B. Johnson, 12 March 1896, SP Folder 6.

[6]GFM to APS, 17 March and 3, 9, 15, 25 April 1896; GLB to APS, 9 April 1896; GFM to APS, 16 April 1896; SP Folder 6.

Walker was known for his retiring disposition and his role as a scion of an old Springfield family. In business, his peers considered Walker "an unusually shrewd and successful businessman."[7]

As his railway neared completion at Miami, Flagler's interest in the waterway's construction continued to decline. At the Florida canal company's annual meeting in St. Augustine held in March, Flagler unexpectedly resigned as president and director after three years. According to Miles who succeeded Flagler, Flagler resigned at Miles' request when Flagler expressed fears the waterway's development might adversely affect railroad rates. To pay back Flagler's cash advances totaling $185,137 to finish the waterway to Miami, canal directors deeded to Flagler nearly 25,000 acres of the company's land grant. Two years later, in 1898, Flagler accepted more canal land in southern Dade County for his remaining interest in the company at a value of $6 an acre, a bargain indeed for the canal company given the generally depressed prices at the time and low quality of the land.[8]

Several weeks after the meeting, Bradley learned more of what occurred at the annual meeting. Although shareholders re-elected Flagler and Parrott as directors, both men resigned during the directors' meeting. Directors then elected George Miles as president and Henry Gaillard as vice president. Meanwhile, a Canadian investor named Wright had been visiting St. Augustine and traveled with Miles to view the company's Indian River lands. If Wright liked the land, Miles expected the Canadian's purchase to provide enough money to finish the difficult Matanzas Cut.[9]

Within the last two years, the Florida canal company had cut through forty miles of coastal barriers. Nineteen miles of waterway had been dredged through high ground at least six feet above the waterline. When the company completed the waterway to a five-foot depth, it was anticipated that the federal government would widen and deepen it. The expansion, as the *New York Times* reported, would bring in considerable trade from the West Indies as well as from Central and South America. With the

---

[7]GFM to APS, 25 April 1896, SP Folder 6. "Senior Member of T. M. Walker & Co. Succumbs to Bright's Disease," " (Springfield, Mass.) *Daily Republican*, 3 October 1905.

[8]Youngberg, "East Coast Canal," 28. GFM to GAY, September 15, 1928, YP Box 4, File 20. Warranty Deed executed by the Canal Company in favor of the Model Land Company on February 28, 1896, and recorded on June 16, 1896, in Deed Book "O," at page 166, of the Public Records of Dade County, Florida. Akin, "Sly Foxes," 33.

[9]GLB to APS, 15 April 1896, SP Folder 6.

completion of the stretch of waterway under construction between Beaufort and Charleston, even more trade was expected to flow into Florida from the north through the inside route. Still the *Times* expressed skepticism about the waterway's viability. "It is difficult to understand," the paper opined, "how this insider route will be of commercial importance." The real worth of the venture, the *Times* speculated, lay in "the possibilities of reclaiming land capable of high cultivation."[10]

In May, three more Canadians appeared interested in buying canal company lands near Rockledge. On the Paintoff venture, Bradley reported poor results when his painter applied the product to some clapboards on the side of his home, "Rathlin." Nevertheless, the next month, the Paintoff company completed the purchase of a factory at Jacksonville, with a railroad spur leading into the factory's yard, on the south bank of the St. Johns River. Instead of cash, the factory's owners took stock in the new company at fifty cents on the dollar, which, Miles bragged, showed the owner's confidence in the enterprise.[11]

After a thorough examination of the Florida canal company's waterway, state engineer Jonathan Bradford reported that the company had dredged seventy-seven miles of waterway between Juno and Miami at a cost of more than half a million dollars. A significant portion of the stretch experienced heavy traffic, with the 170-foot-long steamer *Santa Lucia* routinely carrying eight carloads of freight during the last year. Northern farmers continued to settle in the developing community of Modelo (today's Dania Beach), just south of Fort Lauderdale. Noting the failure of the company to finish the stretch between Jupiter on the Indian River and Lake Worth, Bradford observed that the company's contractor had failed to complete the work despite an extension of six months to finish it. Still the company planned to eliminate the remaining one-mile divide separating the Indian River and Juno on Lake Worth as soon as the company's dredges could be overhauled. But the work ahead to eliminate the Jupiter-Lake Worth divide appeared formidable. In some places, the company had already dredged cuts twenty-

---

[10]"Florida's Rich Rivals," *New York Times*, 18 March 1896.
[11]GFM to APS, 11 May 1896, 1 June 1896; GLB to APS, 17 May 1896; Moses to APS, 16 June 1896; all in SP Folder 6.

two feet deep. So much work had been required that the company built a temporary railroad so that dredged material could be removed by railway cars and the dredges could begin their work.[12]

At the end of June 1896, canal investors scrambled to raise more funds to finish dredging the Jupiter-to-Lake Worth divide. Bradley asked for Sawyer's help in raising at least a portion of the $7,000 needed for what he described as "the little cut between Juno and Jupiter." Finishing the cut, Bradley believed, would prove so profitable for the Boston & Florida that it would be good business for the firm's investors to buy the canal company's unsecured bonds that entitled holders to not only stock but also 500 acres of land for each $1,000 bond purchased.[13]

In early July, Wallace Moses, the Lake Worth Trust's caretaker, reported poor results in the production of Red Spanish pineapple at the Belleville Plantation, suggesting that the Trust switch to planting about 3,000 of the Abbaka variety. Moses planned to ship a quarter of a crate of Abbakas each to Sawyer and Fred Amory as gifts, but by early August he was still encountering difficulties in arranging the shipment north. With no final word from Sawyer, Moses nonetheless began grubbing a portion of the plantation in preparation for planting the Abbakas. Another month would pass before Moses was finally able to get approval to plant the new variety.[14]

Moses believed it was possible to sell the Lake Worth Trust's pine lands near the Trust's Belleville Plantation (southwest of Boynton) for pineapple growing. He recommended lowering prices to meet the prices offered by Flagler and the Florida canal company for similar land in the area. For his part, Miles thought the Boston & Florida company ought to authorize Moses to sell the lands north of the New River at Fort Lauderdale. South of the New River, Miles acknowledged, the Boston & Florida had been trying to sell land to Swedish and German settlers. But Julia Tuttle's plans to charge higher prices caused the company to re-evaluate its plans. Turning to national affairs, Miles thought "the unsettled state of the country" against "brisk business," but expected "better times" with the election of a Republican administration. In Tallahassee, Miles believed it "nothing less than impossible" to get anything done until after the October state elections. The

---

[12]*MIIF*, 16 January 1897, 398-99; *MIIF*, 9 July 1896, 380-81; "More Colonists Coming," *Daily Florida Citizen* (Jacksonville), 17 June 1896. Miles, "Waterway of the Florida Coast Line Canal," 164.

[13]GLB to APS, 26 June 1896, SP Folder 6.

[14]Moses to APS, 8, 17 July 1896; 4 August 1896, SP Folder 7.

canal company had at least one "ace in the hole." The canal company's longest-tenured director, Henry Gaillard, had been nominated for election to the state senate to represent St. Johns County and Miles expected Captain Dimick of Palm Beach, another company friend, to be elected senator to represent Brevard and Dade counties in south Florida another company friend, to be elected senator to represent Brevard and Dade counties in central and southern Florida.[15]

By the middle of September, Miles had entered into a contract with Swedish and German settlers for the sale of Boston & Florida, Flagler railroad, and Model Land Company lands comprising some 8,000 acres. Land prices through December 1 were expected to be set at $12.50 per acre for pine land and $37.50 per acre for muck. After December 1, prices were to rise to $17 an acre for pine land and to $50 for muck land. Miles thought the prospect for making sales in autumn "exceedingly good." The terms were to be a quarter of the selling price down, with the balance to be paid over four years at eight percent interest rate. Julia Tuttle's land initially had been part of the sale of the larger tract but, at the last minute, she withdrew her tracts. At the same time, Miles had also been investigating another venture. He had studied hemp or ramie growing and decided to lay out a plantation at Seville in present-day Volusia County abutting the Jacksonville, Tampa & Key West Railway line, where both he and his brother owned land. He foresaw no difficulty in finding a market for ramie and a new machine that stripped the fiber from the plant economically had just been invented.[16]

The middle of September, the Florida East Coast Railway's land commissioner, James Ingraham, informed Miles of the progress that had been made in the development of the settlements at Modelo and Halland. At Modelo, the Flagler company had built a road and two ditches from the center of the east side of the town across the marsh to the East Coast Canal. The ditches drained the land for a half a mile on each side. To reach pine lands in a section west of the town site, the railway began building a road across the marsh about a half a mile long. At the Halland settlement, James Ingraham reported plans to lay out the town in the southern part of today's Broward County. Flagler's men were digging a ditch eight feet wide at the top and four feet wide at the bottom from the eastern boundary of the town site to what was now called the East Coast Canal. Each purchaser of a lot in the

---

[15]Moses to APS, 17 August 1896, 4 September 1896; GFM to APS, 27 August 1896, SP Folder 7.

[16]GFM to APS, 12 September 1896, SP Folder 7.

new settlement was to be given, free of charge, a lot 50 feet by 125 feet within the town site.[17]

With the first sales of south Florida land consummated, the Boston & Florida land company owed Linton a twenty-five percent commission on the transactions. Miles also weighed in for compensation, asking for a commission for his help in developing the two southern settlements. Elaborating on his extraordinary work in dealing with Julia Tuttle, Miles argued that Tuttle's unreasonable demands for including her lands in the Modelo project caused the joint venture to exclude her holdings from the venture. Miles had also agreed on behalf of the Boston & Florida company to pay half of the $600 expense for the proposed road west of Modelo out of the future sale of company lands. Still unsettled was the location of lands the Boston & Florida was to donate to Flagler to comply with Sawyer's verbal agreement to convey 10,000 acres of land—ten percent of its original purchase from the canal company in 1892—for the railway's extension to Miami.[18]

On October 7, Moses spent the day at Jensen (today's Jensen Beach) attending the annual meeting of the Indian River and Lake Worth Pineapple Grower's Association. The fifty members present heard the report of General Agent E. P. Porcher on the region's pineapple production. Shipments from the area totaled 60,000 half crates or about 80 percent of the marketed product of the entire Florida east coast. Proceeds to each grower averaged $1.50 per half crate on pineapples. But the Lake Worth Trust netted considerably below that figure because of inadequate fertilizing. Moreover, Moses found it difficult to find skilled labor to employ at the Belleville Plantation with so many growers and so few workers and had to train "green men" to satisfy the need for laborers in the field.[19]

In the latter part of October, Cullen Pence, secretary of the Boynton School Committee, asked George Miles for a donation of Lake Worth Land Trust land just west of the original Town of Boynton for a public school site. Albert Sawyer, in turn, asked Wallace Moses, the trust's local agent, to decide the issue. Moses recommended the donation of three-quarters of an acre for the site. In 1913, the Palm Beach County School Board would erect a two-story school house on the Lake Worth Land Trust site, which was used

---

[17]Ingraham to GFM, 18 September 1896, SP Folder 7.

[18]GFM to APS, 19 September 1896. SP Folder 7.

[19]Moses to APS, 6, 8 October 1896, SP Folder 7.

as a public school until 1989. Today the old school building is home to Boynton Beach's popular Schoolhouse History Museum.[20]

In the latter part of October, James Ingraham reported that work progressed well in establishing colonies at Linton (Delray Beach), Boynton (Boyton Beach), Modelo (Dania Beach) and Halland (Hallandale Beach), with new settlers arriving daily. At the beginning of November, Ingraham asked Sawyer for a donation of an 80-acre tract of land owned by the Boston & Florida company at present-day Boca Raton for a sand pit to be used in the construction of the railway. The grant was to be deducted from the still-unsettled 10,000-acre grant the company owed Flagler for the railway's extension to Miami. Miles was glad that Sawyer had asked his advice on the problem, believing Flagler's people "somewhat 'foxy'" and not at all "bashful about asking favours." He recommended a change in the donation's terms in light of Flagler's reduction of prices in the Modelo and Halland colonies. The value of the railway's subsidy—suggesting $100,000—ought to be agreed upon and Flagler should take a half interest in any Boston & Florida land included in any settlement until Flagler received $100,000 worth of land at present-graded prices. The advantage to the Boston & Florida company were the benefits of Flagler advertising and the privileges his railroad granted land purchasers, thus preventing such a "powerful organization" from discriminating against Boston & Florida company lands.[21]

By the end of November, the Flagler railway and Boston & Florida company had sold sixty-five acres at the Modelo colony—fifty acres of pine lands and fifteen in muck land—yielding sales of $1,200, but only a paltry $135.25 in cash, with the balance to be paid over three years. No sales had yet been made at the Halland site because the railway awaited the completion of surveys and drainage ditches. A number of settlers appeared ready to close on their purchases as soon as maps of the area became available.[22]

In December, Moses negotiated with Linton over the sale of the Belleville Plantation tract comprised of 160 acres for $6,000. The banana plants had not been doing well, but were expected to do better in warmer weather. In any event, the plants proved an effective windbreak for the potato crop. By

---

[20]Moses to APS, 16 October 1896; Cullen Pence to GFM, 10 October, 1896; Cullen Pence to APS, 27 October 1896; Moses to APS, 28 November 1896; SP Folder 7.

[21]GFM to APS, 23 October 1896; Ingraham to GFM, 27 October 1896; Ingraham to APS, 4, 11 November 1896; SP Folder 7.

[22]Ingraham to GFM, 24 November 1896, SP Folder 7.

the end of the month, Moses had been haggling with Linton over the sale of the Lake Worth Trust experimental farm. The war in Cuba and the "agitation" in Congress over the confrontation did not "tend to attract investors here," Moses reported back to New England. At the same time, Bradley no longer opposed Miles's plan to mortgage one of the dredges to finance the Jupiter-to-Lake Worth cut, considering that section to be "of the greatest importance." And to raise still more money, Bradley asked Sawyer to consider liquidating their interests in the Paintoff company to finance operations. Good news, though, appeared just around the corner. By the end of December 1896, the New England group learned that the canal right-of-way for the last half mile of the nearly intractable Jupiter-to-Lake Worth divide had finally been secured.[23]

By the close of 1896, state trustees had conveyed some 579,000 acres of public land to the canal company for dredging operations since 1882. Selling some land to raise cash for future dredging operations and conveying other parcels for Flagler's extension of the railway into south Florida, the canal company still owned 97,000 acres, essentially worthless to canal company investors without drainage.[24]

By the beginning of 1897, Florida canal company insiders, concerned about a possible Flagler takeover of the company began formulating plans to place the majority of the company's stock in a trust, essentially vesting absolute control over the enterprise for at least five years in Bradley. Shareholders expected to contribute stock to the venture were Bradley, Bradley's brother Charles, George Miles, and Harcourt and Fred Amory. Eventually, Henry Gaillard, the only original canal company director still serving, would also be asked to join the trust. Bradley asked Sawyer to draw up the necessary paperwork. He positively glowed over the company's prospects. The company already had built about 280 miles of navigable waterway and secured 1,000 acres of land for every unsecured $1,000 bond issued. Assuming that the company could sell the land for $2 an acre, which was not an unreasonable expectation, Bradley thought the unsecured bonds and stock alone ought to be worth the investment without counting the waterway and dredging machinery.[25]

---

[23]GLB to APS, 10 December 1896; Moses to APS, 31 December 1896; both in SP Folder 7.

[24]"The East Coast Canal: Extension of Time;" *MIIF*, 16 January 1897, 396-97.

[25]GLB to APS, 2 January 1897, SP Folder 8.

The Indian River Steamboat Company

Sometime during 1896, probably toward the end of the year, George Miles formed a new steamboat company, the Indian River and Bay Biscayne Inland Navigation Company, to take advantage of the transportation opportunities offered by the completionof the waterway to Miami. The purpose of the venture was to run a line of steamers on the Indian River between Titusville and Lake Worth and a single boat for the less populated waterway link between West Palm Beach and Miami. At Titusville, the northern terminus, the line was to connect with the Jacksonville, Tampa &

Steamboat *St. Augustine* at Rockledge landing on the Indian River, 1880s. The *St. Augustine* was purchased in 1897 by the Indian River and Biscayne Bay Navigation Company, another company related to the Florida Coast Line Canal and Transportation Company, to transport freight and passengers along the developing Florida waterway. (Courtesy, Florida State Archives, Florida Photographic Collection, Tallahassee, Florida)

Key West Railway for further transportation to destinations further north. Miles planned to purchase two stern-wheel steamers—the 219-ton *St. Sebas-*

tian and the 132-ton *St. Augustine* — from the defunct Indian River Steamboat Company for the Indian River run between Titusville and the Jupiter Inlet.[26]

In addition to George Miles as president, the steamboat company's officers included Sam Maddox as vice-president; Henry Gaillard as treasurer; and St. Augustine lawyer George Couper Gibbs (circuit judge from 1913 to 1935 for Nassau, Duval, Clay and St. Johns counties), as secretary. Aside from the officers, George Gleason served as superintendent, while John D. Maclennan served as general agent. A Canadian by birth, Maclennan was a wealthy Cleveland contractor who had superintended construction of Flagler's Jacksonville, St. Augustine and Indian River railroad during the early 1890s and was a perennial winter resident of Flagler's Ponce de Leon Hotel in St. Augustine.[27]

The first week in January 1897, Miles bought two steamers for $6,500. Bradley worked hard behind the scenes to raise $30,000 to place all of the Florida businesses on a solid financial footing, asking Sawyer for assistance in raising capital. But as yet he had heard nothing from the Newburyport banker. On January 5, Bradley pledged to add $10,000 to Edward Walker's subscription of $10,000, leaving the campaign still short by $10,000. A few days later, Bradley learned that Fred Amory had pledged $3,000, with the possibility that Sawyer might get $3,000 from an Arthur Merriam of Manchester, Massachusetts. He suggested that the capital of the proposed third (Walker) trust be increased. Disappointed with the canal company's progress, Fred's brother Harcourt began disposing of his company debentures for fifty cents on the dollar, a substantial loss. But Maddox remained confident that both Henry Plant, then developing another Florida railroad on Florida's west coast, and Henry Flagler wanted to buy the Florida waterway — and badly. Acknowledging Maddox's pledge of $2,000 for the Florida venture, Bradley tentatively agreed to contribute the $5,000 needed to underwrite the $30,000 capital campaign, but, days later, Sawyer finally stepped up with a pledge to raise the remaining $5,000.[28]

---

[26]SM to APS, 27 December 1897; SM to APS, 30 December 1897; GLB to APS, 31 December 1897; all in SP Folder 10. *Atlantic Coast Line*, 55. [no title], *Miami Metropolis*, 17 December 1897.

[27]GFM (Indian River and Bay Biscayne Inland Navigation Company), n.d., YP Box 4, Folder 13, listing officers of the steamboat firm. Biographical sketch of George Couper Gibbs in Cutler, *History of Florida*, III, 364-65. GFM (Indian River and Bay Biscayne Inland Navigation Company), n.d., YP Box 4, Folder 13, listing officers of the steamboat firm. St. Augustine *Tatler*, 20 January 1894; *Tatler* (St. Augustine, Fla.), 4 February 1899, p. 12. Chandler, *Henry Flagler*, 42. *Social Index*, 174.

[28]GLB to APS, 4, 5, 9, 11, 13, 17 January 1897, SP Folder 8.

On January 16, state trustees meeting at Tallahassee learned that in dredging seventy-seven miles of waterway from Juno south to the mouth of the Miami River, the Florida canal company had removed 2.3 million cubic yards of rock, clay, sand and muck at a cost of $500,672. In digging the difficult divide between Jupiter and Lake Worth, the company had removed 481,377 cubic yards of material at a cost of about $100,000. The company optimistically predicted that it would finish the work within the next two to three months. The trustees voted to deed the company 104,092 acres of public land south of Mile Post 126 for completing the 77-mile stretch. They also agreed to pay just over $11,700, as proceeds from the trustees' sale of canal reserve land during the twelve-year period from January 1, 1885 until June 21, 1897. But it would take another six months before the trustees actually approved disbursing any money and then only a mere $1,000 immediately, with the balance on account. The trustees also agreed to allow the company to sell up to 100,000 acres of reserved lands south of Georgiana, three miles south of Rockledge, but the proceeds were to be held until the company had dredged enough waterway to earn the lands.[29]

By January 17, Bradley had advanced $5,500 and Maddox, $1,000, to allow Miles to close on the purchase of two Indian River steamboats. Bradley expected Fred Amory to satisfy his pledge of $3,000 on January 18. Bradley's loan of another $5,000 enabled Miles to start on the Lake Worth Cut between Juno and Jupiter. He anticipated running the two newly-acquired boats on the Indian River in February if arrangements could be made with the Jacksonville, Tampa and Key West Railway for another train to connect with the steamers and a fair division of rates and fares.[30]

By January 23, Maddox, Walker, Sawyer, Bradley, and Fred Amory each had contributed capital for the Florida enterprise. But only Amory had completely satisfied his pledge of $3,000. Walker still owed $6,500 ($10,000 total); Sawyer, $3,000 ($5,000 total); Bradley, $2,500 ($10,000 total); and Maddox, $1,000 ($2,000 total). Bradley now informed Miles that the canal company should deed to Sawyer as trustee 12,500 acres of canal company land for the new investors, organize the new steamboat company and sign a suitable contract between the steamboat and the canal companies.[31]

Sales of Boston & Florida land at the Modelo and Halland settlements had slowed down considerably. Newly arriving settlers preferred the better-

[29]*MIIF*, 16 January 1897, 395-99, 405-410. *MIIF*, 23 June 1897, 410-411.
[30]GLB to APS, 17, 20, 23 January 1897, GFM to APS, 23 January 1897, SP Folder 8.
[31]GLB to APS, 23 January 1897, SP Folder 8.

located Flagler railroad and Model Land Company lands over the Boston & Florida and canal lands at Modelo. Miles questioned whether the Boston & Florida company had made the right decision in locating the Halland colony on land where it was necessary to cut drainage canals and build roads through marsh. Swedish Lutheran settlers there seemed generally pleased with the development, but complained loudly about the outrageous freight charges imposed by the Flagler railway. Some reported paying as much as $20 to ship a few pieces of furniture from Jacksonville south. North of the settlements, west of today's Boynton Beach, at the Lake Worth Trust's Belleville Plantation, a poor crop of pineapples disappointed Moses. The West Palm Beach caretaker predicted the pineapples wouldn't be profitable for at least two years. On the bright side, the potato crop seemed to be growing well.[32]

The canal company chartered the boat *Three Friends*, a steamer owned by Captain Napoleon Bonaparte Broward (later Florida governor from 1905 until 1909) and two friends, to help in the canal work. For some time the tug had been tied up in litigation with federal authorities. Treasury Department officials had seized the vessel on charges that Broward had been running guns to Cuba in violation of federal neutrality laws. Miles planned to use the newly-freed *Three Friends* to tow the company's dredge *Biscayne* up from Biscayne Bay to Jupiter to help in dredging the difficult divide between Lake Worth and Jupiter Creek.[33]

Bradley recalled his plan to pool all of the Florida canal company stock to vest in himself full control over the enterprise. A new stockholder to be included in the pool was Henry Gaillard. The inclusion of Gaillard appears to have been to be an astute political move given Gaillard's election to represent St. Johns County in the Florida Senate. Both the Florida House and Senate, in fact, would be key to any further extensions and additional land grants given the company for completing the waterway.[34]

At the Halland settlement, about 150 acres of muck land, probably Boston & Florida land, priced at $37.50 an acre, had been purchased, with a twenty-five percent down payment. The dredge *Biscayne*, towed by the tug *Three*

---

[32]GFM to APS, 28 January 1897; F. Jacobson, Pastor, Swedish Evanglical Lutheran Bethlehem Church to Ingraham (typewritten copy on Canal Company stationery), 2 February 1897; Moses to APS, 2 February 1897; SP Folder 8.

[33]"Work on the Canal," *Florida Star* (Titusville), 29 January 1897. See, Proctor, *Napoleon Bonaparte Broward*, 122-137, for an account of the federal court litigation concerning the *Three Friends*.

[34]GLB to APS, 3 February 1897, SP Folder 8.

Friends from the New River Inlet to Jupiter for work on the Jupiter-to-Lake Worth cut, was at sea. And finally, the Florida canal company had secured the right-of-way deed to the last parcel at Juno needed to begin work for what today would seem an almost insignificant sum, $201.25, a much smaller amount than Miles had anticipated.[35]

But on February 9, Miles reported bad news. The dredge *Biscayne* had run aground near Jupiter Inlet. Miles feared losing the hull, but seemed assured that the dredging machinery could be saved. He cautioned that he couldn't assess the extent of the damage without a close inspection. In addition to the steamboat and dredging operations, Miles was still trying to push the ramie industry on the Florida east coast. He even wrote of "an old gentleman here (Mr. William Deering), a large manufacturer of Reaping Machines and Binder twine in Chicago, who is much interested in Ramie."[36]

The latter part of February, Miles pressed Ingraham for details on recent land sales at Modelo and Halland. The hang up was that information on the cost of drainage and road construction to be apportioned among all the joint land owners had not been received. About $7,500 worth of Boston & Florida land had been sold in the two colonies, but only a quarter of that amount had actually been received in cash. To reach the western pine land properties, the Flagler railway cut several main drainage ditches and built a road about three-quarters of a mile long because of Julia Tuttle's last-minute withdrawal of land from the proposed Modelo development. While land sales remained relatively slow in the two colonies, Miles reported a bright spot just below Halland. Cuban investors had been negotiating for about 9,000 acres of railroad, canal company and Boston & Florida land in today's northern Miami-Dade County for a sugar-growing operation. The Boston & Florida company's share of the proceeds was expected to be an astonishing $30,000.[37]

At Titusville, the new steamboat company began reconditioning the old steamer *St. Augustine*, which had languished for more than a year at Eau Gallie. Both the *St. Augustine* and the *St. Sebastian* had been purchased from the bankrupt Indian River Steamboat Company. Miles planned to put the *St. Augustine* with a crew of at least eight on daily round trips between Eau Gallie and Titusville to transport pineapples and other fruit and vegetables, with some tourist traffic to supplement the freight business. On March 10,

---

[35]GFM to APS, 4 February 1897, SP Folder 8.

[36]GFM to APS 9 February 1897, SP Folder 8.

[37]GFM to APS, 20 February 1897, SP Folder 8.

the steamboat company's newly-refurbished *St. Augustine* carried passengers — and members of Titusville's Indian River band — on her inaugural trip
down the Indian River to Eau Gallie, with a number of stops along the way.
By the time the steamer arrived at her southern destination, she had taken
on more than 200 passengers. Serving as the boat's purser was none other
than Henry F. Gaillard, the only one of the four original Florida canal company directors from 1881 still in office. Returning to her home port the same
day, the *St. Augustine* arrived just 15 minutes before midnight under a
bright moonlit sky, somewhat later than the scheduled arrival time.[38]

A few weeks later, however, regular service had not yet been established.
More boat repairs were needed. Miles entered into contracts with the Merrill-Stevens Engineering Company at Jacksonville for the refurbishment of
both the *St. Augustine* and *St. Sebastian*. Both flat-bottomed steamers had
been designed especially for service on the shallow Indian River. To handle
the vegetable freight business during the period of repairs, Miles's steamer
company put the old *Sweeney*, formerly owned by the East Coast Transportation Company and re-named the *Della*, on the Indian River. The *Della* also
worked the run between Sewall's Point at today's Stuart and White City,
near Fort Pierce, on the St. Lucie River.[39]

At the Lake Worth Trust's Belleville Plantation west of Boynton, Moses
completed construction of a two-story, wood-frame warehouse for storing
crate material and fertilizer, with the ground floor reserved for making
crates and for wrapping and packing. Public comment, according to Moses,
described the warehouse as "the most imposing structure in Boynton." By
comparison, Moses characterized the Flagler railway station at Boynton as
"quite small and inferior looking." The 30-feet long, twelve-foot wide warehouse sat was located just twenty-five feet from the Flagler railway track.
The connection to the so-called Roberts Platform on the track was by a
bridge at the same level as the platform. Pineapples harvested in the field
were hauled and delivered at one door of the warehouse, then sorted,
wrapped, crated and trucked out the front door, over the bridge, onto the
platform and loaded onto railroad cars. Disappointed with some of the crop
yields, the Lake Worth Trust's caretaker reckoned the potato crop "almost a
complete failure." The tomato yield looked just as bad. In fact, Moses
thought vegetable growing at Boynton "a complete failure" because of the

---

[38]"Steamboat Service Again," *Florida Star*, 5 March 1897; "The J. T. & K.W. Goes A Beg-
ging," *Florida Star*, 5 March 1897; "Excursion on the St. Augustine," *Florida Star*, 12 March
1897.

[39]"Steamboats To Be Repaired," *Florida Star*, 2 April 1897; Hopwood, *Golden Era*, 19.

severe drought. The bright spot continued to be the pineapples, which looked fine, with Moses expecting yields for the next year to generate a surplus above expenses.[40]

By April, subscribers to the Indian River and Bay Biscayne Steamboat Company stock issue included Bradley and Walker, who each agreed to purchase a hundred shares. Sawyer asked for fifty shares and his son, Albert Hayden, bought one share. As trustee for several unidentified shareholders, the senior Sawyer took the greatest number of any of the stockholders—105 shares. Rounding out the list of initial stockholders were Fred Amory, who purchased thirty shares; Sam Maddox, who took twenty; and George Miles and Henry Gaillard (now a state senator) each bought one share.[41]

In the middle of April, Miles explained the delay in getting the New England group's pooling agreement on the Florida canal company stock signed and returned to Newburyport. He had been so laid up with "abscesses" in his ears that he had forgotten to get Gaillard to sign the contract before the St. Augustine senator left for Tallahassee. Miles now had the agreement signed by Gaillard. The two steamers had been docked at New Smyrna for a week awaiting fair weather before going to sea, finally arriving for repairs at Jacksonville, but with the *St. Augustine* narrowly escaping damage on the St. Johns River Bar. Officials expected the vessels to be in operation after repairs by May 10 or May 15, in time to take the Indian River pineapple crop to market.[42]

Toward the end of April 1897, with other stock holdings of mutual interest like the Mergenthaler Linotype Company on his mind, Bradley wrote Sawyer from his home at the nation's capital about the possibility of a sale of the Florida waterway to the federal government. Unfortunately, it would take another thirty-two years, and long after his death, before Bradley's hope would become a reality. In the meantime, Bradley and his colleagues would face numerous calls for additional capital to finance dredging operations, slowing sales of Florida real estate and an intransigent Florida government that insisted on strict completion of the waterway to state specifications before turning over more than a million acres of public land to the privately-owned enterprise for constructing what would eventually become Florida's Atlantic Intracoastal Waterway.[43]

---

[40]Moses to APS, 7, 10 April 1897, SP Folder 8.
[41]Henry Gaillard to APS, 11 April 1897, SP Folder 8; GFM to APS, 19 May 1897, SP Folder 9.
[42]GFM to APS, 13, 19 April 1897, SP Folder 8.
[43]GLB to APS, 21 April 1897, SP Folder 8.

Chapter 5

Steamboating

During the latter part of April 1897, George Miles boasted that Flagler had finally agreed to his plan for the deeding of Boston & Florida lands for the railway's extension to Miami. Miles also sent Sam Maddox a deed from the Florida canal company to Flagler and another from Flagler to Sawyer and Henry Gaillard as trustees, returning to the canal company 94,500 acres of land, conditioned by agreement on the canal company using land sales proceeds exclusively to finance canal construction. Of the acreage deeded, a total of 12,500 acres were to be conveyed to Edward Walker and other investors as bonus lands for purchasing canal company bonds. At the same time, the Clyde Steamship Company expressed an interest in chartering the new Indian River steamboat company's *St. Sebastian* for the summer run on the St. Johns River between Jacksonville and Sanford. Fred Morse, Miami agent for the Boston & Florida and the Florida canal company as well as for the Flagler railway and Flagler's Model Land Company, found a purchaser for ten acres of Boston & Florida land in present-day northern Miami-Dade County at the robust price of $15 an acre, fifteen times the price per acre paid by the company for the company's land in 1892.[1]

The promised Flagler accounting of the lands improved by the drainage canals and roads constructed in Modelo and Halland still had not arrived. Miles sent James Colee — one of the Florida canal company's incorporators — to south Florida to investigate and report back on the holdup. Real estate sales had been picking up in the south. Morse had sold 210 acres of canal company land about two miles west of Lemon City, north of Miami, for $3,150, again at $15 an acre. Despite Miles's fervent assurances that the two vessels would be ready in time for the pineapple trade, the Indian River company's *St. Augustine* and *St. Sebastian* remained laid up at the Merrill-Stevens boat yard in Jacksonville. A federal inspector recommended that the vessels be put in better condition, including sheathing the hulls. The

---

[1]GFM to APS, 21, 23 April 1897; Frederick Morse to GFM, 29 April 1897; SP Folder 8.

cost of the proposed work was $2,500. To raise funds for the additional work, Miles suggested that the steamboat company borrow the money until the pineapple season ended, rather than sell stock, because of the promising long-term outlook for the business.[2]

Meanwhile, the Clyde Steamship Company offered Miles's company $1,750 for a five-month charter of the *St. Sebastian* on the St. Johns River between Jacksonville and Sanford. Miles declined the proposal without conferring with Sawyer but signaled that he might reconsider if the Clyde line increased the offer to $2,000. If the Indian River company chartered the *St. Sebastian*, he thought the enterprise could easily handle the pineapple business with just the *St. Augustine* and the smaller *Della*, and thus, "gradually feel our way on the Indian River." Moreover, the company could operate an independent boat line on the river, if the Flagler railway suspended its own boat operations and afforded the company reasonable rates on all freight delivered to the railroad. That arrangement would leave the new steamboat with "no enemies." Flagler's competitor, the Jacksonville, Tampa and Key West Railway, would have to "work hard for us to get any business for themselves and in order to keep us neutral the East Coast Line [Flagler] would have to deal fairly with us."[3]

By the middle of May, the *Della*, working the pineapple run alone, had not yet yielded a profit. The boat had been too small for the pineapple business and local growers feared the line was only a temporary one. The *Della* might pay within the next two months when business was expected to pick up, Miles thought. He had kept the *Della* in service simply to maintain the company's presence until the two larger steamboats under repair could be put back in service. He discontinued paying $150 a month to a man managing the *Della*, offering to handle the steamer himself, without pay, until business picked up. A later-than-expected pineapple crop afforded the company more time to return the two large steamboats to service. The Merrill-Stevens company eventually completed repairs on the two steamers, with the hulls sheathed, new smokestacks installed, and the boiler repaired; but all of the repairs cost $4,000 more than the $15,000 originally subscribed by the stockholders. With repairs finally completed, Miles made plans to

---

[2]GFM to APS, 11 May 1897, and a second letter the same day but marked "Navigation Co." above canal company letterhead, and a third the following day, 12 May 1897; all in SP Folder 9.

[3]*Ibid.*

travel to Tallahassee to lobby for an extension of the Florida canal company's lapsing waterway charter.[4]

From Lake Worth, Moses reported less than sterling results in crop production at the Lake Worth Trust's Belleville Plantation. Although he deemed the potato crop "almost a complete failure" and the tomato planting "but little," Moses believed that the pineapple crop had been doing well. Before sailing for Europe, George Bradley, at New York's Holland House, made arrangements to pay interest on various notes held by Sawyer's bank at Newburyport and another note by a St. Augustine bank for $5,000 that had been given to finance Florida waterway operations. Sam Maddox reported that Flagler had finally signed the deed returning to Maddox and Sawyer as trustees for the canal company 94,500 acres of land the canal company had transferred to Flagler, complying with an agreement made back in 1895.[5]

In Tallahassee, Miles worked on securing legislation extending the Florida canal company's charter for another four years. Gaillard, now a St. Johns County senator, seemed unable to "reason" a group of legislators opposed to the bill into "a better frame of mind." Although Miles expected the legislation to pass, he remained anxious given a possible sale of the waterway to the federal government. He began assembling a prospectus for a new company to buy not only the company's waterway rights but also all of the Indian River steamboat company's vessels and provide additional capital to finish the waterway to Jacksonville. He intended to send the prospectus to a London banking firm interested in underwriting the proposed company, with the hope that a public offering might yield a good profit for the company's investors. Miles knew Florida's new U. S. senator, Stephen Mallory of Pensacola, and expected his assistance in the sale of the waterway. As a state senator, Mallory had helped the canal company gain legislation aiding the enterprise as far back as 1889.[6]

Facing additional bills from the Merrill-Stevens shipyard for steamboat repairs, Miles believed that if the balance of the Bradley and Maddox pledges were not in hand soon, the steamboat company would have to borrow money to pay the balance on the sheathing contract. He asked for Sawyer's help in getting the directors to authorize taking out a loan, expecting

---

[4]GFM to APS, 18 May 1897, SP Folder 9.

[5]Moses to APS, 12 May 1897; GLB to APS, 16 May 1897; SM to GLB, 16 May 1897; all in SP Folder 9.

[6]GFM to APS, 18 May 1897, SP Folder 9.

the *St. Augustine* to be launched in a few days after completion of the boiler work. The legislature still had not passed the canal extension bill, with Miles claiming that Gaillard had somehow made "many enemies" in the Legislature. Opponents of the bill, while not objecting to the extension, seemed to be "fighting it to get 'even'" with Gaillard.[7]

By the end of May, Maddox advised Sawyer that he had signed a pooling agreement for the steamboat company stock. Maddox also confirmed receipt of the Flagler deed to the so-called "bonus lands," some of which Walker and others were entitled to receive. In the closing days of the session, Florida legislators finally passed a canal extension bill, but only lengthening the time for completion by two years—not the four years that Miles had hoped at the beginning of the session. Miles attributed the difficulties to political enemies of Gaillard "revenging themselves" on the St. Augustine senator. Still fretting over the lack of capital to run both the canal and steamboat businesses, Miles suggested the group borrow $6,000 to finance ongoing operations. Finding himself "used-up," he told Sawyer that once the steamers were back in service, he intended to resign as president of the steamboat company and after completion of the Jupiter-to-Lake Worth cut, he planned to resign as president of the canal company. All alone in running the Florida businesses, and without sufficient financing, Miles could not cope with the difficulties, finding it "impossible to interest others sufficiently to give a helping hand."[8]

The beginning of June, Miles finally received a check from Sawyer for $3,500, desperately needed to finance both the canal and steamboat businesses. Half the money was to be used in the steamboat enterprise, the other half to finance dredging in the Jupiter-to-Lake Worth cut. He sent Maddox the list of the 12,500 acres of land due Bradley, Walker and their associates as bonus lands from the Flagler re-conveyance. Shifting attention to a note owed by William Linton on the purchase of the Lake Worth Trust's, Miles reported that 60-year-old Major Nathan S. Boynton, founder of the Boynton settlement, had been paying Linton's obligation.[9]

Born in 1837 at Port Huron, Michigan, Boynton descended from Sir Matthew Boynton, who reportedly was knighted in the latter part of the seventeenth century for introducing the first sheep and goats into America. He grew up on a farm on the St. Claire River, three miles below Marine City.

---

[7]GFM to APS, 19, 22 May 1897, SP Folder 9.

[8]SM to APS, 25 May 1897; GFM to APS, 31 May 1897; SP Folder 9.

[9]GFM to APS, 5 June 1897, SP Folder 9.

After attending school only in the winter, at the age of 16 he went to Waukegan, Illinois, to take a high school course. Returning to St. Claire County, he started a mercantile business known as Inslee & Boynton at Port Huron. In 1858, he was elected to the state legislature. He earned the title of major serving on the Union side during the Civil War. After the war, he made his home at Marine City and was appointed deputy assessor of internal revenue and postmaster. He also held the offices of village clerk, president, and supervisor of the town. In 1868, he settled in Port Huron, running a newspaper before starting a real estate and insurance business in the summer of 1871.[10]

IIn June 1897, south Florida weather had been so humid it caused the ribbon in Moses's typewriter to blur a letter he wrote to Sawyer. With decent rain, the Red Spanish pineapple had grown to a good size. But sadly, Linton and Boynton had failed to pay their note to Albert Robert, the Lake Worth Trust's first land sales agent. Fred Dewey, the New England group's agent in the Delray area, who had sold the two investors 120 acres at Boynton, also failed to receive payment. And it looked like Boynton was going to withdraw from investing in the Lake Worth area—an ominous thought given the money owed the Trust for the lands sold to the two Michigan investors.[11]

The steamer *St. Sebastian* was soon launched and sent south, with the *St. Augustine* following shortly. Fortunately for the steamboat company, the pineapple crop did not arrive as early as Miles expected. The newly-repaired steamers could still anticipate doing a good business transporting fruit on the Indian River, but Miles planned to test the business by putting the *St. Augustine* on the run first before placing the *St. Sebastian* in service.[12]

By the middle of June, Miles had received, at long last, the much-anticipated Flagler railway accounting of the money spent on roads and canals in developing Modelo and Halland. With the proceeds of lands already sold only enough to pay the Boston & Florida company's share of expenses, Miles estimated that the company had remaining in the area about 1,500 acres, worth $28,800, on average, $19.20 an acre—almost twenty times what the company paid for the land in 1892. And Morse sold forty acres of Boston & Florida land near present-day Hialeah for $600, but only forty dollars

---

[10]"Maj. N. S. Boynton Died in Michigan Home on May 27," *Miami Metropolis*, 19 June 1911.
[11]Moses to APS, 8 June 1897, SP Folder 9.
[12]GFM to APS, 11 June 1897, SP Folder 9.

had been paid down in cash; the balance was to be paid over a three-year period.[13]

Miles expected the upcoming state trustees meeting at Tallahassee to approve paying $11,000 to the canal company on the sale of reserved lands dating as far back as 1885. But the canal company had to pay $4,000 out the payment for expenses. The loss of the dredge *Biscayne* had upset Miles's plans for finishing the Jupiter-to-Lake Worth cut on schedule and heavy rains had caused water rising six feet in the marshes west of the Juno ridge to sweep through the new canal, making it difficult to keep the company's dredge afloat. On the other hand, high water helped in the dry cutting somewhat, and on the whole, Miles expected the deluge to be "more a benefit than a detriment."[14]

Although the Belleville plantation sustained little damage, the potato field at the Huguenot "washed pretty badly," with peas and tomatoes destroyed, Moses reported. Linton and Boynton also failed to make payments on their Lake Worth Trust land purchase. Robert's land had been deeded to both Linton and Boynton, while the Lake Worth Trust land had been titled only in Linton's name. Consequently, Boynton made a payment on the Robert land but paid nothing on the Trust land. Apparently the Lake Worth Trust land was titled in Linton's name alone because Linton thought he could make the payments without assistance. A man named Brinson who sold Linton the 160 acres on which the Linton town site had been located was in the area investigating the situation. Linton appeared to be $400 in arrears in interest payments on the notes for the land. Boynton offered Brinson cash for a twenty percent discount on Linton's note, but nothing toward interest. Brinson felt inclined to accept the offer but only if Boynton also paid the interest.[15]

At the Jefferson State bank at Monticello, just east of Tallahassee, Miles arranged—subject to Sawyer's approval—for a $4,000 loan at eight percent interest for three months to pay for steamer repairs "with the understanding that while the bank will not positively agree to renew the note for another three months, it will do so unless something very unforeseen occurs." On June 18, Miles claimed the loan "a good one," contending the company's steamboats worth $50,000. Giving Sawyer the opportunity to arrange other

---

[13]GFM to APS, 11 June 1897 (this is the second letter written this date; this one written on Canal Company stationery), SP Folder 9.

[14]GFM to APS, 12 June 1897, SP Folder 9.

[15]Moses to APS, 15, 18 June 1897, SP Folder 9.

financing in New England, if he could pull it off, Miles asked him to send a night telegram approving the loan.[16]

Meanwhile, Maddox groused that he'd heard nothing from Miles on the current status of payments on subscriptions for the steamboat company stock. He complained even more about the long name Miles had selected for the Indian River and Bay Biscayne Navigation Company, sarcastically questioning why it was always necessary "to exhaust the English language in selecting names for Florida corporations."[17]

On June 22, Miles attended the meeting of state trustees at Tallahassee to resolve the longstanding debt owed the canal company for land that long before had been reserved for the company but sold without turning over the proceeds. The session was a long one. It began at ten o'clock in the morning and lasted almost nine hours until a quarter to seven in the evening. In the end, the trustees finally agreed to owing the canal company $13,000 on the sale of reserved land from sales as early as 1885, but then agreed to pay the debt only in aggravating installments. On the other hand, the trustees authorized the canal company to sell up to 100,000 acres of reserved lands not yet deeded to the company.[18]

With the new repairs completed, Miles's steamboat company placed the *St. Augustine* on the run between Titusville and the St. Lucie River at Stuart, with the canal company's long-time director, Henry Gaillard, on board for the first trip down the river. Miles was still assessing the strength of the pineapple business along the Indian River and whether to add the *St. Sebastian*, still undergoing more repairs in Jacksonville. The Flagler railway feared the new steamer might undercut railway rates on the Indian River. Miles's steamboat company's policy was to accept freight from both the east and west banks of the river at the same rates, provided the mileage to Titusville was the same. This practice "touched" the Flagler railway at "a tender spot," according to Miles, as the Flagler railway had been "salting the people on the East Side — Merritt's Island, the Indian River Narrows etc. — until they have left them little chance to make anything on their crops." Guaranteeing the Flagler railway absolutely nothing on rate-setting, Miles somewhat ambiguously informed Flagler officials that his company did not intend to cut rates at "competitive points."[19]

---

[16]GFM to APS, 18 June 1897, SP Folder 9.

[17]SM to APS, 24 June 1897, SP Folder 9.

[18]GFM to APS, 25 June 1897, SP Folder 9.

[19]*Ibid.*

The first week of July, Moses shipped 509 crates of pineapple from the Lake Worth Trust's Belleville Plantation west of Boynton. Dewey, from whom Linton had purchased a portion of the Linton town site, had been making new contracts with settlers planning to turn them over to Boynton if he decided to complete the purchase that Linton apparently failed to complete. Moses also reported some talk of the purchase of a large tract of muck land for a sugar cane operation in present-day northern Palm Beach County in the area of today's Juno Beach. On balance, though, the real estate business along the lower east coast had slowed considerably.[20]

The middle of the month, James Ingraham demanded payment for the Lake Worth Trust's share of the expenses of surveying and laying out lots in the Boynton area. Sometime before, Miles agreed to include both the Boston & Florida company and Lake Worth Trust land in the project in order to hasten sales. Moreover, Flagler's land department had even been writing up contracts and drawing notes for the sale of Boston & Florida and Lake Worth Trust properties at no cost to the New England group.[21]

Meanwhile, Miles traveled on the newly-refurbished *St. Augustine* south down the Indian River, reporting on his return the delivery of 1,100 crates of pineapples in the area. Indian River growers and farmers viewed the new steamboat company as "a deliverer from the clutches of a monopoly" and promised "their strong support as long as we give them a fair service." The new company's steamer had been beating the Flagler railway by as much as twenty-four to forty-eight hours in transporting crops to New York markets, using the Jacksonville, Tampa and Key West railway. If the *St. Augustine* was delayed for any reason, the Jacksonville, Tampa railway even ran a special train to ship the pineapple crop. Both company steamers were on the Indian River in good repair. Had the boats been on the run six weeks earlier, the pineapple business would have easily paid the costs of repair. The steamboat company had strong grounds for a lawsuit against the Merrill-Stevens company for extraordinary delays in making the repairs, but "knowing the Florida law," Miles was "doubtful of the wisdom of instituting it." He believed that the company would need to add at least one more steamer on the river by the next winter to meet the burgeoning demand for transportation. He located another vessel, the old steamer *Progress*, which he recommended the company purchase for $750. Writing off her hull as of

---

[20]Moses to APS, 6 July 1897, SP Folder 9.

[21]James Ingraham (Flagler East Coast Railway) to APS, 14 July 1897, SP Folder 9.

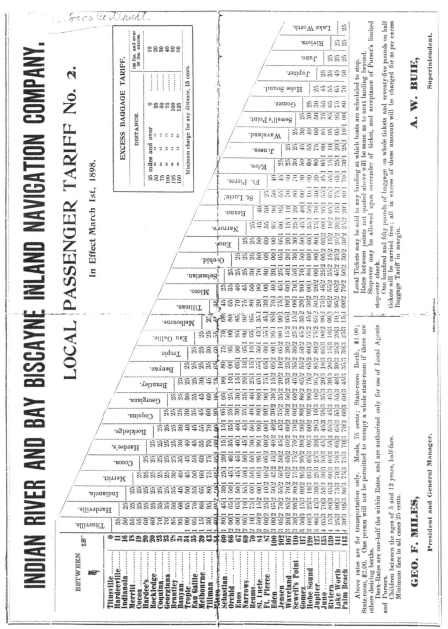

Schedule of steamboat passenger fares of the Indian River and Biscayne Bay Inland Navigation Company, effective March 1, 1898. Putting at first two steamboats on various stretches of the waterway, George Miles and other Florida canal company associates formed the navigation company to take advantage of the construction of what would become known as the Florida East Coast Canal.   (A. M. Taylor Papers, Library of Florida History, Florida Historical Society, Cocoa, Florida)

little value, he thought the machinery still in good condition, and a new hull could be built for something like $2,500 to $3,000. Miles also thought worthwhile the idea of selling steamboat company stock to some of the prominent shippers along the river to strengthen business ties with the growers.[22]

Further south, Flagler announced plans to deepen Biscayne Bay north of the Miami River and Norris Inlet, north of Virginia Key, to twelve feet, and build a steamer costing $215,000 to put on a run between Miami and Nassau. All of these schemes seemed to strengthen opportunities for the New England group. With the arrival of more settlers, Miles recommended increasing land prices to between $20 and $25 an acre, twenty to twenty-five times what the Boston & Florida company paid for canal company land in 1892. Laying up the steamer *St. Sebastian* until the autumn, Miles decided to keep the *St. Augustine* on the river indefinitely. But after the hauling of the pineapple crop, he didn't expect the steamboat operation to turn a profit. He confirmed that all subscribers had paid their contributions to the Florida enterprises. The new subscribers were now entitled to the stock, bonds and land promised when they invested in the Indian River steamboat and Florida canal companies.[23]

Meantime, Boynton finally decided to take over the land contracts he and Linton had signed, but Dewey still was not satisfied with Boynton, who refused to pay any interest on the contract. The matter appeared in limbo. Toward the end of July, Moses found out why Boynton's name was on Robert's notes but not on the Lake Worth Trust's notes. Robert explained that Linton brought Boynton to Lake Worth after the first deal had been made. The two decided that they wanted more land, especially Robert's land. They then made a new deal, involving all of Robert's property—not just land in a square mile section. Robert hesitated at first because he had been working on a plan to get large cash payments up front. Satisfied with the first sale to Linton only, but with a much larger transaction now involved, Robert needed another name on the contract. Boynton also wanted his name on the deed because of his arrangements with Linton. Robert regarded Boynton's name as more good luck than good business. Linton's "sudden collapse" created shock waves throughout the local community. It had been believed that Linton would retain his investment for at least three years, having already invested so much money in the area.[24]

---

[22]GFM to APS, 15 July 1897, SP Folder 9.

[23]*Ibid.*

[24]Moses to APS, 26 July 1897, SP Folder 9.

By the end of July, Miles had secured an application for the purchase of forty acres of Boston & Florida land, located two and half miles west of Biscayne Bay, at $12.50 an acre. At the same time, Miles and Sawyer had been exchanging drafts of the final written agreement with Flagler on the Boston & Florida Company's offer to provide land as a subsidy for the extension of the railway to Miami. Miles insisted that the joint development contract require that in the event Flagler terminated the agreement, Flagler would lose all rights to unsold land in the Modelo and Halland settlements and take the balance of the subsidy from the Boston & Florida's average-graded lands. He believed, and justifiably so, that so long as Flagler's interest in the settlements remained an undivided half portion, his railway land department would stay interested as the "colonizing medium" and thus the Boston & Florida could ride Flagler's "coat-tails" in these developments and participate in the profits without discrimination or undercutting by the powerful railroad magnate.[25]

In the first week of August 1897, Miles planned to travel north to New York and then on to Philadelphia. Without knowing how long he intended to remain there, he also planned to visit Sawyer in Boston, if possible. Florida land sales seemed to be improving along the Florida coast and Flagler planned on making significant investments in Miami. The Florida land baron had purchased a considerable portion of Julia Tuttle's interest in the town for nearly $90,000, which Miles thought "absurd," given that the lands had been "wild" just eighteen months before.[26]

By the first week in September, Stephen Andrews, Keeper of the Orange Grove House of Refuge for shipwrecked sailors five miles south of Lake Worth, lamented that one of his land sales in the Lake Worth area had gone sour. Andrews had sold 120 acres of land east of the canal company's inland waterway to Linton. Linton gave Andrews a note for $1,500 for the first payment. Boynton paid the balance of something over $4,000 in cash. Later, Linton offered Andrews two checks—each in the amount of $750—in payment of the note. But only one of the checks was paid; the other bounced, leaving Andrews $750 short. Andrews attempted to get Boynton to pay the check, but Boynton refused.[27]

Moses still believed that Boynton hadn't abandoned the town bearing his name. In fact, Moses thought that Boynton had been playing "a waiting

[25]GFM to APS, 30 July 1897, SP Folder 9.

[26]GFM to APS, 7 August 1897, SP Folder 9.

[27]Wallace Moses to APS, 7 September 1897, SP Folder 10.

game in hopes of tiring out Linton's creditors and getting a better discount out of them." Boynton had not yet settled up with either Robert or Dewey. Meanwhile, Dewey had been trying to make new contracts with town settlers, but Boynton apparently had already beaten Dewey to the punch. And Boynton was holding the contracts until he could get title to the land from Dewey, thus tying up at least a portion of Dewey's land.[28]

Around the middle of the month, Moses thought Lake Worth Trust land west of Boynton worth between $15 and $20 an acre. But across the board, real estate values in the area had been dropping, with almost no sales in the vicinity of Lake Worth. The price to actual settlers was $17 an acre, with only a small down payment and the balance to be paid over five years. The possibility of future sales there lay in the establishment of the Boynton settlement, the settlers brought in by Linton, and the good quality of land near the town, Moses wrote. But Boynton's plans were still unclear; Dewey had sued him to fulfill his purchase contract. A man named Percival, Boynton's sales broker, had tired of Boynton's delay in closing transactions at Linton and Boynton and ended his relationship with the Michigan investor. Percival had received an offer from Dewey, but didn't write back because Boynton "chose to do his own figuring." Moses believed that the entire matter at the Boynton settlement could have been straightened out if Boynton had left the matter in his hands. But Boynton, "in an effort to be exceedingly sharp and shrewd" had "over reached himself and antagonized everybody by his transparent efforts to grind them down to the last cent."[29]

From New York City on September 22, Miles wrote Sawyer that the Monticello Bank had declined to renew the steamboat company's three-month loan. There had been an understanding—albeit unwritten—that the loan could be extended for at least another three months, at least according to Miles. To protect the group's position, Miles had negotiated a clause in the loan agreement preventing the bank from selling the company's assets to pay the loan for six months. With the note coming due, Miles asked for Sawyer's help in getting a loan elsewhere. Just a few days later, Miles arranged a 90-day extension of the note, but nagging worry over the Florida steamboat and canal companies' fiscal affairs had completely exhausted him. He told Sawyer that unless his colleagues were able to interest "some Northern Banks or Capitalists" in financing their Florida properties, devel-

---

[28]*Ibid.*

[29]Wallace Moses, 16 September 1897, SP Folder 10.

opment would be all uphill work. "We have all the conditions favorable for making it a great success if we had command of a small amount of capital to push it," he lamented.[30]

Sawyer and his colleagues continued to explore other ways to exploit the vast acreage of Florida east coast lands acquired as a result of the company's dredging work. He even sought Miles's advice on forming a company to raise tobacco on some of the land. Although Miles lacked sufficient knowledge about the business to express an opinion, he did state his feelings about the dredging's dismal progress. He recommended that the canal company cease operations immediately "[i]f we cannot arrange the money for the development of our property" and that the properties be placed "in charge of a local man at a small salary in the hope that later on someone may supply the money for its development and that enough of our dredging plant be sold to pay off our present indebtedness." Considering once again resigning as president, Miles wrote that no matter what assets the company had at its disposal, it could not realize sufficient money to continue dredging. In the past Miles felt confident that, with the waterway open between Ormond and Biscayne Bay and the large amount of land available under the state grant, the company could raise enough money, but as he admitted, "I now find that, so far as I am personally concerned, I was mistaken as I have tried hard and failed." However bad the news was on financing the dredge work, Miles relayed the good news from Flagler's associate, James Ingraham, that real estate sales at Halland, Modelo, and White City seemed to be doing very well.[31]

Bradley agreed with Miles's dismal view of the canal company's prospects. Writing to Sawyer from his Pomfret home, Bradley suggested that canal operations be suspended for the present until the mortgaging of canal property could be arranged. From West Palm Beach, Moses had set out pineapples on the canal company's land in the Lake Worth area. The Lake Worth Trust's agent complained about the Flagler railroad's high shipping rates and predicted that the competition from the steamboat would reduce them eventually. "I certainly hope so," Moses wrote, "for although I do not suppose the business of the railroad for this year is, at present, of sufficient volume even at high rates, to pay very much on the capital invested, the [shipping] rates on pineapples is [sic] more than the business will warrant for the season through." Home for the moment from the pineapple growers

---

[30]GFM to APS, 22, 26 September 1897, SP Folder 10.
[31]GFM to APS, 29 September 1897, SP Folder 10.

association's annual meeting at Jensen, Moses told Sawyer that he had discussed the prevailing labor rates for cultivating pineapples with several growers at Lake Worth. Then paying $1.25 a day average for each grove worker, Moses advised of the possibility of reducing wages down to a $1 a day by "a concerted action on the part of the employers," but did not regard that a likely prospect. While he paid wages higher than employers paid for similar labor in the northern part of the state as well as in Georgia where there were many black workers, the Lake Worth area didn't have as many blacks, Moses wrote. Moreover, men hired at a low rate required "much watching," were less experienced and would injure the young plants by cutting the surface roots. Moses had been paying an experienced black worker, King, $30 a month or about $1.15 a day to work in the plantation. He didn't think he could easily replace him. He found King honest, willing and zealous. The general outlook for land sales in the Lake Worth area remained poor.[32]

The second week of October 1897, Bradley received what must have been an unsettling telegram. From St. Augustine, the Florida canal company's treasurer, Henry Gaillard wired, "Do you intend to abandon the Canal answer quick." Without further explanation, Bradley responded with a terse, guarded, and equally ominous eight-word response, "I have explained my position fully to Mr. Miles." There appeared to be no further comment from Miles or anyone else on the subject. But in any event by the middle of October, better news arrived when Miles heard from Ingraham that 600 acres in 10-acre lots had been purchased at Halland and that up to October 1, a hundred tickets had been sold for an excursion of prospects traveling from Jamestown, Ohio, to see the settlement. Miles thought the Halland sale would net both Flagler and the Boston & Florida Company $12,000 after commissions. Ingraham reiterated the terms and conditions of sale at the two south Florida settlements. Each purchaser of an "outside" lot who wished to build in the town was to receive a town lot free, with those lots to be taken alternately, leaving the remaining lots available for sale. Cash buyers were to receive a deed, but if buyers paid over time, they were given an agreement to convey the lot either when buildings were erected or otherwise improved or when buyers paid all of the installments due on the purchase.[33]

---

[32]GLB to APS, 3 October 1897; Moses to APS, 7 October 1897; both in SP Folder 10.

[33]GLB to APS, 9 October 1897, SP Folder 10. GFM to APS, 14 October 1897; James Ingraham to APS, 20 October 1897; both in SP Folder 10.

Beginning in November, Miles took applications for Boston & Florida and Florida canal company land near Fort Pierce for growing tobacco and he sent engineer James Colee down to select land for a tobacco company. Moses confirmed Boynton's failure to carry out Linton's plans for development in the area, although Linton's assignment of his interests to Boynton had not yet been made a public record. Moses supposed it would eventually be made public if and when Boynton ever completed his "trading," hoping that Boynton would either "fix matters up" or get out of the business altogether. By the end of November, company officials began discussing arrangements for the formation of the Walker Trust, an entity formed for the purchase of canal lands just a few months later in February 1898 and to generate much-needed cash for dredging operations. For the Florida canal company, the work was as much a dredging operation as it was a public relations campaign waged with the State of Florida. In a letter to state trustees, Miles wrote that the company expected to complete the long-awaited connection between the Indian River and Lake Worth "in a few days." Inviting them to view the company's work, Miles asked them to "form an opinion of the enterprise." But the trustees did not take up the offer.[34]

The steamboat company's prospects improved considerably with news that Flagler's railway had been considering using waterway transportation in connection with its railroad business. Flagler seemed disposed to give the steamboat company "the whole of their river business," Miles wrote, "without asking us to connect exclusively with them," thus affording the Indian River steamboat company the option to connect with either the Florida East Coast Railway or the rival Jacksonville, Tampa & Key West Railway. By that time, the Florida canal company had almost completed construction of the canal connecting the Indian River with Lake Worth, and the steamer *Courtney* reportedly had already cruised through the passage. Miles also announced the hiring of Captain A.W. Buie of the bankrupt Indian River Steamboat Company as the new steamboat company's superintendent.[35]

In December 1897, Henry Gaillard sent the canal company's Washington counsel, Sam Maddox, a deed signed by the Flagler railway conveying land to Maddox and Albert Sawyer as co-trustees. Made at the request of the company on May 10, the conveyance represented a return of land previ-

---

[34]GFM to APS, 5 November 1897, SP Folder 10. Moses to APS, 12 November 1897, SP Folder 10. SM to APS, 22 November 1897, SP Folder 10. *MIIF*, 22 November 1897, 429.

[35]GFM to APS, 6 December 1897, SP Folder 10; [no title], Miami *Metropolis*, 17 December 1897.

ously deeded to Flagler by the company. As agreed, the land could be sold by the Florida canal company only to complete construction of the Florida waterway.[36]

Prospects for the Boston & Florida's properties in present-day St. Lucie, Palm Beach and Broward counties brightened, while the new steamboat business seemed to increase each day. New settlers arrived at White City, near Fort Pierce and area farmers expected to ship 15,000 crates of vegetables. There was also "a renewal of overtures" from the Flagler railway, which seemed inclined to give Miles's steamboat company "the whole of their business" without requiring the company to tie itself exclusively to the railway.[37]

Thomas M. Rickards, one of the canal company's surveyors, resided at a settlement called "Boca Ratone," a place he had laid out only a few years before in the southern part of present-day Boca Raton. He had prepared a map for the town from a 160-acre tract of canal company land along the Hillsboro River, now the present-day Hillsboro Canal. He charged the firm $75 for laying out the tract in thirty-two five-acre lots and expected a check for $25, with the balance in the form of a ten percent commission on the sale of the lots. He had already gotten applications for the purchase of four or five lots. Rickards could sell all of the lots within a short time, Miles estimated, and net the canal company about $2,400, a sales price of around $16 an acre. With considerable foresight, he predicted that Rickards' "Boca Ratone" community promised to be "about the most prosperous settlement on the Coast."[38]

As the outlook continued to brighten for the Boston & Florida's properties at Halland, Modelo and White City, the company's partner in these projects, Flagler's Florida East Coast Railway, furnished funds for the return of Ormond pioneer John A. Bostrom to his native country, Sweden, to encourage Swedes to settle in the company's south Florida communities like Hallandale. While in Sweden, Bostrom interviewed prospective settlers and published a pamphlet in Swedish advertising the settlements. Because of the Boston & Florida's stake in the same properties, the Flagler company

---

[36]SM to GLB, 1 December 1897, SP Folder 10; Answer of Canal Company, *Florida East Coast Railway Co. vs. Albert Gilchrist, et al.,* TIIF, Chancery Case No. 59, Palm Beach County Circuit Court, 23-27; SM to APS, 27 December 1897, SP Folder 10.

[37]GFM to APS, 6 December 1897, SP Folder 10.

[38]Rickards to GFM, 16 December 1897; GFM to APS, 16 December 1897; both in SP Folder 10.

later suggested that the Boston & Florida group contribute a quarter of the promotion's cost, which totaled $734.61 for Bostrom's passage and expenses. Miles sent the request on to Sawyer, tersely advising that "the expense was not authorized in any way by us." Flagler would later employ another Swede, Olaf Zetterlund, to attract a colony of Swedes to settle in Hallandale.[39]

At the close of 1897, almost a year after Miles's new steamer company began operations, the Florida canal company's secretary, Sam Maddox, mailed a deed to Sawyer transferring some 12,501 acres of company lands in Brevard and Dade counties to Sawyer and Sawyer's son, Albert Hayden Sawyer, as trustees to provide security for the four principal subscribers of stock in the new steamboat company, Bradley, Walker, Amory and Maddox. Also sent to Sawyer were fifteen series "A" canal bonds, each representing $1,000, which were also to be given to the subscribers, all in accordance with the informal agreement reached a year before in the latter part of 1896. Sawyer, Bradley and others had subscribed $30,000 for the benefit of their various Florida interests. Of the $30,000 invested, $15,000 purchased securities of the new steamboat company. The other $15,000 bought canal company securities — $15,000 series "A" bonds, $15,000 worth of stock and 7,500 acres of land. Of the unsecured bonds, $5,000 worth was to go to Bradley, $5,000 to Walker, $1,000 to Maddox, and $4,000 to Fred Amory.[40]

At Lake Worth, the news about the mortgage securing Lake Worth Trust lands west of Boynton sold to Linton went from bad to worse. In December 1897, William Linton-the Flagler, Boston & Florida land, and Florida canal companies' joint agent in south Florida-defaulted on a mortgage he had given the Lake Worth Trust for eighty acres of muck land west of Boynton. Now a Michigan congressman, Linton had subdivided the town of Linton in the early 1890s and sold land there to fellow Michigan settlers before returning home. A few years later — in 1901 — the town would be renamed Delray (present-day Delray Beach) after Delray, Michigan, a suburb of Detroit. Miles recommended foreclosure of the Linton mortgage because he deemed the prospect that Linton might deed back the property in lieu of foreclosure

---

[39]Ingraham to GFM, 14 December 1897; GFM to APS, 16 December 1897; both in SP Folder 10. See, also, Ingraham to Parrott, 1 May 1897, F. E. C. Railway Correspondence, Florida East Coast Railway, Box 1, Folder 9 (1897), for preliminary planning by Ingraham for the trip. For a general biographical sketch of Zetterlund, see Cutler, *History of Florida*, II, 199-200.

[40]SM to APS, 27, 30 December 1897; GLB to APS, 31 December 1897; SP Folder 10.

doubtful, "as others have claims on all his property in Florida." Dewey, the local agent now handling the property for Sawyer, believed that the Lake Worth Trust could make eight or nine sales of the Linton property at an astounding price when clear title could be obtained — $70 an acre! By the end of December, the Lake Worth Trust had already begun foreclosure proceedings, employing longtime Flagler attorney William W. Dewhurst of St. Augustine. Three months after starting the foreclosure suit, in March 1898, President William McKinley appointed Linton to serve as postmaster of Saginaw, Michigan, following the expiration of the erstwhile Lake Worth developer's term of office in the Fifty-fourth Congress.[41]

---

[41]GFM to APS, 7, 21, 30 December 1897, SP Folder 10. Order of Publication, *Albert P. Sawyer, Trustee for the Lake Worth Land Trust, Complainant vs. William S. Linton and Ida M. Linton, Defendants*, Dade County Circuit Court, Chancery, entered on December 29, 1897, legal adv. in *Miami Metropolis*, 14 January 1898. Another example of Linton's growing problems with creditors may be found at "Notice in Attachment (George A. Gale vs. W. S. Linton)," *Tropical Sun* (West Palm Beach), 9 December 1897. *Biographical Directory*, 1398-99. Farrar, *Incomparable Delray*, 12-15, 27. Knetsch's, "One of Flagler's Men," presents an excellent sketch of the life of Dewhurst.

Chapter 6

Seawater Gold

A few days into the new year, Wallace Moses, the New England group's West Palm Beach land agent, sent back devastating news. A cold wave had swept through south Florida, destroying the vegetables at Boynton. On January 2, 1898, the temperature had dropped to 32 degrees. The cold wave was, in Moses's words, "severe," and "nearly as bad" as it had been three years before when a cold wave swept through central Florida, ruining the state's citrus industry. From St. Augustine, Miles confirmed its severity, reporting that the frost had killed off the beans and other early vegetables.[1]

By January 12, Moses guessed the crop at the Lake Worth Trust's Belleville plantation might be diminished by as much as fifty percent, effectively eliminating any chance of a profit for the year. He advised Sawyer's group to put in fertilizer or else abandon "the whole business," cautioning that most of the local planters had already started fertilizing. With all the damage done to the pineapples, Moses found the two-acre potato field scarcely affected. From his home at the nation's capital, Bradley suggested that the trust keep the Belleville plantation for at least another year. But toward the end of the month, Moses still had not heard from Sawyer. He assumed that the Sawyer's colleagues wanted to keep the plantation, but held off on ordering fertilizer until he received approval. Despite the cold weather, the three-year-old Royal Poinciana Hotel at Palm Beach opened for the season with about seventy-five guests. The year-old Palm Beach Inn, later renamed The Breakers, entertained perhaps 200 or more.[2]

The Walker Trust

Completing reorganization of the New England group's Florida enterprises, the Florida canal company transferred 12,501 acres of land to the

---

[1]Moses to APS, 3 January 1898, SP Folder 11. GFM to APS, 5 January 1898, SP Folder 11.

[2]Moses to APS, 12 January 1898, SP Folder 11. GLB to APS, 21 January 1898, SP Folder 11. Moses to APS, 22, 31 January 1898, SP Folder 11

Walker Land Trust, the third Bradley trust, in addition to the Lake Worth and New River land trusts. Created on February 4, 1898, the Walker Trust's beneficiaries included George Bradley, who held 100 of the 250 trust shares, and prominent Springfield, Massachusetts manufacturer, Edward M. Walker, one of Bradley's closest friends, who owned another 100 shares. Sawyer and Fred Amory each owned fifteen shares; Sam Maddox, ten shares; and Arthur M. Merriam of Manchester, Massachusetts, ten shares.[3]

The *St. Sebastian* had been profitable in transporting tourists. But she could have been more profitable, making between $500 to $700 a run transporting commercial freight, had it not been for the freeze that killed off the bean crop just as the steamer had begun to ship large quantities. There was more good news in the canal company's straightening of Lake Worth Creek. In the past, Miles had been forced to transfer steamboat passengers to the lighter-draft *Della* at Jupiter because he couldn't chance running the larger *Sebastian* in the shallow waters of the creek. But with the creek's improvements, Miles expected the *Sebastian* to be able to make the run all the way to Palm Beach without interruption.[4]

There now seemed a fair chance of making a sale of all of the Boston & Florida lands to Flagler. Ingraham apparently had recommended the purchase to Flagler. Miles offered the property in Brevard and Dade counties if Flagler bought all of the lands at once at $5 an acre, with half to be paid in cash and the balance from the first sales of the land as they were sold by the Flagler railway's land department. While the *St. Sebastian* continued to do a prosperous business, the *St. Augustine*, unfortunately, was a day boat and could not operate on the long run between Titusville and Palm Beach. The canal company's inland waterway was now open for navigation to Palm Beach, with the *St. Sebastian* running all the way through to Lake Worth.[5]

But by the middle of February, another cold wave had struck the Lake Worth region, doing no damage in West Palm Beach, but enough at the Belleville Plantation "to do up the beans," practically ruining them, Moses recounted. The tomatoes and young pineapples remained unhurt and the potatoes hadn't yet come up. A new railroad schedule permitted Moses to travel to Boynton from West Palm Beach in the morning and return the

---

[3]Walker Land Trust dated February 4, 1898, and recorded in Miscellaneous Records Book B, at page 77 of the Public Records of Dade County, Florida.

[4]GFM to APS, 31 January 1898, SP Folder 11.

[5]GFM to APS, 9 February 1898, SP Folder 11.

Small boat in the Jupiter Narrows, Indian River, ca. 1900. (Courtesy, Florida State Archives, Florida Photographic Collection, Tallahassee, Florida)

same afternoon, avoiding having to run his sailboat on Lake Worth from West Palm Beach to oversee the Belleville Plantation.[6]

Meanwhile, several members of the New England group, including Albert Sawyer, George Bradley and Edward Walker, had become interested in a new business venture. At Newburyport, Sawyer, a fervent Baptist, helped to promote the stock of the Electrolytic Marine Salts Company, headed by a 32-year-old Baptist minister, Reverend Prescott Ford Jernegan, who served as general manager and vice president. Born on December 17, 1866, Jernegan had graduated from Brown University with a Bachelor of Arts degree in 1889, later graduating from the Newton Theological Institution in 1892. He served as pastor at the Middletown Baptist Church from 1892 until 1895 and the Baptist Church at Deland from 1895 until 1896.[7]

---

[6]4. Moses to APS, 14 February 1898, SP Folder 12
[7]*Who Was Who*, Vol. 4, "Jernegan, Prescott Ford."

Incorporated in Maine in November 1897, just a year after Jernegan's last pastorate, Jernegan's company announced a controversial process for extracting gold from sea water. Sawyer served as a financial agent and sold stock in the company. Company officials represented to prospective investors that "at the lowest estimate, a cubic mile of sea-water contains gold to the value of $65,000,000" and that the sea gold company's process could produce more than enough gold from the waters of Long Island Sound alone to "pay off the National Debt." Quickly selling stock in the venture, Sawyer and other promoters reportedly raised more than $5 million from Newburyport residents alone.[8]

At his Washington residence, Bradley learned a bit of bad news during a visit with Miles. The Florida canal company couldn't pay off the $15,000 note due on February 28, so Bradley had to pay the note himself. Ever the optimist, Bradley believed the outlook for their Florida interests greater than ever. To him, the Indian River Steamboat Company's reports showed "a gratifying profit," with sufficient business for two more vessels than presently employed. With the prospect of war with Spain growing more likely each day, the company, through Bradley, offered the federal government the use of the inland waterway in the event of war, which appeared imminent after the sinking of the battleship *Maine* on February 14 in Havana, killing 260 men. Bradley believed a war with Spain might demonstrate the usefulness of the Florida waterway for national defense and facilitate its sale to the federal government. At the same time, the Flagler railway's land department made considerable sales of Boston & Florida lands. Bradley also learned that "the profitable extraction of gold from sea water was a proved success" and that Walker wanted to invest in the sea gold venture. In fact, so pleased was he with the preliminary reports that merely owning shares of stock in the sea gold company was not enough. He pitched Sawyer to join him in the building of a plant for the conversion of seawater into gold under license from the sea gold company.[9]

From West Palm Beach, Moses reported that the cold had "knocked out" the bean crop and retarded the tomatoes, while the potatoes had made a poor showing. The pineapple crop appeared to be largely unaffected. Al

---

[8]Dodge, "Sea Water Gold." Nelson, *Newburyport*, "The Saltwater Gold Scam." Electrolytic, *A Sketch*; Electrolytic, *Gold*. Hallet, "Great Quoddy"; Mason, "Great Sea-water."

[9]GLB to APS, 2, 5 March 1898, SP Folder 11. See, also, GFM (on Maddox's letterhead) to Secretary of Navy John D. Long (Copy), 3 March 1898, offering the use of the Florida waterway to the federal government, and Long to Miles (Copy), 5 March 1898, acknowledging the offer; both in SP Folder 11.

Robert, the Lake Worth Trust's first land agent, apparently had decided to halt operations at his Huguenot Plantation. In a demonstration of faith in the area, however, Moses decided to care-take Robert's land, at no cost to Robert, for whatever crops he was able to get out of the farm. The freeze had apparently caused prospective settlers to become "shyer than ever." Moreover, the Flagler railroad eliminated the convenient stop at Boynton for lack of business, forcing Moses once again to pilot his sailboat across Lake Worth from West Palm Beach to reach the Lake Worth Trust's Belleville Plantation.[10]

During the middle of March, Miles signed $4,800 worth of contracts for land sold at Halland; all in all, about 300 acres, since February 1. The sales resulted in a credit to the Boston & Florida company in notes of something over $3,000 after paying the company's share of Flagler's cost of constructing roads and drainage improvements. Miles once again asked Sawyer for an extension of his personal note at the Newburyport bank, emphasizing that he had been trying to sell his Paintoff stock to pay the debt off. The prospect of war with Spain had made Florida residents "a little nervous as we have no coast defenses," but Moses hoped that the difficulties might blow over. The impending war, however, was "the engrossing topic" at West Palm Beach. "One day it looks like peace," he mused, "and the next day war. I can only conceive of Spain's [sic] being foolish enough to fight on the assumption that she has lost Cuba, anyway, and if she does not fight and cause us as much damage as possible she will have revolution at home." Especially menacing to Moses was the arrival of the Spanish torpedo flotilla, which had been ordered to Puerto Rico.[11]

Despite the uncertainty of war, Miles's steamboat company advertised a schedule of what must have seemed hefty charges to transport passengers and freight on the Florida waterway from Titusville on the Indian River south to Palm Beach on Lake Worth, with thirty-three stops in between, including Cocoa, Melbourne, Fort Pierce, Jupiter and Juno. A steamboat passenger traveling the entire distance—over 143 miles—expected to pay $4.30 for the trip, with an extra charge of seventy-five cents for a meal. A single stateroom berth cost an additional dollar, while the charge for a stateroom called for $2.00.[12]

---

[10]Wallace Moses to APS, 4 March 1898, SP Folder 11.

[11]GFM to APS, 12 March 1898; Wallace Moses to APS, 28 March 1898; both in SP Folder 11.

[12]Indian River and Bay Biscayne Inland Navigation Company, Local Passenger Tariff No. 2 In Effect March 1st, 1898,"TP."

When war in Cuba finally broke out, the Army's attention initially centered on Tampa Bay along Florida's west coast as a location for stationing troops prior to transport to Cuba. But as time passed, the military's top brass became increasingly interested in the possibility of using transportation facilities along the east coast as an alternative. So tempting was the potential business that Henry Flagler himself lobbied Washington officials to use his railway to transport men and material down the Florida east coast. Florida Congressman Robert W. Davis wrote Flagler on May 3 that he had visited the War and Navy Departments "time and time again" in the interest of the Florida East Coast Railway, pointing out "the superiority of Miami over Port Tampa from a sanitary point of view." Within a few weeks, during a tour hosted by the Flagler railway, Major General J. F. Wade, accompanied by Corps of Engineers Captain David Gaillard and other military aides, visited West Palm Beach and other towns along the east coast to locate camping grounds for troops and determine what means of transportation might be available. Captain Gaillard, a South Carolina cousin of the Florida canal company's Henry Gaillard, would later become famous as the superintendent of construction of the Culebra Cut, the scene of the most difficult blasting and dredging work during construction of the Panama Canal. When Wade and his entourage finally left West Palm Beach after their tour, a local newspaper remarked, "[t]hat some of them fully enjoyed every minute of their stay here they admitted, also their surprise at what and whom they found in this supposed wilderness."[13]

In late May 1898, U. S. Army officials engaged Miles's steamboat company to transport three mortar carriages down the waterway from Titusville to Key West. A local account reported that the steamer *St. Sebastian* bound for Key West carried a 40-ton mortar down the waterway at Juno on May 21. So large was the cannon, according to the report, that "a man on horseback could easily pass through it without dismounting." The Army chose the steamboat company to ship the mortars, Miles later recounted, when Henry Plant's railway and steamship line refused to take the cargo from Tampa to Key West down the west coast for less than $9,000. Miles arranged to have the material shipped by rail to Titusville, then transferred to one of his Indian River steamers for delivery at Key West for only $2,500. Despite its success during the war, Miles's company later abandoned the transporta-

---

[13]Davis to Flagler, 3 May 1898, Florida East Coast Railway Correspondence (1898), Box 1, Folder 10. "Major-Gen. J. F. Wade and Staff," *Tropical Sun* (West Palm Beach), 19 May 1898.

tion business after losing the railroad connection at Titusville when Flagler purchased the Enterprise Junction-to-Titusville branch line.[14]

At the Boynton settlement, Major Boynton had begun construction of a thirty-room beachfront hotel. Moses anticipated shipping six hundred crates of pineapples from the Lake Worth Trust's Belleville plantation. Though the fruit was small in size and late, he hoped for good prices because of the shutting out of Cuban exports and the limited Florida pineapple crop.[15]

While Bradley trusted that all was well with the "sea gold" project in Maine, all was not well. The sea gold scheme turned out to be a fraud on its investors, although Sawyer had not been a part of the deceit. Walker and other Springfield residents had invested in the scheme in addition to Bradley. Bradley himself had invested at least $10,000. Disgruntled investors lodged eight different lawsuits against Sawyer in Maine and Massachusetts, even though Sawyer had done little if anything wrong except sell the stock. Reverend Jernegan appeared, at first, to have been the real perpetrator of the crime. So shocking was the scandal, the scam is still widely talked about in the old town of Newburyport. So embarrassed were Sawyer's Springfield investors, they begged Sawyer to keep the public from knowing they had been duped. Despite the stinging loss, Bradley remained convinced that sea water could someday be converted to gold on a practical basis.[16]

On July 31, sea gold directors issued a terse statement, "The story printed in a New York paper is in the minds of the Directors conclusive evidence of a conspiracy on the part of P. F. Jernegan, General Manager, and C. E. Fisher, Assistant Manager, to defraud the stockholders of the company. They have undoubtedly left the country and disabled the electrical apparatus of plant No. 1." Fortunately, a considerable sum of money had already been recovered, and there were good prospects for recovery of additional funds for the stockholders.[17]

---

[14]Mather, Inland Water-Ways, 13-14. "Juno Jingles," Tropical Sun (West Palm Beach), 26 May 1898; sixteen years later, recounted in "East Coast Canal To Be Bought by Government For Much Less Than It Has Cost to Build," Miami Metropolis, 27 November 1914. GFM to GAY (Note), 26 August 1928, YP Box 4, File 20; Miles, "Inland Waterways," 87. GFM to GAY (Note), 26 August 1928, YP Box 4, File 20.

[15]Moses to APS, 2 May 1898, SP Folder 12.

[16]GLB to APS, 27 June 1898; Dodge, "Sea Water Gold"; Nelson, Newburyport, "The Saltwater Gold Scam." Electrolytic, A Sketch; Electrolytic, Gold.

[17]"Marine Gold Scheme a Fraud," New York Times, August 1, 1898.

Boston officials secured a warrant for the arrest of Jernegan on a charge of obtaining money under false pretenses. Jernegan, however, arrived in Le Havre, France, on August 1 on board the French steamer *Navarre*, but was not taken into custody because of sloppy paperwork. He then left for Paris. But before leaving, he wrote a letter to Arthur Ryan, the sea gold company's president. Jernegan expressed deep regret over the pain and loss caused by his partner, Charles Fisher, but took none of the blame himself, "I fear something has gone wrong with F [Fisher]. He has disappeared from New York, after telling me that the apparatus was ruined and has carried away the formula relating to the making of the machine in combination, which was his own invention, made since the original contract, and which I have been pressing him to make clear to me and deposit a record of." Jernegan went on to assure that "the main machine takes gold from the sea is a certainty." And he promised he would devote the next few weeks to finding Fisher. In any event, Jernegan gave his "word of honor" that he would meet with Ryan "in the near future," but it was a promise he would never keep, even though he did provide Ryan with the combination to the company safe. After a second examination of the plant, a former superintendent found no traces of gold in six of the so-called "accumulators."[18]

On the way to Paris, Jernegan jumped off the train. A police search failed to turn him up. Jernegan and Fisher had between them about $200,000 in company funds, but not a dollar of it belonged to the company, according to legal agreements between the company and Jernegan and Fisher. Ryan asserted that stockholders might be able to recover approximately twenty cents to forty cents on a dollar. To Bradley, Walker and the rest, the probability of recovering their investment in the sea gold scheme must have seemed small indeed.[19]

In Florida, Moses determined that the summer drought had destroyed what crops had been left after the freeze at Lake Worth. So awful were the prospects, Moses refused to assume the caretaking of the Lake Worth Trust's Belleville Plantation for whatever he could get out of it. A new concern, the Lake Worth Fruit Company, however, planned to increase acreage and build a canning factory at Mangonia, three miles north of West Palm Beach. The owners of the enterprise included George B. Swift, mayor *pro*

---

[18]"Jernegan Escapes Arrest," *New York Times*, August 2, 1898.

[19]"Marine Gold Man Vanishes," *New York Times*, August 3, 1898. "Sea-Salt Gold Prospects," *New York Times*, August 7, 1898. "Still Uphold Sea-Salt Gold," *New York Times*, August 17, 1898.

tempore of Chicago in 1893 and mayor from 1895 until 1897, and George R. Davis, director general of the Columbian Exposition of 1893. Aware of the poor results at Lake Worth, Bradley encouraged his Trust colleagues to continue operations for at least one more year.[20]

In August, Moses counseled the Lake Worth Trust to cover at least a portion of the pineapples under cultivation at the Belleville plantation. Moses also offered to maintain the operation at his expense if Sawyer agreed to provide $500 for fertilizer and labor. If the yield didn't produce returns of at least $500, the trust stood to lose only the difference between the investment and the net revenues produced after paying crate and marketing expenses. If the crops yielded more than $500, Moses agreed to pay back the $500 and keep all revenues above that amount for his services. In sum, his plan was simply to keep the plantation going until a buyer could be found.[21]

From Washington, Maddox sent three mortgages to Sawyer to be signed by him as co-trustee, pledging some of the lands conveyed by the Flagler railway as security for three loans totaling $50,000, which had been made by Bradley, Walker and John D. Maclennan of Cleveland, an investor in the Indian River Steamboat Company. Bradley's mortgage, encumbering 30,000 acres, represented a loan of $30,000, while the Walker and Maclennan mortgages each encumbered 10,000 acres of Florida land and represented two different loans of $10,000 to the Florida businesses. Maddox also sent a deed from himself and Sawyer to Sawyer and his son, Albert Hayden Sawyer, as co-trustees, for the lands owned by the steamboat company.[22]

By September 1898, Miles had almost completed the repurchase of Henry Flagler's interest in the Florida canal company through an exchange of lands for securities. The exchange had been essentially a swap of the company's average lands in southern Dade County for company securities at $6 an acre. Because some of the land lay in the Everglades, Miles considered the arrangement "a good one" for the canal company. Flagler had already formed another business, a sugar company with capital of $2 million and had started surveys for the drainage of 200,000 acres of Everglades land west and south of Snake Creek in the northern part of today's Miami-Dade County. The drainage, Miles expected, would improve both Boston & Florida and Florida canal company lands, which lay between the sugar company land and the Atlantic Ocean, because the canals Flagler planned to cut

---

[20]Wallace Moses, 8 July 1898; GLB to APS, 13 July 1898; both in SP Folder 12.
[21]Wallace Moses to APS, 10 August 1898, SP Folder 12.
[22]SM to APS, 15 August 1898, SP Folder 12.

would have to pass through their tracts. Miles also closed an arrangement with the Chicago-based Wilson and Howard Publishing Company for the sale of some of the canal company's land in the western parts of the United States. The Wilson and Howard company owned the *Farm, Field and Fireside* newspaper and, through its Colony Department, had already successfully developed small communities in Louisiana, California, and North Carolina.[23]

Simply to test the market, Moses offered to lease the Belleville Plantation for five years at $500 a year. He remained somewhat doubtful that the property could bring that amount of rent given past returns. Nevertheless, Moses suggested shedding over at least five acres of the land to increase yields. Nearly "sick from heat, overwork and long continued residence at West Palm Beach," he planned to leave on September 18 from Jacksonville via a steamship bound for New York for two or three weeks or "until I get back to my normal condition." Moses hadn't left Florida for more than six years.[24]

Despite the outstanding arrest warrants for the apprehension of Jernegan and Fisher in the sea gold scheme, Bradley remained intrigued with converting sea water into gold. In fact, Bradley wanted to conduct a test of the invention at his expense. If the process worked, Bradley thought he might be interested in forming a manufacturing company, giving the inventor a tenth of the stock in exchange for the exclusive right to use the technology in Massachusetts. Nothing is known of the company's or the inventor's reply, but it is likely that neither testing nor the formation of another company took place given the impending litigation surrounding the sea gold company.[25]

In October 1898, the *New York Times* reported more on the sea gold scandal. Jernegan's father announced that he had received a letter from his son writing from Brussels, saying that he had made up his mind to let the law take its course. The former minister contemplated returning to the United States to surrender himself and return property to the sea gold company's directors. He planned to hand over his cash, books, and bonds and other securities, and if liable, stand trial for his actions and suffer punishment. On

---

[23]GFM to APS, 15 September 1898, SP Folder 12. See, e.g., "Sunset Colonies."

[24]Wallace Moses to APS, 15 September 1898, SP Folder 12.

[25]GLB to J. H. Jery[perhaps Jernegan?], 17 September 1898 [copy], SP Folder 12.

October 11, three stockholders filed suit in the Maine Supreme Judicial Court seeking the appointment of a receiver over the company.[26]

To the disappointment of defrauded investors like Sawyer, Bradley and Walker who had sought redress, neither Jernegan nor Fisher ever returned to New England to face criminal charges or the lawsuits. Jernegan later turned up in the Philippines and became a well-known educator there, employed by the Bureau of Education at Manila from 1901 to 1910. He later lectured in California from 1910 until 1911 before returning to teaching high school and becoming principal at Hilo, Hawaii, serving from 1911 until 1921. He headed McKinley High School at Honolulu from 1921 until 1924. Author of *A Short History of the Philippines* in 1906, the talented minister-turned-schemer even wrote the national song of the Philippines, "Philippines, My Philippines," in 1904.[27]

Jernegan's confederate, Charles Elmer Wilson, had been born in Edgartown, Massachusetts, in 1866 (the same year as Jernegan's birth). A premedical school student for a time, Wilson, by nature, became just another adventurer. Jernegan later reminisced in New Zealand that Charlie had been "a typical soldier of fortune" ready for anything that promised adventure and quick gain, a "dashing, clever, bold and resourceful man." He had "a gentle disarming manner, was successful with women, and was quick thinking and plausible to a degree." Jernegan knew a "soldier of fortune" when he saw one, for he was of that mold himself. Fisher had held a number of jobs, as a cavalryman in both the British and American armies, as a private detective and as a supervisor in a New York retail store. In 1895, Fisher went whaling as master of a ship out of Edgartown. He returned there briefly, going on to Florida to meet up with his friend Prescott Jernegan, who was then preaching at Deland. There Jernegan devised the scheme to make them both a great deal of money, or so the story goes. The two adventurers claimed to be able to turn seawater into gold. Jernegan demonstrated this by slowly lowering boxes of sand off a pier and then bringing them up with flakes of gold mixed in with the grit, gold which Fisher, who was waiting underwater in a ponderous diving suit, had plenty of time to introduce. The scheme nearly caused Fisher's death when his suit leaked and he almost drowned, but in the meantime the charade seduced investors into providing huge sums of capital for Sawyer's sea sold com-

---

[26]SM to APS, 5, 8 October 1898, SP Folder 12. "The Sea-Water Gold Scheme," *New York Times*, October 12, 1898.

[27]*Who Was Who*, Vol. 4, "Jernegan, Prescott Ford."

pany. In July 1898, not long after the scandal broke, Jernegan headed for Europe while Fisher planned to sail for New Zealand. In September, Fisher secretly arrived at Martha's Vineyard to find the scandal had spread all across the local newspapers. Jernegan's father, Captain Jared Jernegan, gave an interview but died within months, a shamed man. Fisher said nothing and sailed off to Edgartown in December 1901. That same week notice of Fisher's death at Sydney, Australia, appeared in the *Vineyard Gazette*, with the cause of death reported to have been consumption. But Fisher's death was a ruse. He was alive and well in New Zealand, where he is believed to have lived the rest of his life.[28]

The beginning of November 1898, Sawyer turned his attention to another of his Florida ventures. He and Sawyer began worked on developing the Paintoff company into a profitable venture. Sawyer formed the New England Paintoff Company to do business in New England. But Miles told Sawyer that he had incorporated a company in West Virginia. Intimating that the group might need another corporation anyway, Miles suggested reorganizing the New England Paintoff Company to do business in New England and New York.[29]

Meanwhile, a few days after returning from his first vacation in six years, Moses proposed in a letter to Sawyer splitting the profits from the operation of the Belleville Plantation. Moses offered to furnish all of the labor and management for two-thirds of the profit. The Lake Worth Trust would receive the remaining third for providing the fertilizer and the land. To Bradley, Sawyer and their New England colleagues, all of their Florida enterprises must have seemed speculative, even a mundane investment like growing fruits and vegetables in south Florida.

---

[28]"Martha's Vineyard in the Bay of Islands," MSS 99/32, pp. 8, 14-19, Auckland War Memorial Museum Library, Auckland, New Zealand, unpublished manuscript with annotations to cited material to Arthur Railton, "Jared Jernegan's Second Family," and "Charlie Fisher, the Perfect Partner," *Duke's County Intelligencer*, volume 28, no. 22, pp. 51-94.

[29]GFM to APS, 2 November 1898, SP Folder 12.

Chapter 7

Ramie

By the middle of February 1899, the demands of financing Florida dredging operations and the agonizingly slow progress in waterway construction had sorely worn down George Bradley, "I am so tired of this Florida struggle," he confessed. He considered halting operations entirely and selling whatever land that could be sold to recoup at least some of the New England group's money. His daughter, Emma, had been very ill, and he was unsure whether or not he would be able to attend the Mergenthaler Linotype Company directors' meeting. Despite the slowing waterway work, he remained confident in the New England group's ability to sell Florida land. Advising Sawyer that neither he nor Miles could raise the capital to finish the waterway and put the steamboat company on its feet, he saw no alternative but to "wind up the business." But on February 22, Bradley, always the optimist, found the reports from Florida "less bad than we might have expected."[1]

Miles had been holding up no better than Bradley. Three years of presiding over the struggling Florida canal company's construction efforts while managing the disappointing steamboat venture had completely exhausted Miles. He soon resigned the presidency of the company. His longtime friend and Pomfret neighbor, George Bradley, succeeded him in the post, rather unexpectedly. Some weeks later, Bradley and Miles met at Bradley's Washington home with one of Flagler's key lieutenants, James Ingraham, to discuss mutual business interests. Miles suggested that Flagler manage the canal company's lands, intimating that the company possessed the financing to finish the Florida waterway to St. Augustine and dredge the channel eight miles more to the St. Johns River to link Jacksonville to the Florida waterway south to Miami. Flagler declined the offer. In a letter to another Flagler lieutenant, Joseph Parrott, Ingraham later warned that if successful, the Florida waterway would "afford competition enough to affect [railway]

---

[1]GLB to APS, 18, 19, 22 February 1899, SP Folder 13.

rates unfavorably." Nevertheless, cooperation between Flagler and the Florida canal company would last until at least the next year when Flagler hired the company to dredge rock and sand from the bottom of Biscayne Bay for Flagler's ocean shipping operation at Miami.[2]

Bradley's attention returned briefly to the sea water gold scandal still brewing in Newburyport. He pointedly asked Sawyer what returns he expected stockholders to receive on their investments and whether or not he and his associate, W.A. Usher, intended to return all of the money they had received as commissions—a total of $100,000—on the sale of stock. He also wanted to know whether he still expected a professor at the Massachusetts Institute of Technology to be able to "get gold from sea water at a profit." With many of their ventures, including the sea gold scheme, souring, Bradley hoped that returns on the Idaho Gold Dredging Company, another of his (and Sawyer's) investments, proved sufficient to make up for some of their recent losses.[3]

In March, Mergenthaler directors gathered for a meeting at the nation's capital. The lack of a quorum prevented them from conducting official business before March 15. The advancing linotype business seemed to Bradley "very prosperous." With the business flourishing, he planned to send the money Sawyer needed for the taxes on the New River Trust land at Fort Lauderdale. On the Florida waterway, Bradley believed that "[i]f we can hold out, I am confident that we shall do well."[4]

By the middle of September, the usually patient Bradley turned insistent with Sawyer about getting some of his money back from the sea gold venture and wanted to know when the company was to make a final payment. He had seen the president of the Baltimore Trust Company in New York who told him that he would recommend that his firm provide financing for the Florida canal company. The matter now rested with the trust company's executive committee. But Bradley had come across another investment opportunity, one that might aid in selling their Florida land. He had seen Phillips Abbott, a 49-year-old New York lawyer who controlled a patent for a revolutionary machine that converted the tropical ramie plant grown in Florida and elsewhere into fiber for use in rope and twine. Abbott believed that the patent could monopolize the ramie processing business.

---

[2]Miles, "History," 8-9. Ingraham to Parrott, 8 May 1899, Florida East Coast Railway Correspondence, Box 1, Folder 11 (1899). U. S. Army Corps, *Annual Report*, 1900 (Part 3), 2009-10.

[3]GLB to APS, 13 March 1899, SP Folder 13.

[4]GLB to APS, 16 March 1899, SP Folder 13.

By the end of September, Bradley had heard from Miles, then in Philadelphia, that tests of the ramie machine were to be conducted in Cleveland. If the machine worked as Abbott represented it, he entertained no doubts about the success of the Florida waterway; land sales would no longer be "an uncertain problem."[5]

As he had done with his sea gold investment, Bradley complained to Sawyer about the slow dividends from his investment in the Smuggler's Union mine near Telluride, Colorado, a venture in which Sawyer also held an interest. At the same time, Bradley pitched Sawyer to invest in Abbott's ramie machine. From his home in Connecticut, Bradley wrote Sawyer at length that the time had come to consider the ramie matter "seriously" and that if the situation were as it appeared, he expected his New England colleagues to make as much money out of it as they had from the Mergenthaler Linotype investment. Bradley had met a South American investor who had spent some $80,000 in trying to get a satisfactory machine to strip the ramie plant. This investor had nearly given up when he encountered the machine which Abbott now controlled. In Bradley's words, the machine's performance was an "unqualified success." An acre of Florida land planted in ramie should yield an annual net profit of $100 using Abbott's machine. An entity named the National Ramie Company was about to be organized with a capital stock of $500,000, Bradley noted. Of this amount, $200,000 was to be used to acquire the American patent interests and $120,000 for Florida lands at $6 an acre. Bradley proposed that of the 20,000 acres needed, 15,000 acres might be contributed from Florida canal company lands, 2,500 acres from Boston & Florida lands and 2,500 acres from the Walker Land Trust in exchange for stock.[6]

Along with Richard Delafield, vice president of the National Park Bank in New York City, the National Ramie Company's board was to be comprised of such leaders of American business as Stuyvesant Fish, John Jacob Astor and August Belmont. Bradley thought that Miles and he might also be on the board. If the machine succeeded, Bradley expected the machine to make "great fortunes for many people," suggesting that he and Sawyer try to get in on the deal. Bradley ended his long pitch to Sawyer surmising that the National Ramie Company stock might some day be worth as many millions as was the Mergenthaler Linotype Company stock.[7]

---

[5]GLB to APS, 11, 28 September 1899, SP Folder 13.
[6]GLB to APS, 23 October, 1 November 1899, SP Folder 13.
[7]*Ibid.*

In the middle of November 1899, Bradley made plans to attend a meeting he claimed to be "of great importance in Florida & ramie matters," welcoming Sawyer to attend. Bradley expected John D. Maclennan to be present, along with his Canadian associates including Sir Sandford Fleming, longtime investors in the Florida canal and Boston & Florida ventures. Edward Walker was also expected to join them. Even now, Bradley had one more new business venture in mind. He had learned of the invention of a new fire retardant material that when applied to the surface of an object prevented it from catching fire. He had already written the inventor about forming a business in Boston to sell the product. But his chief aim now was to tide over "a bad time" for the Florida canal company. He proposed selling 10,000 acres of the canal company's ramie land for cash at $2.50 an acre. Bradley and Sawyer would then form a company with capital stock of $100,000 to be called the Boston & Florida Ramie Company. Of the total stock, $30,000 worth was to be sold for working capital, as needed, and $20,000 worth to be granted to the National Ramie Company for a favorable contract for the use of the machines. Fifty thousand dollars' worth of the stock would be paid for in exchange for 10,000 acres of company land at $5 an acre. Bradley thought that he, Sawyer, Fred Amory, Fleming and Maclennan each might subscribe $5,000 for the purchase of the canal company land and thus acquire stock in the Boston & Florida Ramie Company at just fifty cents on the dollar.[8]

Meantime, in Maine, on November 20, officials of the Electrolytic Marine Salts Company announced a final dividend of six percent to be paid on December 4, winding up the disastrous sea gold firm's affairs. In total, the portion returned to the defrauded stockholders amounted to 36 percent of the nearly $1 million invested, a fairly sizeable percentage given the magnitude of the fraud. A few months before the final dividend, a committee supervising the company's affairs received $75,000 in cash from Jernegan, still on the lam, to be distributed to the unlucky shareholders as dividends. For Sawyer, Bradley and Walker, the sea gold mess was finally over.[9]

At the end of November, Miles wired Bradley some good news on the ramie venture. The National Ramie Company's promoters had accepted the Boston & Florida Ramie Company's offer to buy the machines at double the parent company's cost, which Bradley predicted would barely affect the

[8]GLB to APS, 17 November 1899 (two separate letters), SP Folder 13.
[9]"Cash for Jernegan's Victims," *New York Times*, 12 November 1899.

new company's bottom line given the profits to be reaped from the machines. Bradley had talked with Walker about a scheme to generate $50,000 cash for the Florida canal company's dredging operations. Bradley's plan was for the company to sell to its stockholders its $100,000 worth of National Ramie Company stock at fifty cents on the dollar. Bradley pledged that he would take at least $50,000 worth himself. He then planned to authorize the canal company to buy $50,000 worth of the Boston & Florida Ramie Company stock with 10,000 acres of land and either with it, or by selling it, pay off the notes held by Maclennan, Walker and himself.[10]

With the advent of the new year, 1900, Bradley reflected on the difficulties of a tight money market, but all things considered, remained steadfast in believing the Florida businesses' prospects bright. Willing to contribute something toward the expenses of organizing the Boston & Florida Ramie Company, he confessed he couldn't "carry the whole load." Were the Florida waterway finished to Jacksonville and leased to one of the railroads or even if they ran it themselves, he believed the waterway would greatly enhance the value of their Florida real estate holdings. His desire was to finish the waterway and retain the real estate, not sell it. He sent in $10,000, his final payment for the purchase of Boston & Florida Ramie stock, asking Sawyer to make sure that two $5,000 canal company notes at the St. Augustine bank were paid when they matured. Even after payment of the notes, Bradley was still on the hook for $30,000 of the canal company's paper.[11]

Bradley speculated that he might be able to lease the Florida waterway at a good price to one of several large northern railways connecting to Jacksonville. If that happened, Bradley thought their Florida real estate ought to be worth at least $5 million, increasing in value each year.[12]

At the same time, Henry Flagler seemed willing to consider a new relationship between his Florida East Coast Railway and the New England group's sputtering steamboat company. Miles met with Flagler at Palm Beach, and as Bradley reported, the railroad magnate "seemed to be about as friendly as in the old days." Despite the cordial meeting, the two companies apparently never forged any kind of arrangement. On January 11, 1900, Bradley received two subscription forms acknowledging his payment of $25,000 to the canal company for the new National Ramie Company investment. He reiterated his insistence that the two notes of $5,000 each at

---

[10]GLB to APS, 27 November 1899, SP Folder 13.

[11]GLB to APS, 3 January 1900, SP Folder 14.

[12]GLB to APS. 5 January 1900, SP Folder 14.

the St. Augustine bank be paid. He didn't want to pay the $25,000 in cash without the company paying off the two notes.[13]

Bradley assessed the company's current liabilities at about $50,000, excluding the $10,000 notes due him, Walker and Maclennan. He thought that these notes shouldn't be paid until the $50,000 in company notes endorsed by the three of them had been paid. He reminded Sawyer that at the New York meeting he had suggested that the three take some of the company securities in payment of the notes, but Walker refused to do so because he frankly didn't care about the Florida waterway. Bradley also asked Sawyer to send him a list of Boston & Florida lands sold to Sandford H. Fleming, a longtime investor in both the Boston & Florida and Florida canal companies. Miles had already sent the junior Fleming the figures on the canal company's land sales. About the senior Fleming, Bradley remarked, "Fleming I believe to be a fine fellow, the best of the Canadians.[14]

By the middle of January 1900, Bradley emphasized again that he wanted the two $5,000 notes endorsed by him paid. He hoped that with the taxes on the company lands and both notes paid, Miles would be able to secure loans in Florida without his assistance. He also expected Sawyer to eliminate all unnecessary expenses and just get along with the sale of land already in hand. If they could keep out of debt, Bradley anticipated completing the waterway, securing "a splendid success."[15]

Bradley regretted that he still remained liable on $10,000 worth of canal company paper despite putting up $25,000 cash to pay off some liabilities. But if John Dismukes, president of the St. Augustine Bank, agreed to renew the company notes at no more than six percent interest, he'd agree to let the present cash carry the steamboat business and pay taxes on real estate. About the Florida steamboat business, Bradley thought it "a great thing" if Miles could make a success of the steamboat business that season and it looked as if he could. But, at best, it was only a possibility. He also believed that with three large railway companies and two steamship lines competing for Florida business at Jacksonville, it wouldn't be long before they could secure the financing to complete the Florida waterway. Bradley had two

---

[13]GLB to APS, 8 January 1900, SP Folder 14. GLB to APS, 11 January 1900, SP Folder 14; Two subscription forms as holder of Canal Company stock for National Ramie Company stock, signed by Bradley on 11 January 1900, directed to Miles, Sawyer and Walker, as members of the Committee.

[14]GLB to APS, 12 January 1900, (two separate letters) SP Folder 14.

[15]GLB to APS, 19 January 1900, SP Folder 14.

important prospects interested in buying their Florida land, and he intended to keep at it."[16]

Bradley's group soon interested a few French investors who had made a substantial sum in ramie growing in buying 100,000 acres of the company's land at $6 an acre. Bradley suggested telling these investors that the company planned to use the proceeds to complete the waterway to Jacksonville, which would then offer an easy way to transfer the ramie to market. By the end of January, organization of the National Ramie Company had been completed, a permanent board of directors put in place and promoters didn't intend to sell any stock below par. With this last piece of good news, Bradley considered "our own Canal stockholders very fortunate to be able to buy this stock at 50," or half the stock's par value.[17]

Several of the canal company directors started making plans to attend the annual meeting at St. Augustine on March 15. Bradley, who planned to take his wife Helen, got Sawyer to attend and suggested he prod Walker into going along. He sent Sawyer a check to pay the taxes on the New River Trust real estate and confirmed that Sawyer had sufficient funds on hand to pay the taxes on the Lake Worth Trust property. He suggested that Sawyer attempt to borrow the money necessary to carry the Walker Trust land as he had done for the Boston & Florida properties, with the hope that within a year the loan could be paid off from the land sales, but if that was not possible, Bradley proposed drastic action — assessing shareholders to pay the taxes.[18]

Bradley again considered cutting off steamboat expenses except for caretaker salaries until sufficient waterway funding could be secured. He agreed to find the money to pay the caretakers as well as the taxes owed "until better days." If the ramie growing and processing operations fulfilled expectations in the spring, the task of securing financing might be accomplished more easily . Commenting on Fred Amory's gloomy outlook for the newly formed company, Bradley recalled a time when Amory was as despondent over the Mergenthaler Linotype venture, which ultimately reaped a fortune for his New England colleagues and himself. In fact, at present, the Mergenthaler company boasted a backlog of some eighty unfilled orders.[19]

---

[16]GLB to APS, 20 January 1900, SP Folder 14.

[17]GLB to APS, 22, 25 January 1900, SP Folder 14.

[18]GLB to APS, 30 January; 1 February 1900, SP Folder 14.

[19]GLB to APS, 2, 6 February 1900, SP Folder 14.

Bradley flatly stated that what he planned to propose at the upcoming meeting of the canal company directors at St. Augusine was to close down the company for the present and try to fund the debt somehow, perhaps by selling land. If his colleagues could hold on, the company would have 400,000 acres of land to sell, four hundred miles of finished waterway and three years' time to complete it. "To hold this position until we could find the capital for completion," Bradley thought, "we should have to pay the cost of caretakers, taxes and interest on debt." Land sales would be used to pay these expenses so far as possible, but beyond that, the company might require the stockholders to pay whatever was left unpaid.[20]

From St. Augustine, Miles informed Sawyer that he intended to arrange an extension of the steamboat company loan. Initially, Miles had $3,600 available for canal operations. But since that time, he had drawn down $2,000. Florida trustees had finally paid on their longstanding obligation to pay the company $10,750 on the sale of reserve lands going as far back as the mid-1880s, but Miles had been forced to use the money to pay off a $10,000 company note endorsed by John Maclennan to stave off a threatened lawsuit by the Canadian-born contractor. In Miles's view, in getting the money long due the company for the state trustees, Henry Gaillard, the canal company's longest standing director, had "managed the whole affair with excellent judgment and confirmed my opinion that in dealing with our political interests his services are of great value to the canal company." Miles also thought the *St. Sebastian* had generated "a good business" but until the cleaning out of certain stretches, particularly at Gilbert's Bar, near Stuart, he was not inclined to put the *St. Augustine* back on the Florida waterway. In constructing the canal, he had been working with "an old and incompetent dredge" and pointed out that passengers disliked transferring to a train for the rest of the trip because of low water. In the end, Miles wrote that the steamboat company had been doing "a fair business but nothing to what we would do if the route was open to Palm Beach." Miles hoped soon to be running through, but with "an inefficient dredge" delays seemed inevitable.[21]

At St. Augustine for the annual meeting, Sawyer wrote on March 9, 1900, on canal company stationery to his son, Hayden, at Boston. The senior Sawyer had played golf both at the hotel where he stayed and at the San Marco

---

[20]GLB to APS, 12 February 1900, SP Folder 14.

[21]GFM (Indian River & Bay Biscayne Navigation Co.) to APS, 18 February 1900, SP Folder 14.

Hotel. John Dismukes, the St. Augustine banker, had been "expatiating" on the merits of Paintoff. Although he had no stock in the company, Dismukes believed the paint removing process worked well. A success reportedly had been made of the process in England and at least two railroads had been using the product for two years.[22]

Miles's own note was coming due again at Sawyer's Newburyport bank, and so Sawyer instructed his son to pay the interest and renew it again for three months. The senior Sawyer expected to have $100 to Miles's credit on a land sale within a day or two. The canal company owed Miles a considerable amount of money in sales commissions. When the company paid Miles, he could pay off his loan. Sawyer traveled to Jacksonville and returned to St. Augustine with the Bradleys and the two bachelors, Sam Maddox and Ed Walker. The weather at St. Augustine had been fairly cool and he hadn't changed from his winter clothing, but expected a planned trip to warmer Miami to be "too much for heavy weights."[23]

At the annual meeting of the Florida canal company held on March 14, stockholders elected Sawyer's son, Hayden, a director of the company. The board now consisted of Albert Sawyer, Hayden Sawyer, Bradley, Walker, and Gaillard, the only member of the original group of directors in 1881 still serving. Bradley arranged to leave for Palm Beach on Friday. On March 19, Sawyer planned to go to Fort Lauderdale with James Ingraham and Ed Walker. From there the party planned to cruise aboard Flagler's launch south to Miami. On Tuesday, March 20, the launch party was to cruise in Biscayne Bay south to below Cutler. The elder Sawyer expected to be back at the Hotel Royal Poinciana at Palm Beach on Thursday.[24]

From Palm Beach, at the Hotel Royal Poinciana, Sawyer wrote his son on March 17. Bradley decided not to travel south from St. Augustine after the canal company meeting but instead returned with Helen to their home in Washington.[25]

Fred Amory asked Bradley, now back in Washington, to try to place the Florida canal company's proposed $500,000 bond issue with the old Colony Trust Company of Boston. At the same time, Bradley hoped Walker might succeed in raising funds using his own means. A man named Ross, a large Jacksonville contractor, told Miles that he'd agree to finish the waterway at

[22]APS to AHS, 9 March 1900, SP Folder 14.
[23]APS to AHS, 13 March 1900, SP Folder 14.
[24]APS to AHS, 15 March 1900, SP Folder 14.
[25]APS to AHS, 17 March 1900, SP Folder 14.

"very moderate figures" if the canal company gave him an option to purchase it. Ross was certain that he could sell the waterway to Flagler for two million dollars if the company extended it to the St. Johns River. Bradley, too, could hardly see how Flagler could avoid purchasing it.[26]

In April 1900, Bradley attended the Mergenthaler Linotype Company directors' meeting at New York. The financial affairs of the company appeared in "a very flourishing condition." The canal company's financial affairs were a different matter. Bradley, alone, sent in $200 to Gaillard as a loan to the company simply to maintain the dredges and expected to be repaid from Walker's subscription when he finally paid it. He had one friend in New York trying to arrange financing; another in Baltimore who said he'd do what he could there and in Philadelphia. Eternally optimistic, Bradley remained confident in the waterway's success, believing that "every day that passes makes our property more valuable." He nevertheless regretted that Sawyer, Walker, and Amory didn't share his view. He also worked hard to sell their Indian River steamboat operation. He had even spoken to the famed financier Ogden Mills about getting an introduction to see Clyde Lines steamship officials about selling the company.[27]

Generally sanguine about the Florida businesses, Bradley became somewhat annoyed not only with Miles carelessness in discharging his personal obligations but also with his handling of the Florida canal company as general manager. To make matters worse, Walker had failed to make a subscription payment he had long before promised to make. Walker's payment would have enabled Gaillard to pay all of the Florida businesses' debts. Both Miles and Gaillard had been willing to take practically nothing from the $10,000 that Bradley advanced on March 15 and Walker's subscription and Bradley's $9,000 to be paid on April 5 was supposed to be enough to pay every obligation. But the canal and steamboat companies together had run up debts totaling more than $80,000.[28]

Miles expected the ramie machines to arrive before the end of May and the ramie crop to be in good condition for the upcoming test. Bradley still wished that Walker would complete his subscription. "Much trouble arises from his delay." He regretted that Sawyer as well as he had been having "so much trouble with Mr. Miles" in managing company affairs and hoped that the matter could be resolved without any "hard feelings." Ever the dip-

---

[26]GLB to APS, 5 April 1900, SP Folder 14.
[27]GLB to APS, 18 April 1900, SP Folder 14.
[28]GLB to APS, 24 April 1900, SP Folder 14.

lomat, Bradley thought it of "great importance that good feelings should be preserved between Walker, Amory, Maddox, Miles, Fleming, yourself & myself as in my judgment it would be better to yield some of our rights than to assert them."[29]

By the middle of May, Maddox appeared to feel "pretty sour," which Bradley thought justified, that out of all the money so far paid out, Maddox's bill of $250 for legal services had been left unpaid. Gaillard had written Maddox, acknowledging the debt. Bradley hoped that Sawyer would pay it when Walker paid in his long-overdue subscription.[30]

In a letter to Sawyer on July 21, 1900, James Ingraham, now third vice-president of the Florida East Coast Railway ("Lands and Industrial Enterprises"), noted that the Boston & Florida owned the west and south tiers of 40-acre tracts in one of the sections included in the White City settlement near Fort Pierce. In Miles's absence, Ingraham sent Sawyer an application for a deed to five acres of Boston & Florida land sold by the Flagler railway, along with a small check from the purchaser and a commission receipt. He asked Sawyer to send a deed to give to the purchaser, confirming that the Flagler railway, the Florida canal company and a company called the Florida Cosmopolitan Immigration Company had been selling lands jointly in the small settlement, dividing the net proceeds among the parties.[31]

At the beginning of December, Sam Maddox acknowledged receipt of fifteen series "A" unsecured Florida canal company bonds, a certificate for 1,378 shares of canal company stock and other canal company debt certificates that belonged to Bradley. Fred Dewey, the New England group's agent in the Delray area, informed Sawyer that prospects for Lake Worth Trust land sales appeared "good," and soon he had two potential buyers, both possessing impressive credentials. One was Rousseau Owen Crump, a Bay City, Michigan congressman; the other, Henry H. Aplin, the postmaster of West Bay City. The two had already bought about a hundred acres at Delray and were expected to invest a considerable amount in clearing and planting. The Boynton land pleased them and the pineapple fields nearby impressed them greatly. But Dewey didn't think the men would buy the land if they had to pay cash because they could buy either Flagler railway or Model Land Company land at Delray on terms. Unfortunately, Crump died

---

[29]GLB to APS, 10, 14 May 1900, SP Folder 14.

[30]GLB to APS, 15 May 1900, SP Folder 14.

[31]James E. Ingraham to APS, 21 July 1900, SP Folder 14.

at Bay City just five months later on May 1, 1901, at the age of fifty-six. Nothing more is known of their intended purchase.[32]

Famous advertising executive Charles Austin Bates of New York City invited Samuel Fischman of Newark to join a pool of investors in a new plan to raise money for the Florida canal company's extension of the Florida waterway to Jacksonville and the purchase of six new steamers. The canal company already had a waterway open for 400 miles north from Miami, Bates told him, and held 400,000 acres of land. On completion of the waterway to Jacksonville, the enterprise would be entitled to an additional 300,000 acres. "The desire of the Company to push this work right through has led it to make me a proposition that is more favorable than any I have ever seen or heard of." The company planned to sell 800 gold bonds yielding 25 percent to be sold at par ($1,000 each), with a bonus of $500 of stock in the company and 200 acres of the company's land or a negotiable certificate for $1,000 to be used in payment for any of the company's land at cash prices, then averaging between $5 and $15 an acre. Bates's plan was to form a development company with a limited number of investors, which would subdivide the land and sell it in small parcels or in large tracts. Bates believed that the land could be borrowed against for all that would be needed to improve the land. Within a reasonably short time, the new development company would "get more money out of their sale than we put in originally and still retain our bonds and stock as profit." Bates thought the assets of the company "all right" and the present officers and owners "men of the highest standing and integrity." He elaborated that the company's principal owner was a director of the Bell Telephone Company and the Mergenthaler Linotype Company (Bradley). Another, referring to Sam Maddox, was president of the Bar Association of the District of Columbia. Still another was a large lumber dealer at Springfield, Massachusetts (Walker). Bates wanted Fischman to take five or ten bonds (Bates was to take five) and join the pool of investors. Unfortunately, there is no evidence that Bates was able to pull off a sale of the Florida canal company bonds.[33]

At Boynton, Moses reported back some bad news on the Florida ramie experiment. The ramie roots had come up "very straggling and the seed did not sprout at all." Many of the roots that had been delivered sprouted but soon died as a result of a small white worm having eaten the pith of the

---

[32]SM to APS, 4 December 1900; Fred S. Dewey to APS, 7, 13 December 1900; both in SP Folder 14. Biographies of Crump and Aplin at *Biographical* (1950), 1040 and 787.

[33]Charles Austin Bates to Samuel Allen Fischman, 15 December 1900, (copy), SP Folder 14.

roots. The sansaveria, another variety of the plant, was alive and growing but "not very vigorously." The prospect of land sales in the West Palm Beach area had not been encouraging, although Dewey had made a few sales in Boynton and Delray. If Flagler's experiment of growing citrus trees in the Boca Raton settlement proved successful, Moses thought that such an event alone might increase the demand for citrus lands in the area. He also told Sawyer about a new company in which he had been involved that already appeared successful. Headed by pioneer Rockledge citrus grower Hiram Smith Williams as president and general manager, the Allapatahatchee Fruit & Vegetable Company grew fruit and vegetables seven miles west of Fort Pierce. Moses served as secretary and treasurer. The company had some six or eight stockholders and was capitalized with $4,000, all paid-up except for five shares. Its principal business was citrus growing. The company owned two hundred acres, fifty in hammock, the balance in pine lands, with some vegetables and 1,300 orange and grapefruit trees planted and 20,000 small citrus trees. Moses reported the payroll totaled $125 a month, with one resident manager, a white man, and two black men. Company promoters offered the remaining five shares at $100 a share but Moses presumed the company had already sold three. So he invited Sawyer to buy two shares, with no prospect of any dividend of consequence in less than four years.[34]

In the middle of December 1900, George Miles began stirring up trouble among Boston & Florida land company directors. He demanded a financial statement of the condition of the company, stating that he had never received one and that he had never been able to attend any of the company meetings, which had been held at Portland, Maine. As far as he knew, no statements had ever been given Boston & Florida stockholders. He pointedly informed his New England colleagues that he wished to make "a final settlement of my Florida matters with the Canadians who first joined me in the Canal business, and I require information in order to enable my associates to understand the situation." The question of settling up with Miles and his Canadian colleagues would fester as Bradley, Sawyer and the rest of their New England colleagues, including Miles, struggled to complete the Florida waterway with limited resources over the next twelve years.[35]

---

[34]Moses to APS, 17 December 1900, and second letter the same date along with copy of the Charter of The Allapatahatchee Fruit and Vegetable Company, a Florida corporation SP Folder 14.

[35]GFM to APS, 18 December 1900, SP Folder 14.

Meanwhile, filled with the mirth of the season, Moses wrote Sawyer three days after Christmas that he had asked Hiram Smith Williams to send Sawyer a box of oranges and a few grapefruit from Williams's grove operation near Fort Pierce, expecting them to arrive at Newburyport by the first of the year.[36]

---

[36]GLB to APS, 24 December 1900; Moses to APS, 28 December 1900; both in SP Folder 14.

Chapter 8

Slowing Down

With new capital drying up, Florida canal operations slowed to a snail's pace, awaiting infusions of cash from flagging land sales to finance further dredging. Meantime, Bradley's colleagues continued to explore other investment opportunities. At Hiram Smith Williams's Allapatahatchee Fruit & Vegetable Company operation, near Fort Pierce, one fork of the St. Lucie River on which the farm flourished west of Fort Pierce abounded in fresh water fish, mostly black bass, along with a few alligators. Pinewoods in the area were home to quail, while deer, turkey, and wildcats roamed the hammocks. In October 1899, the firm had bought a tract of 160 acres, part pine trees and part hammock. During the winter of 1899-1900, the company set out 1,200 citrus trees. Twelve hundred more trees had since been added, including those bearing Haver peaches, mangoes, figs, and bananas. An experimental strawberry garden there had also been doing well. The past season, the operation had shipped tomatoes, beans, eggplants, and Irish potatoes.[1]

A few days into the new year, 1901, the New England group's West Palm Beach agent, Wallace Moses, received two checks, each for $100, representing Albert Sawyer's purchase of two shares of stock in Williams's new venture. The pineapple business boomed along Florida's east coast. Garnering an average price of $1.73 a crate, the pineapple crop filled 130,000 crates. But on a disappointing note, Brandenburg & Company, a company invited to help raise new funds for the Florida canal company, had "thrown up their hands" in trying to secure financing. Acknowledging how difficult it was to raise funds for the waterway, Fred Amory conceded that "the only person who can do us any benefit will be Mr. Flagler." If Flagler offered a fair price for the canal company's land, Amory didn't see why a sale wouldn't be "the best way out of it." Amory left it to Bradley's "fertile abil-

---

[1]GFM to APS, 21 May 1901; Prospectus, Allapatahatchee Fruit and Vegetable Co., 1 June 1901; both in SP Folder 15.

ity" to get greater profit out of the Florida canal company because had "so much more faith in this scheme."[2]

At Fort Pierce, Allapatahatchee directors called a stockholders meeting to increase capital stock to $8,000 to finance the firm's expanding operations. At the same time, Bradley sent Phillips Abbott, the New York ramie venture lawyer, a deed conveying 20,000 acres of canal land as its contribution to the promising fiber project. Flagler associate James Ingraham asked Sawyer to draw a deed in favor of a Charles Metcalf for eleven acres of Boston & Florida land the Flagler organization sold in present-day Fort Lauderdale for $165, a robust $15 an acre (fifteen times what Boston & Florida had paid for the land in 1892). Florida land business seemed to be picking up.[3]

Meanwhile, Miles had been at work getting his Boston & Florida stock converted into company land. Without the convertibility feature, he considered the stock of doubtful value, apparently disregarding the high prices the company had been getting for land in Fort Lauderdale. Moreover, he wanted the question of his commissions on past sales resolved. In short, he wanted to get his Florida interests "settled up" as far as possible, as he put it. He had just signed three contracts to sell land owned jointly by the Boston & Florida and the Flagler railway, some thirty acres for $391, with a quarter of the price as a down payment in cash. Ingraham had begun another Flagler venture, the experimental cultivation of the cassava plant, another source of fiber like ramie, probably in St. Johns County. Along with the steady improvement in the tobacco industry, Miles thought Flagler's new cassava operation, if successful, would eventually enhance the value of the New England group's lands in St. Johns and Volusia counties.[4]

The end of February, Miles again brought up the question of his compensation for past services to Boston & Florida. He asked the directors to permit him to convert his land company stock into acreage at "a very considerable discount," suggesting a discount of at least half the present list prices, then averaging about $15 per acre. He thought the plan might work to the advantage of both the company and stockholders because it would not only create a market for the stock but also stimulate the sale of land. "At present the situation is very discouraging," Miles complained, "and I fore-

---

[2]Moses to APS, 3 January 1901; GLB to APS, 14 January 1901; FA to GLB, 14 January 1901; all in SP Folder 15.

[3]Moses to APS, 16 January 1901, SP Folder 15. GLB to APS, 25 January 1901; Moses to APS, 5 February 1901; Ingraham to APS, 14 February 1901; all in SP Folder 15.

[4]GFM to APS, 15 February 1901, SP Folder 15.

see that if the present policy is continued the whole property will be swallowed up in taxes and other expenses." He remained in an awkward position. He and his Canadian colleagues had long before pledged their shares in the Boston & Florida land company as security for loans made by the First National Bank at St. Augustine for some of the early dredging work the group attempted but never completed. If the loans were called, he would be forced to hand over his Boston & Florida shares to John Dismukes, the bank's president. Miles almost seemed to threaten that Dismukes would then seek "a more efficient management" of the company through the courts.[5]

The beginning of March, Fred Morse, Miami agent for Flagler's railway and two land companies as well as the canal company and the Boston & Florida, sold five acres in present-day northern Miami-Dade County. In St. Augustine for the company's annual Florida meeting, both Sawyer and Sam Maddox stayed at the Hotel Alcazar. East coast hotel business had never been better. Walker had already arrived for the meeting and he and Sawyer had been busy discussing canal company business. Bradley had made some progress with a new, and as yet unidentified, party in another proposed reorganization of the company to obtain more financing, but nothing definite materialized. At the annual meeting, stockholders re-elected Sawyer's son, Hayden, a director of the company. The directors, in turn, chose Walker to serve as treasurer, with Bradley still at the helm as president. After the meeting, the senior Sawyer planned to travel south to Lake Worth to look over the canal construction underway, while Bradley remained behind at St. Augustine.[6]

Miles had long expected a resolution from the Boston & Florida Company making his stock exchangeable for land. Thoroughly stymied, he couldn't do anything with the stock until the directors passed a resolution authorizing its conversion. Meanwhile, Ingraham traveled down the coast with Frederick Booth-Tucker of the Salvation Army, scouting out land for Salvationist settlers. Adding to the group's brightening prospects, Miles had heard "wonderful stories" of the fortunes being made in growing tomatoes in south Florida. One grower had already shipped six car loads of tomatoes, netting more than a thousand dollars a car load.[7]

---

[5]GFM to GLB, 27 February 1901, SP Folder 15.
[6]Morse to APS, 4 March 1901; APS to AHS, 12 March 1901; both in SP Folder 15.
[7]GFM to APS, 10, 14 April 1901, SP Folder 15.

Bradley's efforts to attract new capital for the Florida businesses soon appeared to be bearing fruit. Adelbert Hay, Secretary of State John Hay's son, had decided to put $15,000 to $20,000 into the New England group's new and as yet unformed land company and Hay's friend, William C. Whitney, had agreed to put in the same amount. While in New York, Bradley sold Abbott's National Ramie Company a block of stock in both the Florida canal company and the new land company.[8]

Bradley promised one new investor, Dr. John Davies Jones of Washington, that if he could sell a block of new land company stock for $40,000 cash, the land company would hire him at a salary of $5,000 a year. He remarked to Sawyer that they had been getting "such rich men" interested in their projects that it wouldn't be long before Bradley and his colleagues attracted whatever amount of capital they might need. By April 18, 1901, Bradley and his associates had already raised $100,000 for the Florida businesses. The next step was to offer stock to outside investors—two shares of the new land company stock and one share of Florida canal company stock for $100. Using this enticing scheme, Bradley secured $5,000 from one investor and $5,000 from Abbott's ramie company. The third proposition of offering two shares of the new land company stock for $100 and a thirty percent stock commission to brokers had resulted in a sale of enough stock to yield $30,000 or $40,000. All this had been accomplished in less than thirty days. To Bradley, raising $100,000 in cash and securities was enough to finance the completion of the Matanzas Cut. But was it?[9]

In south Florida, longtime Delray real estate agent Fred Dewey sold five acres and reserved five more in two sections for another potential buyer. There appeared to be an increase in real estate activity in the area of West Palm Beach and some activity further south. The vegetable crop at Boynton and Delray seemed large and if prices held up, Dewey expected settlers in the area to have more money than ever to make land purchases.[10]

By April 19, 1901, Miles had finally received company resolutions allowing the conversion of his Boston & Florida stock into land, pronouncing them generally sufficient. But in disposing of his stock, he still needed to show that the stock could be exchanged for land at thirty percent below graded prices. Nothing could make the stock saleable except a resolution making possible exchanges at those prices. Dismukes kept after Miles,

[8]GLB to APS, 17 April 1901, SP Folder 15.
[9]GLB to APS, 18 April 1901, SP Folder 15.
[10]Fred S. Dewey, 18 April 1901, SP Folder 15.

pushing him to secure a formal resolution as soon as possible. The St. Augustine banker held $12,400 of Miles's Boston & Florida land company stock as collateral for Miles's loans. Passing the resolution would make it easier for the bank to carry the loans until he could sell enough shares to pay them off. He planned to sell no more than $9,000 worth of his stock, keeping the rest rather than selling the shares or exchanging them for land.[11]

Bradley talked at length with Louis R. McLain, the Monticello banker who financed the steamboat company in the early years. He wanted McLain, Sir Sandford Fleming and a third contractor named Ross to bid on finishing the waterway as soon as possible. He also hoped to make sales of the new land company stock through Charles Austin Bates, who attempted to broker one of the company's bond issues. Bates agreed to sell the stock, deeply discounted at fifty percent of par value, for a thirty percent stock commission. When Bradley first devised the plan, he went to his old colleagues to raise the money, but he got only $100,000 and that only from Amory, Maddox, Walker and himself. The group was to obtain the new land stock at fifty percent of par with a thirty percent stock commission and a bonus at the rate of one share of canal company stock for every two shares of the new land company stock. Bradley also offered Philip T. Dodge, president of the Mergenthaler Linotype Company, $200,000 dollars worth of new land company stock and $100,000 worth of canal company stock for $100,000 cash.[12]

By April 25, 1901, Miles had been haggling again with Sawyer over his Boston & Florida company stock, wanting it definitely stated that he could redeem his $12,500 worth of stock for land at thirty percent less present graded prices. Bradley, related to Miles by marriage and Miles's Pomfret neighbor, suddenly became annoyed with Miles's insistent requests for a resolution. He didn't like the "Miles business" at all. But he would agree to resolve the issue only because of his relationship to Miles and "to help him out of a hole."

Turning briefly to the crumbling old Indian River steamboat venture, Bradley tersely announced—one more time—that he didn't intend to finance the business another year.[13]

Miles continued to pursue discussions with Sawyer over making the Boston & Florida stock convertible into land. Lots had been upgraded by Miles to keep the property from being sacrificed at low figures. Dade County

[11]GFM to APS, 19 April 1901; GLB to APS, 22, 24 April 1901; all in SP Folder 15.
[12]*Ibid.*
[13]GFM to APS, 25 April 1901; GLB to APS, 30 April 1901, 9 May 1901; all in SP Folder 15.

land near Biscayne Bay had been originally listed at from 75 cents to $5 an acre. Dismukes appeared impatient to have the resolution approving the convertibility either passed or turned down. For Miles, the matter was separate from what commissions had been due him as agent for the Boston & Florida, for which he said he'd take land if it was mutually agreeable. His Boston & Florida claim didn't include commissions owed on the Bradley trust lands sold near Boynton, for which he might take notes in payment.[14]

At the nation's capital, Bradley had a long talk with Jones and Hay. Both appeared happy with what they saw in Florida and ready to fulfill their agreement. Together they agreed to take $80,000 of the new land company stock at fifty percent of par value and serve as directors. Bradley thought Sawyer should go ahead and organize the new company as soon as possible. Sawyer was to serve as president; Bradley, vice-president; and Sawyer, as treasurer. Directors were to be Maddox, Hay, Jones, Sawyer, Walker, Miles, and Bradley.[15]

Meantime, Miles fussed again over the details of his exchange of Boston & Florida stock for land. He disagreed with Sawyer on the interest to be paid on his Boston & Florida preferred stock. The company's original prospectus required the payment of interest on each share of preferred stock since the issuance of shares as early as 1892. To resolve the issue, he offered to accept a new resolution agreeing to accept his shares at fifty percent of the graded prices without interest and to give him a reasonable time, such as until January 1, 1902, by which to select the lands.[16]

From the Black Cat Plantation at the Boca Raton settlement, Captain Tom Rickards, the New England group's land agent there, sent back a deed for acreage bought by one Eli Day for a better legal description. The price was $35. Rickards requested payment of his ten percent commission of $3.50. Suggesting the New England group had been getting a bargain for his services, he pointed out that he had been getting a twenty percent commission selling Flagler railroad land. He forwarded another application for ten more acres in the Boca Raton area at $10 an acre, with twenty-five percent paid down in cash and the balance to be paid in three equal annual installments.[17]

---

[14]GFM to APS, 11 May 1901, SP Folder 15.

[15]GLB to APS, 12 May 1901, SP Folder 15.

[16]GFM to APS, 18 May 1901, SP Folder 15.

[17]Rickards to APS, 20 May 1901, SP Folder 15.

The end of May, Miles sent Sawyer a bill for services he had provided since 1896 as agent of the Boston & Florida land company, excluding commissions on sales made through Ingraham's office or on the sale of various Bradley trust lands made between 1896 and when Wilson and Howard, publishers of the *Farm, Field and Fireside* newspaper, began selling some of the land for a time. He considered the controversy now finally closed. Given the condition of the Boston & Florida company and its inability to pay cash, Miles offered to accept land at a fair valuation in payment of the commissions owed. While prices at which he had sold the lands netted the firm nearly three times the price per acre named in its list prices, the net prices didn't reflect the expenses for drainage and road improvements, which were to be reimbursed Flagler. At Boca Raton, Rickards requested contracts and notes for the sale of eight acres at $10 an acre to Day and for the sale of fifteen acres at the same price to a George Long in present-day Palm Beach County.[18]

At Boca Raton, Flagler railroad lands had been priced for sale at $10 an acre. Rickards couldn't get more than that for the Boston & Florida land. He asked Boston & Florida directors to pay him a twenty percent commission on all lands sold there, the same percentage Flagler had been paying him on the railway lands. Meanwhile, with the exchange agreement made with Boston & Florida directors, Miles had been making significant efforts to sell enough of his stock to pay off the old Canadian syndicate note at the St. Augustine bank as well as a note at the Ocean Bank at Newburyport. Levi Turner, the New England group's attorney, sent Sawyer the directors' record book together with a copy of the original organization papers for the newly formed Florida Land Development Company, including a record of the first meeting of incorporators and also of the meeting held on the June 20, 1901, when regular officers were elected in place of the Maine residents who participated in the original organization. Initial stockholders of the new land company included Adelbert Hay, Maddox, John Davies Jones and Miles. Although the company had been organized, there is no evidence the company ever conducted business in Florida. At Newburyport, Hayden's father, Albert, suddenly became seriously ill. The elder Sawyer's deteriorating physical condition would soon loom large in the New England's group's plans to finish the waterway and develop their massive land grants. At the same time, Miles hoped to secure a deed to some of the Boston &

---

[18]Thomas M. Rickards to APS, 28 May 1901, SP Folder 15.

Florida land which he was to receive under the recent exchange agreement, but he didn't want to pursue the issue until Hayden's father had sufficiently recovered to attend to the business.[19]

The end of June, despite the senior Sawyer's illness, Miles pressed the matter of getting deeds to the Boston & Florida lands to which he was entitled. In the absence or illness of the president and vice president, could a deed be executed by a majority of the directors? "It is a matter of importance to me," because the First National Bank of St. Augustine had been breathing down his neck, and he only needed a conveyance of a small amount of acreage to keep the bank off his back. Apparently unaware of the senior Sawyer's illness, Wallace Moses wrote Sawyer from West Palm Beach that he had sent him a crate of pineapples. So far, the outlook for the pineapple crop looked good. He had shipped north 280 crates at two dollars a crate from the Lake Worth Trust's Belleville plantation and hoped to ship a total of four hundred crates by the end of the season.[20]

In July, Miles asked young Hayden Sawyer to draw a deed to George Couper Gibbs, as trustee, for the lands he had selected. Gibbs had been Miles's stenographer and was Dismukes' nephew. Later, Gibbs would become a prominent St. Johns County jurist. Miles used Gibbs as trustee to avoid the necessity of his wife having to sign a deed every time property was sold. He hadn't heard from Bradley for some time, although he did hear from Helen that she and George intended to leave for Paris in a few days. He had gotten fifteen land contracts from Ingraham for the sale of 175 acres of the New England group's land at an average price of $15 an acre, totaling $2,625. He hoped to hear some word of interest in helping to finish the Florida waterway from Sir Sandford Fleming, which made uncertain when he was to leave for Florida. Fleming had asked Miles to go to Ottawa to meet his partners and Miles told him that he would go. He also indicated to Miles that he might be able to interest a wealthy American in constructing the last improvements to the waterway. Adding to the uncertainty over the completion of the waterway, the senior Sawyer's health continued to deteriorate.[21]

---

[19]GFM to APS, 11 June 1901, SP Folder 15. Levi Turner to APS, 21 June 1901, SP Folder 15; see, biographical sketch of John Hay, Rossiter, ed., *Twentieth Century Biographical Dictionary*, vol. 5, p. 15. for information on Adelbert Stone Hay. GFM to AHS, 22 June 1901, SP Folder 15.

[20]GFM to AHS, 29 June 1901; Moses to APS, 29 June 1901; both in SP Folder 15.

[21]GFM to AHS, 10, 15, & 18 July 1901; Indenture by and between Boston & Florida Atlantic Coast Land Co. and George Couper Gibbs, Trustee of St. Augustine (unsigned); SP Folder 16.

One of the Indian River Steamboat Company's employees, Captain Jarvis, talked with Seaboard Air Line Railway officials about an extension of the rail line to some point along the Indian River to connect up with the steamboat line. The connection would afford the steamers a valuable outlet to railway transportation and railway officials seemed disposed to work out a fair division of rates with the Florida canal company. Miles asked Sawyer for an advance of $300 against his Boston & Florida commissions to travel to Portsmouth, Virginia, to meet with the railway officials to discuss the potential new link to the Florida waterway. Meanwhile, the National Ramie Company had just set out a plantation on its Indian River land. Miles moved ahead with plans to meet the vice president of the Seaboard railway at Portsmouth, who appeared ready to construct a transportation line to Miami via a connection with the Florida waterway, if the parties could agree on certain details. In Philadelphia, Miles had met with Sir Sandford Fleming, who appeared ready to submit a proposal to complete the waterway from St. Augustine to Ormond, the so-called Matanzas-Halifax cut. But first, Fleming wanted Miles to meet with Fleming's partners in Ottawa.[22]

By the first week in January 1902, Miles had just returned from a trip down the Florida east coast to Miami. No damage had been done by recent cold weather. The south Florida settlements seemed to be making good progress, but high railway rates impeded growth. Miles spent a day at White City, near Fort Pierce. The tiny settlement looked in only fair condition, with just sixty families, but the residents seemed content. The outlook for the winter along the coast appeared promising. The St. Augustine railway station handled twenty-four arrivals and departures daily. Lake Worth teemed with men employed in various kinds of work. West Palm Beach had been building up so fast Miles hardly recognized it.[23]

In dealing with the Flagler railway, Miles advised his New England colleagues to either "sell our lands outright" or "keep control of them ourselves." In Miles's view, it was against Flagler's "policy" to allow any money to come their way "if it can be stopped." By the first of February 1902, Bradley had secured the dredge *Suwanee* from the War Department to clean out several waterway channels between the Saint Lucie River and Biscayne Bay. The canal company would have to fund the dredge bills, but Bradley anticipated he could find the money if the company could not. If all

---

[22]GFM to AHS, 26 July 1901, 6, 8, &16 August 1901, SP Folder 16.

[23]GFM to AHS, 3 January 1902; Moses to Cox, 3 January 1902; Dewey to APS, 6 January 1902; all in SP Folder 17.

went well, Bradley hoped to use the dredge in clearing channels north of the Saint Lucie River to Daytona. Bradley was so excited about the waterway's prospects that he confidently pronounced that it attracted more attention now than ever, even though little dredging had actually been pushed in many sections of the waterway.[24]

At Boca Raton, Tom Rickards reported a heavy crop of vegetables bringing good prices, with no damage as yet from freeze, flood or drought. Pineapples bloomed; citrus trees showed good growth. More important to the New England group, Rickards expected to sell a number of lots. Rickards thought it worth the $100 it would cost to hire him to survey the entire section of land owned by the Boston & Florida, staking out the corners of each 10-acre lot. When that work was done, he wrote that more than eighty acres in the section alone could be sold. Describing the rough surveying that lay ahead, he characterized the land as "rough country," anticipating that it would take at least two days to break out a five-acre lot correctly. Without a survey, he argued, it would be nearly impossible to sell the land to prospective settlers.[25]

During the first part of February, Miles received a letter from Albert Sawyer, the Boston & Florida president, for the first time in months. The weather at St. Augustine, though generally cool, had been pleasant since Miles's arrival around Christmas. Light frosts left young vegetables in the northern part of the state undamaged. Oranges and pineapples had been unhurt and the vegetables south of Titusville escaped injury. Miles sought to exchange his Boston & Florida stock for land at fifteen percent less than the company's graded prices. But he knew that if he took the land, he would have to select scattered lots, not a block of land. He needed a single block to attract prospective buyers. In his view, this requirement made development "almost impossible." Meantime, Miles had signed contracts for the sale of land owned by the Boston & Florida amounting to $946, which were mainly sales on time.[26]

Miles regretted that the older Sawyer had decided not to come to Florida for the upcoming annual meeting in March. A month to six weeks in the Florida sunshine would hasten his "full restoration to health," Miles thought. They had experienced an unusually cool winter in Florida, but no

---

[24]GFM to GLB, 17 January 1902; GLB to APS, 21 January 1902; both in SP Folder 17. GLB to APS, 2 February 1902, SP Folder 17.

[25]Rickards to APS, 7, 24 February 1902, SP Folder 17.

[26]GFM to APS, 9 February 1902, SP Folder 17.

severe frosts. Almost every week since Miles had come south the temperature had hovered around the freezing point at St. Augustine, but still no damage had been done to the vegetables or the orange trees. In seven years' time, the orange industry had almost completely recovered after a deep freeze wiped out central Florida's citrus groves during the 1894-1895 season. He expected shipments in 1903 to be as brisk as in the old days. Meanwhile, Sawyer had gotten a resolution passed extending the time for Miles to select Boston & Florida lands in exchange for stock. If more transportation came to the east coast, Miles intended to select his lands as far north as he could in the Indian River section. At the same time, Abbott's National Ramie Company had already been doing fairly good work in planting ramie. The company had drained land near Eau Gallie and planted several acres of ramie roots, constructed buildings, and bought mules and agricultural implements for farming. Miles also understood that a firm called the Florida East Coast Drainage and Sugar Company expected to start draining a portion of the Everglades and establish a sugar plantation.[27]

At the end of February 1902, Abbott kept Miles abreast of more new developments in the National Ramie Company in Florida. A road and bridge builder, sewer contractor and farmer named Belding supervised the construction of a large ditch, cut small laterals, drained small sluices, and limed the bottoms for ramie growing. The operation used a disc harrow to aerate the soil, considered a radical cure for the "sour" bog lands. Drainage had lowered water levels about three feet. Belding thought the sluices would make excellent land. With ditching planned for next year, ramie promoters expected to drain the big sluices west and create at least 200 acres of better land. Professor William Carter Stubbs, of the Louisiana Agricultural Experimental Stations, shipped seventy-five bags of Nevia ramie (the best variety) for the ramie experiment in the Lake Worth area.[28]

From West Palm Beach, Fred Dewey reported an unusual spell of bad weather. So far, land sales in Dade County simply increased as a result of the natural growth of the south Florida settlements. Settlers influenced their friends to join them and to buy adjoining land. Dewey had been trying to locate buyers at the Pompano settlement north of Fort Lauderdale, but found it slow going. At Boca Raton, Rickards reported that all of the land owned by the Flagler railroad within a distance of 24 miles had been priced

---

[27]GFM to APS, 25 February 1902; GFM to GLB, 27 February 1902; both in SP Folder 17.

[28]Phillips Abbott to GFM, 25 February 1902 (copy), SP Folder 17.

at $10 an acre, on terms, but often sold for less. He recommended a price of $10 an acre for the good canal company land and planned to sell the Boston & Florida lands at the same price.[29]

Around the first of July, Walker, the Florida canal company's treasurer, inquired into Hayden Sawyer's efforts in selling subscriptions for an upcoming issue of company bonds. He had hoped that young Sawyer might be able to sell a whole block. The commissions would make "a nice nest egg" for Hayden's new baby boy, he suggested. Alluding to the new addition to the Sawyer household, the Springfield bachelor conceded that although he had "done nothing in that line to speak of," he was always glad to see his friends successful. "The country must be kept populated in some way," he added. He hoped that Hayden's father had been doing better. Things were looking up for the Florida waterway project. Two new waterway dredges pushed south inside the coastal barrier islands from Beaufort, North Carolina, to Jacksonville to work in the Matanzas Cut.[30]

Early in August, Walker needed to talk with Miles on the projected expenses for the cut. Maddox was on his way to Europe, not expected to return until the middle of September. Somewhat annoyed, Walker felt that Maddox should have attended to an old bond matter, then hanging fire, before leaving. In any event, Walker planned to try to resolve the matter himself. He was to meet Miles at the Bay State House hotel at Worcester, Massachusetts. Florida land sales had slowed almost to a halt. Since March 1901, Walker had signed land contracts for the sale of 283 acres of Florida canal company land, generating gross sales of $4,002 and signed deeds for 991 acres, netting $3,722. Sales should have been better, he thought, denouncing them so far "a ridiculously small amount." In fact, he believed the company should be reaping the sums produced so far each month. The two dredges, the *Wimbee* at the northern end and the *South Carolina* at the southern end of the big cut between the Matanzas and Halifax rivers, reportedly had been doing good work.[31]

In December 1902, the senior Sawyer, as trustee of the Lake Worth Land Trust, subdivided a 20-acre tract of land just west of Boynton into twenty-two lots, each approximately 273 feet long and forty feet wide, with two more lots each about a hundred feet square bordering a centrally-located

---

[29]Dewey to APS, 10 March 1902; Rickards to APS, 12 March 1902; both in SP Folder 17.
[30]EW to AHS, 1 July 1902, SP Folder17.
[31]EW to AHS, 3 August 1902, SP Folder 17.

site for the Boynton public school, which the trust had donated to the Dade County School Board in 1896. [32]

On January 1, 1903, the Florida canal company floated a new bond issue of $100,000 to "increase the facilities for a speedy completion of its canals and waterways." Two months later, Walker learned that Dewey had sold 287 acres in the Lake Worth area at $10 an acre. Hayden arrived safely in St. Augustine for the company's annual meeting and had "commenced to appreciate the attractions." At Newburyport, the snow had disappeared and the arrival of the first robin and bluebird had been reported, recalled the senior Sawyer, who had just attended a local bank board meeting. Recollecting that he had just seen his grandson, Hayden Page, the senior Sawyer proudly announced the boy's deportment "perfect."[33]

During the first part of April 1903, Maddox stirred things up among Florida canal company directors when he asked for compensation for legal services long before provided the venture. Bradley planned to consider Maddox's request at a future executive committee meeting but intended first to forward the request to Walker and Miles for their comments. Bradley suggested that Maddox state exactly what he wanted and that he wait for his compensation, as Walker, Miles and Bradley himself had been doing for some time. He felt Maddox's need small compared with the income from his law practice and other business ventures. "The main financial burden comes on me," Bradley tersely reminded him, and, "after all, I am only about one half of the interest. I have made and am making, great sacrifices in selling various sorts of property to meet the vital expenses of the Canal Company." All three dredges in Florida had been doing well. But Bradley pointedly warned that if March expenses could not be met, "our whole structure falls."[34] Could they be met? Would the "whole structure" fall?

---

[32]Plat of Sawyer's Addition to the Town of Boynton, recorded in Plat Book B, Page 68, of the Public Records of Dade County, Florida, on December 11, 1902

[33]Deed of Trust (Mortgage) executed by Canal Company in favor of American Security and Trust Company of the District of Columbia, Trustee, on January 1, 1903, and filed on January 13, 1903, in Mortgage Book "N," Page 219, in the Public Records of St. Johns County, Florida. EW to AHS, 1 March 1903, SP Folder 17. AHS to APS, 9 March 1903, SP Folder 17.

[34]GLB to SM, 8 April 1903, SP Folder 17?

Chapter 9

Death and Uncertainty

On Saturday, November 19, 1903, tragedy struck the New England group when Albert Page Sawyer, the Boston & Florida land company's president and a trustee of the three Bradley trusts, died suddenly at his home in Newburyport. Also a director of the Florida canal company, Sawyer has reportedly been one of Newburyport's wealthiest citizens when he passed away at age sixty-one. Sawyer's son, 32-year-old Albert Hayden Sawyer would succeed his father as trustee of the Bradley trusts and as president of the Boston & Florida company.[1]

State Freezes Canal Company Land Grants

Within seven months of Albert Sawyer's death, and with only nine miles of cuts apparently remaining before the completion of the Matanzas-Halifax connection in the Florida waterway, more bad news came, this time from Florida. In June 1904, the first of a flurry of lawsuits emerged over the state land grants promised Flagler's railway and the Florida canal company well before the turn of the century. Grants already made to the St. Augustine-based canal company for dredging the Florida waterway amounted to 475,015 acres. Frustrated over the failure of the canal company to carry out waterway construction with sufficient speed, state trustees froze further grants south in what is now Miami-Dade County, even ordering a return of 92,070 acres regarded as erroneously deeded. In litigation brought in Tallahassee, the canal company countersued to keep state trustees from disposing of public lands reserved for the waterway's completion. A Leon County judge temporarily stopped the state. As Miles observed at the time, the State "cannot give valid title but they may put us to much inconvenience if

---

[1]"Death List of a Day - Albert P. Sawyer," *New York Times,* 22 November 1903, p. 7, column 5; "Laid at Rest," *Newburyport Daily News,* 23 November 1903. See, Sawyer, Albert H., "Comparison of Vital Statistics of Groups of Towns of Various Populations in Massachusetts," Thesis (B.S.)1894, Massachusetts Institute of Technology, Institute Archives, Cambridge, Mass.

we permit them to do so." More suits and countersuits followed, tying up the public lands so tightly that neither the state nor the canal company could dispose of the state lands.[2]

With George Bradley at the helm, the Florida canal company had completed the waterway between Ormond and Miami—a distance of about 300 miles by the close of 1903. Two dredges working at opposite ends, the *Wimbee* and *South Carolina*, kept dredging the nearly intractable Matanzas-Halifax canal, soon to connect St. Augustine with Ormond to the south. First begun in 1883, the canal, when completed, would extend a distance of twenty-four miles and require the excavation of more than 1.6 million cubic yards of material. A popular magazine of the day described the completed stretch of waterway south of Lake Worth as "more than thirty miles...leading to the Hillsborough river," and then "forty miles to New river, twelve miles carrying us to Snake creek and Biscayne Bay, down which we float twenty miles to Miami," where steamship lines made shipments to Nassau, Key West and Havana.[3]

In the southern part of the peninsula the Florida canal company's dredging work had moved forward but slowly and with great difficulty. The cut connecting Boynton with the Hillsboro River at Deerfield to the south stretched fifteen miles, and the river itself had to be dredged for a distance of five miles. Dredging between the Hillsboro River and the New River Sound at Fort Lauderdale required a cut nine miles long. Another cut nine miles long had been made south to Silver Lake, and then a cut through solid earth and rock one mile long dredged into Dumfoundling Bay. Finally reaching Biscayne Bay, the company had dredged waterways fifty feet wide and six feet deep through sand, earth, and rock for a distance of eight miles in completing the last stretch.[4]

But in October 1904, Walker brought sobering news. Land sales had fallen off drastically and the dredges had done poor work, especially the *Wimbee*, which advanced only 4,000 feet in September. Repair bills staggered stockholders. Walker called on Bradley for $3,000 to pay September bills amounting to almost $4,000. Still, by the end of the month, Miles had been

---

[2]GFM to AHS, 3 June 1904, SP Folder 18. *Canal Company v.* TIIF, Leon County (FL) Circuit Court, *Lis Pendens*, filed June 10, 1904, and recorded in *Lis Pendens* Docket A, at page 84, of the Public Records of Dade County, Florida.

[3]Mather, "Inland Water-Ways," 9, 10-11; Miles, "Waterway of the Florida Coast Line Canal," 163.

[4]Mather, 12.

circulating a plan to drain their swamplands to stimulate lagging land sales. Sir Sandford Fleming, an early investor in the Boston & Florida land company, seemed to Miles "impatient to realize something" on his investment. Fleming expected him "to do everything in my power to see that some substantial results are obtained," Miles recounted, because he had persuaded Fleming to buy stock in the company in the early 1890s. Miles wrote Fleming to offer his resignation as a director of the Boston & Florida in favor of Flemings' son, Sandford H. Fleming, but hadn't heard from the senior Fleming. Sawyer hoped that Miles wouldn't resign and suggested adding Fleming's son to the board. Miles suggested that Sawyer carefully consider the question of appointing real estate agents who were not "mixed up" with the Flagler companies, believing better results could be obtained without using Flagler's agents. With no money generated from the sale of canal lands, Bradley agreed to furnish funds for October's dredging expenses. Walker, for his part, wanted the younger Sawyer to travel to St. Augustine for the upcoming canal company board meeting but the new head of the Boston & Florida company didn't think the piddling Florida business justified his going.[5]

By the first of November, Miles reported back to New England on an interview he had with Flagler associate James Ingraham. Ingraham emphatically stated that young Hayden Sawyer had agreed on behalf of the New England group to join in the drainage underway at Lantana, south of West Palm Beach, and to pay a portion of the costs according to the land benefited by the effort. If Hayden agreed to the plan, Miles didn't believe that he could back out. Hayden had spoken with Ingraham when he and Ingraham met, along with Miles, at Newburyport. Ingraham told Miles that both Sawyer and Tom Rickards had called on him, asked him to undertake the drainage, and it was clearly understood that the work was to be borne jointly by the railway and the Boston & Florida company. Turning to the Florida waterway, Miles reported the dredges had been doing good work. He also planned to take Florida's newly elected governor, Napoleon Bonaparte Broward, a former St. Johns River boat captain, down the waterway from St. Augustine to Miami to inspect the work accomplished so far.[6]

---

[5]EW to AHS, 14 October 1904, SP Folder 18. GFM to AHS, 26 October 1904; AHS to GFM, 29 October 1904 (copy); both in SP Folder 18. EW to AHS, 26 October 1904; AHS to GLB, 29 October 1904 (copy); both in SP Folder 18.

[6]GFM to AHS, 2 December 1904, SP Folder 18.

Meanwhile, local newspapers widely reported great optimism over the waterway's success. In West Palm Beach, while repairs continued on the *Tomoka*, a dredge that had been working in the canals south of Lake Worth, George Gleason, Miles's superintendent, reported that a divide eight miles long separated the two dredges working in the Matanzas-Halifax river cut. Steamers were expected to run between St. Augustine and West Palm Beach within 12 months' time and special boats built for tourists. According to the West Palm Beach *Tropical Sun*, Gleason predicted that no finer boats would be seen anywhere, with well-furnished staterooms, spacious decks, and "modern table service." The paper even opined that it was a "certainty" such a steamer line would succeed. [7]

In the middle of December 1904, Miles headed a group of prominent travelers including governor-elect Broward on an inspection cruise down the company's Florida East Coast Canal, now extending 326 miles south of St. Augustine to Miami, with the exception of the still unfinished Matanzas-Halifax cut begun in 1882. For the eight-mile stretch, Miles's group drove by automobile for a few miles and took a rowboat for a mile and a half to reach the dredge *South Carolina*, cutting north from the Halifax River. Joining Broward for the combined inspection trip and tour were defeated congressional candidate and close Broward friend John M. Barrs (soon to become prominent in the purchase of large tracts of the Florida canal company's massive land grant not yet delivered), St. Johns County State Senator W. A. MacWilliams, and Merrill-Stevens boat works executive A.R. Merrill of Jacksonville, along with Miles and Gleason. Although the trip south from the dredge *South Carolina* at the Matanzas Cut proved largely pleasant and uneventful, the *Cherokee* managed to strike a snag and sink. The accident occurred in the Indian River when the large vessel struck a submerged U. S. Government beacon in ten feet of water, going down with all provisions on board in about five minutes' time. Miles then chartered another launch, the *Ethel*, losing only an hour or two because of the accident. On Tuesday, December 13, the entourage reached Miami. Arriving at the Magic City in the afternoon, Miles's party dined at the Biscayne Hotel, then quickly boarded the northbound train at seven o'clock in the evening bound for St. Augustine and Jacksonville. Broward appeared well pleased with the trip, having surveyed the work and assessed what it would take to make present untillable lands productive and marketable. He also seemed surprised not

---

[7]"Magnificent Inland Waterway," *Tropical Sun* (West Palm Beach), 19 November 1904.

only with the amount of work the Florida canal company had done so far but also with the way in which the canals held both their width and depth. The dredges worked efficiently, with no trouble in shallow water. Despite the slight mishap on the *Cherokee*, the trip with the newly-elected governor on board had been "a great success" and "of much benefit" to the company, Miles reported back to his northern colleagues.[8]

But by Christmas Eve 1904, Bradley despaired over the lack of adequate financing for dredging operations, despite Miles's optimistic report. The constant grind of securing financing for the waterway project had caused Bradley much anxiety. He had loaned the enterprise a total of $12,500 since October 1, 1903, and now expected that completing the Matanzas Cut would take another ten months of dredging at a cost of $4,000 a month. Dredging north from the North (Tolomato) River to the St. Johns River would cost at least another $50,000. In the end, Bradley did not see how he could afford to pay for the remaining work without help. Nor did he find early sales of land made through Miles encouraging. Bradley proposed that young Sawyer form a syndicate to purchase from their Florida businesses 10,000 acres of land at a very low price. The scheme would, in Bradley's view, generate $25,000 in revenue for the canal company's bare coffers and a large profit for investors, adding that the Florida entities involved would pay Sawyer a liberal commission for selling the land.[9]

No further news of Florida business reached Sawyer until the end of March 1905 when Miles submitted a formal plan to improve the group's Florida lands. Miles believed that north of Fort Lauderdale, at the Pompano settlement, a limited amount of acreage could be easily and quickly drained, as compared to the lands west of West Palm Beach, where acreage west of the coral ridge required considerable sums to drain. But Sawyer declined to accept the plan.[10]

During the first part of April, while Bradley planned to dine with Maddox at the nation's capital to discuss the Florida businesses, Miles indicated that he might resign as a director of the Boston & Florida Company, giving stockholders the opportunity to elect Sandford H. Fleming as a director. During the last fifteen years, Miles didn't think he had attended more than two or three meetings, believing that he might be more useful to his col-

---

[8]"Gov. Broward and Party Here," *Miami Metropolis*, 14 December 1904; GFM to AHS, 16 December 1904, SP Folder 18.

[9]GLB to AHS, 24 December 1904, SP Folder 18.

[10]GFM to GLB, 31 March 1905 (copy), SP Folder 19.

leagues on the ground. He proposed to buy company land in the Lake Worth area at $6 an acre on terms. There were at least 10,000 acres in the tract. If he sold 500 to 1,000 acres to Lake Worth residents alone, he'd consider that he'd done well, but he couldn't do it without convincing them that he could drain the land. It would rest upon residents to persuade the railroad interests to join in the drainage. This would leave between 9,000 and 10,000 acres profit for the company. But he had gotten a considerable piece of bad news—the Dade County Board of County Commissioners asserted that it possessed the power to drain swamp lands within county boundaries and assess the costs among the land owners. The dismal prospect was to be a whopping tax bill for the New England group.[11]

In May, Miles appeared before the Florida House Committee on Canals and Telegraphs to testify on a bill to extend the time for the waterway's completion, which had been set to expire on May 31 by legislation passed in 1903. The hot-blooded Miles believed the committee's chairman "a henchman of Jennings," referring to former Florida Governor William S. Jennings. The chairman was joined by "a very unprincipled man" on the investigating committee (whom Miles did not identify) who had been "fighting us, though he signed a favorable report on the works." He expected "a hard time" obtaining passage of the bill, but assured his associates that "I shall leave no stone unturned to succeed." He had been trying to stay away from Tallahassee whenever possible "as I have been pestered by Lobbyists to such an extent (trying to bleed us) that I find it to be better to be out of their reach." Every time he declined "the overtures of these people," he'd made an enemy, with this session "the worst I have ever seen." At the same time, in hastily trying to get a plan for drainage west of West Palm Beach started, he had gotten himself in hot water with West Palm Beach residents and his New England colleagues over what was understood to be his agreement to buy 190 acres of Boston & Florida swamp land at six dollars an acre. Miles hoped that both Sawyer and Bradley might sanction the sale for around $1,200, arguing that he'd gotten the West Palm Beach Board of Trade to pass a resolution requesting members to do everything they could to get the legislature to extend the Florida canal company's charter.[12]

---

[11]GLB to AHS, 8 April 1905, SP Folder 19.

[12]GFM to GLB, 18 May 1905 (copy); GFM to AHS, 20 May 1905 (copy); both in SP Folder 19. Answer of Canal Company, *Florida East Coast Railway vs.* TIIF *et al.*, Chancery Case No. 59, Circuit Court in and for Palm Beach County, filed December 31, 1910, pp. 18-19.

Former Governor William Sherman Jennings (standing, left) and Governor Napoleon Bonaparte Broward (standing, right), one of Florida's biggest promoters of inland waterway development, on a tour of the Everglades drainage project in 1906. (Courtesy, Florida State Archives, Florida Photographic Collection, Tallahassee)

On May 23, Bradley lunched with a George Woolsey in New York to discuss selling the waterway. Woolsey reportedly had solid people to take up the project. One of Woolsey's London partners happened to be in New

York, while Bradley made plans to set sail the next day for London. Woolsey wanted his partner to meet Miles to discuss the Florida project as soon as Miles returned north. In Bradley's view, this was "the sort of work, I think, where Mr. Miles can be of most use to us."[13]

From St. Augustine on June 8, Miles reported the devastating news that Florida's new Governor Broward had just vetoed the bill extending the canal company's charter, which had been passed by the legislature after considerable lobbying on the part of the company. Miles nevertheless began working on a contract with state trustees on terms he thought were equal to what had been in the proposed legislation. He didn't know whether he would succeed or not, but "I mean to do all in my power to do so." He had no fear of losing any of their lands; still he wanted to avoid litigation. "Governor Broward positively promised me in the presence of a witness, that he would approve our extension bill, but through the influence of ex-Governor Jennings he broke his word," Miles later recalled. On the progress of canal work, now its twenty-second year, Miles reported that the Florida canal company's dredges had been making "good progress," but "I am a good deal put out, and disheartened, over the Governor's action, as I feel that the state is in the hands of a very unreliable set of officials."[14]

Vacationing at Lucerne, Switzerland, in the summer of 1905, George Bradley, despaired again over the failure of the enterprise to generate sufficient capital to finance dredging operations, "I am utterly worn out with this business of the Florida canal and, if it is not possible to get out of it altogether, I, at least do not wish to get in any deeper." The firm lacked both the means and a suitable organization for continuing the work. He proposed that the company settle the litigation with Florida trustees on the understanding that when the canal company's dredges finally reached St. Augustine, the trustees would grant an additional 100,000 acres of land for the waterway's extension north to the St. Johns River. Such a plan would mean 400,000 acres of land for the canal company, Bradley believed, and "more than 100 cts. on the dollar for all of our securities." If the trustees rejected such a proposal, the canal company's president and biggest investor recommended that the company "'stand pat' and fight for our lands in the courts."[15]

---

[13]GLB to AHS, 23 May 1905, SP Folder 19.

[14]GFM to AHS, June 9, 1905, SP Folder 19.

[15]GLB to GFM, 23 July 1905 (copy), SP Folder 20.

Walker Dies

In early August, Bradley, learned news during his vacation abroad nearly as devastating as the report of Albert Sawyer's death in 1903. The company's 59-year-old vice president and treasurer, Edward M. Walker, lay dying. Suffering from the final stages of Bright's disease, Walker was expected to live for only a short while. With Bradley in Europe and its vice president and treasurer near death, the company struggled to secure releases to sell company land to sustain dredging operations. It had entered into a contract to sell 5,100 acres of land, however, a mortgage given to secure a loan made by Walker tied the sale up. To sell the land, the company officials needed Walker's permission to substitute other canal company land for the acreage the company wanted to sell as security for the Walker mortgage. On August 9, Hayden Sawyer traveled to Springfield to obtain the dying Walker's signature on the papers required for the substitution. While acknowledging the "great loss" that Walker's impending death would bring, Bradley wrote young Sawyer from Switzerland to memorialize that he had personally loaned the company a total of $46,300 since October 1904.[16]

The usually optimistic Bradley suddenly turned pessimistic, believing now that the New England group should shut down the Florida canal and transportation companies, "From my own point of view, considering my age, health, etc. etc., and from the view of my associates as I see their interests, I am satisfied that the Canal Co. after reaching St. Augustine, should not undertake any further construction nor undertake the carrying on of a transportation business." He suggested instead that Miles might be able to form a company to complete construction of the waterway to the St. Johns River and on it, carry on a transportation business. After construction, the new company could then lease the waterway from the existing company. Considering the work to be undertaken, Bradley surmised they might grant the firm between 75,000 and 100,000 acres of land. But no new company was formed, nor did Bradley shut down the Florida canal company.[17]

By the end of August 1905, even more shocking news stunned Florida canal directors. The 59-year-old Bradley—the enterprise's president and

---

[16]GFM to AHS, 2 August 1905; AHS to GFM, 9 August 1905; GLB to AHS, 11 August 1905; all in SP Folder 20.

[17]GLB to GFM, 12 August 1905, SP File 20.

biggest investor — had undergone an "imperative surgical operation" in London. Meanwhile, in Florida, Flagler's associates pushed Miles to join in litigation to challenge the heavy tax burden imposed on the company's lands by the Lake Worth Drainage District, which had been formed to drain West Palm Beach-area lands. But no action could be taken on the company's part because of the unavailability of Bradley and the desperate illness incapacitating Walker, two of the three members of the company's executive committee.[18]

On September 8, more bad news reached canal company directors. Miles received two letters from Bradley reporting that his London doctor had pronounced surgery on his tongue "imperative." Bradley's wife, Helen, also cabled Miles twice. The first telegram advised that Bradley's operation had been "successfully performed." The second telegram, however, reported that another surgery had been scheduled for August 25. Writing Sawyer from his Connecticut home, Miles expressed "fear that another operation [had been] necessary on that date. We are all greatly distressed here as we do not know what the trouble is, but that it is serious there is no doubt whatever." Turning briefly to the Florida waterway, Miles reported that San Francisco-based Howard Trumbo had put in a bid to dredge the waterway from St. Augustine north to the St. Johns River.

The middle of September brought still more bad news. Walker's death appeared imminent. And Bradley's first operation had been performed "to save his life." Another surgery was to be performed on Bradley's neck. Walker's illness, Miles commented, "makes me to feel that we are likely soon to lose such a good friend."[19]

Turning to waterway business, Miles informed his colleagues that he planned to use Trumbo's bid to negotiate a settlement with the trustees on the lingering land grant.

Despite the canal company's persistent money problems, young Hayden Sawyer planned to add to his mother's holdings in the Oro Fino Company, a mining venture organized in Maine, as had been both the Boston & Florida and Indian River steamboat companies, in order to minimize organizational expenses. Hayden expected his father's old partner, George Piper, the Boston & Florida's treasurer, to invest an additional $4,000 to $5,000 in the min-

---

[18]GFM to AHS, 30 August 1905; GFM to AHS, September [2?], 1905; GFM to AHS, September [4?], 1905; all in SP File 20.

[19]GFM to AHS, 8 September 1905; AHS to SM, 15 September 1905; GFM to AHS, 16 September 1905; all in SP Folder 20.

ing enterprise; and Fred Amory, the holder of more than $12,000 worth of stock, to buy still more shares in the company. Of the 24,000 shares of authorized stock, only 4,000 shares at $10 a share remained available for purchase. From Pomfret, Miles reported astounding news—Dade County commissioners had assessed the Lake Worth-area lands owned by the Walker Trust, as well as the Boston & Florida and Florida canal company, $68,753 in taxes for drainage improvements made by the West Palm Beach Drainage District.[20]

Yet news somehow turned positive despite the series of bad reports. A board of army engineers had been appointed to study the possibility that the federal government might construct an inland waterway twelve feet deep along the Atlantic coast from the Chesapeake Bay south to Florida, connecting Jacksonville to Baltimore. A Florida paper opined that such a waterway would not only have great strategic value in time of war but also offer considerable economic advantage for coastwise trade. The board was to hold sessions at Baltimore and at other places along the route including Norfolk and Wilmington, North Carolina, before a formal survey could actually begin.[21]

Less than two years after Albert Sawyer's death, Edward M. Walker passed away at his home on October 2, 1905, at the age of 59. Walker had been a director of Springfield's First National Bank and a life member of the City Library Association. He had never married. His only immediate family member was his brother, William, a junior member of the Springfield building firm of T.M. Walker & Company, founded by Walker's father. Walker's estate provided a lifetime income for his brother, and upon his brother's death, an income for the life of his cousin, Katherine Richardson. William would pass away just six years later in 1911; Katherine, 28 years later. After Katherine's death in 1939, Walker directed that the income of his estate be forever split equally among three charities—the Springfield Hospital, the Springfield Science Museum and the City of Springfield's Forest Park. Three weeks after Walker's death, Bradley and his wife, Helen, returned to New York City aboard the transatlantic liner *Celtic*, somewhat delayed because of rough weather and fog. Fellow passengers on the cruise home included the Phippses (steel), the Charles W. Ogdens (shipping), and

---

[20]AHS to SM, 21 September 1905; GFM to AHS, 21 September 1905; both in SP Folder 20. Inventory of Estate of GLB, vol. 26, pp. 592-95, Pomfret (Conn.) probate records.

[21]"A Twelve-Foot Canal," *The Weekly True Democrat* (Tallahassee, Fla.), 20 October 1905.

the Lorillards (tobacco) — the *crème de la creme* of upper-crust American society.[22]

Despite the devastating loss of Walker, Florida canal company officials pressed on with the work that lay ahead. Miles surveyed the east coast canal's condition, making a trip as far down as Palm Beach. The Haulover at Titusville, recently pumped out, he found in good condition with no less than six and a half feet of water. From the head of the Halifax River through the south end of the Matanzas-Halifax canal to the dredge *South Carolina* (18 miles north of Ormond), there had been excellent progress, but some of the hard work required blasting. On November 18, to fill the vacancy created by the death of Walker, company directors selected Albert Hayden Sawyer (already trustee of the three Bradley trusts) to serve as treasurer of the firm. From St. Augustine, Miles reported some encouraging news. The U. S. government dredge *Florida* had passed through the canal company's new Halifax River cuts as well as the Haulover and Oak Hill canals drawing five to seven feet of water. Meanwhile, at Boston, Hayden Sawyer consented to the Bradley land trusts and the Boston land company joining in federal court litigation already underway challenging the onerous five-cents-an-acre Everglades drainage tax plan.[23]

By early January 1906, Sawyer received word that December expenses totaled about $4,000 and asked Bradley to send a check to pay them. Miles met with Charles Cooper, the Florida canal company's Jacksonville lawyer, to discuss the status of ongoing settlement negotiations with state trustees over the land grant situation. The company should try to get as much land upfront as possible, Miles believed, with the balance to be delivered on a specified date. The company had already been entitled to some 160,000 acres of state land. Land deeded outright could be used to finance the northern cut from St. Augustine to the St. Johns River. Although Miles was not very hopeful of accomplishing much with the trustees, he wanted negotiations to continue until at least the completion of the Matanzas Cut when the canal company would be in a much stronger position to claim its lands. On yet another venture, Miles planned to go to Orlando to see a peat pro-

---

[22]Last Will and Testament of Edward M. Walker, and accompanying probate proceedings, Hampden County (Mass.) Register of Probate; *McKechnie v. City of Springfield*, 41 N.E. 2d 557 (Sup. Jud. Ct. Mass., Hampden, 1942). "Three Belated Liners In," *New York Times*, 23 October 1905.

[23]GFM to AHS, 2 December 1905; AHS to GFM, 16 December 1905; GLB to AHS, 18 December 1905; George W. Gibbs to AHS, 23 December 1905; AHS to GLB, 30 December 1905 (copy); all in SP Folder 21.

duction plant there, but he was waiting for it to start up. Excessive rains had shut down work on the plant temporarily. Meantime, the dredge *Wimbee* had been doing good work since her overhauling. But the repairs on the dredge *South Carolina* slowed getting her back into service. Even Miles's personal life presented a challenge. His wife, Helen, had suffered "a species of nervous collapse" at St. Augustine, experiencing a sudden headache and dizziness. After a local physician attended her, though, she appeared to be getting better.[24]

Directors began making preparations for the annual meeting of the Florida canal company to be held at the Ancient City on March 13. A new stockholder, William McKechnie, a Massachusetts lawyer serving as executor of Walker's estate, planned to attend. Hayden Sawyer scheduled a trip down to St. Augustine aboard the Florida Special using the Atlantic Coast Line route, leaving Boston about two o'clock in the afternoon and arriving at St. Augustine about 4:50 p.m. the next day. The annual meeting was to be held at the company's St. Augustine offices located directly over the First National Bank's first-floor quarters. The congenial group of directors soon gathered for the annual meeting, which invariably consisted of ample amounts of Florida sunshine, a few rounds of golf, some bridge playing and a little business. No less a recorder than the the the *New York Times* confirmed the recreational aspects of the meeting. The paper reported that George and Helen Miles had given a tea party for George and Helen Bradley, with Sam Maddox also attending, on Sunday, March 11. But just a few weeks later, after returning from an apparently uneventful stockholders meeting, George Lothrop Bradley died at his Washington home on March 26, 1906, at the age of fifty-nine, the third major Florida canal company figure to die within three years' time.[25]

---

[24]AHS to GLB, 8 January 1906; GFM to GLB, 12 January 1906; both in SP Folder 21.

[25]McKechnie to AHS, 17 February 1906; AHS to McKechnie, 19 February 1906 SP Folder 21. "At St. Augustine," *New York Times*, 18 March 1906, p. 9.

Chapter 10

More Uncertainty

The unexpected death of George Lothrop Bradley, the Florida canal company's president and largest investor, dealt a major blow to the firm's operations, leaving in doubt the Florida waterway's completion. Fortunately, Bradley's will left open the possibility of continued financing. His will also provided for the founding of what would become the nation's first psychiatric hospital for children—the Emma Pendleton Bradley Hospital at East Providence—in memory of George and Helen Bradley's only child.

A healthy child until age seven, Emma Pendleton Bradley was stricken in 1887 with what is now understood to have been encephalitis. The sickness left Emma epileptic, retarded, and afflicted with cerebral palsy. Bradley wrote his will in 1904 when his daughter was twenty-five years old, establishing a trust following his death to assure her future care and support. A few months after completing his will, Bradley became ill requiring an operation on his tongue and a second procedure on his neck. Following another operation in New York City, just a few weeks after returning from the Florida canal company's annual meeting in St. Augustine, Bradley died of pneumonia at his Washington home on March 26, 1906. His daughter Emma would die only twenty-one months later on December 26, 1907, at the Bradley summer home in Connecticut, at the age of twenty-eight. The bulk of Bradley's $4.6 million estate, following the death of his wife Helen, would go toward the establishment of a hospital in memory of their daughter Emma.[1]

Bradley Will Backs Florida Waterway

Bradley's will placed all of his Florida canal company securities in trust, designating as trustee his long-time friend and business associate Edward Walker, who, unfortunately, had succumbed only a year before to Bright's

---

[1]"George L. Bradley Dead," *New York Times*, 27 March 1906; "Death of Mr. Bradley," *The Tatler* (St. Augustine), 31 March 1906; Johnston, *Out of Sorrow*, 7-13.

disease. The will exuded great faith in the importance of the unfinished Florida waterway, "I have confidence in the ultimate success of the enterprise in which said Company is engaged, and the business for which it was organized." Acknowledging that keeping the company securities might be "hazardous and not such as would be approved by the Courts for the investment of trust funds," Bradley directed that the securities be retained for "a limited period and be disposed of or collected when the works and improvements now in progress shall be more nearly completed." In disposing of his canal company holdings, Bradley instructed his trustee—now the Rhode Island Hospital Trust Company—to protect smaller shareholders by requiring his trustee to obtain the same price for their shares as the trust might garner for the Bradley shares.[2]

Of his other investments Bradley recommended keeping his stock in the Mergenthaler Linotype and Newport Land Company for their "great income." During the early 1880s, Bradley had become interested in the iron ore-rich Gogebic Range in northern Michigan through renowned geologist Raphael Rumpelly (1837-1903), who, like Bradley, had studied geology at the widely regarded Freiberg mining academy in Germany. Rumpelly, George Bradley, Judge Bradley (George's father), along with Arthur and Hamilton Emmons of Newport, each held a twenty percent stake in the Newport Land Company. The company bought a square mile of iron-ore property in the Gogebic Range on the Michigan-Wisconsin border. When Bradley's father died in 1888, Bradley received another 10-percent share of the company from his father's twenty percent interest. Leased to subsidiaries of the United States Steel Corporation and Youngstown Sheet and Tube Company, the Gogebic tract would yield the Newport company royalties for nearly 75 years until 1965. Considered at the time the richest of the iron ore mines in the Lake Superior region, the Newport mine yielded an astounding 887,000 tons annually, averaged over the three-year period ending in 1913. From 1919 until 1934, Bradley's investment netted what would become the Emma Pendleton Bradley Hospital dividends amounting to almost $2 million.[3]

---

[2]Last Will and Testament of GLB executed on November 1, 1904; codicil executed on November 1, 1904; second codicil executed on December 7, 1904. Transcripts recorded in Vol. 26, at pages 520-543 of Pomfret (Conn.) probate records.

[3]*Ibid*. Gardner, "18th Anniversary; *Newport Mining Co. v. City of Ironwood*, 152 N.W. 1088 (Mich. 1915); Champlin, *Raphael Pumpelly*, 17, 83; Pumpelly, *Reminiscences*, 584-91.

Bradley bequeathed one painting to his old friend, Fred Amory, and all remaining paintings, including works by Corot, Courbet, David and Delacroix, to the Corcoran Gallery of Art at Washington. He left his collection of 2,054 engravings, drawings, and etchings, including works by Cranach, Durer, Rembrandt and Van Dyck, to the Library of Congress. One of the more striking prints was Albrecht Durer's "Large Triumphal Carriage of Maximilian," a fifth-edition multi-block woodcut print made in 1589 by the German printer Jacubus Chinig. When assembled, the Bradley print measures eight feet long and one and a half feet high. To the Cosmos Club of Washington, of which Bradley had been a member since 1883, Bradley gave his rare book collection. Almost sixty years later, in 1965, the Club loaned the Folger Shakespeare Library twenty-eight early printed books from the Bradley bequest, including seven incunabula (books printed between 1455 and 1501). These books bore a special Bradley collection bookplate with an inscription that dedicated the work "for wider appreciation and use by literary scholars."[4]

Foremost among the Bradley incunabula was Francesco Colonna's romantic allegory, *Hypnerotomachia Poliphili* ("The Strife of Love in a Dream"), printed by the Venetian printer Aldus Manutius in 1499 and considered by many to be among the most beautiful early printed books in the world. The Folger Shakespeare Library displayed the Bradley collection at the nation's capital in 1947 and again in 1972. The introduction to the 1972 Folger catalogue overlooked Bradley's contribution to the development of both the Bell Telephone and Mergenthaler Linotype companies. Focusing instead on the entrepreneur's role in the Florida canal company, the catalogue proclaimed that Bradley "encouraged expansion of Florida as an agricultural and resort state." In 1978, seventy-two years after George Bradley's death, the Cosmos Club auctioned off the Bradley collection, yielding a substantial sum for its endowment fund. Almost twenty years later, in the fall of 1997, a single

---

[4]Last Will and Testament of GLB executed on November 1, 1904; codicil executed on November 1, 1904; second codicil executed on December 7, 1904; all transcripts recorded in vol. 26, at pages 520-543 of Pomfret (Conn.) probate records. Library of Congress, 63-64; *Cosmos Club Bulletin* (September 1972):10; Washburn, *Cosmos Club*, 202-204; Letter from Folger Shakespeare Library to author, 7 August 1999, enclosing a copy of the bookplate and a copy of the catalog cards for each work in the Bradley collection on loan. Works bequeathed to the Corcoran identified by Laura Coyle, Curator of European Art, Corcoran Gallery of Art, in a communication to the author dated February 20, 2004. Information on Durer's "Triumphal Carriage" may be found in Stiber, "The Triumphal Arch."

copy of an imprint of Manutius's *Hypnerotomachia* sold for almost a quarter of a million dollars at a Christie's auction.[5]

Although Bradley's executor, the Rhode Island Hospital Trust Company (known today as Bank of America), initially reported many of his investments as "doubtful" in value, his Florida holdings alone would add almost a half a million dollars to his estate during the next twenty years. Meantime, the remaining Florida canal company directors struggled to meet the costs of waterway operations. Writing from Washington shortly after Bradley's death, George Miles, the company's longtime managing director, hoped to arrange payment of March canal expenses.[6]

Around the middle of April, Miles reported that the Flagler railroad apparently had taken notice of the usefulness of the developing Florida waterway. The railway was about to take forty barges down the waterway from Mosquito Inlet, near New Smyrna, to Biscayne Bay, a distance of almost 300 miles, for use in the construction of the overseas extension of the railway to Key West. Meanwhile, Fred Amory, another longtime director, still hadn't heard whether or not Bradley's trust company would continue funding the Florida canal work and suggested to his old friend Sam Maddox, the company's secretary and lawyer, that it might be worthwhile for someone like him with his "knowledge and persuasion" to go to Providence to lobby for the project. For his part, Amory confided that he no longer could invest additional funds in the Florida waterway and didn't suppose that Maddox would either. In any event, Amory didn't know why Bradley's estate wouldn't protect its interest and the minority stockholders at the same time.[7]

Hayden Sawyer, another director and president of the Boston & Florida land company, delayed writing Maddox in the hope that the trust company might have something definite to say. So far, the trust company had been seeking information but had stated "nothing." Sawyer had only enough

---

[5]Cosmos Club, "Exhibition," 1947; Cosmos Club, "Collector's Choice"; Washburn, *Cosmos Club*, 202-204; Thomas, *Great Books*, 60-61; *American Book Prices Current*, vol. 104, p. 418.

[6]Inventory of Estate of GLB, January 15, 1907, vol. 26, pp. 592-95; and Accounting of Estate of GLB, April 5, 1934, vol. 32, pp. 201-18; found in Pomfret (Connecticut) probate records. See, also, *Rhode Island Hospital Trust Co. v. Bradley*,103 A. 486 (R. I. 1918), for the Rhode Island Supreme Court's discussion of Bradley's Florida investments after his death in litigation brought by Helen against the trust company shortly before her death to compel distribution of the Florida profits. GFM to AHS, 10 April 1906, SP Folder 21. AHS to McKechnie, 14 April 1906 (copy); McKechnie to AHS, 18 April 1906; both in SP Folder 21.

[7]GFM to AHS, 14 April 1906; FA to SM, 17 April 1906; both in SP Folder 21.

money in various bank accounts to pay the company's March expenses. Apart from the Florida ventures, Sawyer and his partner George Piper each had gambled about $8,000 on the development of the Oro Fino mine, a speculative venture in the Southwest. Fred Amory had invested $19,000; the Bradley estate, perhaps $28,000. Reflecting on the loss of the waterway's biggest backer, young Sawyer wrote that Bradley's death did not come as a shock to him, although he expected him to live for several months, possibly as long as a year. The blow nevertheless was "a hard one." "When Mr. Bradley was on this side of the water," Sawyer recalled, "almost every mail brought something from him to the office. You can imagine how much we miss him."[8]

James Ingraham, one of Henry Flagler's key associates, invited the Florida canal company and Boston & Florida to join the Flagler railway and five large land companies that controlled six million acres of land in the organization of an "Immigration Society." The Society was expected to promote settlement of their lands and influence state legislators to encourage immigration. Organizers anticipated a land assessment of between six and ten mils for advertising and development work. Miles recommended that his colleagues join if the assessment proved affordable. He saw at least one objective of the association as protecting their lands from "practical confiscation by irresponsible politicians." If Governor Broward carried out his drainage plan, Miles foresaw an annual tax of *10 cents* an acre on their property, an outrageous extraction given current land prices hovering around only two dollars an acre. With primary elections for the state House of Representatives set to take place on May 15, the association hoped to help elect "conservative men" to office.[9]

Maddox reiterated his inability to invest more money in the waterway. All of his cash had been tied up in speculative stock purchases, with one investment slowly declining in value. He suggested that Sawyer and Amory work out the nagging cash problems, while he and Miles worked on the technical details of finishing construction. At first tempted to write Bradley's trust company, Maddox finally decided against it, concerned that a letter might "manifest over-anxiety on the part of the canal directors." Besides, he felt, "if they need my advice in connection with this decision they will write and ask it." On another front, Miles thought an investigation

---

[8]AHS to SM, 18 April 1906, SP Folder 21.
[9]Ingraham (Florida East Coast Railway) to GFM, 18 April 1906, SP Folder 21.

into the gas properties of peat found on some of the New England group's Florida lands was promising. Some St. Louis gas engine manufacturers had said they could use the peat economically to generate gas to run in their engines. Meanwhile, some progress had been made in completing the waterway. At the south end of Lake Worth, the canal company's dredge *Tomoka* moved some 800 to 1,100 cubic yards of material a day.[10]

Toward the end of April, Miles traveled south down the coast to Jensen to discuss a St. Lucie County state legislator's purchase of around a hundred acres, half Florida canal company land; the rest, Boston & Florida acreage. After leaving Jensen, Miles spent a few hours on the suction dredge farther south at Boynton, then moving from 1,200 to 1,500 cubic yards of material a day and doing excellent work. Although the dredges *Wimbee* and *South Carolina* encountered large quantities of rock, both worked through it well. Still further south, at West Palm Beach, Miles inspected the group's holdings west of town for a potential drainage project to be undertaken with Flagler. Suffering from a severe toothache for several days, Miles had been attended to by both a doctor and dentist. His gums were swollen, the result of an "ulcerated tooth." [11]

Ignoring requests from Bradley's trust company to assist in financing the Florida project, Fred Amory insisted instead that Bradley's estate should continue investing in the venture, at least to reap the large grants that would be available to the estate for completing the waterway. "I always understood most particularly from George Bradley," Amory wrote, "that whatever happened to him that the Canal should be built through to St. Augustine, and had supposed that all required arrangements had been made for that purpose. I know that Mrs. Bradley who was very familiar with all that George did there, and what he hoped to do, would wish most particularly that his desires should be carried out, and that whatever money she had for that purpose should be supplied by the Executors of the Estate." To that end, Amory suggested a meeting with Providence trust officials to discuss what needed to be done to acquire the 400,000 acres to which the canal company was entitled. Amory thought Miles best to in argue the case for the waterway, "You know that George Miles is the best talker amongst us, and I think he should come up and do what he can with his persuasive

---

[10]SM to AHS, 19 April 1906, SP Folder 21. GFM to AHS, 23 April 1906, SP Folder 21.
[11]GFM to AHS, 30 April 1906, SP Folder 21.

ability." But months more would pass as Bradley trust officials deliberated over the problem of financing the waterway.[12]

In May, the Flagler railway sent a few lighters south down the canal company's inland waterway for the railway's Key West extension. A tow of three barges, each 100 feet long and forty feet wide, went though without incident. But for another tow, Flagler associates thought it more economical to use the outside ocean route. Unfortunately, this tow, with three large barges worth $6,000 a piece, went ashore one night near Boynton with calamitous results, completely disintegrating the next day with the loss of all of their cargo. Miles wryly commented that the incident might "impress on them [the Flagler railway] the value of the inside waterway." By the first week in June, Miles had returned from a four-day trip from Lake Worth south to Biscayne Bay. Real estate development in the area had been progressing. Near Boynton, Miles carefully looked over the drainage operations slowly developing near the settlement. To the north, West Palm Beach merchants told Miles they would purchase 1,000 acres of drained land west of the town at $25 an acre if the Flagler railway helped drain the land. Flagler associate James Ingraham expressed an interest in pooling Flagler railway and Model Land Company lands with those of the New Englanders in draining the lands. Further south, Miles met with Andrew Christian Frost at Dania, just south of Fort Lauderdale. Frost, the Dania settlement's founder, had been working on persuading Ingraham to get a canal cut from Dania to the waterway. He told Miles that if such a canal was cut, he could get thirty dollars an acre for the group's marshlands. Meanwhile, in the northern stretches of the waterway, Miles had made some headway toward selling Boston & Florida land in St. Johns County, near St. Augustine, until a man named Carter produced what appeared to be permits from the Boston & Florida company allowing him to cut timber on the land.[13]

Around the middle of June, having just completed his inspection of the waterway, 51-year-old John Ripley Freeman, the Bradley trust's consulting engineer, seemed well pleased with what he had seen, though Miles doubted his appreciation of the value of a proposed extension of the waterway to the St. Johns River. Still, Miles felt confident that he could change Freeman's mind, thinking the Providence-based engineer "a particularly competent man." In fact, so competent was Freeman, he later became a

---

[12]FA to SM, 30 April 1906 (copy), 9 May 1906 (copy), SP Folder 21.

[13]GFM to AHS, 15 May 1906; GFM to AHS, 15 May 1906; GFM to AHS, 3, 8 June 1906; all in SP Folder 21.

consulting engineer for the federal government on the construction of the Panama Canal.[14]

Four months after Bradley's death, trust officials wrote to both Amory and Sawyer, asking whether either felt inclined to invest more money in the Florida project. Not unexpectedly, both declined. In fact, Amory bluntly rebuffed Bradley's trustee, informing the trust that "out of personal friendship alone" for Bradley he had bought as much as 600 shares of Florida canal company stock and owned only six bonds. On the other hand, Bradley held 4,105 shares of stock and at least a hundred bonds. Bradley "had always told me that I should never be called upon for any more money," Amory insisted, and that "he had arranged in case of his death that the whole of this construction to St. Augustine should be paid out of his Estate."[15]

In July, Miles received a bill from Alexander St. Clair-Abrams, a well-known Jacksonville lawyer, for his work in handling a drainage tax suit that resulted in a victory for all the landowners affected by the court decision. The bill for the New England group's share of the expense totaled an astounding $3,000. Miles suggested no further legal action be taken. He believed, however, that the Florida canal company ought to bear its proportionate share of the legal expenses already incurred. The company's lands had benefited from the favorable court decision the land and railroad companies had secured for all the land owners. Now at Pomfret, Miles groused a bit over his unfinished house there and a whole lot more on the loss of his furniture on the train trip back to Connecticut, forcing a stay at the Pomfret Inn where Helen Bradley had been residing for a few days before leaving for Bar Harbor. In Florida, the dredges had been doing such fine work that workers on one dredge could see the other dredge closing in on the completion of the crucial cut between the Matanzas and Halifax rivers.[16]

At Providence, Miles finally spent some time with members of the executive committee of the trust company controlling Bradley's estate. Committee members appeared to be in a dilemma over what to do with the Florida

---

[14]For a biographical sketch on Freeman, see "John R. Freeman, Engineer, Is Dead," *New York Times*, 7 October 1932. GFM to AHS, 18 June 1906, SP Folder 22. FA to SM, 21 June 1906 (copy), SP Folder 22. Miles, "History," 10; cf., "Governor Vetoes Canal Bill," *Weekly True Democrat* (Tallahassee, Florida), 16 June 1906.

[15]Clark (RIHTC) to FA, 3 July 1906; Clark (RIHTC) to AHS, 3 July 1906; FA to Clark (RIHTC), 6 July 1906 (copy); all in SP Folder 22.

[16]GFM to AHS, 4 July 1906, SP Folder 22.

project.   According to the terms of Bradley's will, the trust company appeared to lack authority to advance money for the canal except out of whatever income that Helen Bradley didn't need. Helen's lawyer, Stephen O. Edwards of the law firm of Edwards & Angell, who had drawn George's will, agreed.   Committee members had not been "in a happy frame of mind," considering that Bradley had invested between $500,000 and $600,000 in the project , which they expected would be completely lost without finishing the Matanzas-Halifax Cut. Miles argued strenuously that the waterway would be a "rate regulator," even if it were not fully constructed, and he gave them a report of the statistics for an "inside waterway from Norfolk south" then being pushed by a "Congressmen from that district," probably North Carolina Congressman John Humphrey Small, an early leader in the inland waterway movement. Small's report showed that while barges could haul a ton of freight for one mile at a cost of a fifth of a mil, it would cost as much as forty times that figure to haul a ton the same distance by rail. Finally, the Bradley trust committee's decision arrived, dealing a devastating blow to the canal company. It was bad news indeed. Further financing of the waterway could be obtained only through Helen Bradley's willingness to forego income from her husband's trust in favor of the project.[17]

In July, Miles suggested to Edwards that money could be advanced to complete the Matanzas Cut by using the Maddox trustee land as security for loans from the bank serving as Bradley's trustee. This land, especially the land in the Indian River area with large stands of valuable timber, was free and clear and could be sold to pay off advances made to finance dredging. Talks also began between the Florida canal company and state officials about settling the litigation that had tied up the public lands since 1903. Governor Broward had met with Charles Cooper, the company's lawyer, about a settlement over the lands owed the company. Cooper believed that if the company agreed to extend the waterway to Jacksonville, investors might be able to obtain a satisfactory settlement. Cooper had the promise of Bion Barnett, president of the National Bank of Jacksonville, that he would do his best to secure a settlement. Barnett, Cooper noted, was supposed to have financed Broward's gubernatorial campaign.[18]

---

[17]GFM to AHS, 11 July 1906, SP Folder 22.
[18]GFM to AHS, 16 July 1906, SP Folder 22.

To encourage the Rhode Island Hospital Trust Company to aid the Florida enterprise, Amory wrote Robert H. Goddard, a Providence cotton broker, to enlist his aid in getting trust officials to help in completing the Florida canal. In his letter to Goddard, Amory argued that for such "a magnificent present of a future home for persons afflicted with nervous or other chronic diseases to your State," the trust company ought to undertake to carry out this work for "its future profit." After a time, the trust finally approved a series of loans to the Florida canal company. Sawyer also worked on a plan to get Helen Bradley personally involved in loans to the company. Sawyer told Helen that she could easily expect an income from the Bradley estate of not less than $60,000 a year and that it would be "a grave mistake" to take the chance of losing valuable Florida lands by not completing the waterway to St. Augustine."[19]

Helen answered the call, endorsing a canal company note for $4,500 to pay June construction vouchers. Apparently unaware of Helen's plan to provide financing out of her own funds, the strain of making land sales to finance dredging operations had brought Miles to the breaking point. Miles asked for an urgent meeting at Boston, warning that "we must face the prospect of receivership." Florida land sales had produced a paltry $4,000. A few days later, he reported better news. He had gotten a telegram from an investor seeking an option to buy 60,000 acres of Brevard and St. Lucie county lands at $2.50 an acre. He countered at $3 an acre. The prospective buyer, in Miles's mind, ought to make a killing off the pine-laden land—at least $4 an acre from turpentine sales alone and nearly the same amount from timber sales.[20]

After a visit with Maddox and Sawyer in Newburyport in early August, Miles thanked Sawyer for his hospitality; he and Maddox had thoroughly enjoyed themselves. Meanwhile, the dredges in the Matanzas-Halifax Cut had advanced nearly 3,000 feet during July. The machines were now only about 8,800 feet apart, but Miles warned of the likely presence of rock in the remaining divide. Maddox reported that Helen Bradley didn't seem likely to agree to the plan to bail out the company he outlined in a long letter to her. He hadn't sent a copy to Miles because Helen appeared to imply in their conversations that Miles's missed predictions for completion were the

[19]FA to Robert H. Goddard, 17 July 1906, SP Folder 22. AHS to Mrs. George L. Bradley, 18 July 1906 (copy), SP Folder 22

[20]AHS to FA, 21 July 1906; FA to SM, 23 July 1906; GFM to FA, 24,27 July 1906; all in SP Folder 22.

cause of the waterway's troubles. Miles was, in Maddox's words, "a sensitive soul." The lawyer thought Miles might quit the project if he knew Helen had expressed such reservations about his abilities. Uncharacteristically protective of Miles, Maddox the bachelor dismissed Helen as "only a woman" who thought that an engineer should be able to foretell "with the accuracy of a Jeremiah or a Hosea" the precise time at which the Florida cut should be finished through the swamps between the Matanzas and Halifax rivers, without knowing in advance what obstacles were sure to be encountered. He added that he could raise all the money if that is what he wanted, but he would only earn six percent on his money, while Bradley's estate garnered the real benefits of completing the waterway. "If anybody is to take further risks," Maddox thought, "it ought to be the fellow who will reap the gains of success."[21]

Demands for more money for dredging began to wear as much on Maddox as they had on Miles, acknowledging that receipt of a telegram from Sawyer alerting that the Florida canal company still needed $2,500 to meet July expenses produced "an awful gasp." Whereupon the well-connected lawyer arranged to borrow $2,500 for thirty days at six percent interest with a commission of two percent, secured by twelve 1903 bonds. Trying to summarize but always failing, the verbose Maddox told Sawyer, "In other words, and stripped of circumlocution, I guaranteed the note without endorsing it," adding that endorsing notes was "a practice I promised myself many years ago never to be guilty of for friends, clients, relatives or anybody else, and I have never departed from it." He made it quite clear that he was only borrowing the money out of friendship, "Were it not for the keen personal interest in the general situation, acquired by an association of more than twenty years, I should certainly throw up the sponge and let the Rhode Island Hospital Trust Company, the practical owner as the executors of the will, of the entire property, treat it in any way they see fit."[22]

For his part, Amory thought Helen should finish the waterway in George's memory and keep his promise that "even if he should die the work would be finished under his will." At Pomfret, Miles added his two cents that it was, to him, "rather discouraging" that the trust company had been "so indifferent as to what becomes of the Florida property" after all their

---

[21]GFM to AHS, 8 August 1906; SM to AHS, 9 August 1906; both in SP Folder 22.
[22]SM to AHS, 14 August 1906, SP Folder 22.

hard work, but, he believed, "it is not our fault, and so far as I can see every-thing that can possibly be done by us to save the situation is now being done."[23]

To help finish the waterway, Helen made plans to raise $30,000 by pledg-ing her Mergenthaler Linotype Company stock, with the understanding that she was to be paid back out of the first sales of canal company lands. The end of August, Maddox had just spent a week at the old family home in Washington County, Maryland. It rained every day, keeping everyone indoors most of the time. Helen appeared discouraged over her Florida prospects. If Helen declined further assistance, the company directors would be "at the end of their tether," Maddox concluded. The "bugaboo" to Helen was the uncertainty over the amount of rock remaining in the Matan-zas Cut. Miles, he thought, ought to be able to take borings and make a determination with an investigation requiring two men not more than a day or two. To prod Bradley's trustees into action, he suggested that instead of bringing lawsuits, Amory and McKechnie (Walker's executor) join him in making formal demand on the trust company to complete the Matanzas Cut. The basis of the demand would be the promise made by Bradley to complete the waterway when they all put up $10,000 for the purchase of stock in 1902. But just after dictating the letter, Maddox cautioned care before launching a lawsuit. It later appeared in correspondence received from Amory that Helen had been more interested in the waterway than he first thought. At Bar Harbor, Amory wrote that he had met with Helen Bradley. Helen showed him a letter from her lawyer in which he warned against the possibility of a lawsuit against George's estate to force the finish-ing of the Cut. Amory, however, told Helen that he wouldn't pursue litiga-tion because "I did not want bad publicity" about the group's failure to finish the waterway during Bradley's lifetime. If nothing else could be done, Helen told Amory that she'd raise the $30,000, using her own securi-ties.[24]

At the beginning of September, Sawyer had a long visit with Ingraham at Newburyport. Flagler's right-hand man was disturbed hearing that Miles didn't think a Flagler meeting with the group a good idea. In his opinion, the political situation in Florida appeared precarious. If the efforts to drain lands west of West Palm Beach fell through, an amendment to the Florida

---

[23]FA to SM, 14 August 1906; GFM to AHS, 15 August 1906; both in SP Folder 22.

[24]Helen McH. Bradley, 22 August [1906?]; SM to AHS, 30 August 1906; FA to SM, 30 August 1906 (copy); all in SP Folder 22.

Constitution would surely pass. The amendment would remedy the constitutional defect in Governor Broward's drainage tax legislation that resulted in a favorable court decision for the group and thereby impose a heavy tax burden on everyone's land. Ingraham offered Miles $7.50 an acre for all the lands in the drainage district owned by the group's companies or an exchange of lands if the group didn't want to join them. It seemed plausible, at least to Sawyer, that they could make a sale of both Florida canal company and Boston & Florida lands because of Flagler's commitment to drainage.[25]

Around the middle of September, Miles' assistant, George Gleason, reported from Florida that the dredge *Tomoka* had been doing good work, pumping over a 17-foot bank. But the dredge encountered rock as well as trouble moving forward because of small anchors. Gleason ordered wire rope and a new anchor to pull her ahead and made a sketch for a ratchet and drum to draw up the rope and anchor. With these improvements, the company's superintendent expected her to do at least a third more work than the old rig. The *Tomoka* moved into the Matanzas-Halifax Cut at the rate of fifty to seventy-five feet an hour, digging out from one to two feet of material. Gleason cautioned, however, that without a lookout, she was likely to bend a shaft or break a chain after striking logs or rocks.[26]

By the middle of September, the company's lawyer, Charles Cooper, had written Governor Broward about reaching a final settlement with the state trustees. Then Cooper saw the governor on the street in Jacksonville one day and Broward said that he would come to Cooper's office. But a few days passed before Cooper saw him again on the street, when Broward finally agreed to meet in Cooper's office that afternoon. Broward favored making conveyances to the canal company, with some lands held in escrow, but only if the firm released its claim to 34,000 acres. Some trustees, however, wanted to save more public land, demanding that the canal company release 50,000 acres, a figure exactly half of the 100,000 acres some trustees had requested. Professing completion of the waterway north to Jacksonville to be of "the greatest importance," Broward warned that two state trustees were not at all favorably disposed to the canal project or even a settlement. He offered that he would be willing to support conveying 150,000 acres to the Florida canal company immediately if directors showed an ability to

---

[25]AHS to GFM, 5 September 1906 (copy), SP Folder 23.
[26]Gleason to GFM, 12 September 1906, SP Folder 23.

secure financing to complete the waterway to the St. Johns River. Cooper considered the time right for the company to strike a deal with the state trustees.[27]

Florida dredges again had been doing well, with approximately a mile to go in the cut between the Matanzas and Halifax. The dredges lay about 65 stations or 6,500 feet apart. The *Wimbee* cut through soft rock that her dipper moved without blasting. The *South Carolina*, on the other hand, moved ahead with heavier dipping. Each day the *Wimbee*'s work grew lighter. "How long the rock will remain soft," Miles wondered, "is however an uncertain quantity." Moreover, Miles's crew had been doing a considerable amount of re-digging at the north end of the canal because of shifting sand.[28]

From Helen Bradley's $1,500 loan, Sawyer paid August dredging expenses. James Ingraham was expected to arrive at Boston to discuss with Sawyer once more the West Palm Beach drainage project, which affected some 2,000 acres of company land. Miles had made no direct offer to Ingraham to sell at $7.50 an acre but told him instead that he would submit an offer, if made, of $10 an acre to the company's directors. In New York City, Helen Bradley wrote to Sawyer, hoping that he could make a sale to Ingraham so that she could redeem her Mergenthaler Linotype stock that had been pledged for loans to the canal company. Uncomfortable with the city's warm weather, Helen longed for cooler climes. "I rather sigh for the Bar Harbor sea," she conceded. By the end of September, Ingraham had accepted the canal directors' offer to sell 2,500 acres of canal company land in the West Palm Beach area at $10 an acre. But it would be months later until the details of the sale could be worked out and the deal closed. Until then, the canal company would struggle each month to pay dredging expenses.[29]

With both the West Palm Beach land sale to Flagler made but not yet closed and Helen Bradley's pledge to provide $4,000 for September dredging expenses, Sawyer left the first week of October on a ten-day vacation, featuring a trip by automobile to Jackson, New Hampshire, in the White Mountains. Sawyer would soon regret leaving Boston. A fire destroyed the

---

[27]C. M. Cooper to GFM, 13 September 1906 (copy), SP Folder 23.

[28]AHS to P. H. Gardener (RIHTC),14 September 1906 (copy); GFM to AHS, 14 September 1906; both in SP Folder 23.

[29]AHS to SM, 17 September 1906 (copy); Helen McH. Bradley to AHS, 19 September [1906?]; AHS to Mrs. George L. Bradley, 29 September 1906 (copy), all in SP Folder 23.

dredge *Wimbee* at 2:50 a.m. on Saturday, October 13. It started in the galley in the early morning hours after someone had come down for coffee. The *Wimbee*'s captain, Fred Dupont, woke up and sounded the alarm. He jumped out of a window on the port side to escape the fire. He lost his watch, most of his clothes, and all of his tools. One of the crew jumped overboard into ten feet of water, dog-paddling to safety because he couldn't swim. Another lost all of his money, but thanked God no one was hurt. "We are all shoeless but two," a crew member confessed. Flames had gutted the dredge inside and out, leaving nothing but a shell. The *Wimbee* had been burned to within four inches of the water line.[30]

Miles wrote immediately to the company's insurance brokers, Blake & Rice, to insure the dredge *South Carolina*, which had cost $21,000, for a minimum of $12,000. Now back at Newburyport after his 400-mile automobile trip though the White Mountains, Sawyer brought Helen the bad news, but assured her that, according to Miles, both crews on the *South Carolina* could finish the cut "very speedily," with a stretch of only 4,400 feet left to be dredged. He also brought some good news, at least for himself. At the annual meeting of the Mergenthaler Linotype Company, shareholders elected young Hayden Sawyer a director to fill the vacancy on the board created by George Bradley's death, a fact reported by the *New York Times* on October 18. Stockholders also learned that despite the devastating San Francisco earthquake, the company generated sales of $2.7 million, a half a million dollars ahead of the last year's revenues. Sawyer thanked Mrs. Bradley for her help in getting him on the board with an eloquent statement of his commitment to fill George's shoes, "There is a sadness in taking positions that have been held by men so dear to me and whose abilities have been so far beyond my own, but I shall do my best to help in the various enterprises I am connected with." About the loss of the *Wimbee*, Sawyer admitted that it was "a hard blow to us," but urged that "we must do our best to complete the cut with the dredges left." The company's treasurer, Edward Walker, and Miles, Sawyer wrote, had frequently discussed obtaining insurance for both dredges in the cut, but because of the high rates and because both vessels had been supposed to have been well protected by watchmen and various fire protection devices, decided not to secure coverage. The *Wimbee* cost about $12,000 but Miles expected to use much of the

---

[30]AHS to Mrs. George L. Bradley, 2 October 1906 (copy); Helen McH. Bradley to AHS, 6 October 1906; both in SP Folder 23. Crewman aboard *Wimbee* to GFM, 13 October 1906; Geo. Holleman to GFM, 15 October 1906; both in SP Folder 23.

machinery again. The company had secured coverage for the *South Carolina* and increased its coverage on the dredge *Tomoka* working at Fort Lauderdale.[31]

Writing from St. Augustine nine days after the fire, Miles himself reported first-hand on the loss of the *Wimbee*. She appeared "a sad sight," with nothing left above water but her boom, boiler and a part of the turntable. The hull had been burnt in "a most thorough manner." He confessed how "heart rending" it was to see such a short space separating the two ends of the cut. To finish the work, the determined Miles arranged to place a gang of three blasters ahead of the *South Carolina* to break up the rock with dynamite. If the dredge could withstand the strain of a double crew, he didn't think the enterprise would be "much belated" in completing the cut.[32]

While the New England group struggled to finish the cut with only one dredge, Henry Flagler's ambitious project to extend the Florida East Coast Railway overseas to Key West sustained its own hard blow when a hurricane destroyed a portion of the railway on October 18. The devastating event also resulted in a loss of life initially estimated at 150 to 600 men. Miles supposed that "we will never really know the correct figures, as the Railroad people cannot afford to publish the full extent of the disaster" and doubted that, if the true figures were known, the Flagler organization could secure enough men to continue the work. Interestingly, no mention of the disaster was made in the railway's official account of the extension published in 1912. In his biography of Flagler, Akin notes the incident as the greatest single loss of human life on the project. Based on what appear to be Flagler sources exclusively, however, the author cites only 50 deaths resulted when a vessel broke from her moorings with 150 men aboard.[33]

Near the New River at Fort Lauderdale, the dredge *Tomoka* escaped the ravages of the storm, with only a screen door blown out. At the Matanzas Cut, two crews worked the *South Carolina* day and night. Miles walked over the unfinished portion of the work in about fifteen minutes' time. Helen Bradley's nephew, J. Manton Bradley, reported that he had someone inter-

---

[31]GFM to AHS, 16 October 1906, SP Folder 23. AHS to Mrs. George L. Bradley, 16 October 1906 (copy), SP Folder 23. "Net Receipts of the Linotype Concern Larger by $529,000," *New York Times*, 18 October 1906.

[32]GFM to AHS, 22 October 1906, SP Folder 23.

[33]GFM to AHS, 22 October 1906, SP Folder 23. FECR, *Announcement*; Akin, *Flagler*, 215. For a first-hand account of a survivor of the wreck of Houseboat No. 4 at Long Key, see Saunders, "Wreck."

ested in buying the group's Florida interests. Manton was to see Miles on his return to Pomfret and then arrange to travel south with Miles to look over the situation. Worried over Flagler's indirect involvement in a possible purchase of the group's interests, Sawyer confided that Manton "feels sure that the man in question is not interested with the Standard Oil people." Back home at Pomfret in the beginning of November, Miles hoped to dine with Helen and learn the identity of the prospect. Given the prevailing political climate in Florida, Miles cautioned that negotiations be handled "very tenderly" if the company were to avoid a conflict with "our present socialistic state administration in Florida." If he had a free hand in handling the question "as I think best," Miles boldly claimed that he could get the lands reserved for the company without litigation, awaiting the arrival of a blasting gang to break up the remaining rock ahead of the *South Carolina* in a matter of days.[34]

At the nation's capital, Maddox also advised deliberation before hastily agreeing to a sale of the entire Florida property. He expected a better sales price once the company finished the cut and settled with Florida officials over the land grant. By November 6, Flagler associate Joseph Parrott had returned from New York City where he had conferred with the railway magnate about closing on the purchase of the Boston & Florida and Florida canal company lands at West Palm Beach. A snag developed. Flagler wanted interest waived on the delayed purchase during the period of drainage construction, perhaps for as long as eighteen months. The New England group eventually agreed to the sale with payment to be made in Flagler railway notes with a five-year maturity bearing interest at five percent and the canal company waiving interest for the first eighteen months. Still unsettled, however, was the question of the Florida canal company's entitlement to almost half a million acres of state land the company believed it had earned for dredging the waterway between St. Augustine and Miami for the past twenty-three years.[35]

---

[34]GFM to AHS, 27 October 1906; AHS to GFM, 31 October 1906 (copy); GFM to AHS, 2 November 1906; all in SP Folder 23.

[35]SM to AHS, 2 November 1906; Ingraham to GFM, 6 November 1906; GFM to AHS, 13 November 1906; all in SP Folder 23.

Chapter 11

Dry Old Gentlemen of Providence

Less than nine months after Bradley's death, Florida improvement fund trustees and the Florida canal company finally settled the lawsuits that for nearly three years had tied up the state land reserved for the enterprise. Company directors agreed to pay $50,000 for more than 200,000 acres of land and to escrow with Jacksonville banker Bion Barnett 100,000 acres to be sold for the construction of a waterway from St. Augustine to Jacksonville. For its part, the State of Florida deposited two deeds in escrow with Barnett, each representing more than 117,000 acres of state land, for the construction of the remaining portions of the waterway.[1]

The Details of Settlement

A month before the settlement, in November 1906, Charles Cooper, the company's lawyer, urged Florida canal company directors to move quickly in settling with state trustees because of the recent election defeat of a proposed amendment to legislation creating an Everglades Drainage District, with the power to impose taxes on property within the area. Governor Broward had lobbied hard for the measure's passage in order to cure a defect that caused one court to rule the original law unconstitutional. Rebuffed by the voters, Broward now seemed more determined than ever to dispose of all available state-owned lands to fund drainage projects below Lake Okeechobee. Some of the railroad companies appeared ready to sue the trustees to freeze the transfer of state lands. There had even been a rumor that the trustees planned to sell the canal company's lands to people

---

[1]Bill of Complaint, June 31, 1904, *Florida Coast Line Canal & Transp. Company vs. Trustees of Internal Improvement Fund*, Leon County Circuit Court, cited in sworn Answer of the Canal Company in subsequent litigation, *Florida East Coast Railway Co. vs. Albert W. Gilchrist, et al.*, TIIF, Chancery Case No. 59, Palm Beach County Circuit Court (hereinafter "*FEC vs. TIIF (Palm Beach)*"), pp. 30-37. A copy of the 1906 Agreement is attached to the Answer. See, also, Elliott, "Report on Florida Coast Line Canal."

outside the state. Cooper suggested that if canal directors accepted Broward's suggestion to release 50,000 acres in alternate sections of land so that the trustees could sell them to fund drainage, the move might persuade the trustees to deed the remaining lands due on the grant if the company also agreed to extend the Florida waterway north from St. Augustine to the St. Johns River.[2]

On November 26, following an urgent meeting held at Boston but adjourned because of Sam Maddox's absence, directors reconvened at Maddox's Washington law office to authorize Miles and Maddox to settle with the Florida trustees. Miles left for Florida, with Maddox close behind. Meanwhile, Bradley trust officials still resisted fully backing the Florida venture. His trustees seemed "so much at sea," afraid to do anything without consulting their lawyers, Sawyer told one of his colleagues. The Florida venture remained an uncertain one, even with the prospect of a finished waterway from Jacksonville to Miami and the deeding of over 400,000 acres of prime land.[3]

By December 6, Miles had returned from Florida after completing the settlement with the trustees. The precise terms were the deeding of the entire land reserve due the company, approximately 435,000 acres, for $50,000 cash; the deposit of 100,000 acres in trust for the construction of a St. Augustine-to-Jacksonville canal, with the proceeds to be used for construction only; 50,000 acres deeded to the canal company unconditionally; with the balance of approximately 234,000 acres held in escrow pending completion of the waterway. This left 50,000 acres of reserved land unaccounted for, which were to be sold to Bion Barnett, president of the National Bank of Jacksonville, for $50,000 to pay cash to the trustees and to cover the expenses of negotiation, including a $10,000 commission to be paid to the man who helped negotiate the compromise, William J. Bryan, a Jacksonville lawyer just thirty years old. Appointed a year later to the U. S. Senate to fill the vacancy caused by the death of Stephen Mallory, the politically astute Bryan would serve only from December 26, 1907, until his untimely death on March 22, 1908, at the age of thirty-one.[4]

---

[2]C. M. Cooper to GFM, 13, 15 November 1906, SP Folder 23.

[3]Minutes of meetings of Canal Company, 23, 26 November 1906, SP Folder 23. AHS to Mrs. George L. Bradley, 27 November 1906, SP Folder 23. AHS to Messrs. Brandeis, Dunbar & Nutter, 5 December 1906, SP Folder 23.

[4]GFM to AHS, 6 December 1906 (copy); SM to AHS, 6 December 1906; SM to FA, 6 December 1906; AHS to FA, 12 December 1906 (copy); all in SP Folder 23.

Maddox thought the Florida settlement "an admirable piece of work" by Miles and Cooper. Yet, reflecting on the reluctance of the trust company to help the company, Maddox no longer cared to spend his time "at the cheap rates" he had been getting as the company's lawyer for the past twenty years, and then when success is in sight, have "our throats cut" by a sale of the Florida interests to someone not friendly to the minority stockholders. He intended to forego active participation in the affairs of the company after the stockholders meeting in March, claiming that he was "too old to continue this grind much longer." In Boston, Amory, on the other hand, took a more favorable view, thinking that Flagler might buy the Florida canal company for at least $2,500,000.[5]

Other members of the group tended to the business of paying bills. Sawyer saw Helen Bradley in New York City to complete arrangements for a $5,500 loan to the canal company, which when added to other funds proved only enough to pay November expenses. Further, this appeared to be the last money Helen intended to loan the company. Helen wanted the canal company's directors to use Flagler railway notes from the sale of the Lake Worth acreage to pay further waterway expenses.[6]

At Providence, Miles informed Sawyer that he had given an option to Barnett to purchase some 22,000 acres at $3 an acre from the 50,000 acres to be transferred to the company. Sawyer, however, thought the acreage might be worth double that amount. Miles explained that Barnett had been helpful and thought it good business to keep in good graces with him. Still skeptical, Sawyer thought the group ought to know more about the remaining 28,000 acres before fixing a price. He wrote only to Maddox about the transaction "because even a carefully worded letter to Mr. Miles in the way of criticism produces a storm."[7]

Defending the transaction, Miles argued the option covered only about 11,500 acres. And the price of $3 an acre stood a dollar higher than "anyone seemed disposed to pay for it up to date." Obviously irritated by the questioning of his judgment, Miles caustically replied that he had "been pestered for years to sell lands a low prices," a policy with which Miles strongly disagreed. Despite the pressure of the canal work, the slow land sales, and

---

[5]*Ibid.*
[6]AHS to GFM, 13 December 1906 (copy), SP Folder 23.
[7]*Ibid.*

what he felt had been unjustified criticisms, Miles enjoyed some time away from the drudgery of dredge work, hunting quail at St. Augustine.[8]

But by the end of the year, problems in completing the Matanzas Cut still plagued Miles, with delays in the delivery of dynamite by the railroads and labor shortages heading the list of annoyances. He also faced the difficulty of installing a dam behind the *South Carolina*. North winds had lowered the water there so much that it was difficult to keep her afloat, even though the dredge had been digging below grade.[9]

By the beginning of 1907, Amory had grown skeptical that Helen Bradley or trust officials would allow the minority stockholders to reap as much as the Bradley estate from the sale of the waterway, even though Bradley's will explicitly stated otherwise. Sawyer talked with Helen by telephone. Helen assured him that she would protect minority shareholders. Amory, meanwhile, hoped that current publicity over negotiations for the sale of the canal company might tempt Flagler to take over the enterprise. In his view, Flagler was "the one that really ought to have it."[10]

By the end of January, Amory had grown more confident that Bradley's trust would not leave the company's minority stockholders like himself, Maddox, and Walker's estate out in the cold. On a possible sale of the waterway, he speculated that $5 an acre for the company's 500,000 acres might not be too much for anyone to pay "and have the Canal thrown in for nothing." Frustrated over Miles's handling of construction, he told Helen Bradley that he would like "to stick pins in our friend Miles." Helen wondered whether they might be bonnet pins. "Yes, way up to the head," Amory replied, "for I consider that George F. Miles owes the Company about $60,000 for working over time with incapable people."[11]

For nearly a year after Bradley's death, there had been no one at the helm of the company and, in February 1907, discussions began over the possibility of Amory heading it. From Florida, Miles wired his approval of a land sale in Florida to close as soon as possible, with hopes that the proceeds might cover the January vouchers. If the sale went through as planned, the company could pay back the $15,000 loaned by Helen Bradley to pay expenses. Meanwhile, Sawyer expressed support for Amory's selection as president, arguing that his election would prevent the sale of the company

[8]GFM to SM, 19 December 1906 (copy), SP Folder 23.

[9]GFM to AHS, 29 December 1906, SP Folder 23.

[10]FA to SM, 17 January 1907 (copy); SM to AHS, 19 January 1907; both in SP Folder 24.

[11]FA to SM, 24 January 1907 (copy), SP Folder 24.

at an unreasonably low figure and at the same time keep the management of affairs as they had been before Bradley's death. By February 15, the busy Amory had agreed to accept the presidency, but only on a temporary basis until a successor could be found. He planned to leave Boston by train for the annual meeting in Florida on Friday, March 8, and arrive in Washington sometime Saturday morning. He asked Maddox to join him. Their time on the train would give them an opportunity to talk over business before the meeting on the following Tuesday, March 12. Amory hoped that Maddox could persuade Helen to join them. He reiterated that taking the presidency would be only "a temporary arrangement," believing himself "the least suited for that kind of work" and Maddox better equipped. Once again he expressed his dismay over Miles's handling of the canal project, "I do not like the idea of Mr. Miles being connected either directly or indirectly with that Canal, for I do not think that he does work economically or quickly." For her part, Helen Bradley appeared undecided about attending the meeting. So soon after her husband's death, she felt her attendance in his place might take more courage than she possessed.[12]

While making preparations to attend the annual meeting, Sawyer asked William McKechnie, Walker's executor, to accept a substitution of unencumbered lands near present-day Vero Beach so that other lands burdened by Walker's mortgage could be released and sold to finish canal work. Since his death in March 1906, Bradley's estate and Helen Bradley had advanced the canal company almost $30,000 to continue dredging operations in the Matanzas Cut.[13]

A few days after his election as president at the St. Augustine meeting, at his Boston home once again, Amory candidly wrote Helen that his interest in the project had been almost exclusively for her and "dear George." He hoped that the demands for financing wouldn't cause the directors to sell too much land at low prices before finishing the extension to the St. Johns. In the end, Amory thought George's estate might recover $700,000, perhaps $800,000, on the sale of the waterway or twice what George had already been put in the project and suggested that Helen advance the money to finish the work, taking company bonds secured by the company's land grant.

---

[12]AHS to Mrs. Bradley, 2 February 1907 (copy); Mrs. Bradley to AHS, February 5, [1907]; AHS to GFM, 7 February 1907 (copy); AHS to Mrs. Bradley, 15 February 1907 (copy); FA to Wells, 15 February 1907 (copy); FA to SM, 15 February 1907 (copy); Mrs. Bradley to AHS, 15 February 1907; all in SP Folder 24.

[13]AHS to McKechnie, 15 February 1907, SP Folder 24.

Sawyer also wrote Helen to persuade her to aid the completion of the waterway. The company had title to 110,000 acres, and with the Tallahassee settlement, acquired 370,000 more on the condition the waterway's extension to the St. Johns River wouldn't cost more than $200,000. The escrowed lands were worth at least $3 an acre. It would be "suicidal" not to undertake the extension to the St. Johns, he thought. To finance the project, Sawyer recommended the issuance of bonds worth half a million dollars versus selling land at cheap prices, with the sale of bonds only to the original investors. To his way of thinking, the bond's first mortgage on the real estate and the waterway franchise represented the "cream" of their assets. The "cream" ought to be retained by those who had "borne the burden and heat of the day" and not "passed over to eleventh hour converts." Bradley's estate owned fifty-seven percent of the stock and a still larger proportion of the unsecured debt. In Sawyer's view, the Bradley estate had "more at stake than all the other interested parties put together." His own desire was to make the canal a success "after so many years of struggle," declaring that his interest now had become "almost purely sentimental."[14]

Meantime, at St. Augustine, on Monday, March 18, Miles and his wife Helen hosted a festive afternoon party aboard a launch, with a guest list that included Sawyer, along with Bradley's nephew, J. Manton Bradley, and Herbert Wells of the Rhode Island Hospital Trust Company, Bradley's trustee, the *New York Times* reported in its Sunday, March 24 edition.[15]

From his Jacksonville law office, Cooper not only urged directors to complete the Matanzas Cut quickly but emphasized as paramount the beginning of actual work on the cut between St. Augustine and the St. Johns River within the time limits required by the Tallahassee settlement. Merely surveying the route and clearing right-of-way would not be acceptable to state trustees, some actual excavation must be done immediately. Maddox doubted Miles's estimate of the time and cost for completing the waterway. In fact, since Miles had been associated with the enterprise, dating back to 1884, the estimates of all of the engineers, including Miles, had been "far afield." Just last year, Miles thought that the Matanzas cut could be completed within twelve months at a cost of not more than $30,000. "Now it appears that it is going to cost double that amount," Maddox complained. Conceding that rock dredging could account for some increase in cost, still

---

[14]FA to Mrs. Bradley, 18 March1907; AHS to Mrs. Bradley, 20 March 1907; both in SP Folder 24.

[15]"Season at St. Augustine," *New York Times*, March 24, 1907.

he didn't understand why encountering rock could not have been discovered at the beginning, using soil boring tests or some other method to gauge the difficulty of the work that lay ahead. Compared to what little money the minority stockholders had invested in the enterprise and were likely to reap in return, Maddox estimated that Helen might receive as much as $800,000 from the sale of the canal property before the rest of the shareholders.[16]

Dismissing or perhaps unaware of Miles's apparent lobbying of Wells at St. Augustine, Amory complained directly and forcefully about the fiery-tempered engineer's handling of the dredging work. The work on the Matanzas Cut should have been pushed "more energetically." He hoped that the investigation of the extension north of St. Augustine to Jacksonville turned out to be thorough in determining more precisely what material had to be removed. On the two old steamers laid up for some time on a back river at Eau Gallie, Amory didn't believe that the company or anyone else would ever use them and thought they should have been disposed of long ago. To solve the canal company's persistent cash shortages, Amory suggested Miles attempt to get the promised Flagler railway notes from the sale of the Lake Worth acreage and turn them into cash to pay back Helen what she had already advanced for dredge work.[17]

A few days after Amory's letter, the overly sensitive Miles fired back. The Matanzas Cut work had been delayed quite obviously by the *Wimbee*'s destruction by fire. Moreover, he didn't want to risk the "absolute collapse" of their last dipper dredge, the *South Carolina*, which he characterized as "a very old machine," by pushing her beyond her limits. At bottom, Miles didn't believe Amory had sufficiently studied Miles's annual report. Had Amory read the report thoroughly, he would have been "perfectly aware" of the rock present in the divide. "We were handling the coquina rock cheaply and quickly with the dredge *Wimbee*, which was on a high level, with 10 feet of water under her, and able to break rock in this depth without drilling." The destruction of the *Wimbee* "upset everything" and made it necessary to employ drillers and use large quantities of dynamite exploded under two to four feet of sand and earth and in layers of rock almost ten feet deep. On the other hand, the *South Carolina*'s narrow hull prevented her from working in deep water with a long boom. Pitifully, only 900 feet of rock remained in the divide. In all, the *South Carolina* had only to dredge

---

[16]Cooper to GFM, 23 March 1907; SM to GFM, 1 April 1907; SM to AHS, 3 April 1907; all in SP Folder 24.

[17]FA to GFM, 8 April 1907 (copy), SP Folder 24.

another 1,550 feet to complete the cut, but the work proceeded slowly, painfully so. On a single day, the dredge advanced just fifty feet; on another, seventy feet.[18]

Reacting to Amory's suggestion to dispose of the two old Indian River steamers, Miles thought it bad policy to dispense with the caretakers overseeing the dredge machinery and steamers the group had bought in 1897. Their machinery and superstructure certainly could be saved. Only the hulls need be abandoned. The *St. Sebastian* cost the New England group a significant sum—about $34,000. She could be placed in working order with a new wooden hull for about $6,000 to $7,000. The *St. Augustine* could be repaired for the same amount. In the past, both Bradley and Walker had known that in buying the two old dredges they had to expect "many and serious accidents." Both understood that for $11,500 they couldn't expect that the dredges could do the work of machines that cost $70,000. In addition to "indifferent machinery," work had been plentiful in Florida but men scarce, "so much so, that in the efforts of Mr. Flagler's agents to secure laborers for the Key West extension, some of these agents are now indicted for peonage," Miles added. Insulted by Amory's criticisms, Miles thought it necessary to leave Florida and travel north to seek "a clear understanding with the Company."[19]

To make matters worse, a few days later Amory considered resigning both as president and as a director of the Florida canal company, believing Miles more useful to the enterprise. He even thought about forgetting the relatively small amount of money he had invested but decided to await "further developments" before doing so. In any event, he noticed "a committee" had been appointed during the last session of Congress to investigate the nation's inland waterways. The Florida waterway, he thought, might be "a very principal subject for consideration." Amory's reference to the creation of what would become the Inland Waterways Commission was significant. The body would play an important part in an advancing national inland waterway movement and the birth of what would become the Atlantic Intracoastal Waterway, stretching from Trenton, New Jersey, to the tip of the Florida peninsula.[20]

In the middle of April, Florida legislators began turning their attention to determining how much, if any, of the waterway had been completed under

---

[18]GFM to FA, 13 April 1907 (copy), SP Folder 25.

[19]*Ibid.*

[20]FA to SM, 18 April 1907 (copy), SP Folder 25.

the settlement made with the trustees in December 1906. Charles J. DuPont and W. A. MacWilliams, members of the state House of Representatives, formally notified Miles that a resolution had passed the Senate and was now in the House for consideration that recommended the appointment of a committee to inspect the waterway. Another representative, C.F. Ohmstead, introduced a resolution naming three members from the House and two from the Senate to inspect the canal.[21]

Toward the end of April 1907, George Bradley's nephew, J. Manton Bradley, who was working in the company's offices at St. Augustine, reported to Sawyer that he had been making tracings of all of the land maps, marking all the land owned by the canal company, including those held in escrow by Barnett. He also noted that the company's only dredge, the *South Carolina*, headed by Captain Nipson had been making good progress during the past few weeks. Less than 800 feet remained in the Matanzas Cut. Although Nipson had made significant strides in the work, he was now laid up with a bout of suspected malarial fever. Manton himself thought the divide could be eliminated in three weeks' time. Moreover, the survey north to the St. Johns River progressed favorably, and so far, no rock had been encountered.[22]

Miles, however, gave a less than enthusiastic account of the company's progress, reporting "a bad week now" and an unsatisfactory showing. A dipper-arm brace broke on the *South Carolina*, requiring several days for repairs. When she started up again, she broke a cylinder ring and bent a piston shaft, requiring still more days of repair work. Nipson then took the dredge to Palatka where he became seriously ill, probably from malaria. He then hauled the vessel to St. Augustine. Captain Gleason started south with a shaft ring and had the dredge again at work within two days. But Nipson arrived at St. Augustine from Palatka with chills and had to be hospitalized, his temperature approaching 105 degrees. Nipson's doctor thought the captain had succumbed to typhoid or malarial fever. In Miles's view, the loss of Nipson might prove to be "the worst blow" to canal operations so far. With rock work at the Matanzas nearly finished, Miles expected to send a foreman up the North (Tolomato) River to make a start there in time to comply with the Tallahassee contract for work between St. Augustine and Jacksonville. The survey between the North River (Tolomato) and Pablo Creek had

---

[21]Chas. J. Dupont and W. A. MacWilliams to GFM, 18 April 1907; C. F. Olmstead to GFM, 19 April 1907; both in SP Folder 25.

[22]J. Manton Bradley to AHS, 26 April 1907, SP Folder 25.

advanced so far that Miles now believed the company knew what sort of soil conditions it might encounter in finishing the work. Survey crews again found no rock ahead except a section of small pebbles that extended for only a short distance, which Miles believed could be easily handled by a dredge without blasting. He estimated the quantity of material to be moved in the extension to be between a million and a half and two million cubic yards.[23]

In Boston at the end of April, Amory approved paying bonuses to the men on the *South Carolina* for the extra hours spent in completing the cut. He also approved what might be construed as a "payoff" to a local legislator. He left it to Miles's discretion to determine whether or not he was satisfied that State Representative C.F. Ohmstead's "services" were worth several hundred dollars to the Florida canal company, enough to sell him eighty acres of canal land at four dollars an acre.[24]

At the beginning of summer, Miles recommended increasing Nipson's salary from $125 to $150 a month to meet a competing offer from a Charleston-area phosphate company. Nipson was to take charge of the entire dredging operation on the Jacksonville extension. He was able not only to run the machines but also to design any type of dredge needed and to build it himself. In sum, with Gleason and Nipson leading the dredging, Miles expected no trouble in the northern cut if the *Wimbee* were rebuilt and the *South Carolina* overhauled properly.[25]

The middle of June, Sawyer informed Helen Bradley that the company would not be able to pay back her $11,000 loan by selling the Flagler railway notes. Settlement of the notes had turned complicated over making them negotiable. John Dismukes, president of the First National Bank of St. Augustine, would not discount them without the negotiation feature. Stymied at first, Sawyer quickly arranged a loan through the First National Bank of Newburyport to secure enough money for the company's current expenses but not enough to pay off Helen's loan. In Florida, unaware of Sawyer's efforts, Miles had already remedied the problem. Before leaving St. Augustine for Baltimore, Flagler associates Parrott and Ingraham agreed to take deeds for Flagler's West Palm Beach land and give mortgages and ordinary promissory notes instead of the conditional paper which held up

---

[23]GFM to AHS, 26 April 1907(copy), SP Folder 25.

[24]AHS to GFM, 26 April 1907(copy); J. Manton Bradley to AHS, 19 May 1907; both in SP Folder 25.

[25]GFM to AHS, 7 June 1907, SP Folder 26.

discounting them for cash. At the Ancient City, it had been a scorcher. On Sunday, June 9, the temperature had reached 103 degrees in the shade.[26]

From his offices in Washington, Maddox reported the occurrence of a rather odd event. George Miles had just been in his office to settle an old debt. "Way back in 1887, when you were still in short clothes," Maddox rather condescendingly related to the junior Sawyer, he had loaned $2,000 to Miles's brother, W. G. Miles, who, in return, had given Maddox a mortgage on an orange grove at Seville, Florida, as security. George posted a bond to pay the loan if his brother didn't pay. Unfortunately, a severe freeze killed off all the orange trees, instantly making the Seville grove worthless. To pay off his brother's note, George Miles agreed to turn over to Maddox some of the land sales commissions the canal company owed him. Maddox thought it sufficient simply to request payment of the $2,000 from the firm's treasurer, Hayden Sawyer, charging the amount against the commissions owed Miles, and asked Sawyer to send him a check in payment of the debt.[27]

Toward the end of June, directors held a meeting at Providence at the offices of the Trust Company. Miles agreed to ask Barnett to come up to Providence or Boston to talk about providing financing. Amory still had not given up hope that Flagler might buy the company's waterway and the lands earned in the course of construction. He also believed that the federal government would inevitably acquire the Florida waterway, asserting that the government "must have it sooner or later."[28]

By the end of July, canal lands held by Maddox as trustee amounted to 47,288 acres, with only 10,000 acres mortgaged to Walker's estate, leaving 37,288 acres unencumbered and saleable. In the first part of August, Maddox attended another meeting of the trust company at Providence. It now appeared the company might advance the necessary funds to pay July expenses. "My notion is that the Bradley estate must finish the St. Johns Extension, as I told them at our Boston meeting." One of the new canal board members appointed by the trust company, P. J. Matteson, indicated that he was now against selling any land for less than what "we think it is worth." He suggested that money ought to be found to at least begin the St. Johns River extension. Herbert Wells, whom Maddox characterized as "the

[26]AHS to Mrs. George L. Bradley, 12 June 1907 (copy); GFM to AHS, 13 June 1907; both in SP Folder 26.

[27]SM to AHS, 20 June 1907, SP Folder 26.

[28]FA to SM, 27 June 1907, SP Folder 26.

big fat gentleman," was now also strongly in favor of the extension to win the Florida lands. Maddox nonetheless congratulated Wells for adding Matteson as a director to the canal company's board.[29]

Delighted that Maddox had traveled to Providence and "stirred up those dry old gentlemen," Amory hoped that the mortgage Maddox was to draw for the additional financing might meet with their approval. Miles had been in Amory's Boston office "as digressive and evasive as ever." He wanted either to go slow or stop work on the extension north of St. Augustine. But Amory believed that the money could be found to carry on the work without selling much, if any, land and estimated the land to be gained worth at least double its present value. By the middle of August, Helen Bradley had bought additional company land to enable directors to meet July expenses. But Wells, at Providence, seemed to Sawyer to be "about as much at sea as ever" on company affairs.[30]

Whether "at sea" or not, Maddox thought that unless the Bradley estate completed the St. Johns River extension, "the rest of us might as well throw up the sponge." Edwards seemed to recognize that without the extension, the estate might lose most of the estimated $560,000 Bradley had already invested in the project, perhaps as much as $400,000. By the end of August, Bradley trust officials had stopped their "hand-wringing" over the Florida waterway and took steps to authorize, for the first time, the rebuilding of the dredge *South Carolina*, which had been out of commission for almost a year, at a cost of between $7,500 and $8,000.[31]

At Providence, Wells tried to get a handle on expenses for the *South Carolina*'s reconstruction and the repair of the *Wimbee*, which he expected might total $51,000, along with some operating costs. To keep the two dredges running for six months, he thought costs might total $7,000 a month, in addition to $7,000 budgeted for miscellaneous expenses. In total, he anticipated the costs of the operation for the coming twelve months to amount to around $100,000. To extend the canal north to the St. Johns River, expenses should total at least $300,000. Miles, always underestimating the expenses in Wells's view, predicted a total cost of only $180,000. Miles had forecast the amount of material to be moved at two million cubic yards, with the

---

[29]GFM to AHS, 31 July 1907; SM to AHS, 8 August 1907; SM to GFM, 8 August 1907; all in SP Folder 26.

[30]FA to SM, 8 August 1907 (copy, with postscript to AHS); AHS to SM, 15 August 1907 (copy); both in SP Folder 26.

[31]SM to AHS, 16 August 1907; Wells (RIHTC) to AHS, 20 August 1907; both in SP Folder 26.

work consuming only 606 days or less than two years to dredge the extension.[32]

The beginning of October, Bradley's trustees authorized advancing $100,000 to complete the St. Johns River extension. Maddox believed that once the trust company started down the road of financing the completion, it could not stop without finishing it. Barnett thought that with the right machinery the cut to the St. Johns River could be made in one year.[33]

Wells made it clear that he did not want the Florida canal company to call on the Providence trust company to pay September expenses. Sawyer called instead on Helen Bradley for $6,000. Although disappointed with the request, thinking last month's payment would be the last, she sent Sawyer a check for $6,000, requesting payment in land rather than company paper. Maddox, as surviving trustee of the Maddox-Sawyer trust lands, transferred 1,749 acres of Brevard County land to Helen in payment of her loans which now totaled $35,000.[34]

Directors now began the process of gathering information on setting tolls along the waterway, soon to stretch the length of the peninsula from Jacksonville to Miami. At the end of October, Miles traveled to Philadelphia to meet with officials of the privately-owned Delaware and Chesapeake Canal Company to discuss the toll issue and to gather information. Just as important, the Florida canal company ordered two new excavators from the Hayward Company to dredge the St. Johns extension. On a cheery note, Sawyer expected George Bradley's investment in the Automatic Clerk Company, a New Jersey firm that manufactured chewing gum vending machines, initially thought defunct, would eventually become profitable. The company, founded in 1902, was now generating earnings of $5,000 a month. If earnings kept on at the same pace, Sawyer anticipated the resumption of the payment of dividends within a year.[35]

The Florida canal company and the Rhode Island Hospital Trust Company now embarked on a large-scale plan to finance construction of the waterway and collect the hundreds of thousands of acres earned in dredg-

---

[32]Wells to AHS, 28 August 1907, SP Folder 26.

[33]SM to AHS, 3 October 1907, SP Folder 26.

[34]AHS to Mrs. George L. Bradley, 8 October 1907; Helen McH. Bradley to AHS, 10 October 1907; SM to AHS, 9 October 1907; GFM to AHS, 18 October 1907; all in SP Folder 26.

[35]GFM to AHS, 23 October 1907; AHS to Wells, 28 October 1907; AHS to Mrs. George L. Bradley, 31 October 1907 (copy); all in SP Folder 26. 'Incorporated in New Jersey [Automatic Clerk Company]," *New York Times*, 29 May 1902.

ing it since 1882. Acceding to the plan Sawyer had floated months earlier, on November 1, 1907, the Florida canal company issued $500,000 worth of bonds. This amounted to a transfer, in total, of 492 $1,000 bonds to Bradley's trust and eight to Helen Bradley, secured by a first lien on all of the company's assets, including the waterway and the state land grants. At the same time, Miles traveled to Philadelphia to find out whether he might be able to read a paper on the Florida project before an assembly that would become pivotal in the development of the modern Atlantic Intracoastal Waterway. Capping an inland waterway movement gathering steam with each passing month, the Atlantic Deeper Waterways Conference, organized by Congressman Joseph Hampton Moore, was to convene on November 19 or 20 at Philadelphia. By November 15, Miles had returned and found the conference likely to be "a large and important gathering." He had also been chosen by Governor Napoleon Bonaparte Broward to serve as Florida's delegate to the assembly. Enclosing a letter from Moore, he urged Sawyer to read it and "from it you will see that something is doing." Something indeed was "doing." Along the entire Atlantic coast from Maine to Florida, the movement continued to gather enough steam to dramatically affect the improvement of inland waterways, including the Florida project, for at least the next forty years. [36]

---

[36]Bill of Complaint, and, Report of Special Master, *Rhode Island Hospital Trust Company, etc. vs. Florida Coast Line Canal and Transportation Company, et. al.,* Chancery Case No. 1408, St. Johns County Circuit Court, filed June 28, 1923. GFM to AHS, 12, 15 November 1907, SP Folder 27.

Chapter 12

The Philadelphian

In 1907, spurred on by an inland waterways movement sweeping the country, 43-year-old Joseph Hampton Moore, a first-term Philadelphia congressman, began organizing what would become the Atlantic Deeper Waterways Association to lobby Congress for waterway improvements along the Atlantic coast, including the nearly completed Florida waterway. The impetus behind the association was a three-day meeting Moore headed in November at Philadelphia's newly-built Hotel Bellevue-Stratford, now the Park Hyatt Philadelphia, at Broad and Walnut Streets. Along with delegates from Arkansas and Washington, D.C., representatives from fifteen states along the Atlantic seaboard from Maine to Florida gathered at the Atlantic Deeper Waterways Conference. At the opening dinner held on November 18, more than 500 conferees dined on cleverly-named Atlantic coast fare such as Cape Cod Oysters, Connecticut Kingfish with South Carolina Sauce, and Florida Tomato and Delaware

Joseph Hampton Moore, considered the father of the modern Atlantic Intracoastal Waterway, in his first term as a Philadelphia congressman Moore spearheaded the formation of the Atlantic Deeper Waterways Association in 1907 to promote the waterway's creation and presided over the organization until 1947. After serving in Congress from 1906 until 1920, Moore served as mayor of Philadelphia from 1920 until 1923 and again from 1932 until 1935. He died in 1950. (Gutekunst, n.d., Society Portrait Collection, The Historical Society of Pennsylvania)

Lettuce. Among Florida's representatives were Bion Barnett, William J. Bryan and Charles Cooper, all three important supporters of the state's waterway, as well as Tallahassee Congressman and former Florida Attorney General William B. Lamar of Tallahassee. Congressman Stephen Mallory of Pensacola also attended.[1]

Rounding out the list of guests at the first conference was none other than the canal company's former president and long-time general manager, George Francis Miles. At the Wednesday session, just before lunch, Miles was to deliver a speech entitled, "Inland Waterways from the Florida Viewpoint," which included a review of what was now called the Florida East Coast Canal, but a bad cold prevented him from speaking loud enough to be heard and another delegate read the speech for him. Three days later, Moore announced the formation of the Atlantic Deeper Waterways Association, listing Miles as a vice president representing Florida. For the next decade, Miles would represent both Florida and the canal company at the association's large annual meetings, routinely delivering papers on the waterway's progress. For four more decades, the association would convene each year to make plans to lobby Congress to fund what would become known as the Atlantic Intracoastal Waterway.[2]

Born on March 8, 1864, in Woodbury, New Jersey, after attending school there and studying law, Moore served as a reporter at the *Philadelphia Public Ledger and the Court Combination* for thirteen years from 1881 until 1894 when he became chief clerk to the city treasurer of Philadelphia, serving for three years. In 1900, Moore became secretary to the mayor and served as city treasurer from 1901 until 1903. In January 1905, President Theodore Roosevelt appointed the fast-rising Moore to serve as the first chief of the Bureau of Manufactures of the Department of Commerce and Labor, but Moore resigned after six months to become president of a Philadelphia trust company. After serving as a member of Congress from November 6, 1906, until his resignation on January 4, 1920, Moore was elected mayor of Philadelphia and served in that office for the next three years.[3]

In his first term in Congress, Moore tried but failed to secure passage of a measure to deepen the lower Delaware River to thirty-five feet. The fresh-

---

[1]Formal Invitation, "Atlantic Deeper Waterways Conference, Philadelphia, November 18th, 19th, 20th 1907, Hotel Bellevue-Stratford," Folder November 16-20, 1907; "Program, Atlantic Deeper Waterways Conference," and "The Atlantic Deeper Waterways Association, Philadelphia, Nov. 21, 1907," open letter, in Society and Miscellaneous Collection, Atlantic Deeper Waterways Conference, Box 8B, Folder 10, JHMP.

[2]*Ibid.*

[3]"Moore, Joseph Hampton," *Biographical Dictionary of the American Congress, 1774-1949*, 1582.

man congressman, however, would not be deterred. In an October 1907 speech before the Trenton, New Jersey Chamber of Commerce entitled, "The Scope of the Conference," Moore called for the immediate organization of a deeper waterways association along the entire Atlantic coast. He concluded that the scope of the proposed gathering might be summed up in one word, "Agitation." The improvement of inland waterways was "government work," Moore argued, but the government must have "inspiration, and that inspiration must come from the persistent agitation of earnest men." "Let us have a broader conference than that called by the Chamber of Commerce of Trenton. Let us invite the Governors of the various states affected to send representatives to such a conference." Immediately following Moore's remarks, the assembly, comprised of representatives of various Pennsylvania, New Jersey and Delaware business groups, passed a resolution calling for "a general conference of commercial bodies along the Atlantic coast" to which the governors of the coastal states were asked to send official representatives.[4]

A month before the Trenton speech, Moore had begun corresponding with a North Carolina congressman, John Humphrey Small, a Democrat and a strong proponent of federal inland waterway improvements along the Atlantic coast, particularly those contemplated between Norfolk and Beaufort, North Carolina. Small sent Moore publications on the proposed improvements along the Virginia-North Carolina coast, including an article written by Small that appeared in the August 1907 issue of *World's Work* magazine. Small congratulated Moore for his interest in improving inland waterways and endorsed the federal government's purchase of the privately-owned Chesapeake and Delaware Canal as well as its acquisition of New Jersey's Delaware and Raritan Canal. Moore and Small soon became close friends in the inland waterways movement and the most important figures in the creation of the Atlantic Intracoastal Waterway.[5]

Born in Washington, North Carolina, the 49-year-old Small—six years older than his Republican counterpart—had taught school, practiced law, served as superintendent of public instruction in Beaufort, edited and run the local Washington (North Carolina) *Gazette* newspaper, and served as mayor, all before his election to Congress on the Democratic ticket, representing Beaufort County in 1899. Small would serve ten terms in that posi-

---

[4]Burk, Addison B, Secretary (ADWA), "History of Atlantic Deeper Waterways Association, Extract from summary of Atlantic Deeper Waterways Conference, Philadelphia, November 18, 19th and 20th, 1907," Folder November16-20, 1907, JHMP.

[5]Small to Moore, 30 September 1907, Folder June 1-Sept. 30, 1907, JHMP.

tion until his defeat in 1920. In 1917, he became chairman of the prestigious Committee on Rivers and Harbors, the holder of the purse strings over appropriations for inland waterway improvements along the Atlantic coast and the rest of the country. Two years later, no longer chairman of the waterways committee, Small became president of the National Rivers and Harbors Congress, leading this important and influential organization until 1940. During his twenty years as a congressman, Small, like Moore, became a leading expert on the nation's inland waterways. He pushed bills appropriating funds for improvements in the inland waterway connections along the Atlantic coast, especially between Norfolk and Beaufort. Although Small wouldn't see that section's completion until after he left government service, he did see that section improved, even the entire Atlantic Intracoastal Waterway completed, by the time he ended his service as president of the National Rivers and Harbors Congress.[6]

A renewed interest in inland waterways created what might be described as a national renaissance in waterway improvements at the turn of the century. In 1903, New York residents voted to spend $101 million to transform the old Erie Canal system into the New York State Barge Canal. Four years later, President Theodore Roosevelt appointed members to the Inland Waterways Commission to study and report on the nation's inland waterways. Along the Atlantic Coast, New Jersey's Delaware and Raritan Canal, the Chesapeake and Delaware Canal, Virginia's Albemarle and Chesapeake Canal, along with the Dismal Swamp Canal, represented important privately owned toll ways, each imposing a different schedule of charges.[7]

At the grassroots level, no fewer than thirty-five citizens groups, including the National Rivers and Harbors Congress (1901) and the Atlantic Deeper Waterways Association (1907), came together to lobby Congress to embark on a massive program of inland waterway improvements. Attending the first meeting of the National Rivers and Harbors Congress held at Johns Hopkins University in October 1901 was none other than Jacksonville

[6]"Small, John Humphrey," *Biographical Dictionary of the American Congress, 1774-1949*, 1822. Watson, *John Humphrey Small*, 1, 103, 110. Watson's unpublished thesis represents an important source of information about Small's life and career and the pivotal role the North Carolina congressman played in the creation of the Atlantic Intracoastal Waterway. The work draws heavily on the Small Papers at both Duke University and the University of North Carolina, Chapel Hill.

[7]Association of American Railroads, 7; Moulton, *Waterways*, 3. U. S. Inland Waterways Commission, 310-11. ADWA, 25th Annual Convention (October 1932):73-74.

banker Daniel G. Ambler—the Florida canal company's first private banker in the early years. Ambler not only represented his home state but also served as the state's only representative on the Committee on Organization and Rules. In 1906, five years after the first national waterway convocation, two more important waterway meetings convened—the St. Louis Convention, which led to the formation of the Lakes-to-Gulf Deep Waterway Association, and the Washington Session of the National Rivers and Harbors Congress, which persuaded President Theodore Roosevelt to appoint the Inland Waterways Commission. At the Washington Session, Ambler again served as Florida's sole representative, with the meeting ending in the NHRC's reorganization. A second meeting took place ten and a half months later at the nation's capital with 58 cities, 29 states, 161 organizations, and 2,708 attending. Stephen Sparkman, a Tampa congressman, attended as state vice president. An important purpose of this organization was to demand that Congress appropriate not less than $50 million annually for a period of ten years for the improvement of the nation's inland waterways. The budget request—an "all-for-one, one-for-all" proposition—united many of the smaller regional organizations like Moore's ADWA in making requests for the nation's inland waterway projects. In 1907 the second Lakes-to-the-Gulf convention, headed by Missouri's William Kavanaugh, assembled at Memphis. This group, whose motto was "River Regulation is Rate Regulation," advocated improvements in the Mississippi River and its tributaries. Florida's Governor Broward joined seventeen other state governors as a member of the Lakes group's advisory board.[8]

Why had so many citizen's groups come together to press Congress for waterway improvements? The railroad industry's monopoly over the nation's transportation system was one motivation. A second was a transportation need greater than what the railroads could meet. The Inland Waterways Commission, in its report to Congress in 1908, found that "railway interests have been successfully directed against the normal maintenance and development of water traffic by control of water-fronts and terminals, by acquisition or control of competing canals and vessels, by discriminating tariffs, by rebates, by adverse placement of tracks and structures, and by other means." Among many other measures, the commission recommended improvements in the nation's inland waterways, including the development of the Mississippi River and the construction of an Atlantic

---

[8]Moulton, *Waterways*, 1-4. NHRC, 8-9 October 1901:8; NRHC, 15-16 January 1906:23; NRHC, 6-7 December 1906:4, 35. Lakes-To-The-Gulf.

coast inland waterway. From this point forward, improvements in the nation's inland waterways would no longer be made predominantly by private companies monopolizing inland waterways, but by the federal government slowly and deliberately meeting waterway transportation needs with taxpayers' funds.[9]

A few days after the November 1907 conference in Philadelphia, George Miles arrived at Baltimore after a trip through the privately owned Chesapeake and Delaware Canal with the president of the company. The Atlantic Deeper Waterways Conference, Miles reported, had been "a much larger and more important affair" than he had anticipated, with more than 500 guests and a large number of congressmen and senators attending. An attempt had been made to limit recommended waterway improvements to the Atlantic coast between Boston and Beaufort, but as a member of the Committee on Resolutions and by influencing some New York and "Carolina" congressmen, Miles succeeded in enlarging the group's recommendations to include "the whole coast from Boston to Key West." He planned to return to Philadelphia to discuss future ADWA policies with Moore. Although unable to deliver his own speech at the conference, Miles boasted that following its reading, Senator Francis Newlands of Nevada, chairman of the Inland Waterways Commission, said that he had "no idea that the new waterway was such a large and important concern" and "half promised" that he would visit the Florida project. Almost parenthetically, Miles reported to company directors that he had been appointed by Governor Broward as a delegate to the National Rivers and Harbors Congress to be held at Washington, on December 4, 5, and 6.[10]

By the first of December, Miles returned from a three-day trip down the Florida waterway rather tired. A new dock for the start of the extension canal appeared well constructed, but between the waterway and the dock, the *South Carolina* struck running sand, stalling her repeatedly. After a few days in the Sunshine State, Miles left for a three-day meeting of the NRHC, still suffering from the lingering cold that had kept him from reading his speech at the Philadelphia conference.[11]

On December 4, Miles joined nearly 2,000 delegates representing 463 cities in thirty-three states attending the National Rivers and Harbors Congress at

---

[9]Johnson, *Transportation by Water*, 546. "$200,000,000 for Waterways," *New York Times*, 21 October 1907, 12, column 1. U. S. Inland Waterways Commission, 19.

[10]GFM to AHS, 23 November 1907, SP Folder 27.

[11]GFM to AHS, 1 December 1907, SP Folder 27.

the nation's capital. Prominent among those attending were twenty-three governors and fifty-one mayors. Another Florida representative was Tampa congressman Stephen M. Sparkman. Four years later, Sparkman presided as chairman of the powerful House of Representatives' rivers and harbors committee and represented Florida at the opening of the first link in the Atlantic Intracoastal Waterway system from Maine to Florida on the banks of the waterway near Beaufort, North Carolina. Miles heard "some very good speeches" at the conference, but, all in all, he reported back to his New England colleagues, the NHRC seemed to be paying more attention to proposed improvements in the Mississippi River than to needed changes elsewhere and he thought Moore's Atlantic Deeper Waterways group more important to the Florida canal company's nearly complete waterway.[12]

Back in St. Augustine, Miles's cold seemed much better. His doctor, however, placed him under severe restrictions that allowed him to go outside for only a few hours each day. Despite this limitation, he concerned himself with work on the new dredges. With both 54-foot booms for the two new excavators already built, work had begun on the frames. Miles planned to have all of the timber in place and bored for bolts for assembly at St. Augustine. But the engines and the large steel buckets for the two excavators hadn't yet arrived. Miles had warned the manufacturer, the Hayward Company, that time was critical in providing the machinery. Finally, by December 20, nearly five weeks behind schedule, the Hayward Company had shipped all of the machinery for the excavators, excusing the delay on providing stronger and better machinery than what the specifications called for, which Miles admitted was true. Nevertheless, the Hayward Company's tardiness in sending the drawings for the frames had kept Miles from assembling the lumber for them and put the project significantly behind schedule.[13]

Early February 1908, Miles saw no possibility of the excavators being in operation before his return to the North and predicted that it would take at least three weeks before the machines actually began digging in the northern extension. His assistant, George Gleason, made plans to run the excava-

---

[12]"All Canal Plans To Have Fair Show," *New York Times*, 5 December 1907, p. 2, col. 5. NRHC, 4-6 December 1907: 3; "Rivers and Harbors," *Tampa Tribune*, reprinted in *Miami Metropolis*, 8 November 1911; Rerick, *Memoirs*, I; 385, 390-91. "Maine to Florida Waterways Route," *Everglade Magazine* (February 1911):4, reporting an undated article appearing in the *Florida Times-Union*. "Open New Canal For Use Of Trade," *New York Times*, 30 July 1914, p. 6, col. 2. GFM to AHS, 8 December 1907, SP Folder 27.

[13]GFM to AHS, 14, 20, 23 December 1907, SP Folder 27.

tors day and night. Gleason obtained a large amount of information on lighting systems, thinking an acetylene gas-generating lighting system on the excavators would faciltiate this around-the-clock schedule. At North (Tolomato) River work with Gleason, carpenters had been busy erecting portable houses for the men and getting a camp into shape. Captain Spiers, who for years served as first mate on one of the Indian River steamers, superintended construction, which ran day and night. Despite the steady progress, the delays annoyed Miles's New England colleagues, prompting one to criticize the lack of progress. "It seems to me that the enterprise now is afflicted with too many superintendents and that we sadly lack conscientious, capable workmen," Hayden Sawyer commented from Boston.[14]

Around the middle of February, a launch from Jupiter arrived at St. Augustine with excavator machinery. Spiers filled two lighters to take the rest of the excavator machinery on a single trip. To improve the *South Carolina*'s performance, he decided to put in the large engines from the old *Biscayne* and install a three-cubic-yard dipper, with more timber needed in the hull. Within days, the two last lighter loads of excavator machinery went up to the head of the North (Tolomato) River. Gleason returned from the *South Carolina*, reporting that its boiler, which had been taken from the old steamer *St. Augustine*, was not only too small to operate a three-yard dipper but weak in several places.[15]

On February 24, 1908, company directors met at the offices of the Rhode Island Hospital Trust Company and approved Miles's schedule of tolls for the waterway. Although not immediately implemented, the tolls, when collected, would never amount to much for almost twenty years. At the end of February, the dipper dredge *South Carolina* was under repair at an improvised dry dock twenty-five miles south of St. Augustine. Carpenters from Merrill-Stevens, a Jacksonville shipbuilding firm, were doing the wood work while Captain Nipson overhauled the machinery. One of the Bradley trust's engineering consultants, Frank W. Hodgdon, attempted to retain a dredging expert to look over the canal company's work for the estate. Like John Freeman, Hodgdon was a nationally known engineer. In a few years' time, Hodgdon would become a consulting engineer supervising the construction of the Cape Cod Canal, completed in 1914.

---

[14]AHS to Wells, 9 February 1908 (copy), SP Folder 27.
[15]GFM to AHS, 17, 20 February 1908, SP Folder 27.

At the same time, Fred Amory and the trust company's representative, Herbert Wells, decided on March 16 as the best date for a trip down the waterway. They hoped that the ADWA's Moore and other congressmen might be able to join them on this adventure and see the tremendous progress that had been made. Sawyer also hoped to be there. In St. Augustine, Miles remained in close contact with the ADWA gathering momentum and strength every day along the Atlantic coast from Boston to Miami. He wrote to Moore to invite the Philadelphia congressman to tour the Florida waterway, which was nearing completion. [16]

As Moore began formulating his plans, he also considered inviting Louisiana Congressman Joseph Ransdell, president of the National Rivers and Harbors Congress, and North Carolina Congressman John Small to join the waterway tour. Miles informed Moore that Jacksonville board of trade members expressed considerable interest in his proposed trip and assured him of a warm welcome there. Confident that Savannah would be equally interested, Miles already had taken steps to "wake up" the Brunswick people too. He knew also that St. Augustine and the smaller towns along the Florida east coast would take a keen interest in the ADWA movement. His plan was for Moore to come directly to St. Augustine around the middle of the month. He would then take him down the inland waterway on a four-day trip to Miami. From Miami, Moore could return either by boat or by rail to the Ancient City where he could address the local board of trade on the waterway movement. For the trip back to Philadelphia, Miles suggested a trip by boat inside the Atlantic coast to Brunswick, Georgia, with an intervening stop at Jacksonville for a board of trade talk and perhaps additional stops farther north at Savannah and Charleston. An added attraction of an arrival at St. Augustine was an opportunity to meet the Florida canal company's directors, whom Miles described as "influential men" from Rhode Island and Massachusetts interested in the development of the nation's inland waterways.[17]

---

[16]Unsigned minutes of meeting of board of directors of Canal Company dated February 27, 1908, approving tolls at a meeting held on February 24, 1908, but confirmed in AHS to GFM, 27 February 1908 (copy), SP Folder 27. AHS to Frank W. Hodgdon, 28 February 1908 (copy); AHS to GFM, 28 February 1908 (copy); both in SP Folder 27. "Frank W. Hodgdon, Engineer," *New York Times*, 27 January 1923.

[17]Moore to GFM, 24 February 1908, Folder February 20-24, 1908; GFM to Moore, 2 March 1908, Folder March 1-3, 1908; GFM to Moore (Telegrams), 26 and 27 March 1908; GFM to Moore, 26 March 1908; Addison Burke to Moore, 26 March 1908; Wm. B. Stillwell (Savannah Board of Trade) to Goodyear, 27 March 1908; all in Folder March 24-27, 1908; John Small to Col. C. P. Goodyear (Copy), 29 March 1908, Folder March 28-31; all folders in JHMP. See, also, J. Hampton Moore (ADWA) to GFM, 17 February 1908 (copied on Canal Company stationery), SP Folder 27.

On March 28, 1908, the dream of a modern federally-sponsored and continuous Atlantic Intracoastal Waterway came partially into existence when Moore introduced a resolution in the House of Representatives calling for a inland waterway survey from Boston to Beaufort Inlet. Almost immediately after filing the measure, Moore left Washington to join George Miles for a cruise down the Florida East Coast Canal from St. Augustine to Miami. Joining them on the trip were the ADWA's treasurer, Addison Burke; Wayne Cunningham, a prominent Savannah Harbor contractor; and W. D. Barnett, brother of Bion Barnett; as well as Colonel Lansing Beach, Florida chief of the U. S. army engineers. Arriving at Miami on Monday, March 30, the group left at noon aboard the launch *Truant* for a cruise headed north, reaching Fort Lauderdale late in the afternoon. After supper, they traveled up the New River Canal to view the dredges working to drain the Everglades. Late in the evening, members returned to Fort Lauderdale for a night's rest. At six o'clock the next morning, Miles's group continued their journey along the waterway north to Lake Worth, returning by train to Jacksonville from Palm Beach.[18]

On Thursday afternoon, April 2, after arriving at Jacksonville, Miles's guests cruised aboard the handsome yacht *Harmar*, owned by Harold Weston. Now joined by Jacksonville's Mayor Sebring, Bion Barnett, and Governor Broward, the entourage spent Thursday afternoon cruising the St. John's River, exploring four possible routes to connect the Florida waterway with Jacksonville. The company's survey showed that construction of the waterway via the Pablo Creek route might result in a savings of between $150,000 and $200,000 over what it would cost to dredge any other route. Fifty-six-year-old William Alsop Bours, president of the Jacksonville board of trade, called a meeting of the members to order at eight o'clock that Thursday evening to hear Moore express his views. Promoting the virtues of a connected Atlantic inland waterway, he expounded on the beauty of the Florida waterway, telling the crowd that "[i]f a man needs inspiration he needs only to spend four days along the East Coast canal, as I have just done. Why, if the beauty of that canal was fully appreciated in the north, I dare say that next season would find the waterway jammed with craft laden with pleasure-seekers." Comparing the Florida waterway to the gargantuan federally funded Panama Canal project then under way, he added, "I

---

[18]Concurrent Resolution Number 35, 60th Cong., 1st Session; see, also, ADWA, October 1932:74, for a good legislative history of the Atlantic Intracoastal Waterway. "Members of the Deep Waterway Com's'n Deeply Interested," *Miami Metropolis*, 1 April 1908.

think that it would be advantageous to the builders of the Panama canal to see the way the East Coast canal has been built. I am sure money and time could be saved by the experience." The next morning, Moore left Jacksonville for Savannah where he was to give another speech to the board of trade there. He was the movement's most articulate and active booster and he had a message he wanted to share. Georgia, like Florida, had much to gain from an inland waterway.[19]

On April 8, just six days after his Jacksonville speech, Moore, Small and four more inland waterway boosters, met with President Theodore Roosevelt in Washington to discuss the "project of a great inland waterway from Boston to Key West." Roosevelt publicly expressed his general support for the improvement of the nation's inland waterways. That same day, Small, Moore's mentor in the waterway movement, introduced another resolution in the House to survey the section from Beaufort Inlet to Key West. With both Moore's and Small's resolutions now in the House, the monumental project could now begin. For the next twenty-seven years, the influential pair's schemes for waterway funding would spur a series of Army Corps of Engineers studies of the Florida waterway and other privately owned canals along the Atlantic coast, culminating in 1935 in the completion of the Atlantic Intracoastal Waterway, extending from Trenton to Miami.[20]

Meanwhile, Miles closed a real estate deal with an important Jacksonville landowner named Pitt. He now had the deeds to all of the right-of-way for a waterway between the North (Tolomato) River and Pablo Creek, and hoped to secure similar rights through the Pablo Marshes without any serious trouble. Miles described Pitt as "a most ardent canal man and talks of doing wonderful things with his large tracts of land bordering the canal," an expanse of property he estimated amounted to some 23,000 acres between St. Augustine and Jacksonville. Pitt also sent Miles a letter written to him nine years before, in 1899, by Brigadier General Alexander MacKenzie, then Army Chief of Engineers, which ordered that the bridges across Pablo Creek be put in such a condition as to allow navigation. Miles thought this meant the federal government's recognition of the creek as navigable water — good news for the canal company. If true, Miles foresaw little

[19]"Coast Line Canal To Be Discussed," *Florida Times-Union*, 2 April 1908; "Waterways Men Address Meeting," *Florida Times-Union*, 3 April 1908.
[20]"Boston to Key West Via Inland Route," *Florida Times-Union*, 9 April 1908; Concurrent Resolution Number 39, 60th Cong., 1st Sess.

trouble in demanding drawbridges at both the railroad and county road crossings for their waterway.[21]

Isaac Calderwood, another Bradley trust engineer, and the canal company's Gleason returned from the excavators. The 36-year-old Calderwood, then superintending dredging work for the St. Lawrence River Power Company, seemed satisfied with the work, but reported an excavator boom broke trying to lift a large palmetto stump out of a cut. He thought the weakness in design could be overcome by making side braces. In Miles's opinion, the break had been caused by a weakness in design developed by the Hayward Company. Although the excavator's repair was not to delay them more than one or two days, Miles entertained grave doubts over ordering two more Hayward excavators. In his opinion, Calderwood did not know what kind of conditions might prevail when normal rainfall returned. Although it had been dry for eighteen months, returning rain would seriously hinder the removal of tree stumps along the way. The only way to remove the stumps economically was by first breaking them up with dynamite and then burning the remnants by heaping fuel on them and setting them on fire. But burning couldn't be done if the land were underwater. Because it was necessary to remove all obstructions for excavators to work effectively, nothing but a dipper dredge could be relied upon to do the work for a considerable portion of the route. On some sections along the line of the waterway, there were stands of cypress trees nearly a hundred feet high with large stumps, which even in the dry season were partly submerged. In Miles's opinion, only a dipper dredge could cope with these stumps easily and economically.[22]

Around the first of April, both Sawyer and Amory, after consultation with Wells, rejected Miles's advice and instructed the St. Augustine office to order two more excavators. Calderwood had returned from the North (Tolomato) River after surveying the proposed northern line of the canal with James Colee, one of the canal company's original directors and long-time engineer on the ground. The canal company could get out of the swamp by moving the line either to the west or east of the present location but Miles was not certain this was feasible. He believed the original line, had been well located as long as machines of the type they had expected to use were employed on the work. In any event, he promised to have another

---

[21]GFM to FA, 28 March 1908 (copy), SP Folder 27.

[22]*Ibid.*, On Calderwood's life, see "Bits of Stone," *The Daily Times* (Maryville, Tennesee), 14 August 2005.

Dipper dredge in the southern reaches of the Florida East Coast Canal (Intracoastal Waterway) in Delray Beach or Boynton Beach, early 1900s. (Courtesy, Florida State Archives, Florida Photographic Collection, Tallahassee, Florida)

survey made in hopes that Calderwood might be right. If Calderwood proved to be correct, Miles conceded the excavators could cut a longer section of the waterway than Miles ever thought they could. The line, as originally located, would minimize the cutting as long as the operation avoided cypress stumps so that excavators could be used instead of a dipper dredge. On the other hand, the line suggested by Calderwood would result in more material being moved because it was higher than land along the present line. In short, Miles urged that the dredging operation stick to the present line. They could send the *South Carolina* around to the St. Johns River and allow her to work her way south. Workers could get at the cypress stumps with a dipper machine and finish the southern portion of the work with the *Tomoka* and the excavators.[23]

In April 1908, longtime West Palm Beach real estate agent W. L. Bragg informed the company of his interest in building a road in the southern part of the state from Lake Worth west to the old Military Trail, which ran south through Dade County. The amount of land he asked for did not amount to

---

[23] AHS to Wells, 2 April 1908 (copy), GFM to AHS, 6 April 1908; both in SP Folder 28.

much and there was no doubt that the road "will give some impetus to the settlement of the country lying west of the fresh water lakes," Miles confirmed. The canal company owned two square miles of land affected to some extent by the proposed road and had been asked to contribute only 113 acres. At the same time, Excavator Number 1 worked steadily in the northern extension, but had not been able to remove as much material as had been expected. She moved sand, but the points of her bucket did not penetrate the material easily. A new boom on Excavator Number 2 had been installed. Miles hoped that she could return to work soon. With the arrival of an acetylene gas generator to light the dredge work at night, Miles telegraphed the lighting company's engineer with orders to install the equipment. Miles promised his colleagues, "We shall then run the machines night and day."[24]

And night and day they would run.

---

[24]GFM to AHS, 9 April 1908, SP Folder 28.

Chapter 13

Almost There

The middle of April 1908, a shortage of workers to clear canal right-of-way between Saint Augustine and Jacksonville forced Florida canal company officials to fall back on Italians and Greeks, George Miles claimed, arguing that he had been unable to hire black laborers at "anything like reasonable wages" for the northern extension work. He immediately hired twenty-five Greek and Italian workers. If these men performed well, he planned to hire twenty-five more. The downside was that hiring more men required building more housing. Miles decided to transport the machinery as well as lumber for the frames for the two additional excavators from Jacksonville down to Pablo Creek, and then to the station where the excavators were to be built. George Gleason, Miles's assistant, located a boat about forty feet long with a small engine at a cost of $350 to haul supplies on Pablo Creek. To clear the right-of-way and haul supplies from Pablo Creek to the new excavators, Miles also needed a couple of horses or mules. He considered it cheaper to buy the animals than to hire them by the day, estimating a pair of mules might cost $500. The outlook for Florida real estate looked dim, however. As a result of a depression in the naval stores market, pine land prices continued to fall, further dampening the canal company's prospects for land sales to fund the northern waterway extension.[1]

Meanwhile, Gleason asked for changes in the two new excavators, including added weight in the buckets and substitution of steel booms for wood at an additional cost of around $300. To operate excavators six miles apart, the company also needed depots at both points stocked with gasoline, provisions and other supplies. With twenty-six Greeks and Italians at work, Miles hoped to employ forty or fifty more.[2]

Miles suggested to Sawyer that he might run up to New York to check with the Hayward Company's offices about the two additional excavators

---

[1]GFM to AHS, 13 April 1908, SP Folder 28.
[2]GFM to AHS, 15 April 1908, SP Folder 28.

the canal company had ordered, since he thought the Hayward firm had been trying to run up the price on the two excavators after Gleason's suggested changes. Hayward had wired a price of $8,290 for the machinery with the requested changes, but if the company wanted friction instead of jaw clutches, the cost increased by $470. At the same time, an acetylene gas company employee was installing gas lights on the first two excavators where double crews would soon be digging, night and day.[3]

In Boston, both Sawyer and Amory liked Miles's proposal to hire Greek and Italian laborers for the northern extension work and encouraged him to hire twice as many more. In Florida, though, the buckets on the first two excavators had been doing poor work, coming up with little more than half, and sometimes a third, of the anticipated load, which Miles attributed to the character of the material dredged, not the excavators' operators. He regretted ordering two additional excavators much too hastily. He also disagreed with Isaac Calderwood's (the Bradley trust's engineer) recommendation that the name of the *South Carolina* be changed. For his part, Miles argued that the *South Carolina* in "a crippled state" had performed well finishing the lower reaches of the Florida waterway, with much of the hull still in good condition. He saw no chance of any confusion in retaining her name. He also suggested a change in the northern extension work, recommending first taking off the top of each cut and removing palmetto and other stumps as the excavators moved back, and wherever the excavators found a section where the buckets could be filled up, they could dig to grade. But where the excavator work proved unfavorable, the machines should move on, with the suction dredge *Tomoka* moving the intransigent material instead. If the *Tomoka* wasn't able to handle that material, the company could rely on the old, reconditioned *South Carolina*. Toward the end of April, the enterprise had fifty-two men clearing the right-of-way north of St. Augustine. Miles had been negotiating with a large landowner named Pitt to haul lumber and machinery for the new excavators in lighters from Jacksonville up Pablo Creek to the landing where Pitt owned a turpentine distillery. Miles once again criticized the decision to use excavators over standard dredges. The excavators had to be hauled over uneven ground and placed on rails. Standard dredges, which moved on water, did not need to be relocated over indifferent roads.[4]

---

[3] GFM to AHS, 17 April 1908 (copy), SP Folder 28.

[4] AHS to GFM, 18 April 1908 (copy); GFM to AHS, 22 April 1908 (copy); both in SP Folder 28.

From Boston, Sawyer joined in the criticism of the excavators, remarking to Herbert Wells that the excavators ought to be doing better than 10,000 cubic yards a month in one twelve-hour shift. In Washington, Maddox had been ailing with a bad case of ptomaine poisoning, which forced him out of the office for a least a week. Sawyer hoped that a brewing disagreement over the new 1907 bonds could be settled when Maddox returned to work. Before turning over the new bonds to Wells for waterway construction advances, a release had to be executed by the Washington-based American Security & Trust Company for the 1903 bonds, which Maddox was to secure.[5]

In Florida, wages for the right-of-way men in the northern extension dropped to $1.25 a day, with the men paying for their own food. The company had built a commissary and issued checks which, when used for food and other supplies, were deducted from employee wages.[6]

The beginning of May, Miles tried out a pair of mules, which could be bought for $400, for use in clearing the right-of-way. With wagon and harness thrown in, the cost rose to $495. He had experienced little success in securing an independent contractor to clear the right-of-way north. The size and type of timber that lay ahead frightened off nearly all of the contractors that hoped to bid on the work. The only bid at first was $125 an acre, which Miles did not take seriously. The two excavators at work still had been having difficulty moving the packed sand in the cut and couldn't pick up full buckets. If the company didn't strike better material soon, the work would prove more expensive than Calderwood had estimated, Miles argued. For a time, the dredging seemed to improve somewhat. Excavator No. 2 moved ahead forty-seven feet on double crews during a 24-hour period. Excavator No. 1 made twenty-eight feet on a single 12-hour shift. Crews couldn't work double shifts on Excavator No. 1 until the tracks were built to move the machine easily. Moreover, heavy standing timber ahead posed a serious obstacle. Early May, Miles received a bid of $79 an acre to clear the right-of-way and asked for authority to accept the bid if he couldn't get a better price.[7]

---

[5]AHS to Wells, 23 April 1908 (copy), SP Folder 28.
[6]GFM to AHS, 23 April 1908, SP Folder 28.
[7]GFM to AHS, 4 May 1908, SP Folder 28.

Miles expected a Hayward Company representative to come down shortly to inspect the first two excavators in the northern extension. The excavators' castings had shown great weakness. In Miles's view, the Hayward Company miscalculated the castings' strength. In fairness though, as he conceded, Hayward had given the canal company much heavier buckets than it normally supplied and the booms were four feet longer than the company's standard booms. His men encountered tough going hauling equipment and lumber for the two additional excavators through the woods from Jacksonville. Meanwhile, Excavator Number 1 had been removing 400 to 500 cubic yards in a 12-hour shift, digging to full depth. The Number 2 machine, still lagging behind, moved ahead only forty-seven feet every twenty-four hours, digging to a depth of eight feet. Miles advised his colleagues he was "particularly anxious" to close on the contract to clear the right-of-way, as he believed "our white men have all they want in the woods." In fact, Gleason thought that the men were likely to abandon the work "in a body." The clearing crew had cut the trees down about a mile ahead of the excavators, but a significant amount of the fallen timber had not yet been removed.[8]

Calderwood advised against spending $4,000 to $5,000 to refit the old dredge *Tomoka*, favoring her doing the same work she had been doing with existing equipment. He also recommended against Gleason's idea of using an orange-peel bucket on the *Tomoka* because she sat too low in the water. Meanwhile, Miles arrived in Washington on Monday, May 10, 1908, to attend two important conferences—the National Drainage Congress, whose mission was to reclaim the nation's wetlands for housing and agriculture, to be held on Tuesday and the Conference of Governors, the nation's first presidential conference on the problems of conservation, on Wednesday, Thursday, and Friday. A week later, on Wednesday, May 19, Miles saw President Theodore Roosevelt for a few minutes to discuss the Florida waterway. Roosevelt seemed quite interested in the enterprise and even stated that the Florida company had been engaged in "a great work which had only just commenced to be understood," Miles wrote afterward. He planned to spend Friday morning, May 21, at the House of Representatives, and afterwards to lunch with Hampton Moore, John Small and a few other congressmen.[9]

---

[8]GFM to AHS, 9 May 1908, SP Folder 28.
[9]Calderwood to AHS, 9 May 1908 (copy); GFM to AHS, 11, 20 May 1908; both in SP 28.

That same day, Miles joined a committee of six Atlantic coast congressmen, including Pennsylvania's Hampton Moore, as chairman; John Small of North Carolina; Adin Capron of Rhode Island; Joseph Goulden of New York; and Irving Wanger of Pennsylvania; along with Theodore Burton of Delaware, in calling on Theodore Roosevelt to congratulate him on the success of the recent Conference of Governors and on the vote in the House in favor of continuing the Inland Waterways Commission. But Burton, chairman of the House Rivers and Harbors committee, informed the group that there would be no funding for inland waterway surveys during the current session, but a liberal appropriation would be made the next. Still, Atlantic coast representatives planned to push passage of a plan for a continuous inside waterway from Boston to Florida. Reporting on the White House meeting, the *Washington Star* glowingly described the Florida canal company's George Miles as "the directing constructor of the canals along the east coast of Florida from St. Augustine to Key West."[10]

By Monday evening, May 24, Miles had returned to the Ancient City. Both excavators had now been working with double crews in the northern extension. Five days later, Miles traveled to Jacksonville and spent two hours with Bion Barnett. Barnett advised against offering company lands for sale as long as lumber, turpentine, and rosin prices remained depressed. But Bradley trust officials wanted to sell the land to pay expenses even if they had to be sacrificed at low prices. If Barnett didn't want to buy more land, Miles intended to form a syndicate to purchase 75,000 to 100,000 acres and to ask for Barnett's help in financing it. Barnett thought an offering price of $2.50 an acre much too high, but said he'd think over the plan. In a letter to Sawyer, Miles enclosed a copy of former Governor Broward's platform for his Senate campaign, which Miles thought "strongly favors waterway improvements." Barnett, who apparently had been contributing to Broward's campaign, asked Miles for the company's help. In Barnett's opinion, Broward's election to the Senate would mean the sale of the Florida waterway to the federal government. Although Miles did not feel quite so cheery about the prediction, he remained convinced that Broward's election would materially help their cause.[11]

By June 1, 1908, the new 1907 Florida canal bonds had been signed by Amory. When Sawyer got them, he hoped to be able to turn over many of

---

[10]"At the White House," *Washington Star*, 21 May 1908, SP Folder 28.
[11]GFM to AHS, 28, 30 May 1908, SP Folder 28.

them to the Rhode Island Hospital Trust Company in exchange for cash advances made to pay for waterway construction since November 1907 and to redeem the old 1903 bonds.[12]

Maddox wrote Sawyer that the small 1903 mortgage would be released by the American Security & Trust Company on his request and that of the trust company. The American Security company agreed to accept the new bonds in exchange for those of the old issue. Maddox wrote that he would do the same to the extent of $6,000 worth of his own bonds, but as for the other five $1,000 bonds he did not control, he confessed that he was liable to redeem them himself if the company didn't.[13]

The trust company agreed to take $150,000 worth of bonds for security as collateral for $100,000 in cash already advanced for dredging operations. Sawyer apparently arranged for Maddox to take eight new bonds as collateral for a $5,000 note to take the place of Maddox's five bonds of the 1903 issue. To obtain cash for construction, he asked Maddox whether or not he would make available the so-called Maddox trustee lands if sales of these lands could be made when Maddox planned to be abroad on summer vacation. The land represented the only company asset which was not held in escrow by state trustees. Cordially inquiring whether he planned to stop by Newburyport on his way to Europe, Sawyer promised Maddox "quiet and bracing east winds" during his stay. However, in Florida with land sales falling off dramatically, Miles considered resigning as vice president and managing director of the canal company. No sale could be closed in time to pay the month's expenses.[14]

Just before going abroad, Maddox expressed wonder over Sawyer's ability to meet canal expenses with so little available resources. He attributed the skill to plain old heredity, "But from the discovery of Plymouth Rock down, the thorough-bred New Englander has been a type of thrift and ability to get money, so I take it the art comes to you naturally by inheritance." With over-the-top verbosity, he related that if his European trip didn't take place, it would "give me great pleasure to try once again the effect of those bracing East Winds of yours up there at Newburyport, and I shall be strongly tempted so to do in the event that for any reason the European proposition does not materialize."[15]

---

[12]AHS to SM, 1 June 1908 (copy), SP Folder 28.

[13]SM to AHS, 2 June 1908, SP Folder 28.

[14]AHS to SM, 12 June 1908 (copy); GFM to AHS, 14 June 1908 (copy); SP Folder 28.

[15]SM to AHS, 15 June 1908, SP Folder 29.

In Florida, Miles discussed with Gleason his idea of putting the new excavators on lighters and working them in from Pablo Creek toward the cypress swamp to provide two miles of solid dredging in the northern extension. In fact, he thought all the work through the Pablo Creek marshes could be done with these machines. To do so would eliminate the expense of building a track for each excavator. At present, they had to move through the woods while working on land, which was the expensive part of using the Hayward excavators. As Miles reminded Sawyer, the machines needed to be kept absolutely level to do their work.[16]

Following the Florida elections, Barnett had been depressed over the defeat of Broward for a Senate seat. He hoped the company wouldn't lose anything by the nomination of Duncan U. Fletcher for the Senate and Albert Gilchrist for the governorship and outlined a plan for Miles to obtain $100,000 in financing to press the waterway extension.

But Miles's wife, Helen, had been unwell and he notified Sawyer that he needed to leave Florida with Helen immediately.[17] At the end of June, she remained quite ill. Both Helen and George planned to return to Pomfret as soon as possible. In a letter to Sawyer, Miles asked whether Barnett's proposed plan for financing the waterway appeared "acceptable to the Gentlemen of Providence" and to Amory and Sawyer. Enclosing a copy of Hampton Moore's speech on the waterway appropriation bill introduced in Congress the previous session, Miles pointed out that the address contained "some interesting references to our Waterway."[18]

Miles recommended putting Excavators 1 and 2 on hulls or lighters instead of building expensive tracks and "so do away with a small army of men for moving purposes." He also recommended removing the acetylene gas light generators from Excavators 1 and 2 and putting them on Excavators 3 and 4, and that Excavators 1 and 2 be worked only during the daylight hours. Moving tracks at night hampered the work. He favored employing double crews on all floating machines except the *Tomoka* unless she could handle the solid marsh material. If the *Tomoka* proved able to handle that material, he recommended a double crew. Up north, the "dry old gentlemen of Providence," as well as Amory and Sawyer, approved Barnett's financing plan and authorized Miles to accept it. The terms were the sale of 100,000 acres held by Barnett as trustee for $100,000, with the com-

---

[16]GFM to AHS, 17 June 1908, SP Folder 29.

[17]GFM to AHS, 20 June 1908, SP Folder 29.

[18]GFM to AHS, 23 June 1908, SP Folder 29.

pany reserving the right to redeem the land within a year for the sum of $106,000 plus any taxes owed. The committee gave Miles the authority to negotiate the best terms, perhaps an extended two-year period of redemption.[19]

On the first of July, Miles had been summoned to Providence to attend a canal company meeting called to act on pending matters before Maddox's departure for Europe. Miles presented Barnett's offer to the directors. While the directors took no formal action, they asked Miles whether Barnett could arrange a sale of 100,000 acres at a dollar an acre, with the right to repurchase the land at the end of a year for $106,000, or $115,000 at the end of two years. Miles also sought a provision giving the company the right to repurchase 50,000 acres if directors decided they could not buy back all of the acreage. On July 6, Maddox told Preston Gardner, a Bradley trust official, that he needed cash for the six bonds he held for others. In his mind, the trust company thought Maddox should put up $6,000 of his own money to redeem the bonds and surrender them for the same number of bonds which the company thought was adequate collateral at eighty cents on the dollar. Unfortunately, Maddox was to leave for Europe the next day at ten o'clock in the morning. "I don't know where I'll find the cash to obtain the release of the old mortgage," Maddox despaired. If he was unable to raise the money, the matter would have to wait until September when he returned.[20]

Arguing against Miles's negative view of using the new excavators on rails, Isaac Calderwood thought the excavators better able to do the dredging work than the old dredge boats. They were capable of depositing material a greater distance from the canal bank than the old dipper dredge, thus reducing the overall cost of the work. The canal company should stay the course and follow his original plan. To increase the excavators' productivity, he recommended placing Excavators 3 and 4 on scows, working them down through the marsh toward the St. Johns River instead of into the solid work. Orange peel buckets would make a big showing in the marsh, but they would be useless in the solid cut on scows. The scows would have to dig down ten feet deep to float themselves and the first hard material they encountered would require building a dam behind them to keep them

---

[19]GFM to AHS, 27 June 1908 (copy), SP Folder 29. Minutes of Canal Company Executive Committee, n.d., SP Folder 29.

[20]GFM to Bion H. Barnett, 3 July 1908 (copy), SM to AHS, 6 July 1908, SP Folder 29.

afloat. In Calderwood's view, either one of the two excavators could make the cut without any trouble.[21]

But Miles thought that the old *South Carolina* could move material at far more economical rates. In fact, Miles believed the old dredge could move material at between four to five cents a cubic yard. Excavators 1 and 2 should be moving material at ten cents a yard. Excavators 3 and 4, if placed on lighters and run night and day, ought to be moving material at six cents a yard. The great problem with the excavators had been the cumbersome laying of tracks. In short, Miles saw no prospect of getting the work done at much less than ten cents a yard using land-based machines. To prove his point, he noted that as of February 28, 1907, some 1.8 million cubic yards had been removed from the Matanzas-Halifax Cut under his supervision at an average cost of 8.21 cents a yard. Of that amount, 75,000 cubic yards had been comprised of rock, which Miles pointed out, usually cost the federal government between $2.25 and $3.80 per cubic yard to remove. By comparison, rock excavation generally cost the canal company a modest fifty cents to seventy-five cents a cubic yard.[22]

During the middle of July, Maddox, to Amory's considerable dismay, departed for Europe without obtaining a release of the 1903 bond issue, which held up issuance of the new 1907 bonds. The company had no money to construct a dredging plant, to clear the right-of-way north to Jacksonville or to meet even routine operating expenses. Amory needed $30,000 to $35,000 just to pay expenses for the next two months and hoped to give new 1907 first mortgage bonds as collateral for new loans. At Pomfret, Miles had a telephone conversation with Herbert Wells of the trust company, which had finally agreed to advance money for the next couple of months to meet construction expenses. Wells said something Miles couldn't hear distinctly about leaving the arrangements of the excavator crews in Captain Gleason's hands. Miles had recently questioned Gleason's abilities, but there was "noise" in the receiver, and, somewhat disbelieving and indignant over Wells' instruction, he asked him to write him at St. Augustine. Miles disagreed with the notion that Gleason should be placed in charge of the excavator work and insisted that Fred Amory, the company's president, inform him what his duties were as "a Managing Director." "In Mr. Bradley's time," Miles recalled, "I represented the Company in Florida,

---

[21]Calderwood to AHS, 8 July 1908, SP Folder 29.

[22]GFM to AHS, 11 July 1908, SP Folder 29.

and had full charge of the Construction plant, with the understanding how-ever that on all matters of importance I should have the approval of the Executive Committee." With Executive Committee approval, Miles appointed Captain Gleason as a superintendent. Miles thought that Glea-son had been a good man with machinery, that he understood heavy wood-work, that he knew the inside waters well and that he was a first-class gasoline engineer. But Gleason couldn't handle men well and had even made some of the workers his "pets." To bring in the Matanzas-Halifax Cut at a fraction over eight cents a yard, with a 100,000 yards of rock in the work, Miles had taken the supervision of the two construction dredges out of Gleason's hands for nearly two years, leaving him in charge of mainte-nance work only. "I cannot consent to be responsible for the work *unless* I have the direction of it," Miles insisted.[23]

From his summer residence Bar Harbor, Amory lectured Miles in a long letter about the responsibilities of leadership. As treasurer and manager of his family's two cotton mills for over the past thirty years, he had placed responsibility for the work on the mill's resident agent. He required his overseers to do their work satisfactorily without interference. But if the work had been done unsatisfactorily, he dismissed them. Over the years, he had fired two resident agents and several overseers. George Gleason was Miles's responsibility. If Gleason couldn't perform, Miles should hire some-one else, but only with Executive Committee approval.[24]

In St. Augustine, waterway operations had been running smoothly in the northern extension. At first, the *South Carolina* anchored south of the bridge because Captain Nipson feared running her through. She finally got through safely and started up the North (Tolomato) River and was expected, to be already at work. Miles asked newly elected Governor Albert Gilchrist for help in getting draw spans put in at the Pablo Creek bridges. The War Department thought the Florida canal company should share in the expense. Miles had been trying to get the president to order the War Department to force the Flagler railway to install the draw spans. If Miles couldn't get federal cooperation directly, he intended to get the state to intervene and raise the question with the Secretary of War of the bridge's blocking a navigable waterway. He expected the fight to last a long time,

[23]SM to FA, 14 July 1908 (copy); FA to Wells, 20 July 1908; GFM to FA, 22 July 1908 (copy); all in SP Folder 29.

[24]FA to GFM, 27 July 1908 (copy), SP Folder 29.

thus recommending that the hulls for the proposed Excavators 3 and 4 be built south of the railroad bridges to avoid the interference.[25]

By September 8, "hard up" with a boil on his arm at Newburyport, Sawyer hoped to be back in his Boston office in a day or two. He needed $8,924 for the August canal expenses plus another $2,000 for a total of $10,924 for waterway dredging. A few days later, Miles saw Wells and again criticized Gleason. And there was more bad news to report from Florida. Both excavators and the *South Carolina* had been idled for a week, "which subjects somebody to criticism," Wells complained. "Just where the criticism should lodge, I am not prepared to state."[26]

Miles agreed that the company had not been getting the results it should with the machinery in use. Although the *South Carolina* was again a new machine in first-rate shape, her boiler steamed poorly. She had broken her spud, resulting in four days without digging. Why had there been no extra spuds on board to replace broken ones to anchor the dredge? Wells asked. Moreover, a report had reached him confirming that two-thirds of the spoil material removed from the Matanzas Cut during the month of August had slid back into the cut. The excavators in the northern extension had been delayed because the trees ahead had not been cut down in advance of the dredging. The timber, Wells thought, should have been cut at least 500 feet in advance.[27]

By September 26, Miles had arrived at the Day Kimball Hospital at Putnam, near his Pomfret home, to undergo a serious operation for an unidentified illness that had plagued him for some time. He planned to travel the short distance to Providence to see Helen Bradley's lawyer, Stephen Edwards, to offer his view on the importance of maintaining the cuts in the Florida waterway but was unable leave home. He thought Florida's new governor, Albert Gilchrist, an "uncertain quantity." If Gilchrist gave the group trouble, he didn't want Edwards nervous. To ensure getting the remainder of the canal company's land grant, Miles recommended that the company secure a dredge immediately to maintain the waterway sections already dredged.[28]

---

[25]GFM to AHS, 30 July 1908, SP Folder 29.

[26]John W. Denny to Wells, 8 September 1908; Wells to AHS, 12 September 1908; SP Folder 29.

[27]Wells to FA, 12 September 1908, SP Folder 29.

[28]GFM to AHS, 26 September 1908, in SP Folder 30.

At Washington once again after his return from his trip to Europe, Maddox blew up over demands made by young Sawyer to exchange the 1903 issue of bonds in his possession for less than their full value in cash. In a three-and-a-half-page letter, he lambasted Sawyer for writing his law partner to request the release of the old mortgage bonds and for misrepresenting what Maddox agreed to take in exchange for them. Sam's old friend, Fred Amory, tried to console him. "I am sorry that you are still thinking about that miserable business of getting properly remunerated for the assistance you gave George Bradley in his life time towards this Florida Canal business." "If I were you," Maddox's friend softly counseled, "I would deliver over all the securities to those in charge of the Rhode Island Hospital Trust Co. who are looking after our Canal business, and settle up the best way I could with Wells and Mr. Edwards, and get out of the whole thing and resign as Secretary." Amory wrote that he planned to resign as president, not immediately, but at the end of the year. Having gotten the Bradley estate to complete the waterway, he considered himself no longer a part of the project, leaving it to Wells, Sawyer and others to carry on. He saw no point in continuing to serve with the trust so firmly in control of company affairs. Commiserating over the auction sale of textiles at the family mills during the summer, he looked forward to an improved economy, rejoicing that William Jennings Bryan would *not* be occupying the White House. Even though he had declared his intention to resign by the end of the year, Amory continued to serve as president of the canal company another fourteen years. Maddox, however, announced his intention to resign immediately his positions as secretary and director of the Florida canal company, citing, at least on the face of it, the inconvenience in attending board meetings called at short notice, and sometimes by telegram, to convene at Boston or Providence. Reminiscing over the fact that he had been a director of the company for more than twenty years, Maddox expressed "extreme regret" at having to sever his relationship with the board of directors.[29]

Maddox again ruminated over what he understood to be Sawyer's belief that he, Maddox, ought to turn in his six bonds for cancellation without getting cash. He had always insisted on payment of bonds secured by a mortgage before consenting to a release of the encumbrance. He lectured Sawyer that he preferred cash for his bonds. "Although your plan seems to have the sanction of the President of a large trust company in Providence, I infinitely

---

[29]SM to AHS, 2, 24 October 1908; FA to AHS, 6 October 1908; all in SP Folder 30.

prefer the old fashioned method in vogue here, and by that I must abide." Always the gentleman, though, he acknowledged the news from Florida that flood water and fever among the workmen had hindered progress in the northern extension during the summer, expressing great regret that more bad news plagued the Florida canal company.[30]

By October 24, Miles had spent almost a month in the Putnam hospital. Recovering well, Miles planned to return home the next day with a nurse because his surgical wound hadn't completely closed. The operation had been more serious than expected and he was still exceedingly weak. But in spite of it all, he felt better than he had in several years, and in fact, he had been told that he looked like a new person. Three days later, at a director's meeting held in Providence, Frank Hodgdon, another of the trust's dredge consultants, reported on the Florida waterway. Although Sawyer believed the Florida group fortunate to have an engineer with thirty years' experience assisting in the Florida operation, the cost per yard of the work on the St. Johns River cut had been more than the cost of the work south of St. Augustine.[31]

A month or so after his surgery, Miles finally was able to sit at his desk at his Pomfret home. Gaining strength daily, he felt better than he had for years, but was not strong enough to travel. He had read in an edition of Jacksonville's *Florida Times-Union* that the First National Bank of St. Augustine building where the Florida canal company maintained its offices had been struck by fire. The company's offices narrowly escaped destruction but had been flooded with water from efforts to save the building. He had received Hodgdon's report recommending changes in the Florida waterway work but wanted to talk with the engineer before the company carried out any of his suggestions. On the proposed idea to increase the beam of Excavator 4, for example, Miles observed that if the hull were made 40 feet wide, she wouldn't be able to pass through the drawbridges at Ormond, Daytona and Port Orange.[32]

Sawyer met with Amory to tell him of Helen Bradley's wish that he continue to serve as president of the canal company. But Amory didn't feel that he could take on the responsibility another year, afraid he couldn't even attend the annual meeting in Florida the following March. Besides, he felt

---

[30]SM to AHS, 21 October 1908, SP Folder 30.

[31]GFM to AHS, 24 October 1908; AHS to Mr. George L. Bradley, 28 October 1908 (copy); FA to Wells, 29 October 1908; all in SP Folder 30.

[32]GFM to AHS, 30 October 1908; GFM to AHS, 3 November 1908; both in SP Folder 30.

that by then construction would have progressed so far that his serving as president would no longer be necessary. At a conference in Providence with representatives of the Bradley estate and the canal company, it was finally decided that Helen's lawyer, Stephen Edwards, would contact Maddox regarding the eleven bonds he held, a decision which thoroughly vexed Maddox who already had become embarrassed because of the company's delay in settling the old bond issue. He now threatened to return the bonds to their owners and let the owners take the action needed to collect on them. Weary of the whole situation, he complained that it now looked like that he would indeed be forced to sever all connections with the company so that as counsel he could represent the holders of the old bonds against the company.[33]

In another letter to Sawyer on November 11, Maddox confessed again his embarrassment over the six bonds he did not own. He had gone to the American Security & Trust Company and withdrawn the eleven bonds he owned or controlled. If he returned them to their owners, he was certain that Sawyer would hear from six of them. If that happened, "good faith on my part" would require that he represent them because he had induced them into making what seemed to be "an unfortunate investment." He reiterated his intention to resign as company secretary. With regard to the five bonds he owned outright, Maddox again agreed to accept the notes and collateral Sawyer had sent him on July 1. But that was to be done without delay or he planned to ask the American Security & Trust Company to enforce payment. In any event, Maddox demanded cash for the six bonds he held for other investors.[34]

Three days later, Sawyer advised Maddox that he had spoken with Edwards. Edwards said that he planned to advise Wells to pay cash for Maddox's six bonds at once. Apologizing for the misunderstanding, Sawyer argued that he had tried to carry out the wishes of the president, acting in the capacity of treasurer only. "Had the matter been in my hands alone," Sawyer said, "I should have seen you in Washington long before this." Some months past, Wells had referred everything affecting the Bradley estate to Edwards and, in Maddox's case, he was not called in as counsel, but as Helen Bradley's representative. Sawyer suggested that on receipt of the $6,000 cash for the six bonds he held for others, he inform Wells of his

[33] AHS to Mrs. George L. Bradley (copy); 6 November 1908; AHS to SM, 6 November 1908 (copy); SM to AHS, 7 November 1908; all in SP Folder 30.
[34] SM to AHS, 11 November 1908, SP Folder 30.

willingness to take the other five for bonds of the new issue, bond for bond. In closing, Sawyer wrote, "Take this for what it is worth; the suggestion may be gratuitous but it is made with the best of intentions."[35]

Despite Sawyer's insistence that Edwards had agreed to a settlement, Maddox wrote Amory again that he had just received a wire asking him to delay a few days longer in calling for payment on the six bonds. Maddox pointed out that he was not just being disagreeable. He had, after all, fore-gone collecting on the bonds he owned for a long time. "The Maryland man, however — the other one — wants his money and has been wanting it since I wrote you way back in May," he insisted. "Even though the Taft election has added very handsomely to my financial stature, I do not care to sell out anything to pay bonds of the Canal Company, and I am still more loathe [sic] to borrow money for that purpose." Maddox recollected that when Bradley sold five bonds to the Newburyport bank, it was understood that Bradley himself should underwrite the bonds. No director seemed surprised that the bank would ask that the bonds be paid at maturity. "Purely as a matter of sentiment I stepped to the front — 'butted in', as they say over in Georgetown — and procured the bonds to be carried under a guaranty similar to Mr. Bradley's agreement with the bankers up there on the Merrimac [Newburyport]." But when the purchaser he found asked for his money, "following the example set by the canny bean-eating bankers," Sawyer raised "a hullabaloo" and said that he ought to take back the bonds and surrender them for a long-term bond of a new and much larger issue, basing his contention on the mistake of a stenographer and "a letter bearing my name that I had not signed or even seen." To make matters worse, Maddox wrote that if "a bit of lawyering" is what Sawyer and Wells wanted, then that was "my business and such things add no little to the pleasure I get out of life."[36]

On November 23, 1908, Maddox wrote Sawyer that it had been most unfortunate that Sawyer elected to settle the bond dispute the very week he had long planned to take for a hunting trip in the Virginia mountains. He had accepted an invitation to join friends for the trip back in June. The weather, though, had been bad during the trip with four inches of snow. The only fit day to be out hunting had been a Thursday, but he returned home that same day so that he didn't delay Sawyer. The trouble was now

[35] AHS to SM, 14 November 1908; SM to FA, 14 November 1908; both in SP Folder 30.
[36] Ibid.

over and the work of developing the Florida waterway could now proceed as smoothly as it might have progressed had he, Maddox, not, most unfortunately, as it now appeared, "in a moment of sympathy for an ill man," agreed to take five bonds. "Here was the initial error which in its ramification has led to a lot of bickering" and, as Maddox feared, some ill-feeling, which he greatly regretted. "If in any of my letters to you on the subject I was intemperate in my choice of words or modes of expression," he apologized, "you must not attribute it to any want of regard or respect for yourself but rather to the highly nervous strain under which I have labored since the middle of April." The nervous condition persisted, and it was possible that he might have to give up work for another six months to spend time out in the open. The brouhaha over the bonds was over. But it had taken a heavy toll, straining old relationships. After more than twenty years' association with Amory and the Sawyers in the work of the Florida canal company, Sam Maddox had withdrawn from further involvement in Bradley's dream of a completed Florida intracoastal waterway.[37]

---

[37]SM to AHS, 23 November 1908, SP Folder 30.

Chapter 14

Gaining Speed

While Florida canal officials struggled to finish the waterway "land poor," members of Moore's newly born Atlantic Deeper Waterways Association gathered at Baltimore for the organization's first convention in November 1908. The ADWA's committee on resolutions recommended the extension of several inland Atlantic coastal waterway routes as well as a survey of the Florida east coast. Early in 1909, drawing attention to the nation's desperate need for inland waterway improvements, President Theodore Roosevelt declared in a major speech that "[u]ntil the work of river improvement is undertaken in a modern way, it cannot have results that will meet the needs of a modern Nation." "These needs should be met," he exhorted, "without further dilly-dallying and delay."[1]

Meanwhile, in Florida, canal directors sought state trustees' approval of a toll schedule for vessels plying the nearly completed waterway. But in November 1908, Nathan P. Bryan, one of the company's lawyers and two years later a senator representing Florida in Washington, found it difficult to secure their consent. Former governor William S. Jennings, now the counsel to the state trustees, took the position that the trustees had no authority to fix toll charges, contending that the legislature had vested sole power over the matter in the state's Railroad Commission. The commission's attorney, on the other hand, took the opposite view. In the end, the trustees, including Jennings, voted to permit the canal company's directors to set such tolls as the company "may desire and deem reasonable" until the trustees took further action, a resolution which neither denied nor authorized the collecting of tolls on the waterway.[2]

Charles Cooper, the company's principal lawyer and a former Florida attorney general, had spoken with Governor Broward about getting the tolls

---

[1]Hull, *Origin*, 31.

[2]Bryan to GFM, 25 November 1908, SP File No. 30; MIFF, 19 November 1908, 460. N. P. Bryan to GFM (and enclosed Minutes of TIIF), 25 November 1908, SP Folder 30.

approved. Bryan would have been successful in getting approval, Cooper believed, but for Jennings' advising the trustees that they lacked the power to do so. Cooper went on to criticize the former governor, "This is about like most of his legal opinions—worthless as an opinion on the law but given and used as a pretext for the Trustees not specifically approving the schedule of tolls." Broward, though, told Cooper that he favored the tolls, saying they were entirely reasonable.[3]

With state trustees essentially taking no position on the toll issue, doubts arose over the ability of the directors to enforce a toll schedule without state consent. Although the record is unclear, it appears that the company delayed in collecting tolls until 1911 when officials stretched the first toll chain across the waterway at today's Dania Beach. And in fact, the trustees took no action to expressly approve the company's tolls until 1913. Two years later, however, in 1915, the Florida Legislature passed a law resolving the problem, giving the Railroad Commission the sole authority to set tolls on the waterway.[4]

While resting briefly at Baltimore's Hotel Sherwood the middle of December 1908, Miles had been under the care of two physicians and wondered if he could travel safely to Boston with its colder weather. To Miles, the "prospect of being a confirmed invalid" was not "alluring." Still Miles's doctors allowed him to spend a few hours in Washington to attend meetings of the National Conservation Commission, which had been authorized to inventory the nation's natural resources, and the National Rivers and Harbors Congress. In Washington, he heard from Governor Broward that Flagler railway officials had been lobbying for withdrawal of the War Department's order opening the Pablo Creek bridges. He also made peace there with former Florida Governor Jennings. Miles lunched with both Jennings and Broward at the famed Willard Hotel. Jennings reportedly told Miles that in the future he would favor "every move" to push the development of water transportation, including the Florida waterway.[5]

With some degree of relief, Miles learned he had been replaced as the canal company's managing director because of his lingering, unresolved medical condition. He believed the new manager, Captain Seth Perkins, would be able to complete the work north of St. Augustine at the same cost

---

[3]Chas. M. Cooper to GFM, 2 December 1908, SP Folder 30.

[4]Bryan to GFM, 25 November 1908, SP File No. 30; MIFF, 19 November 1908, 460. N. P. Bryan to GFM (and enclosed Minutes of TIIF), 25 November 1908, SP Folder 30.

[5]GFM to AHS, 14 December 1908, SP Folder 30.

as the cost of the work had been between St. Augustine and Biscayne Bay. The lack of rock in the northern extension and the proximity of the dredges to machine shops should make the work cheaper, the ailing engineer thought, provided the new excavators worked properly.[6]

By Christmas Eve, Perkins presented the terms of his contract for completing the northern extension. He agreed to manage the work for $5,000 a year and $1,000 a year for expenses, with full authority to hire and fire employees and spend up to $10,000 for equipment with the consent of the company's consulting engineer. He also agreed to be bound by an "upset" or maximum price for the cost of the work per cubic yard. If the actual cost fell below that price, he could to keep half of the savings to the company as a bonus.[7]

Despite the uncertainties of the ongoing dredging operations, by the end of the year the Florida canal company had made great strides in constructing the private waterway along the Atlantic coast, opening up large expanses of property lying on both banks of the waterway to real estate development and farming. Known now as the Florida East Coast Canal, the inland waterway stretched from St. Augustine to Biscayne Bay, a distance of 400 miles. Work on the final cut between Jacksonville and St. Augustine had already begun, with completion expected in two years' time. And even though the entire waterway hadn't yet opened up to larger craft, it still attracted small yachts from northern ports. In fact, Florida residents during the winter of 1908 saw a continual procession of smaller yachts cruising down the waterway from St. Augustine.[8]

In the first week of 1909, Sawyer sent checks payable to the Providence law firm of Edwards & Angell totaling twenty-five dollars to Stephen Edwards, Helen Bradley's lawyer, for services connected with the Lake Worth and New River land trusts, financing vehicles for the canal company that Sawyer's father had set up in 1892 for Bradley, Sawyer and their colleagues. Sawyer spent some time in New York City with Frederick Warburton, secretary and treasurer of the Mergenthaler Linotype Company, and a director of the American Graphophone Company, an early manufacturer of phonograph devices. Sawyer and Bradley had been associated with War-

---

[6]GFM to AHS, 19 December 1908 (copy); Wells to AHS, 22 December 1908; both in SP Folder 31.

[7]Perkins to FA, 24 December 1908, SP Folder 31

[8]"Florida Coast Line Canal," *St. Augustine, St. Johns County, Florida, Illustrated* (Pictorial Edition of the *St. Augustine Evening Record*, [1908?]), p. 22.

burton in the Automatic Clerk Company, a chewing gum vending machine business incorporated in New Jersey in May 1902. But the general manager, Isaac Mansfield, turned out to be totally ineffective. Wealthy California banker D. Ogden Mills turned over the voting rights to two-thirds of his stock in the company to Warburton and other large shareholders turned over their rights as well in an effort to revive the company. Bradley had invested perhaps $25,000 in the venture and probably owned a substantial amount of common stock. Sawyer asked Herbert Wells, a Bradley trust official, to give the voting rights to Bradley's stock in the venture to Warburton in order to preserve Bradley's stake in the company. Meanwhile, back in Florida, financial difficulties continued to plague canal directors. December expenses for dredging the Florida waterway amounted to $8,870, with little cash in the company's coffers to pay them.[9]

By the middle of January 1909, Florida real estate sales started to pick up. Miles had received a letter from now ex-Governor Broward, who had left office just days before. The former riverboat captain wanted to inspect the canal company's waterway near Jacksonville for a group of investors. Miles had also been negotiating with a lumber firm in South Carolina interested in buying land along the Indian River. But he also received some rather disquieting news from an old friend. Eighty-four-year-old Sir Sandford Fleming, former chief engineer of the Canadian Pacific Railway, wanted to know more about his lackluster holdings in the Boston & Florida land company from which he had derived no earnings since investing in the company in 1892. Fleming's son, Sanford H. Fleming, planned to come down to Florida the next winter to look into the value of the remaining unsold lands. The senior Fleming believed Miles was responsible for his investment and felt that Miles ought to take some steps to ensure at least a decent return on his stock. Miles also heard dismal news from Bion Barnett, the Jacksonville banker holding hundreds of thousands of acres of Florida canal company land in escrow, awaiting completion of the Florida waterway. Barnett's timber cruiser's assessment of the Boston & Florida lands was soon to be completed. Miles expected the survey to show half the lands in useless marsh, making it unlikely that company stockholders would get anything close to $2.50 an acre for the land.[10]

---

[9]AHS to Edwards, 4 January 1909 (copy); AHS to Wells, 8 January 1909; both in SP Folder 31. "Frederick John Warburton," *New York Times*, 3 November 1917. "Incorporated in New Jersey," *New York Times*, 29 May 1902 (Automatic Clerk Company).

[10]GFM to AHS, 14,15 January 1909, SP Folder 31.

Miles received another communication from Broward, just twelve days after the inauguration of his successor, Albert Gilchrist, on January 6, 1909. One of Broward's customers expressed interest in buying large tracts of Florida land, preferably Everglades acreage, and particularly the Florida canal company's land. His as yet unnamed customer desired to make installment payments on purchases over a period of two to five years. Broward asked for Miles's best prices and terms for tracts ranging in size from 100,000 to 300,000 acres. Miles replied that the ex-governor's letter had been referred to the company's directors, but cautioned that the escrow lands south of Fort Pierce probably wouldn't be offered for sale until the acreage had first been carefully evaluated.[11]

Barnett thought two dollars an acre too a high price for the sale of the escrow lands. Still Miles argued Barnett ought to give directors the opportunity to sell the lands at prices as high as $2.50 an acre. He suspected Barnett relied on Broward and his partner, William S. Jennings, also an ex-governor and a former canal company opponent, to find purchasers for the New England group's properties. But because of their political connections, Miles hesitated on starting negotiations with the two former governors, doubting his New England colleagues would get the best prices from them.[12]

Toward the end of January, Miles insisted that Sawyer furnish a financial statement on the Boston & Florida Company to give to the senior Fleming, who owned twenty-five percent of the company's stock. Miles admitted that he hadn't been able to attend the annual meetings at Portland, nor had he ever seen any of the annual financial reports. Somewhat irritated, Miles asserted that he ought to have some voice in the management of the company after nineteen years. He soon received a financial statement, but it was an incomplete one. If Sawyer needed to employ a bookkeeper to prepare a more complete statement, Miles suggested, he wanted him to secure one and he agreed to pay for the service "to satisfy Fleming that he has not been unfairly treated." "He has not stated that he considers this to be the case," Miles added, "but his letters are of such a nature that I wish for my own protection to have him fully informed on all points relating to this invest-

---

[11]Broward to GFM, 18 January 1909; GFM to Broward, 19 January 1909; both in SP Folder 31.

[12]GFM to AHS, 22 January 1909, SP Folder 31.

ment, as it was made at my solicitation and he looks to me to see that he receives some return on his money."[13]

Herbert Wells lectured Hayden Sawyer on marketing Florida land, telling him to ignore people saying the Florida canal acreage was worth anything like $4 to $10 an acre. At least 50,000 to 100,000 acres of land should be sold immediately to pay dredging expenses. To Wells, it was better to sell at $2.50 an acre than wait for land prices to rise. Meanwhile, Miles met with Captain George Spalding, the Army's chief engineer in Florida, to review the canal company's plans. On March 3, Congress appropriated funds for a survey along the Atlantic coast for an inland waterway between Boston and Key West. The survey included an assessment of the cost of a ship canal from Boston south to Beaufort, North Carolina, and the cost of a shallower barge canal no more than twelve feet deep from Beaufort, North Carolina, south to Key West. Congress also authorized Army engineers to recommend a shallower waterway if traffic didn't support a waterway twelve feet deep. Colonel Dan Kingman, chief engineer of the South Atlantic Coast Division (formerly, chief engineer in Florida, 1906), headed the survey for the deeper barge canal, along with four assistants — all U. S. Army engineer officers, including Captain Spalding. Miles hoped that he could persuade the engineers to inspect the Florida waterway to appreciate what the canal company had accomplished. He also learned that they might ask the company's price if the federal government decided to buy the waterway. Spalding asked Miles to accompany the engineers on the survey if Kingman made the trip to Florida.[14]

The middle of March, the Florida waterway opened for light-draft vessels from St. Augustine south for some distance while canal directors struggled to eliminate the last solid cut between St. Augustine and the St. Johns River. For a few miles south of the river, the company had been dredging in Pablo Creek. To the considerable satisfaction of the company's directors, the War Department ordered the Florida East Coast Railway to place a draw span in the bridge crossing the creek by July 1, which was needed for unrestricted navigation. Sawyer understood that a vice president of the Flagler railway expected the order to be withdrawn and now was anxious to speak with

---

[13]GFM to AHS, 23 January 1909; GFM to AHS, 30 January 1909 (copy); AHS to Wells, 2 February 1909; all in SP Folder 31.

[14]Wells to Sawyer,13 February1909; GFM to FA, 20 March 1909; both in SP Folder 31. H. Doc. 229, 63rd Cong., 1st session contains Kingman's report of survey of July 11, 1911, to the Board of Engineers for Rivers and Harbors.

Jacob Dickinson, President William Howard Taft's secretary of war, before a final decision was made.[15]

Meanwhile in Tallahassee, a commission appointed by state legislators completed its investigation of the management of the state's internal improvement fund. Unfortunately for former Governor Broward's detractors, commissioners reported that the fund's management during his administration's push for Everglades drainage had been faultless. "Try as hard as they wish, the opponents of Broward's drainage plan cannot find corruption," the *Miami Metropolis* proclaimed. "Broward has a clear conscience and he looks a man straight in the face when talking to him in a manner that makes his hearer know that he is a sincere man with an honest purpose in life to accomplish." The paper added that money to Broward was "a minor consideration." For Broward, his first consideration was his family; second, his state and country; and only last, money. Broward was "a great and good friend" of the state, the paper opined, neither "a corruptionist," nor "a grafter, as the Octopus Press and its little Sand-Spurs would have the unenlightened believe." After reviewing the report, Miles thought that Broward maintained "a strong hold politically" in Florida. In fact, he wouldn't be surprised if Florida voters elected Broward to the United States Senate the following year. Following a review of the commission's report, state legislators directed a committee of eight members (three from the state Senate and five from the state House) to examine and report on the work of the Florida canal company on the northern extension between St. Augustine and the St. Johns River.[16]

By the first of May, Florida canal directors learned that under President Taft's instructions, the secretary of war's order directing the construction of the Flagler railway's Pablo Creek draw bridge had been rescinded. The company's only hope for a draw bridge appeared to be in the state legislature. There was also some good news. In fact, great news. Miles had gotten one of ex-Governor Broward's associates, John Barrs, to pay $2.65 for an immense tract of Dade County land owned by the company but held in escrow by Barnett, with the terms of payment to be agreed upon between Barrs and Florida canal company officials.[17]

---

[15]AHS to Nathan S. Davis, 22 March 1909 (copy); AHS to Edwards, 7 April 1909 (copy); both in SP Folder 31.

[16]"Broward Vindicated," *Miami Metropolis*, 23 April 1909. GFM to AHS, 24 April 1909, SP Folder 31

[17]GFM to AHS, 1, 3 May 1909, SP Folder 32.

By the middle of May also, Miles inspected the southern stretch of the completed waterway south of Lake Worth with the state legislative committee. He boarded a launch to meet the party between St. Augustine and Daytona to go over the northern section. Former Governor Broward, went along for the ride, and committee members stopped off at Daytona and inspected the work in progress between the Matanzas and Halifax rivers and between St. Augustine and the St. Johns River. To Miles, the legislators seemed favorably impressed.[18]

Meantime, Frank Hodgdon traveled to Florida to superintend the work in March. He spent a month there before coming down with a light case of typhoid fever. For seven weeks, he was confined to bed but had to convalesce for several more weeks because of a reinfection. Captain Spalding formally wrote Miles asking him what price the company wanted if Congress decided to purchase the waterway. Miles did not immediately respond. A member of both the ADWA and the National Rivers and Harbors Congress, he thought it the wiser course to consult first with ADWA president Hampton Moore and Louisiana congressman and NHRC president Joseph Ransdell on what path he should follow. By the end of May, Miles dropped plans to sell Boston & Florida land in the St. Augustine area. Flagler was selling railroad lands there for only two dollars an acre, considerably below the Boston & Florida's asking prices.[19]

During the first part of June, Fred Dewey, the New England group's longtime south Florida real estate agent, gave up brokering land in south Florida. Before hiring a replacement, Sawyer first needed to know how much territory Fred Morse, the group's agent at Miami, wanted to handle to eliminate any conflict that might arise with Dewey's successor in the Fort Lauderdale area.[20]

Miles meanwhile advised against Sawyer lobbying Secretary Dickinson to rescind the Pablo Creek bridge order because Excavator 3 was now either digging through Flagler railway lands or heading toward them. Flagler had given Miles only informal verbal approval to cut through his lands and could stop the work if the New England group tried to get the bridge order rescinded. Miles further warned against claiming ownership over strips of

---

[18]GFM to AHS, 1 May 1909; GFM to AHS, n.d. [16? May 1909]; both in SP Folder 32.

[19]AHS to Calderwood, 18 May 1909; GFM to AHS, 25 May 1909; GFM to AHS, 25 May 1909 (second letter this date); all in SP Folder 32.

[20]AHS to Morse, 2 June 1909 (copy); GFM to AHS, 4, 17 June 1909; AHS to GFM, 10 June 1909 (copy); all in SP Folder 32.

land on either side of the canal through the Pablo Creek marshes because the canals were being cut as an improvement to a navigable creek under a permit from the War Department and would become public property after completion of the work. To address the Pablo Creek bridge problem in a different way, Miles helped to secure legislation at Tallahassee authorizing the state to remove impediments to navigation like the fixed railway bridges blocking the canal company's waterway and hoped the governor would sign it. But a few days later, Governor Gilchrist vetoed the bill, asserting that existing law already had given him sufficient authority to order the opening of bridges for inland waterway navigation.[21]

In July, along the coast of the Gulf of Mexico, a new civic group lobbied for regional inland waterway improvements. The Mississippi-to-Atlantic Inland Waterway Association, led by Duncan U. Fletcher of Jacksonville, one of Florida's senators, pushed for an inland waterway connecting the Mississippi and Apalachicola rivers across the Florida peninsula to the Atlantic Ocean. Fletcher's group also advocated linking the proposed cross-Florida waterway with the Florida East Coast Canal. Meanwhile, at Providence, Herbert Wells learned from Barnett that he had secured a firm offer of a meager $1.75 per acre less commissions for one of their tracts comprising 100,000 acres. Wells suggested calling a directors' meeting to accept the offer. Still trying to secure a draw bridge over their waterway at Pablo Creek and despite Miles's warning, Sawyer left Boston for Plattsburg, New York, to meet with Secretary of War Jacob Dickinson. President Taft was also staying there, but never talked with Sawyer. By July 11, Frank Hodgdon was up and about, again taking an active part in Florida waterway work. But Seth Perkins, the contractor doing much of the work, had not done as much with the suction dredge as he had expected. There had been a number of breakdowns. By the middle of July, Sawyer was trying to meet with Dickinson at Washington, while Miles planned to travel from Pomfret to New York City to see Richard Bolles of Colorado Springs, "the leading spirit in the Everglade land companies." Eight months before, in December 1908, Bolles had made the largest purchase ever of Everglades land under Governor Broward's drainage program, buying 500,000 acres of state land

---

[21]*Ibid.*

for $1 million dollars, with the commitment that the Colorado promoter spend half a million dollars on drainage.[22]

A few weeks later, Miles spent a few days in New York City, but it is unknown whether or not he actually met Bolles. Nevertheless, he could find no trace of a working dredge that could be bought or chartered to work in Florida. Several leading dredging companies had been looking for dredges, including the Atlantic Gulf & Pacific Dredging Company, the largest marine contracting company in the United States. Miles wrote to another dredging contractor, Howard Trumbo, to ask him for his dredge but doubted he would get it, "as he is in Mr. Flagler's clutches." He even asked his assistant, George Gleason, to travel north to inspect the Savannah Dredging Company's machines en route to Florida.[23]

During August, state trustees couldn't spare an engineer to survey and report on the progress of the waterway extension between Jacksonville and St. Augustine. The trustees recommended that the company employ another engineer, J. W. Bushnell. Barnett had known Bushnell for a long time and recommended him to Miles as a competent engineer. For many years Bushnell had been chief engineer for the Florida Central & Peninsular Railroad (then the Florida division of the Seaboard railway). Bushnell offered to perform the investigation for $15 a day plus expenses or $350 a month if the investigation took thirty days or longer and was ready to go to work immediately. But Miles disagreed with Barnett over employing Bushnell. He thought Bushnell chiefly a railway engineer, preferring another engineer to inspect the dredging. The company needed accurate measurements of the dredged material moved to date. Although he was sorry another engineer he preferred was unable to do the work, he liked D. D. Rogers of Daytona because of his considerable experience in dredging work, but more particularly because he had made the original surveys for the northern extension above St. Augustine. Rogers knew exactly where to find all of the benchmarks for the surveys and had all the necessary notes on the low water levels at both ends of the waterway.[24]

---

[22]"Mississippi-Atlantic," *Manufacturers' Record*, 8 July 1909 (announcing first annual convention at Jacksonville in fall 1909); "Mississippi to Atlantic Inland Waterway Association," advertisement, *Everglade Magazine* (September 1911):10. *Mississippi to Atlantic Bulletin*. Wells to AHS, 4,9 July 1909; Denny to GFM, 8 July 1909 (copy); Seth Perkins to AHS, 11 July 1909; AHS to Wells, 15 July 1909 (copy); GFM to AHS, 19 July 1909 (copy); all in SP Folder 32.

[23]GFM to AHS, 3 August 1909, SP Folder 32.

[24]Bion Barnett to Wells,10 August 1909 (copy); GFM to Bion Barnett,13 August 1909 (copy); both in SP Folder 32.

Consent of the state trustees for the sale of the Dade County escrow lands to Barnett's customers was given, with the provision his engineer reported favorably on the work north of St. Augustine. It also seemed probable the trustees would agree to release the second escrow deed before the first. Fearing the trustees might take offense if company directors insisted on a different engineer, Miles finally agreed to Bushnell's employment.[25]

For the week ending September 11, 1909, Florida dredging operations in the northern extension produced astonishing results. The excavators and the *South Carolina* removed 53,352 cubic yards of material, the largest excavation ever reported for one week's work. By September 27, the perennially unwell Miles had returned to Pomfret from Florida feeling well. But he had gotten into cold damp weather, and as a consequence complained, "I am now laid up with a threatened attack of bronkitis." [26]

In October, Governor Albert Gilchrist and several other state governors joined a delegation of St. Louis business leaders aboard the steamer *Alton* cruising down the Mississippi River, bound for New Orleans for the second annual convention of another waterway booster group, the Lakes-to-the-Gulf association. Introduced as an apostle in the "great cause of conservation," Gilchrist urged not only implementation of conservation policies and the improvement of inland waterways but also the development of waterway transportation. The beginning of November, Miles and Sawyer made plans to attend the ADWA's second annual conference at Norfolk. The group also heard from Sawyer's partner, George Piper, that $49,000 in cash had come into Florida coffers from the sale of Boston & Florida real estate. The more Amory thought about it, the more he thought it necessary for Sawyer to join Miles and Charles Cooper, one of the Florida canal company's longtime lawyers, in Norfolk for the meeting.[27]

At Norfolk, Sawyer joined George Miles, Duncan Fletcher of Jacksonville, and W. A. McWilliams of St. Augustine in representing Florida. Florida sent only six delegates out of a total attending of 743. Moore's Pennsylvania delegation comprised of 310 overwhelmed the remaining fourteen state delegations. Miles presented a paper entitled, "The Inland Waterways of East-

---

[25]GFM to AHS, 18 August 1909, SP Folder 32.

[26]Wells to Mrs. George L. Bradley; 21 September 1909; GFM to AHS, 27 September 1909; both in SP Folder 33.

[27]Stevens, *Log*, 29-30. See, also,"From Lakes to Gulf," *Manufacturers' Record*, 8 April 1909, for brief references to the three Lakes-to-Gulf conventions already held. GFM to AHS, 5 November 1909; FA to AHS, 15 November 1909; both in SP Folder 33.

ern Florida," which included a summary of the work of the St. Augustine company in constructing the Florida East Coast Canal. But another delegate, not Miles, read the paper because Miles, again suffering from a cold, couldn't read the paper in a voice loud enough to be heard by the delegates. The paper detailed not only the company's development of the inland waterway but also the state's Everglades drainage program and the state's dredging of the Miami and New River canals to Lake Okeechobee. These state-dredged canals, he claimed, would soon permit navigation across the peninsula from the Atlantic Ocean to the Lake and then down the Caloosahatchee River to the Gulf of Mexico. Miles also informed the delegates that his company had been engaged in "opening up an inside passage along the whole east coast of Florida, from the mouth of the St. Johns River to Key West," noting that the company's canals between the St. Johns River and St. Augustine had not yet been fully completed. Rather than block Flagler's efforts to develop his railway, Miles boasted, Florida canal directors granted the railway magnate a land subsidy of a quarter of million acres to extend his railway to Miami.[28]

In January 1910, state trustees meeting at Tallahassee formally approved the company's sale of land, an immense tract comprising 150,000 acres of Palm Beach and Dade County land still in escrow with Barnett, to Jacksonville lawyer John Murdoch Barrs on the condition that Barrs drain and reclaim the land. Barrs, a close friend of Napoleon Bonaparte Broward, agreed to buy the canal company's land at $2.65 an acre. Barrs later sold some of the property to George O. Butler, a state representative for Palm Beach and Dade counties, and to G. D. Bryant, a Tampa resident. At the time, Butler and Bryant had been making headlines with plans to build a rock road eighteen to twenty feet wide flanked by a drainage canal between Lake Okeechobee and Lake Worth running through lands owned by both the Flagler railway and the Florida canal company.[29]

Tuesday morning, January 25, Herbert Wells arrived in Washington for a visit with Sam Maddox. The weather was cool, clear, and comfortable. Maddox appeared in better health than Wells had expected, considering

---

[28]Miles, "The Inland Waterways of Eastern Florida," ADWA, November 1909: 86-91, 226.

[29]*MIIF*, 31 July 1909, 166-67; *MIIF*, 10 January 1910, 285-87. Answer (Sworn) of Canal Company, *FEC vs. TIIF* (Palm Beach), pp. 35-36. See, Proctor, *Napoleon Bonaparte Broward*, 128, 133, and 306, for background information on the close relationship between Barrs and Broward. "Looking After Canal Surveys Between Two Florida Lakes," *Miami Metropolis*, 18 October 1911; "Plan Fine Road for Automobiles," *Florida Times-Union*, January 10, 1910.

Maddox's attack of ptomaine poisoning several months before. But to Wells, Maddox seemed disinterested in the waterway. In fact, Wells couldn't even get Maddox to turn over company records.[30]

Where Wells had failed, Amory tried to get his old friend to turn over the canal company's papers, hoping Sawyer had written Maddox asking him to send all of the documents to his office "even if they should fill a flour barrel either large or small." Amory felt Seth Perkins had done good work in the northern extension between St. Augustine and Jacksonville and expected the company to complete the Matanzas Cut in just two months' time, with the exception of the suction dredging, which had been following up the top-digging by the excavators. He had gone down south to survey the cut between the Matanzas and Halifax, which he felt Miles and Gleason had never finished as thoroughly as they should have. Wells recalled that Miles believed that Perkins's work was too costly but chalked up the pessimistic assessment to "a great deal of rivalry" and bad feeling between the two. On the real estate side of the business, it was becoming easier to sell land at three dollars an acre. The Barrs sale was expected to bring in $420,000, with twenty-five percent of the purchase in cash, with the rest in one-, two-, and three-year notes, secured by mortgages on the 150,000 acre transaction. Company directors asked Barnett to sell 30,000 acres to 40,000 acres more from the escrow lands, which might bring as much as $4 an acre. In the end, Amory thought, the canal company might be able to squeeze enough out of the land to reap the Bradley estate profits amounting to $100,000 to $150,000, leaving the entire waterway for the stockholders. The sale of the waterway alone for $1 million could yield stockholders $140 a share based on a total of 7,000 shares of Florida canal company stock outstanding.[31]

The end of January, while watching over the impending sale of escrow acreage to Barrs in St. Augustine, Sawyer became quite ill. His strength had been coming back rapidly, but his doctor advised him not to return home for a week and, if possible, to remain in Florida longer. Barrs had been getting anxious over the delay in the paperwork. Lawsuits challenging the Everglades drainage tax were about to be settled. State improvement fund trustees had let contracts for the dredging of five drainage canals from Lake Okeechobee to the Atlantic coast. And there were plenty of state funds to finance drainage. Back taxes owed to the drainage district amounted to

---

[30]Wells to AHS, 25 January 1910, SP Folder 33.

[31]FA to SM, 27 January 1910 (two letters same date, both copies) SP Folder 33.

$600,000, with future drainage tax collections estimated to be about $150,000 a year. Trustees had available about $700,000 in cash and future sales of state land could be made to pay for drainage. Flagler associate James Ingraham reported that sugar cane and rice were to be grown in the drained lands. Capital was already in place to build mills to process sugar cane.[32]

Sawyer spoke with W. L. Bragg, the New England group's West Palm Beach real estate agent, who had been working with Barrs on buying Florida land. Bragg had shown Oscar Crosby, a wealthy Virginia engineer and entrepreneur, some of the company's lands held in escrow by Barnett. Bragg also reported that two prospective purchasers, Fred Ballard and John Tucker of Colorado Springs, formerly mining brokers there, planned to buy at least 10,000 acres, and perhaps, as much as 30,000 acres. Sawyer knew both Tucker and Ballard well. Ten years before, the two brokers had bought a couple of mines for the New England group. Sawyer considered them honest men with good reputations. At the same time, Sawyer sold 240 acres of Boston & Florida land at $20 an acre to former Governor William S. Jennings (the canal company's former nemesis on the toll setting issue), with $2,000 in cash paid as a down payment. On Flagler's side, three hundred acres of railway land had reportedly been sold at $12.50 an acre for a town site about four miles north of Fort Lauderdale in what today would probably be in or near Pompano Beach.[33]

In February 1910, Herbert Wells met with Helen Bradley, Amory, and Helen's lawyer, Stephen Edwards, at Providence. All wanted to sell land immediately to pay the canal company's operating expenses. Wells instructed Sawyer to close a sale at $2.75 if nothing better came up, with as much cash up front as possible. He also directed Sawyer to accept Barnett's offer to advance funds on the mortgage notes held by the company and to use his best efforts to get $3 out of Barnett for 40,000 acres. Edwards had just received the proposed Barrs contract from Charles Cooper, planned to look it over and hoped to close on it in a few days. The four also discussed Miles's disturbing actions over the last several months in meddling with Seth Perkins's Florida dredging contract. They considered suggesting that Miles perhaps take 'a little vacation', as he hadn't been well after his operation. He might also think about lobbying in Tallahassee, they thought, or perhaps form another transportation company so that Perkins could have a

---

[32]AHS to Wells, 28 January 1910 (copy); AHS to FA, 28 January 1910 (copy); both in SP Folder 33.

[33]Ibid.

free hand on the work south of St. Augustine in the Matanzas Cut. Helen took all the conversation in but said very little.[34]

A few days after Edwards' receipt of the Barrs contract, the New England group learned that the contract had not been drawn to Edwards' satisfaction. The closing would be further delayed, aggravating the company's financial situation. But by the end of February, directors received some encouraging news. During the year 1909 alone, the Florida canal company excavated more than a million cubic yards in dredging the northern extension. And by March 15, more good news arrived. The company had completed a crucial connection between the North River and Pablo Creek, affording open water on the last heavy dredging between St. Augustine and the St. Johns River. Three days later, Perkins piloted his launch *Dispatch* through the newly-constructed waterway from St. Augustine to the St. Johns River, the first vessel to come through the extension to Jacksonville. Now, light draft boats could pass through the waterway north. Directors expected to have the entire canal ready for state inspection in seven or eight months' time. In August, news circulated that the Florida canal company had completed the inland waterway from Jacksonville to Miami. But a boating party traveling down the waterway from Jacksonville, which included Senator Duncan Fletcher and the company's general manager George Miles, turned back when it reached St. Augustine. The waterway still had not been completed and certainly was not ready for inspection by state trustees.[35]

Flagler Sues Canal Company

The company's impending sale of public lands to John Barrs forced Henry Flagler to sue both the state of Florida and the company to stop the state's planned conveyance to the company of a substantial amount of the public lands held in escrow by Bion Barnett. In a lawsuit filed in Palm Beach County in October 1910, Flagler's railway claimed the canal company owed the railroad state land for extending the line south to Miami under several agreements dating back to 1892. The litigation sought 1,500 acres of state

---

[34]Wells to AHS, 4 February 1910 (copy); FA to AHS, 5 February 1910 (copy); both in SP Folder 33.

[35]Wells to AHS, 9 February 1910 (copy); AHS to W. G. McKechnie, 25 February 1910 (copy); AHS to W. G. McKechnie, 31 March 1910 (copy); all in SP Folder 33. Davis, *History of Jacksonville*, 236. "Intercoastal Canal Completed," *Everglade Magazine*, August 1910.

land for every mile of railway constructed for the railway's extension beyond Palm Beach to Biscayne Bay.[36]

While Flagler pressed the West Palm Beach litigation, two years later, in December 1912, the Flagler railway filed another lawsuit against the Florida canal company seeking the same relief, but this time the suit would be lodged in St. Johns County Circuit Court at St. Augustine. Judge George Couper Gibbs, because of a possible bias, disqualified himself from hearing the second case and transferred the litigation to Putnam County. The judge's father, George W. Gibbs, had served as assistant treasurer and chief executive officer of the Florida canal company and the judge himself had been employed by the St. Augustine Canal Company in 1894 and for a few years after that date. While the fact that Judge Gibbs had served as secretary of the Indian River and Bay Biscayne Inland Navigation Company in the late 1890s may have provided additional grounds for recusal, the St. Johns jurist nonetheless didn't mention it in his recusal order. Both lawsuits would move slowly through the court system until finally the Flagler and canal companies reached a settlement, resulting in the dismissal of the West Palm Beach suit in January 1913 and the Putnam County litigation seven months later. To settle both suits, the Florida canal company agreed to convey another 20,002 acres of land in Dade, Orange, and Brevard counties to the Flagler railway.[37]

Despite the first Flagler lawsuit filed in October 1910, state trustees delivered the second escrow deed conveying over 117,000 acres of land to the company on December 28 as payment for the completion of the St. Augustine-to-Jacksonville link. The first escrow deed, however, would remain in trust with Barnett, awaiting the completion of the cut between the Matanzas and Halifax rivers, which the company had begun dredging in 1882.[38]

On November 18, 1910, the Florida canal company conveyed a large expanse of Palm Beach County land to John Barrs, former Governor Broward's close friend. What would become known as the Palm Beach Farms tract included parcels comprising an immense area of some 234 square

---

[36]Bill of Complaint, *FEC vs. TIIF* (Palm Beach).

[37]Bill of Complaint, *FEC vs. Canal Co.* (St. Johns/Putnam). Order Changing Venue, *FEC vs. Canal Co.* (St. Johns/Putnam), May 19, 1913, filed May 26, 1913, and recorded in Minute Book E, at page 286, St. Johns County Circuit Court. Progress Docket, page 2, *FEC vs. TIIF* (Palm Beach); Order of Dismissal, August 2, 1913, *FEC vs. Canal Co.* (St. Johns/Putnam). Perkins to GAY, 21 April 1928, YP Box 4, File 9.

[38]Answer of Canal Company, *FEC vs. TIIF* (Palm Beach County), p. 37.

miles, stretching from a point just west of West Palm Beach thirty miles south to Boca Raton. Eight months before on March 21, Barrs had already agreed to sell the same land to Harold J. Bryant of Colorado Springs. On May 19, Bryant, in turn, assigned his agreement with Barrs to the Palm Beach Farms Company, a Colorado corporation. When the canal company conveyed the land to Barrs on November 18, Barrs deeded it on the same day to the Palm Beach Farms Company. Eight years later, in August 1918, Barrs died unexpectedly of a stroke at the age of sixty-one while visiting the St. Augustine offices of his banker, John T. Dismukes of the First National Bank. A year later, in a lawsuit brought against Barrs' estate at West Palm Beach, the Florida canal company foreclosed on a mortgage given by Barrs to finance his purchase of other substantial tracts of Palm Beach County land. The final decree would order the sale of more than 21,000 acres for Barrs's failure to pay the mortgage and taxes on the property.[39]

But by November 1910, the Florida canal company still had not completed the Florida East Coast Canal, after more than twenty-eight years of hard dredging. Westcott's dream still was only that...a dream.

---

[39]Warranty Deed executed by Canal Company in favor of John Murdoch Barrs on November 18, 1910, and recorded in Book 8, at page 235, of the Public Records of Palm Beach County, Florida. Agreement between J. M. Barrs and Harold J. Bryant on March 21, 1910, and recorded in Book 7, at page 24, of the Public Records of Palm Beach County, Florida; Assignment executed by Harold J. Bryant in favor of Palm Beach Farms Company on May 19,1910, and recorded in Deed Book 8, at page 250, of the Public Records of Palm Beach County, Florida; Warranty Deed executed by John Murdoch Barrs in favor of Palm Beach Farms Company on November 18, 1910, and recorded in Deed Book 8, at page 242, of the Public Records of Palm Beach County, Florida. "Well Known Lawyer Dies," *Miami Herald*, 20 August 1918. Decree of Sale and Foreclosure, *Florida Coast Line Canal and Transportation Company vs. Lydia Barrs, as Executrix of the Last Will and Testament of John Murdoch Barrs, Deceased, et al.*, Chancery File No. 1012, Palm Beach County Circuit Court, Chancery Order Book No. 4, at page 123. On November 26, 1912, the canal company would convey another tract of escrowed state land to the Colorado Florida Land Company. *Colorado Florida Land Co. v. Roebuck*, 83 So. 502 (Fla. 1919).

Chapter 15

Canadian Trouble

Florida legislators, especially those serving east coast constituencies, had become uneasy over the lack of progress in completing the waterway as well as efforts to maintain it despite the record-setting amount of dredging done in the north. Recently re-nominated as Brevard County's state representative, longtime citrus grower R. B. Stewart pointedly asked George Miles in May 1910 what the Florida canal company intended to do about maintaining its nearly completed waterway. "We are very anxious to secure this water-way and the <u>assurance</u> of its <u>maintenance</u>," the 56-year-old Stewart insisted. "The people feel they have given their lands to secure some thing that will be a benefit, and relieve them from having to pay the Railroad Co. exorbitant freight rates." He had been told that the waterway had been poorly maintained in several places, adding that the stretch from Jacksonville to St. Augustine wouldn't be of any great use without a continuous connection south to Biscayne Bay. Despite the pressures to complete the waterway and maintain it to state specifications, the canal company subdivided for sale a tract of land a quarter-mile square in St. Lucie County along today's Federal Highway south of Fort Pierce.[1]

Meanwhile, trouble brewed in Canada. Miles endured ever-increasing criticism from his Canadian colleagues about their underperforming Florida holdings. Sir Sandford Fleming himself expressed disappointment over the lack of any profits earned on his Boston & Florida investment made almost twenty years before. Fleming held Miles personally responsible. Miles considered recommending that Fleming send a representative to the annual meeting to be held at Portland on Thursday, June 16. Regarding the Florida canal company in which Fleming also held shares, Miles did not think that "the Gentlemen who control the Co. in New England at all realize the situation in Florida." Trouble also was brewing among Florida legislators at Tal-

---

[1]R. B. Stewart to George Gleason, 26 May 1910, SP Folder 34. Plat of Florida Coast Line Canal & Transportation Co., recorded in Plat Book 1, at Page 43, of the Public Records of St. Lucie County, Florida.

lahassee over the failure to maintain the inland waterway's depth, violating the firm's 1906 agreement and thereby potentially jeopardizing entitlement to hundreds of thousands of acres of state land. To make matters worse, the state's authority to charge tolls expired and the company couldn't renegotiate them until directors provided assurances that the company intended to maintain the waterway. On the bright side, Miles learned that former Governor Broward, an ardent inland waterway supporter, had won the recent primary election to the United States Senate. Sawyer had no doubt about the boom in Florida and considered the New England group's investments there "a mighty good gamble." With Amory putting a value of at least $1.5 million on the waterway, Sawyer offered it for sale at $2,750,000.[2]

After thanking Helen Bradley for her loan of $7,500 to the Florida canal company, Sawyer boasted over some $140,000 in notes receivable that had come in from recent land sales. Bradley's trust, however, refused to loan more money because of complications with the Second Escrow Deed and the perceived negative attitude of the Florida trustees toward the company. The Barrs sale depended on securing title to the land, but the land was still tied up in escrow with Barnett. All in all, the company needed cash to operate, not promises to pay. Helen made it clear that her husband had never wanted to put money into a waterway north of St. Augustine. Although she had made some advances for the work, she didn't want to invest more money, despite the rosy reports emanating from a few persons in Florida. According to Gleason, more than 50,000 residents had settled along the Florida waterway, noting that a boat line had been operating between Jacksonville and Miami, that at least one resident in St. Augustine shipped and received goods using the waterway between Jacksonville and Miami and that "parties familiar with the Canal Company affairs assure us of considerable business along the line of the Canal." To Herbert Wells, all of these facts indicated that the waterway had "at least some value" as a means of transportation. Sawyer informed Helen that the work north of St. Augustine had progressed so well that the end appeared in sight, with weekly reports showing the northern extension completed to full depth. An expenditure of $60,000 to $90,000 should complete the work, Sawyer thought, but a much greater amount would be necessary to complete the waterway to its full width and depth below St. Augustine. The company already had been required to re-dredge several points south, at the Haulover, at both ends of

[2]GFM to AHS, 5 June 1910; AHS to SM, 11 June 1910; AHS to Arthur Merriam, 27 June 1910; all in SP Folder 34.

Lake Worth, and down south into the canal leading into Biscayne Bay. The work that lay ahead in the south seemed so indefinite that it appeared impossible to estimate its cost.[3]

While the Florida canal company pressed to finish the waterway, ADWA members assembled at Providence for the four-day annual meeting beginning on August 31, 1910, and Miles again represented Florida as state vice president. Florida's former governor and now Senator-elect Napoleon Broward delivered one of the keynote addresses. Bragging that the state had spent about $3 million to dig canals across the state, Broward announced that the work would not only reclaim the Everglades but also furnish "commercial cross-State travel." With 250 miles of canals, the waterways would serve as links in "a chain of a system of interstate canals from the Rio Grande to Boston." Taking on the railroads, Broward asked the audience whether or not "the commercial greatness of the country [ought to] be restricted to the wish of people who invest their money in railroads, or shall our prosperity, our commercial greatness depend upon the needs of transportation?" To the applause of delegates, Broward brashly asserted that "[w]e are not asking Congress to appropriate their money, but we are asking them to appropriate our money." Arguing that inland waterway improvements wouldn't consume too much time or money, he recalled how he rebuffed those in the Sunshine State who insisted that $50,000 over four years' time must be spent for accurate surveys before the actual work of draining the Everglades could be undertaken. To those critics the former Jacksonville river boat captain wryly responded that in Florida "we don't dig canals with [surveying] levels, we dig them with dynamite."[4]

Defending congressional appropriations for inland waterway improvements, Broward argued that expenditures of public money would not only promote military defense but also increase trade and commerce and provide competition for the railroads and thus reduce rates. Envisioning the completion of an extensive inland waterway system from Boston to the Rio Grande, Broward urged that coal barges working the route could supply American battleships while American torpedo boats attacked enemy ships

---

[3]AHS to Helen (Mrs. George L.) Bradley, 15, 19 August 1910 (copies); Wells (RIHTC) To FA, 8 August 1910; AHS to Helen Bradley (Mrs. George L.), 19 August 1910 (copy); all in SP Folder 34.

[4]"Atlantic Deeper Waterways," *Manufacturers' Record*, 25 August 1910; Broward, "Florida View"; "Broward Represents Florida at Deep Waterways Convention," *Everglade Magazine*, September 1910.

at will behind the protection of the barrier islands lining the Atlantic coast. As for the enormous cost of inland waterway improvements, he asked delegates rhetorically to suppose that if it cost $5 billion to improve the privately owned railroads to meet the rising demands for transportation, would it not make sense to pay $500 million—a tenth of the railways' cost—to improve the nation's waterways? Later touting Broward as "heart, soul and body, a waterway advocate," the St. Augustine *Meteor* newspaper noted that he would take office the following March. The paper expected the former riverboat captain to "go up the mighty Mississippi" and, "looking the representatives of the great cereal producing States squarely in the face with a Broward look," show them "the placid path to cheap and ever ready transportation, and they will be found 'coming across'." But Broward would never face "the great cereal-producing States." Within a month of his Providence speech, Broward—one of Florida's greatest waterway boosters—suddenly died at the age of fifty-three on October 1, 1910, at his home in Tallahassee.[5]

Meanwhile, writing from West Palm Beach, Willard Bragg, longtime agent for both the Flagler and New England group's several land interests, related a humorous story to Sawyer about one of Florida's tax assessors. Jacksonville's assessor, a man named Adams, held a free pass to use Flagler's railroad, which Flagler suddenly canceled. In response, Adams wrote to Flagler asking him to send a statement of his personal property for taxation purposes. Flagler immediately reinstated Adams's pass.[6]

In December, the nation's inland waterway movement continued to gather steam. Just two months after the ADWA assembly, more than 3,000 delegates assembled at the nation's capital for the annual convention of the National Rivers and Harbors Congress. The convention adopted resolutions urging the federal government to promote immediately a "broad, liberal, comprehensive and effective policy" of river and harbor improvements. Urging again that Congress adopt a rivers and harbors bill that provided fifty million dollars annually for the next ten years, the gathering rejected resolutions calling for regulation of the railroads. One speaker suggested that Congress empower the Interstate Commerce Commission to regulate competition between rail and inland waterway carriers, while the NHRC's president, Louisiana Congressman Joseph Ransdell,

---

[5]Broward, "Florida View." "Great Traffic for Inside Waterway," *Everglade Magazine*, September 1910, citing the reader to the *St. Augustine Meteor*.

[6]Willard L. Bragg to AHS, 26 October 1910, SP Folder 34.

urged cooperation, not competition, among rail and waterway lines. He also recommended that the government issue bonds for waterway improvements whenever general revenues proved insufficient to meet the need. In building the nation's railway systems, he pointed out, railway companies issued some $8.5 billion in bonded debt—more than nine times the size of the federal government's debt at the time.[7]

In Florida, Sawyer had been doing well in dealing with state engineer James O. Wright and it appeared certain that Seth Perkins and George Gibbs could do the remaining dredging work. But as of February 27, the company's balance sheet showed finances decidedly upside down. The company owed a total of $1,560,459 against notes receivable of only $221,318. In April, Amory learned that Miles appeared to doing anything except canal work and had been trying to set up a transportation company.[8]

Conceding that Miles may have been an engineer "many years ago," Amory didn't believe that Miles measured up against someone like Frank Hodgdon, who had an active waterway engineering practice in the Bay State. Miles had "deceived us thoroughly" about the completeness of the work he supervised, Amory asserted. He found no fault with the new manager, Seth Perkins, and in fact, believed that Miles had given the directors the wrong impression about Perkins. "Not only that, but he [Miles] is so near Mr. Flagler and the Florida railroad, that we sometimes think it is quite unsafe for us to have him take any interest in both Companies." Miles had not only delayed the work in the north but imbued Wright with "so many ideas" that found their way in his report to Florida trustees, which could have been eliminated had Perkins been able to consult with Wright. Not missing the recent loss of George Gleason in the canal work, Amory wanted Miles out of Florida, no longer needing his assistance with those "political opportunities which have been so advantageously given to us in the past." Moreover, in his opinion, Charles Cooper and Bion Barnett proved more effective in dealing with Florida politics than Miles. As if Amory hadn't said enough, he went on to add, "Another thing I should say is that Mr. Miles was almost always anywhere except doing the work for which he was hired—most of the time loafing—and that was the reason why Gleason's

[7]"A Congress Unanimous for Development," *Manufacturers' Record*, 15 December 1910; Ransdell, "National Rivers and Harbors Congress, *Manufacturers' Record*, 6 January 1910.

[8]FA to AHS, 28 February 1911, SP Folder 35. Balance Sheet of Canal Company as of February 27, 1911, SP Folder 35. FA to SM, 26 April 1911 (copy, first page only); FA to SM, 10 May 1911 (copy); both in SP Folder 36.

resignation was accepted, and cannot be considered a loss to the Company." Miles had been jealous of Perkins's work. While Helen Bradley felt optimistic about the venture, Fred Amory didn't expect to get anything out of the waterway and offered his resignation as president and director. If Helen wanted Miles as president, Amory would yield to her desire.[9]

On Saturday, May 6, Miles met with Sam Maddox at his office in Washington. Miles, as Maddox described him, had been "in a very ugly humor — in the sort of mood that Samson was in when he pulled down the pillars of the temple and killed himself in order that he might get square with thousands of his enemies." Two days later, a different Miles appeared in Maddox's office, the Miles "we knew many years ago." George Bradley, Maddox recalled, had originally gotten into the waterway project on Henry Cooke's representation that it "was destined to become the eighth wonder of the world." Cooke, the financier Jay Cooke's nephew, had been in an "immense hurry" and urged Bradley that if he didn't get in quickly, the waterway would be finished and the boats running "before he could turn around." Bradley invested in the Florida scheme "more as a toy than anything else — he wanted a place he could own, as it were, and spend winters in a house boat up and down his canal." But Bradley's money wasn't enough "to even scratch the surface." Miles then appeared, and with his "Canadian friends" began prosecuting the work, but they, too, soon gave it up. Miles still believed in the waterway, figuring as the company's engineer that when boats began running from Jacksonville to Miami, he would have "a place in the hall of fame second only to De Lesseps." With canal affairs now placed in new hands, Miles seemingly has been cast aside. The new order had come about from "the bungling interference of that great bookkeeper of Providence," Herbert Wells. Maddox thought Wells possessed no real authority within the trust company, deriving such power as he had only from the board of directors. The same "bookkeeper" had "queered" Maddox "early in the game" and had been responsible for his getting out. Maddox still hoped that Amory could restore harmony and keep Miles in the project. But such would not be the case.[10]

Toward the end of May, Miles finally wrote Edwards that he was sending in his resignation as general manager of the company. But if the directors still wanted to use his long experience to help work out problems, he would

---

[9]*Ibid.*
[10]SM to FA, 8 May 1911, SP Folder 36.

do so, as long as he kept the vice presidency. Since he remained the general manager until the acceptance of his resignation, he felt entitled to express his views on the work and did so at length. Among other things, Miles argued that considerable dissatisfaction had arisen among Palm Beach and Dade county residents over the company's failure to send a dredge to the southern portion of the waterway. Residents feared that the federal government's appropriation for dredging Gilbert's Bar at Stuart would be lost because of the canal company's failure to secure a dredge within the required time.[11]

By June 13, Amory was out of money again and unable to pay June expenses. Writing from London in July, Helen asked Sawyer for a report on the waterway's progress. Sawyer told her that the state's engineer, James Wright, who maintained some authority over the company's work under the 1906 agreement, at first refused to approve the June vouchers but then later approved them.[12]

Meanwhile, at Washington, in July 1911, a board of the Corps of Engineers brought what may have seemed lukewarm news at best to the Florida canal company. In considering two different Florida routes, board members reported favorably on a proposed continuous federally-maintained waterway from Beaufort to Key West. One proposed route followed the Florida canal company's waterway. But the board preferred an alternate westerly route that followed the deeper St. Johns River south from Jacksonville to Sanford, then by way of a proposed artificial canal to Titusville, and only then down the line of the remaining stretches of the Florida canal company's waterway to Biscayne Bay. The board recommended that the federal government enlarge the waterway to a depth of ten feet and a width of one hundred feet at a cost of almost $7 million.[13]

In an article appearing in the Baltimore trade paper *Manufacturers' Record* in August, Lewis M. Haupt, a well-known maritime engineer from Pennsylvania and the proponent of an Atlantic intracoastal waterway in the same publication more than nineteen years earlier, echoed the National Rivers and Harbors Congress's motto, "A Policy and Not a Project." Haupt advocated a $500 million government bond issue and the expenditure of $50 mil-

---

[11]GFM to Stephen Edwards, 25 May 1911 (copy), SP Folder 36.

[12]FA to Edwards, 13 June 1911 (copy); Helen Bradley to AHS, 11 July [1911]; AHS to Mrs. George L Bradley, 20 July 1911 (copy); all in SP Folder 37.

[13]H. Doc. 229, 63rd Cong., 1st Sess., July 1, 1911. See, also, Youngberg, "East Coast Canal," 28. Edwards to FA, 19 August 1911, SP Folder 37.

lion each year for ten years for inland waterway improvements. In the same issue of the Record, the Florida canal company advertised for bidders to complete the work in the 20-mile-long cut between the Matanzas Inlet and the Halifax River. Company directors expected the work to require the excavation of 1.2 million cubic yards of earth. The opening of bids was be at noon on Wednesday, September 20, at the offices of the company in St. Augustine. Interested bidders were invited to inspect plans for the work at the company's offices at St. Augustine or at Sawyer's offices at 19 Pearl Street in Boston.[14]

In October, delegates gathered for the fourth annual meeting of the ADWA at Richmond. Attendees unanimously adopted resolutions calling for a deep-water inland channel extending from below Cape Hatteras north to Boston Harbor covering a distance of six hundred miles and then south to Florida and the Gulf of Mexico. Among the Florida participants were the canal company's former general manager, George Miles, who attended again as state vice-president, and Charles Cooper, the company's long-time attorney, who represented the Sunshine State as a delegate. One ADWA resolution claimed that thirty million residents along the Atlantic coast would reap the benefits of the "flow of commerce" if only a hundred miles of obstructions were removed from the mostly naturally occurring intracoastal waterway. Thousands of lives and millions of dollars worth of cargo had been lost in Atlantic seaboard shipping between 1900 and 1909. Reciting a "laundry list" of benefits to be reaped from a continuous Atlantic intracoastal waterway, the resolution proclaimed, "The time for talk about this great project has ended, and the time for action has come." And in what must have been one of the longest sentences ever written for an ADWA resolution, the proposal further argued, "A project plainly indicated by nature against which no reasonable argument has ever been presented, which has encountered no open opposition, which will hurt nobody, which will give cheaper transportation, lower costs of food, and a larger scope for commerce to one-third the people of the nation, and which will involve an outlay not larger than that required for the construction of half a dozen battleships, should be carried forward to consummation without further argument or consideration." A Jacksonville paper reported that the Army engineers' projected Atlantic intracoastal waterway route using the St. Johns River raised hopes among waterway boosters that Jacksonville

---

[14]Haupt, "A Policy and Not a Project," and "Notice to Dredging Contractors," both appearing in *Manufacturers' Record*, 7 September 1911.

would become an important station for coal and other commodities that would pass through in barges bound from inland points and from the Gulf of Mexico to destinations up and down the proposed Atlantic seaboard waterway.[15]

In November, Samuel A. Thompson, a national leader in the inland waterway movement, published a letter in the *Miami Metropolis* urging Miami residents to send a delegate the following month to the National Rivers and Harbors Congress convening at the nation's capital. He pointed out that Congress had enacted rivers and harbors bills only every three years from 1893 until 1910 (except for a two-year interval between the 1905 and 1907 bills), but in 1910, however, the chairman of the House rivers and harbors committee, D. S. Alexander, had announced his intention to pass a bill every year. Noting that Tampa Congressman Stephen Sparkman had recently replaced Alexander as chairman, Thompson assured Miami readers that Sparkman would continue the practice of passing an annual waterway bill. Massachusetts Congressman Ernest W. Roberts argued in widely circulated newspaper comments that "the day has gone by when river and harbor appropriation bills can be log-rolled through Congress." The day of "pork barrel" legislation was over, he added, promising scrutiny of every item "with a view of seeing to it that only meritorious projects are taken care of." Roberts further assured his readers that projects not approved by the Corps of Engineers would not be funded. In December 1911, three thousand waterway enthusiasts assembled at the New Willard Hotel in Washington to hear General William H. Bixby of the Corps of Engineers, Jacksonville's Duncan Fletcher and Congressman Stephen Sparkman boost inland waterway improvements, including the Florida waterway nearing completion.[16]

From the St. Augustine's Valencia Hotel, Miles offered to assist Sir Sandford Fleming's son, Sandford H. Fleming and his friends in securing lodging in good hunting country around New Smyrna, about seventy miles south of the Ancient City. The dove, quail and duck shooting in the area had been

---

[15]"Atlantic Deeper Waterways," *Manufacturers' Record*, 26 August 1911; ADWA, 17-20 October 1911. "Resolutions for Deeper Waterways Proceedings of Richmond Meeting," *Miami Metropolis*, 1 November 1911. "Engineer Board To Meet Here on November 8," *Florida Times-Union*, 2 November 1911.

[16]"Urges Miami To Send Delegate to Rivers and Harbors Congress," letter to editor by S. A. Thompson, Acting Secretary, National Rivers and Harbors Congress, *Miami Metropolis*, 11 November 1911; "Better Waterways An Aid to Railroads Says Bay State Man," *Miami Metropolis*, 10 November 1911. "Waterway Men Cheer General Bixby Wildly," *Washington Times*, 7 December 1911; "Canal Is Chief Topic," Washington *Post*, 7 December 1911.

exceedingly productive. The outlook for the sale of Florida land appeared good but since Bradley's death, his trustees had been trying to manage the Florida properties from Providence, 1,200 miles away. He carefully watched the situation so that when the time came he could protect his and his Canadian colleagues' mutual interests in the courts, if necessary. He guessed that the remaining Boston & Florida land was worth between $600,000 and $700,000 at current prices, but in order to realize any returns on the land, radical changes in the management of the company needed to be made.[17]

In Boston at the annual meeting of the Boston & Florida land company, shareholders elected Sir Sanford Fleming's lawyer and son-in-law, E. D. H. Hall, as a new director. Unlike the Florida canal company, the Boston & Florida had no debt. Of the 100,000 acres the company originally purchased in 1892, approximately 69,500 acres remained available for sale but only 60,000 acres were considered saleable. Current terms of sale required a fifty percent down payment in cash, with the balance to be paid within two years. Some 10,000 acres had been set aside for the Florida East Coast Railway as the land company's contribution for the extension of the Flagler railway. Of that amount, 7,000 acres had already been transferred. More than 2,000 acres had been deeded to Miles for commissions. Taxes and expenses amounted to an astounding $10,000 a year. Yet, net sales for the last five years averaged $9.39 an acre. During that time, the firm sold 12,690 acres, grossing $121,545. Receipts totaled $78,833 in cash, with $43,736 in deferred payments. The land side of the group's business seemed to be taking off.[18]

Florida seemed to be experiencing something of a land boom. On January 1, 1912, Sawyer learned from a confidante that Flagler railway had been part of a movement to curb the Boston & Florida's land sales. The railway wanted to sell its land on the coast first, which depressed the Boston & Florida's inland land prices. But the Flagler's freight operations had been doing no better. The railway had been sued for $2 million for the loss of perishable freight the railway couldn't move quickly enough. Flagler settled the litigation for an enormous sum at that time—$600,000. Still, it took an astounding five days to transport perishable goods by rail from Miami to Jacksonville even though the railway had double-tracked forty miles of the

---

[17]GFM to Sanford H. Fleming, 5 December 1911, HGP

[18]Boston & Florida Atlantic Coast Land Co., Thursday, December 14, 1911, (Memorandum), HGP. AHS to Wells, 1 November 1911, and Moyer & Briggs, CPA's to AHS, 1 November 1911, with accompanying financial statements, HGP.

route in the fall of 1911 and purchased thirty-five new engines. Flagler was convinced he couldn't control the situation and welcomed any transportation that could help the railroad out. Reportedly some purchasers who bought Florida land from a Colorado Springs real estate developer on the assumption that he would spend some of the money on canals or drainage ditches, now feared he would spend none of it on improvements. Purchasers had already started legal actions to protect their investments. A competing railway, the Atlantic Coast Line, was expected to build a line from Fort Myers across the Everglades to Miami. Another railway company began securing rights-of-way for a rail line from Tampa to Miami and an electric railway was to provide a connection between Fort Myers and Palm Beach.[19]

There was also speculation over the construction of a inland waterway from Monroe County on the Gulf directly across to Miami, thus enabling the moving of freight in Lee and Monroe counties to Miami for further shipment by rail north. For his own account, Miles had sold 11,000 tons of soil at $6 a ton to the Virginia-North Carolina Chemical Company. The company also purchased and enlarged a mill and bought 2,000 tons of soil at eight dollars a ton. The mill was expected to ship a hundred tons a day down the Florida East Coast Canal to Miami. The Tatum Brothers of Miami bought 9,000 acres south of Miami from the Empire Land Company at $4.50 an acre and sold it at $60 to $75 an acre. Comprised of three brothers — Bethel Blanton, Johnson Reed and Smiley M. — the Tatum firm purchased 12,000 acres more from the Flagler railway at $15 an acre. The three were getting anywhere from $80 to $120 an acre for the land. In only nine months' time, Comfort, a candy manufacturer nine miles above Miami, had already grown sugar cane 14 feet tall, a crop estimated to yield more sugar an acre than any land in Cuba. As soon as Comfort had 10,000 acres planted in cane, he planned to build a sugar mill. And Broward's old friend, John Barrs had earned a profit of $400,000 on his land deals so far. With 60,000 acres left and no installment payments to be made for a year, Barrs held out for twenty dollars an acre, refusing offers at ten dollars an acre.[20]

Meanwhile, back in Canada, Sandford H. Fleming, who had been told that the land was now worth at least 10 times its 1892 value, asked Hall to look more closely into his father's investment. In Florida, Miles agreed to take some of the Barrs' notes for the balance due on his commissions for land

---

[19]Morrell to AHS, 3 January 1912, SP Folder 37.
[20]*Ibid.*

sales. According to Sawyer, Miles now lived in "most comfortable apartments" at St. Augustine's Hotel Alcazar, devoting his time to various outside interests and perennially writing letters of both advice on, and criticism of, Florida canal company affairs to Helen Bradley's lawyer, Stephen Edwards, in Providence.[21]

Cruising the Waterway

George Miles had indeed busied himself on outside interests. He had already started a second transportation company — the Florida Coastal Inland Navigation Company — to run steamers on the Florida East Coast Canal. Sometime in December 1911, Miles began to move the company's headquarters, initially based in Savannah, to Jacksonville. By April 1913, Miles's company had completed the relocation. For a time, the company operated the steamboats *Geneva, Emmett Small*, and *St. Lucie*, as well as the *Swan*, between Jacksonville and St. Augustine and between St. Augustine and towns south on the East Coast Canal. The steam packet *Swan*, a luxury cruiser with a crew of twenty, was said to have been so light as to "float on a dewdrop" while cruising the Florida East Coast Canal on its regular two-and-a-half-day run from Daytona south to West Palm Beach. Formerly a Mississippi River cotton boat, the 156-foot vessel was a steel-hulled triple-decker, with a stern paddlewheel and accommodations for eighty passengers and forty automobiles. Well-heeled passengers arrived at Daytona in chauffeur-driven automobiles like the Stoddard Dayton, the Pope Toledo, the Lozier, and the Stanley Steamer. Nearly every resident turned out to see the vessel depart.[22]

Late in the afternoon, the *Swan* anchored in the Indian River, off Rockledge. Dinner aboard the packet was a sumptuous affair — chicken, southern style; candied sweet potatoes; fresh lima beans; chopped lettuce heads with Russian dressing; assorted hot biscuits; and shortcake. After dinner, passengers played the table games of the day like whist, Parcheesi, and backgammon. The second night of the trip, the *Swan* made fast to a palm tree near Vero Beach for an overnight stay. The next morning, the *Swan*'s

---

[21]S. H. Fleming to Hall, 23 January 1912, HGP. AHS to SM, 10 February 1912 (copy), SP Folder 37.

[22]Bill to Foreclose Lien, *Walter Mucklow, et al. vs. Florida Coastal Inland Navigation Company*, Case No. 5509 (Equity), filed October 22, 1913, Duval County (Florida) Circuit Court. Wheat, "Florida Waterways."

Owned by the Florida Coastal Inland Navigation Company headed by George Miles, the *Swan* plied various sections of the Florida East Coast Canal (Intracoastal Waterway) from St. Augustine to West Palm Beach, transporting automobiles or freight in the open spaces below with passenger cabins above, ca. 1912. (Courtesy, Florida State Archives, Florida Photographic Collection, Tallahassee, Florida)

journey resumed, ending at West Palm Beach a few hours later. A ticket for the one-way trip, including meals, cost what seemed a modest seven dollars a person.[23]

But the *Swan*'s existence would be short-lived. Although the *Swan* had been refitted and the company planned to build three more boats, Miles eventually abandoned the venture because of poor waterway conditions and lack of maintenance.[24]

By the end of February 1912, the Florida waterway had cost the canal company a total of $3,004,259. The company valued its remaining land at

---

[23]*Ibid.*; Hellier, *Indian River*, 70.

[24]"New Boat Lines for Florida's Inland Waterway," *Everglade Magazine* (September 1911):4. GFM to Ranson (copy), 12 January 1926, YP Box 4, Folder 20. Miles, "Florida Coast Line Waterway."

$181,656. Notes receivable owed the company on land sold rose to $67,797. The so-called Special Fund Assets held by Barnett, consisting of land escrowed under the 1906 agreement, totaled $513,027, included $325,349 in remaining lands unsold under the first escrow and the Barrs notes on land sold under the second deed. Of the Barrs notes, $47,000 became due on November 1, 1911, and $63,341, on January 29, 1912. In all, company assets totaled $3.9 million. On capital stock of $700,000, the company's accumulated earnings topped $977,529, hardly the dismal picture painted by a few of the company directors. Still, there existed little cash to continue operations. Uncollected money owed by land purchasers tied up much of the firm's available assets to pay bills.[25]

From St. Augustine on March 3, Miles promised Sandford H. Fleming that he would do everything possible to make Hall's impending visit to Florida a pleasant one. "If he is interested in the development work now going on in the state I shall make arrangements to have the various projects shown to him," he pledged, and "if he wants to keep to the civilized sections of the country, and play golf, I can arrange that character of programme for him too without trouble."[26]

By the end of March, Hall arrived and settled in St. Augustine. Miles hoped to introduce Hall to his lawyers, Hudson and Boggs, whom he had asked to relate to the Canadian lawyer everything they knew about Fleming's Florida interests. "I have spent over twenty of the best years of my life in trying to make our Florida interests valuable," Miles complained in a letter to the junior Fleming, "and, as I think you realize, I had done so when the New England Gentlemen assumed control of the situation and deliberately wasted the assets." Despite efforts to meet at Washington and Richmond, Hudson was never able to visit with Hall at either place. The first week in April, Hudson and Boggs wrote Hall following his return to Canada to offer a formal legal opinion on the feasibility of a lawsuit against the current management of the Florida canal company. Recommending a bondholder's suit, Hudson and Boggs thought it "practically certain" that they could obtain Miles's appointment as receiver to seize control of the company. Reiterating his past concerns, Sir Sandford wrote Hall on April 8 that he had been "most anxious" that his interests there be watched, asking him

---

[25]Moyer & Briggs, Report of Audit of Florida Coast Line Canal & Transp. Co., March 16, 1912, HGP.

[26]GFM to S. H. Fleming, 3 March 1912, HGP.

to ferret out more information on the Boston & Florida land company and to take whatever action he deemed necessary to protect his interests.[27]

On April 12, Miles informed Helen Bradley's lawyer, Stephen Edwards, of the "[a]gitation now in progress" in Florida which he believed was likely to overturn all the good work that had been accomplished the past November at Tallahassee, apparently referring to some state legislators' attempts to hold up the canal company's land grant. The disruption hindered Miles's plans for selling lands near Fort Pierce. Turning to his main point, Miles felt that he had to "place facts" before his Canadian associates, who along with him almost twenty years before had formed a syndicate with a considerable interest in the canal company, about the company's poor management for the last three and half years.[28]

Miles made it clear to Hall that he had done his best to protect his associates' interest and that he had been able to do so in the face of "unaccountable opposition" met from directors representing George Bradley's controlling interest in the company. At the end of 1907 when Gleason, and later Perkins, replaced Miles as manager, the company controlled nearly half a million acres of lands and a waterway which, although incomplete, was open so that boats of considerable size could run from St. Augustine to Miami. Under the 1906 agreement with state trustees, the company was to extend the waterway north to Jacksonville and restore the existing canal south to its required dimensions. This now required the removal of approximately 3.3 million cubic yards in the northern section. If done at the rate at which he had performed the work in the past, the work should have cost $300,000, including machinery. In three years' worth of correspondence, Miles had been able to persuade lawyers representing his Canadian associates that he had done everything in his power to prevent the canal company directors from taking an unwise course, which he felt had resulted in the squandering of several hundred thousand dollars. Before Sawyer and the trust company's lawyer, Frank Swan, arrived in St. Augustine for the canal company's annual meeting, Miles asked them to notify the board of directors that he didn't want to be re-elected vice president. But he heard a few days later that despite his decision, he had been re-elected. He still wanted to be relieved of the office. The company had failed to furnish a dredge for

---

[27]GFM to F. M. Hudson, 26 March 1912; GFM to Hudson (telegram), 28 March 1912; F. M. Hudson to GFM, 31 March 1912; Hudson & Boggs to Hall, 2 April 1912; (Sir) Sandford Fleming to Hall, 8 April 1912; all in HGP.

[28]GFM to Edwards, 12 April 1912 (copy), HGP.

maintenance work in the southern stretches of the waterway running through Palm Beach and Dade counties after agreeing to provide one to induce state trustees to release the Second Escrow Deed, which embarrassed the company in the southern counties.[29]

Meanwhile, on April 23, 1912, Governor Gilchrist led an impressive group of notable state officials and important newspaper reporters from around the country traveling with him by steamboat up the Caloosahatchee River from Fort Myers on the Gulf coast, across Lake Okeechobee and down the newly completed New River Drainage Canal, arriving at Fort Lauderdale on the Atlantic coast on April 25. Completed as part of the state's Everglades drainage program, the route became Florida's first cross-state waterway. Steamboats soon made regular three-day trips between Fort Myers and Fort Lauderdale until the silting in of the upper reaches of the waterway several years later made passage impossible.[30]

Atlantic intracoastal waterway enthusiasts intensified efforts to lobby Congress for more money to purchase or at least improve at least a half a dozen privately-owned canals for a proposed Atlantic Intracoastal Waterway along the east coast. In September 1912, ADWA members met at New London, Connecticut for the organization's fifth annual convention. No longer general manager, Miles presented to the delegates a wide-ranging paper entitled, "Florida's Inland Waterways and Harbors," summarizing the Florida canal company's success in connecting the various natural rivers, lagoons, and sounds along the Florida east coast into a continuous intracoastal waterway — entirely without locks or tide-gates — 500 miles long. At first claiming the waterway now open for its entire length, Miles conceded that several dredges still worked to widen and deepen canals in some stretches of the work. He boasted that the company had not only built the inland waterway for which the Florida legislature had granted lands but aided in the construction of "a first-class railroad [now all the way down to Key West] and a great system of hotels along the East Coast" by sharing its land grant. But the railroad had been unable to meet the demands of the state's burgeoning commerce. Miles argued that the canal company's

---

[29]GFM to Edwards, 12 April 1912 (copy), HGP.

[30]"Official Opening of the Everglade Drainage Canals," Miami *Herald*, 18 April 1912; "Governor Gilchrist and Party of Officials and Newspaper Representatives Will Come to the Magic City as Guests this Afternoon," *Miami Herald*, 26 April 1912; "Miami Gave a Royal Welcome to Her Distinguished Visitors," *Miami Herald*, 27 April 1912.

waterway offered a cheap alternative for the transportation of fruit and vegetables as well as "low class freight" such as fertilizer and lumber.[31]

A resolution adopted at the New London conference commended Congress's steps to provide for a link in the proposed Intracoastal Waterway extending south from Norfolk to Beaufort Inlet and, on the appropriation of $500,000 for the purchase of the Chesapeake and Albemarle Canal. The group's resolution also included a "demand" that Congress appropriate funds to purchase the Chesapeake and Delaware Canal or otherwise provide for alternate route. It further requested the adoption of the New Jersey sea-level canal project to connect the southern waters with those of New England and New York. Finally, ADWA delegates urged a survey for the extension of the Intracoastal Waterway northward from Boston to Maine.[32]

Despite the obvious disinterest in the Florida waterway at the New London conference and the Corps of Engineers' lack of interest in its purchase, good news for the New England group was just around the corner. Within a matter of weeks, the canal company would receive the last of the massive land grants for constructing what would become Florida's Atlantic Intracoastal Waterway. Meantime, Boston & Florida land company directors began developing a large block of land in south Florida, while Miles and his Canadian colleagues continued to press the company's directors to generate at least some earnings on their investment made twenty years before. On November 5, 1912, Boston & Florida directors subdivided for sale two square-mile blocks of land, each into sixty-four 10-acre lots straddling the Hillsboro Canal in what is now the northern part of Deerfield Beach in Broward County and the southern part of today's Boca Raton in Palm Beach County.[33]

---

[31]Miles, "Florida's Inland Waterways and Harbors," ADWA, September 1912: 307-315.

[32]"Resolutions Adopted at the Fifth Annual Convention," ADWA, Annual Convention, Miscellaneous, JHMP.

[33]Plats recorded on November 5, 1912, in Plat Book 2, Pages 62 and 63, of the Public Records of Palm Beach County, Florida.

Chapter 16

A Land Grab From The Start?

Six years after Bradley's death—almost three decades after the Florida canal company first began dredging—state trustees finally accepted the Florida East Coast Canal as finished according to specifications. In November 1912, Fred Elliott, the state's drainage engineer, confirmed the company had completed the 30-mile Matanzas-Halifax Canal between St. Augustine and Ormond, just above Daytona, with the exception of a three-and-a-half-mile strip. Despite the unfinished work, in December, the trustees made their final land grant to the company, resulting in a total of 1,030,128 acres of public land granted to the privately held firm for dredging 268 miles of inland waterway. The conveyance was the last in series of thirteen transferring land to the company, dating back to 1883.[1]

Meanwhile, Miles stirred up trouble in Canada. Miles wrote Sir Sandford Fleming's son that he had been considering whether "the New England Directors" of the canal company had squandered "our assets" and, if so, whether he could recover the losses from George Bradley's trustee. Some of their investments had been held by St. Augustine and Newburyport banks as security for the old Canadian syndicate's debt, which grew out of Miles's and his Canadian colleagues' attempts to dredge the northern part of the waterway in the late 1880s under a contract with the Florida canal company.[2]

Despite all his saber-rattling, Miles hesitated over litigating the Canadian group's Florida interests. "The estate represented by the New England Gentlemen belongs to Mrs. Bradley, my wife's cousin and only relation in the

---

[1]*MIIF*, 19 November 1912, 575-79; "Intracoastal Waterway from Jacksonville, Fla. to Miami, Fla.," House Document No. 586, 69th Cong., 2d Session. Letter from the Secretary of War transmitting Report from the Chief of Engineers on Preliminary Examination and Survey of Intracoastal Waterway from Jacksonville, Fla., to Miami, Fla., 10; Youngberg, "East Coast Canal," 5. General biographical material on Elliott may be found in Cutler, *History of Florida*, III, 109.

[2]GFM to S. H. Fleming, 29 November 1912 (copy), HGP.

world: and one of my best friends," he explained. A lawsuit would likely cause strained relations. Miles proposed to the company's directors that if they would give him the right to sell the company's remaining lands and the waterway itself on a commission basis, with commissions to be credited, not to Miles personally but to the syndicate, he would do his best to make sales. But Miles never heard from them. Still Miles remained optimistic about Florida's prospects for development. His Canadian associates, he thought, would find a trip down of considerable interest "as the country is developing rapidly," adding that "Cuba is being drawn so near Florida by improved transportation that great opportunities are opening up there also."[3]

News that the canal company was to receive the last of the huge land grants that had subsidized the waterway's construction touched off a fire-storm of controversy, with cries that the company had not lived up to the state's charter requiring the waterway's maintenance. The West Palm Beach-based *Tropical Sun* predicted that if state trustees transferred the last land grant that "[t]he Boston syndicate will have their lands and be gone this time, and there won't be canal enough to float a canoe to show for it, if action is not taken to point out conditions and have them remedied." The plan of the canal company, "a combination of Boston capitalists," the news-paper declared, had been "a land grab scheme from the start." Even though five boats ran between Daytona and Jacksonville every week, with freight rates nearly half railway charges, the stretch of waterway between Jupiter and Fort Lauderdale had been seriously neglected. A few miles south of Delray, the company's dredge *Minkee* struck a mile-and-a-half-long stretch of rock in three feet of water at low tide, but the captain was ordered "to skip it." Below Lake Boca Raton a few miles south to the Hillsboro drainage canal at today's Deerfield Beach, the paper found the worst section of all, with no more than twenty-six inches of water at low tide.[4]

But the *Tropical Sun*'s protest and those of many others arrived too late. Sometime between November 20 and 26, state trustees conveyed 117,000 acres of valuable public land lying along the Florida east coast to the Florida canal company. Despite objections lodged by boards of trade at Miami, Fort Pierce, Cocoa, Titusville, New Smyrna and Daytona, state trustees approved

---

[3]*Ibid.*

[4]"Inland Waterway and Daytona," *Tropical Sun* (West Palm Beach), 28 November 1912; "Bad Condition of Coast Canal," *Tropical Sun* (West Palm Beach), 28 November 1912.

the transfer. Even former waterway advocates such as George Gleason opposed the move. Before the trustees' decision, Gleason asserted that "[a]s matters now stand, the canal is of little or no use in the transportation of freight. Between Jacksonville and Daytona the boats are constantly hung up and the freight waiting to be forwarded is piling up mountain high. Miami is virtually out of it entirely."[5]

While the canal company's acceptance of the last of the land grants generated considerable debate, the state trustees' compromise with Flagler over the lands grants promised his railway provoked hardly a whisper of protest. On December 20, to settle litigation brought against the state and the company over lands held in reserve for both the railway and canal companies, state trustees quietly agreed to deed the railway 250,000 acres of public land, 200,000 acres of which lay in the extreme southern portion of the Everglades, with the remaining 50,000 acres located north of the new town of Fort Lauderdale.[6]

News of the trustees' decision in Tallahassee over the company's final grant failed to reach Jacksonville until December 27, when the *Jacksonville Metropolis* headlined a report from Gleason that the trustees had already delivered the deeds to 117,000 acres of public land. State trustees, including Governor Albert Gilchrist, attempted to explain their actions as simply complying with the settlement made in 1906. The trustees argued that a new escrow of funds from the sale of lands had been more than sufficient to pay for any remaining work. They pointed out that because of the canal company's financial problems the trustees agreed to allow the company to sell some of the land set aside to guarantee the work, with the understanding that all of the proceeds would be used to finish the canal and, in addition, that $50,000 would be set aside to finish the waterway south of Daytona. But the *Metropolis* continued to push for an explanation, pointing out that

---

[5]"The State Delivers 117,000 Acres to Atlantic Coast Line Canal Co.," *Miami Herald*, 22 December 1912.

[6]"Compromise Effected With State Over Florida Lands," *St. Augustine Record*, 20 December 1912.

even Miles, a former president of the canal company who had made the waterway his life's work, opposed the transfer.[7]

Weighing in on the controversy, the Miami *Herald* clearly didn't believe the trustees' explanation, "Either the canal is completed or it is not. From the statement of the board [of trustees] we are to conclude that it is. From its action we are driven to the conclusion that it is not. As a matter of hard fact, all residents of the east coast of the state know that the canal is not in condition to be used successfully, and there are grave doubts as to whether the amount retained by the board will fully complete it." A few months later, another Jacksonville paper published a lengthy diatribe by Charles Jones. Jones defended the canal company's work, arguing that the Flagler railroad and newspapers it controlled had misrepresented the facts behind the trustees' decision to discredit both the trustees and the company.[8]

Although Miles publicly criticized the waterway's uselessness, his Florida Coastal Inland Navigation Company announced just weeks before the trustees' decision that in addition to the five boats already running between Jacksonville and Daytona, the company planned to add a new vessel, the 125-foot steamer *City of Daytona*. The company also chartered the *Emmet Small* and had been negotiating a charter of the *Biscayne*. With the arrival of the *Biscayne*, the firm owned or controlled enough boats to provide transportation between Jacksonville and Daytona every other day. In addition, the McCoy brothers began operating the steamer *Republic* between St. Augustine and Daytona, with the steamer *U.S.A.* running between Daytona and Palm Beach. The thrice-weekly trip on the *Republic* began at St. Augustine at eight o'clock in the morning, arriving in Daytona at about four o'clock in the afternoon.[9]

---

[7]"State Delivers 117,000 Acres to Coast Line Canal Company Despite Protests of the People," *Jacksonville Metropolis*, 27 December 1912; "Editor, _____, Tallahassee, Florida, December 28, 1912," by TIIF, an open letter, in "Old Railroad Bonds, etc.," "Drawer 3," Land Records and Title Section, Division of State Lands, Florida Department of Environmental Protection, Tallahassee, Fla., was published in, e.g., "Governor Explains Why Trustees Signed Deeds," *Jacksonville Metropolis*, 1 January 1913; "State Trustees Have Safeguarded the People in the Celebrated Inter-Coastal Canal Deal," *Miami Metropolis*, 3 January 1913; "Improvement Fund Trustees Issue Complete Statement About Turning Over Lands." *Daytona Gazette-News*, 7 January 1913; "The Florida East Coast Line Canal," *Dixie* (Jacksonville), 5 April 1913.

[8]*Miami Herald*, 1 January 1913. "The Florida East Coast Line Canal," *Dixie* (Jacksonville), 5 April 1913.

[9]"Coastal Company To Put on Three More Steamers," Daytona *Daily News*, 28 December 1912; "Company Hopes To Furnish One Boat Every Other Day," *Daytona Gazette-News*, 18 January 1913. "McCoy Brothers' Line Down East Coast Begins Service," *St. Augustine Record*, 21 January 1913.

State trustees advertised for bids on the cleanup work in the Florida waterway, with most of the work to be done in the approach to the Halifax River to be paid for out of the new escrow fund established by the canal company. At the same time, east coast residents began working with representatives of Hampton Moore's Atlantic Deeper Waterways Association to address the long-neglected Florida waterway situation. Local representatives planned to attend an April hearing before Brigadier General William Bixby, chief of engineers, on the federal government's plans to complete a waterway connection between Beaufort (home town of North Carolina Congressman John Small), and Key West. Overlooking the Florida canal company's many failures in dredging and maintaining the waterway, state trustees permitted the enterprise to collect tolls at various points along the waterway as early as 1911 when the company began collecting tolls at a chain stretched across the waterway at today's Dania Beach. Three years later, the company would stretch toll chains across canals at North River, Smith's Creek, and the Haulover, in addition to the Dania Beach chain. In 1916, two more chains would be added at Juno and Boynton, while the company moved the toll chain at Dania south to today's Hallandale Beach.[10]

At the end of January 1913, Fred Elliott, the state's acting chief engineer, toured the section of the east coast canal between Daytona and Miami, along with several canal company officials, including the firm's general manager, Seth Perkins, and even Hayden Sawyer, the canal company's treasurer since Walker's death. Elliott admitted finding bad places north of West Palm Beach but pledged that the shoaling would be dredged out. The local West Palm Beach *Tropical Sun* opined that the engineer would find as many poorly dredged locations on the inspection trip south. Later, Sawyer assured local residents that the shoals would be eliminated within a few weeks.[11]

But discontent over the canal company's land grab and its dereliction in completing the waterway continued to fester among east coast residents. The *Palm Beach County* newspaper pronounced the waterway a flop: "That the Inter-Coastal Canal in Florida is a flat, dead failure, even after the projectors of the enterprise have received 800,000 acres of land for the faithful

---

[10]"Trustees Push Canal Work," *Tropical Sun* (West Palm Beach), 6 March 1913; "Coast Canal To Be Completed," Palm Beach *News*, 7 March 1913. "Would Incalculably Benefit This Section," *Tropical Sun* (West Palm Beach), 13 March 1913. Perkins to GAY, 12 November 1927, YP Box 4, File 2.

[11]"Canal Officials Getting Busy," *Tropical Sun* (West Palm Beach), 30 January 1913; "Houseboat Fast in Canal," *Tropical Sun* (West Palm Beach), 13 February 1913.

completion of the terms of the contract [with the state], is admitted by all who have occasion to use that waterway." Describing the travel of Corps of Engineers Major John Slattery down the waterway, the paper reported "a slow and dreary trip" from St. Augustine to Miami. The trip was abruptly halted at Fort Lauderdale after consuming five days in the struggle and Slattery gave up on ever reaching Miami by water.[12]

Meanwhile, by the early part of the summer, Sandford H. Fleming had returned to Canada from "a fairly satisfactory visit to Boston." The Boston & Florida land company had declared a healthy seven and one-half percent dividend on the preferred stock. Miles objected to a good many things at the meeting but was "quite pleasant," the younger Fleming reported, and believed that "his troubles have blown over after he made his objections to the management which were put on record." Fleming couldn't contact Miles to make a settlement of the Canadian syndicate's holdings but promised to do something. He estimated the Boston & Florida stock worth an astounding $350 to $380 a share. But Hall apparently had been mistaken when he informed Fleming that Miles had gotten over his bad feelings about the Florida canal company. Miles had started a lawsuit.[13]

On July 1, in a letter to the Montreal counsel for the MacDonell estate to discuss the claim of Allan R. MacDonell against the Florida syndicate composed of MacDonell, John D. Maclennan, Sandford H. Fleming, and himself, Miles stated that he held certain Florida Canal and Boston & Florida land company securities for the benefit of the four-man group. Against these securities had been a claim for the syndicate's debt when it gave up its contract with the canal company. Miles had paid part of the debt over the past two decades out of his personal funds to prevent legal proceedings against him and his partners. In Miles's view, the Bradley interests controlling the canal company had dissipated most of its assets by gross mismanagement and, if permitted to do so, would wreck it completely, thereby rendering their securities worthless. So far, he had been unable to secure sufficient interest from his Canadian colleagues to prevent this, but in any event, he hoped for their cooperation in the litigation or at least for a free hand to litigate on behalf of his own interests.[14]

---

[12]Quoted in "The Intracoastal Canal, Once Bad, Now Excellent," Ziemba, *Martin County Heritage*, pp.,194-95.

[13]S. H. Fleming to Hall, ? May 1913; 5 July 1913; both in HGP.

[14]GFM to Campbell, McMaster & Papineau, 3 July 1913 (copy), HGP.

Toward the end of July, Miles appeared willing to withdraw his lawsuit and, by the end of August, Miles and the Florida canal company had reached a settlement. Sawyer informed Fleming that the settlement with Miles had only been agreed upon because of the unwillingness of Helen Bradley to engage the company in a legal battle with Miles and because of "expediency" in eliminating any possibility of a cloud on the title to the land the company had already agreed to sell to others.[15]

On September 10, Acting Secretary of War Henry Breckenridge forwarded to the Speaker of the House of Representatives the long-awaited report of William H. Bixby, the Army chief of engineers, of a survey for a proposed continuous inland waterway from Boston to the Rio Grande. The chief's report, entitled "Report on Intracoastal Waterway — Beaufort, North Carolina, to Key West Section," endorsed the improvement of the section of the waterway between Beaufort and the upper St. Johns River in Florida to a seven-foot depth at an estimated cost of $14,400,000. But beyond the St. Johns River and south along the Florida east coast, Bixby found the population "sparse" and the means of boat travel "occasional." In sum, to the disappointment of Florida waterway supporters, Army engineers had deemed a seven-foot channel along the Florida coast for Atlantic coast travel "not at present urgent." A federal takeover of the Florida canal company's waterway would have to wait.[16]

In Canada, young Fleming approved a proposed division of the Florida securities among the Canadian group. He also knew that Miles held $70,000 in debt securities of the Florida canal company in escrow, as well as 163 shares of preferred stock and 165 common stock shares in the Boston & Florida land company, along with, perhaps, a few bonds in the canal company. By October 9, a settlement on the securities held by the Miles was completed. The settlement was based on the assumption that Boston & Florida shares were worth $300 each. Miles, MacDonell and the Maclennan estate each were to receive $17,127 worth of stock after accounting for the claims of each partner against the syndicate.[17]

In Florida, the controversy over the state trustees' conveyance of the final land grant to the company continued to simmer. The burden of tolls along

---

[15]S. H. Fleming to Hall, 22 July 1913; AHS to S. H. Fleming, 25 August 1913; Murray, Prentice & Howland to S. H. Fleming, 29 August 1913; all in HGP.

[16]H. Doc. 229, pp.10-11.

[17]S. H. Fleming to Murray, Prentice & Howland, 8 September 1913; S. H. Fleming to Hall, 9 October 1913, with attached reconciliation of shares among three syndicate members; both in HGP.

the waterway, together with the canal's poor maintenance, provoked local residents into action. Boards of trade up and down the Florida east coast stepped up lobbying efforts seeking the waterway's turnover to the federal government and formed several inland waterway associations to advance the cause. In November 1913, enthusiasts meeting at Jacksonville formed the Florida East Coast Canal Association to cooperate with the larger ADWA to persuade the federal government to take over the Florida waterway. Board of trade members meeting at St. Augustine, Daytona, New Smyrna and Eau Gallie passed resolutions supporting a federal takeover. In turn, ADWA delegates incorporated the measures in proposals adopted at a meeting held at Jacksonville and — a year later — at a second one convened at New York. At the ADWA's sixth annual meeting at Jacksonville, on November 18, 19, 20, and 21, 1913, hundreds of delegates arrived aboard a special Seaboard Air Line Railway train from New York and via three different steamships — the *Persian*, the *Somerset*, and the *Huron*. A hundred delegates, including J. Hampton Moore, president of the association, traveled aboard the *Persian* from New York City. At Jacksonville, attendees paid homage to the late Napoleon Broward by adorning the speaker's rostrum at the Board of Trade auditorium with a life-size portrait of the former governor who had died just three years before at the age of fifty-three.[18]

While ADWA delegates gathered at Jacksonville, cross-Florida waterway enthusiasts headed inland for Palatka on the St. Johns River for the third annual meeting of the Mississippi to Atlantic Inland Waterways Association. Beginning on Monday, November 17, twenty-two speakers, including former Governor Albert Gilchrist and Congressman Stephen Sparkman, addressed the delegates assembled at Palatka's Howell Theater on a variety of waterway issues during the course of the three-day event. In a patriotic gesture, the United States Navy sailed two torpedo boats, the *Tingey* and the

---

[18]"Big Meeting at Stuart," *Fort Lauderdale Sentinel*, 23 October 1914; "Clans Meet at Stuart," *Fort Lauderdale Sentinel*, 13 November 1914; "Florida Canal Men Meet," *Fort Lauderdale Sentinel*, 27 November 1914. "All Ready for Two Great Conventions in City this Week," *Florida Times-Union*, 16 November 1913; "A.D.W. Association Opens Sixth Annual Convention in City," *Florida Times-Union*, 18 November 1913; "Special Train Brings Big Northern Party to Waterways Convention," *Florida Times-Union*, 18 November 1913; "Matters of Interest About Those Attending the Conventions Here," *Florida Times-Union*, 20 November 1913; "Seaboard's New York-New Jersey Special to Waterways Convention," [Section Two banner headline, with photograph of train] *Florida Times-Union*, 19 November 1913; "Coastal Canals Would Save Lives and Be Facility in Contingency of War," *Florida Times-Union*, 20 September 1913; "J. Hampton Moore Again Elected President of Waterways Association," *Florida Times-Union*, 21 November 1913.

Thornton, up the St. Johns River to the town and moored them at the Hart wharf. One resolution urged the federal government's improvement of the St. Johns, Ocklawaha and Withlacoochee river route as the most feasible cross-Florida inland waterway route. At the conclusion of the Palatka assembly, both the *Tingey* and *Thornton* returned to Jacksonville to join a third vessel, the destroyer *Preston,* for the ADWA convention.[19]

Miles, the Florida canal company's former general manager, attended the Jacksonville meeting again as the association's vice president. Florida's other delegate to the gathering was Charles M. Cooper, the company's lawyer. Speeches included a welcome address by Governor Park Trammell, Congressman John Small's remarks on the South's interest in a completed Atlantic coastal waterway, and Congressman Stephen Sparkman's summary of the work of the House rivers and harbors committee on inland waterway improvement.[20]

On the third day of the Jacksonville meeting, Senator Duncan Fletcher told the Jacksonville delegates of the progress being made by the Mississippi to Atlantic Inland Waterways Association in creating an inland waterway connection between the Gulf of Mexico and the Atlantic Ocean. Describing his tiny group as "the Indian dugout" as compared to the ADWA's "trans-Atlantic liner," he informed the delegates that a good portion of the work had almost been completed at the western end and that when the route for the next stretch of work through Alabama, Georgia and Florida was selected, additional construction could begin.[21]

Just a few weeks after the conclusion of the ADWA meeting, almost a thousand delegates attended the 10th annual National Rivers and Harbors Congress, held once again at the nation's capital, in December 1913. Standing in for President Woodrow Wilson, Interior Secretary Franklin Lane strongly urged the states to preserve their harbors from the grasp of railroads seeking terminal sites while also warning against harming the railroad industry. All of the speeches focused on the need for a broad policy

---

[19]"Flotilla in Port Now for Conventions," *Sunday (Florida)Times-Union,*16 November 1913; "Naval Vessels Interesting to Sunday Crowds," *Florida Times-Union,* 17 November 1913; "Waterways Convention To Open in Palatka Today," *Florida Times-Union,* 17 November 1913; "Mississippi-To-Atlantic Inland Waterways Association," *Florida Times-Union,* 19 November 1913."

[20]"Official Programme, Atlantic Deeper Waterways Association, Sixth Annual Convention, November 18, 19, 20, 21, 1913, Jacksonville, Florida," ADWA, Annual Convention, Miscellaneous, JHMP.

[21]ADWA, *Proceedings,* 18-21 November 1913: 165-173.

and cooperation between the federal government and the states. In one more waterway appearance, the ubiquitous Senator Duncan Fletcher emphasized the value of the cross-Florida waterway, while both Congressman John Small and Pennsylvania's J. Hampton Moore espoused the cause of the Atlantic Intracoastal Waterway.[22]

Meanwhile, at the Tallahassee meeting of the state trustees held on December 12, 1913, canal company officials submitted a schedule of tolls for formal adoption. Finally agreeing to the proposal after considerable debate, the trustees noted the approval of George Miles, who was still connected to the canal company and was also president of the Florida Coastal Inland Navigation Company, and the concurrence of A.W. Corbett, mayor of St. Augustine and president of another line of steamboats operating on the waterway. The trustees believed that enabling the company to collect tolls would allow the enterprise to finance proper maintenance of the waterway. Cognizant of the substantial business already generated by waterway improvements, the trustees acknowledged the losses in tolls previously sustained by the company and noted that "a large amount of commerce and traffic [is] now using the canal, consisting of freight boats, passenger boats, yachts, etc., and the Canal Company is sustaining heavy loss by not collecting tolls."[23]

By January 9, 1914, Sawyer and Frank Swan, attorney for the Rhode Island Hospital Trust Company, had been in Florida for almost three weeks. Engaged in Florida canal company affairs, including the vexing toll questions, the two directors had been over the entire length of the waterway and considered several suggestions to spur land sales, which had been increasing nonetheless. The company had been using several land agents in Maine and West Palm Beach as well as a Jacksonville agent named Tomlinson. According to Sawyer, Tomlinson had sold about a million dollars' worth of company land.[24]

But trouble had been boiling along the lower east coast over the tolls the state trustees had just authorized. On January 21, members of the West Palm Beach Board of Trade unanimously adopted a resolution calling on the trustees to suspend all tolls. The measure called the toll rates "practically prohibitive" and referred to many sections along the waterway blocking passage of vessels drawing more than two feet of water. Three days later,

---

[22]"Harbors Congress Meets," *New York Times*, 14 December 1913.

[23]*MIIF*, 12 December 1913.

[24]AHS to S. H. Fleming, 9 January 1914 (copy), HGP.

the Florida East Coast Canal Association, whose executive committee was headed by George Gleason, met at Daytona. Gleason's group passed a resolution protesting any waterway that failed to meet state specifications. Members pointed out that yachts of all sizes had been cruising along the outside route instead of using the inland waterway because of high tolls and shoddy maintenance, all of which resulted in lost economic benefits to the area.[25]

To counter Gleason's resolution, the canal company submitted affidavits supporting the toll schedule. George Gibbs, the company's assistant treasurer for the previous ten years, asserted the enterprise had turned out to be a financial failure for the original investors. The net cost of the waterway to the company had been $1,770,000, after deducting the land grant and the $75,000 escrowed by state trustees for future maintenance. In 1909, when Miles was a director and vice president of the company, he and Gleason had surveyed the tolls charged for passage through canals in other states. Based on Miles's survey, the canal company submitted a toll schedule that had been approved for a six-month period on October 22, 1909. Very few tolls, if any, were collected in the northern stretches of the waterway. The schedule was complex and a simpler one had been desired. Gibbs had heard no complaints about the tolls and, in fact, understood in speaking with a few knowledgeable people, that the company's tolls were less than other canal companies had been charging. The question was then presented to Miles, still a director of the company and also a director and vice president of the Florida Coastal Inland Navigation Company, who had both formulated and approved the new toll schedule.

A toll chain had recently been put in between St. Augustine and the St. Johns River where tolls had been collected for only a few weeks. Toll chains had also been installed across the cut between the Matanzas and Halifax rivers, across the Haulover between the Indian River and the Mosquito Lagoon, and another near Dania. For the twenty-day period from December 29, 1913 until January 18, 1914, the company collected tolls amounting to $456 at the North (Tolomato) River chain, where tolls for passage through all of the chains could be collected at the beginning of a trip. The chain at Smith's Creek had just been established and no report had been received

---

[25]Resolution of West Palm Beach Board of Trade, January 21, 1914; Resolution of the Florida East Coast Canal Association, January 24, 1914; both in "Old Railroad Bonds, etc.," "Drawer 3," Land Records and Title Section, Division of State Lands, Florida Department of Environmental Protection, Tallahassee, Fl.

Florida Coast Line Canal & Transportation Co.

Operative December 15th, 1920, at noon, the following Schedule of Tolls will go into effect.

To be collected for one chain for each of the following divisions of the Florida Coast Line Canal:

St. Johns & N. River Canal
JACKSONVILLE TO ST. AUGUSTINE

Matanzas & Halifax Canal
ST. AUGUSTINE TO DAYTONA

Haulover Canal
DAYTONA TO JUPITER LIGHT

Jupiter & Lake Worth Canal
JUPITER LIGHT TO PALM BEACH

Lake Worth & New River Canal
PALM BEACH TO FT. LAUDERDALE

New River & Biscayne Bay Canal
FT. LAUDERDALE TO MIAMI.

(ALL MEASUREMENTS ARE DECK LENGTH)

Pleasure Boats and House Boats

10c per foot through each chain.
8c per foot through each chain for Launches 40 ft. and under
(not engaged in business.)

Freight and Passenger Boats

5c per foot through each chain and 5% on gross rates from
Freight and Passengers.

Barges and Lighters in Tow

LOADED — 8c per foot through each chain and 5% on freight.
8c per foot on Tug through each chain.
EMPTY — 5c per foot through each chain.
Tugs towing empty lighters 5c per foot through each chain.

Fish Boats —3c per foot through each chain.

Schedule of Tolls, effective December 15, 1920, Florida Coast Line Canal and Transportation Company. The Florida canal company stretched chains across six different sections of the waterway from Jacksonville to Miami until 1929 when the State of Florida's Florida Inland Navigation District purchased the waterway and turned it over to the U. S. Army Corps of Engineers for improvements and future maintenance. (Courtesy, Department of College Archives and Special Collections, Olin Library, Rollins College, Winter Park, Florida)

from the chain at the Haulover. Tolls collected at the chain at the New River, near Dania, barely paid the expense of the toll keeper for the past year.[26]

The company's general manager, Seth Perkins, also signed an affidavit supporting the firm's toll schedule. Perkins pointed out that the schedule had been examined by "one or more experts on transportation and received their endorsement," without mentioning the experts' names. The present schedule was considerably lower than the 1909 approved schedule of tolls, he contended. Information on other canal tolls was sparse because two-thirds of the nation's canal mileage east of the Mississippi River was owned and operated by the federal government or by several states and not by private companies. Of the so-called private canals, ninety percent were controlled by the railroads and used chiefly in connection with their own rail transportation. The current tolls collected at the North (Tolomato) River Canal approximated what would be obtained by applying a unit of measure that had been adopted by the State of Ohio of four mils per thousand pounds per mile, with freight charges and tonnage estimated.[27]

At their January 26 meeting, state trustees heard complaints about the newly approved tolls. Representatives from the Florida East Coast Canal Association, the West Palm Beach Board of Trade, the Woodmen of the World Camp 141 of Titusville and pioneer citrus grower Hiram S. Williams of Rockledge all criticized the tolls' unfairness. In response, the Florida canal company agreed to suspend collecting tolls at its southernmost chain at today's Dania Beach because it failed to produce enough income to meet expenses. With most of the protests coming from residents south of the Haulover at Titusville and no other chains in the southernmost reaches, the trustees approved the company maintaining its toll chains north of the Haulover.[28]

---

[26]*Affidavit of George W. Gibbs, Assistant Treasurer of Florida Coast Line Canal and Transportation Company, Concerning Tolls,* "Old Railroad Bonds, etc.," "Drawer 3," Land Records and Title Section, Division of State Lands, Florida Department of Environmental Protection, Tallahassee.

[27]*Affidavit of Seth Perkins, Concerning Canal Tolls,* "Old Railroad Bonds, etc.," "Drawer 3," Land Records and Title Section, Division of State Lands, Florida Department of Environmental Protection, Tallahassee.

[28]*MIIF,* 26 January 1914. A representative sample of the sudden notice of the second meeting may be found at "Resolutions Adopted by the Trustees," *Fort Lauderdale Sentinel,* 23 January 1914.

It would take another year before the southern toll chains would be restored. On January 29, 1915, state trustees allowed the company to reinstall the three toll chains south of the Haulover. But just four days later, after hearing protests from the Miami Board of Trade, the trustees rescinded their action. Moreover, the trustees no longer appeared interested in arbitrating toll disputes, asking the Florida legislature to relieve them of the burden of approving canal tolls and instead to authorize the state's Railroad Commission to set the charges. A few months later, the legislature responded by empowering the Railroad Commission to regulate tolls along the Florida East Coast Canal.[29]

Meanwhile, waterway association activities gathered steam all along the Florida coast. Just a few months after the large and important ADWA meeting at Jacksonville, representatives from Daytona, New Smyrna and other towns along the coast gathered at St. Augustine on February 5 to discuss government ownership of the east coast canal and to persuade the Corps of Engineers to change its recommendation favoring the St. Johns River route over the East Coast Canal. Speakers at this meeting, which was chaired by J. C. R. Foster of the St. Augustine Chamber of Commerce, included Charles F. Burgman of Seabreeze and H. I. Hamilton of New Smyrna. Burgman, a native of Germany who had been one of four organizers of the American Federation of Labor, would later become a key figure in the federal government's takeover of the waterway and the first chairman of the Florida Inland Navigation District. At the meeting's end, the group voted to form a committee composed of one representative from every town and city along the east coast to draft a report for the Corps of Engineers demonstrating the superiority of the East Coast Canal over the St. Johns River route.[30]

The next month, Senator Duncan Fletcher introduced a joint resolution in Congress authorizing the president to appoint a commission to consider the feasibility of the government constructing an inland waterway along the Atlantic coast from the St. Johns River to Key West. The body was to be comprised of an officer or retired officer of the engineer corps of the Navy and one person from civilian life. "This contemplates the possible taking

---

[29]*MIIF*, 29 January and 2 February 1915. Since 1868, canal companies had possessed the authority with the approval of the state trustees to fix tolls not only on each vessel passing through the each artificial channel cut but also upon any merchandise carried on such vessel through the canal. *Laws of Florida* (1868), c. 1639, § 12. *Laws of Florida* (1915), c. 6888, § 1.

[30]"Big Waterways Meet at St. Augustine Wednesday, *Florida Times-Union*, 3 February 1914; "Government Ownership of Florida Coast Canal An Important Move," *Florida Times-Union*, 6 February 1914.

over of the Florida East Coast canal if suitable terms can be arranged," Fletcher said at the time. "Provision is made for a somewhat parallel route in case satisfactory terms cannot be reached with the canal company. The object is to establish a free inland waterway for transportation along the East Coast of Florida to be maintained by the government." Fletcher's resolution was referred to the commerce commission. Fletcher hoped that the resolution would be favorably reported and acted upon by the House of Representatives. "It appears that the Florida East Coast canal, while open practically all the distance, is in some places very shallow and not well maintained or marked, and that the charge for tolls in some instances is excessive. This canal is very much needed in order to afford facilities for moving the products along the East Coast, as well as for the carrying of passengers and for use by pleasure yachts and boats," Fletcher said.[31]

By the end of June 1914, Boston & Florida stockholders in Canada and New England received heartening news of increasing Florida land sales. Company directors declared a whopping sixteen percent dividend on the stock, which meant a return of sixteen dollars for each share of stock. Officers of the Florida canal company now included Amory as president; Helen Bradley's lawyer, Stephen O. Edwards, as vice president; Sawyer as secretary and treasurer; past president John W. Denny as assistant secretary and George W. Gibbs as assistant treasurer.

Still more Florida waterway gatherings took place. In November, supporters expected a thousand people to gather at Stuart for the first annual convention of the Florida East Coast Canal Association. A group of Florida east coast newspaper publishers, including *Miami Herald* publisher Frank Shutts, a strong inland waterway advocate, and J. J. Birch of the *New Smyrna Breeze*, another waterway supporter, also began forming the Florida East Coast Press Association twenty miles north of Stuart at Fort Pierce.[32]

So great had been the anticipated attendance at the Stuart meeting, the Florida East Coast Railway — the East Coast Canal's rival — advertised a special rate for participants traveling to the town. The price of a round-trip ticket would be the usual one-way fare plus an additional twenty-five cents

[31]"Free Inland Waterway Is Now Wanted," *Florida Times-Union*, 7 March 1914.

[32]George W. Piper (Boston & Florida company) to Hall and Ritchie, in trust, 30 June 1914, HGP. "East Coast Canal To Be Bought by Government For Much Less Than It Cost to Build," *Miami Metropolis*, 27 November 1914. "Big Meeting at Stuart," *Fort Lauderdale Sentinel*, 23 October 1914; "Clans Meet at Stuart," *Fort Lauderdale Sentinel*, 13 November 1914; "Florida Canal Men Meet," *Fort Lauderdale Sentinel*, 27 November 1914. "Florida East Coast Press Ass'n Formed," *Miami Herald*, 24 November 1914.

for the return trip home. Leaders at the three-day gathering included George G. Currie of West Palm Beach, who led the association as president; J. C. Hancock of Stuart, vice president, and H. I. Hamilton of New Smyrna, secretary. During the meeting, Stuart lawyer C. C. Chillingworth reflected on the history of the Florida East Coast Canal, while Governor Park Trammel outlined the waterway's current status. Chillingworth's speech honored the achievements of the Florida canal company' directors, observing that the "struggles, the hardships, the heartbreaks, the disappointments, and the despair of its owners have never been and never will be recorded, but let us honor the men who have fought the fight to the finish and who truly deserve the praise of all men for the good work they have done." Delegates to the large Stuart gathering passed resolutions urging Congress to finance a survey and appraisal of the Florida waterway as well as a study of the cost of constructing a waterway parallel to the canal.[33]

The featured speaker at the Stuart meeting was another of Florida's U. S. senators, Nathan P. Bryan—and one of the Florida canal company's most influential lawyers. Bryan addressed the convention on the most effective way to get the federal government to take over the privately owned waterway, vowing that the Florida congressional delegation would support the proposed plan, but cautioned that he expected opposition from members of Congress representing other parts of the country who advocated a rollback in inland waterways funding. As the meeting drew to a close, delegates selected St. Augustine over Miami as the site for the next convention, although the entire Fort Lauderdale delegation prefered the Ancient City over the Magic City. Delegates also re-elected the group's officers for another term and elected numerous vice presidents to represent counties along the east coast, including Harry Goldstein of Fernandina, also a delegate to the Atlantic Deeper Waterways Association, to represent Nassau County and *Miami Herald* newspaper publisher Frank Shutts for Dade County. A few weeks later, members of the Palatka and Sanford boards of trade announced plans for a convention at Palatka on December 21 to organize a competing association to lobby Congress for funds to construct a con-

---

[33]*Ibid.* "Special Rate Is Given to Stuart," *Miami Herald*, 8 November 1914; "He Praised Our City, *Fort Lauderdale Sentinel*, 25 December 1914 (verbatim report of Mathew's speech); "East Coast Canal To Be Bought by Government For Much Less Than It Has Cost to Build," *Miami Metropolis*, 27 November 1914; "East Coast Survey," *Fort Lauderdale Sentinel*, 18 December 1914.

tinuous inland waterway linking Florida's east and west coasts using the St. Johns River.[34]

The choice of routes was such a hot potato the ADWA leadership avoided the issue, preferring to await the Corps of Engineers' final recommendation. An ADWA publication, however, predicted that boats of eight-foot draft would soon be able to ascend the St. Johns River a distance of 170 miles from Jacksonville to Sanford on Lake Monroe. Along the Florida east coast between the St. Johns River and Biscayne Bay, existing channels offering only a four-foot draft needed improvements, but the Corps recommended against further expenditures under the current uncertain political conditions. The Corps expected that an improved route between the St. Johns River and the Gulf of Mexico would cross the state and add to the existing cross-state link between Fort Lauderdale on the New River and Fort Myers on the Caloosahatchee. Supporters for the Florida East Coast Canal route would have to wait another day for encouraging news.[35]

---

[34]"Enthusiasm Marked Meeting of Fla. East Coast Canal Ass'n at Stuart," *Miami Herald*, 24 November 1914; "St. Augustine Gets the Next Meeting of Florida East Coast Canal Ass'n," 25 November 1914, *Miami Herald*. "Trans-State Waterways," *Fort Lauderdale Sentinel*, 18 December 1914.

[35]ADWA, *Atlantic Intra-Coastal Waterway*, 3.

Chapter 17

Waterway Madness

While Florida canal directors looked forward to the possibility of a sale of the Florida East Coast Canal to the federal government, more good news arrived for Boston & Florida shareholders. On June 18, 1915, directors declared a robust cash dividend of twelve percent or twelve dollars a share on the company's stock, reflecting steadily improving land sales. At the same time, lower east coast board of trade representatives began forming another if less effective group known as the Florida East Coast Chamber of Commerce to promote waterway improvements and other matters of local interest. On July 20, representatives met at the Lake Park Hotel at West Palm Beach to elect officers and formulate an agenda for future action. Among the topics discussed were the cooperative marketing of agriculture, improving livestock, and publicizing the advantages of the east coast. Delegates elected Richard Paddison, head of the West Palm Beach Board of Trade, as president, after Fort Lauderdale resident Samuel Drake declined the nomination. Attendees then chose Drake as vice president and J. W. Reeves of Jupiter to fill the offices of secretary and treasurer. Son of Captain Richard Paddison, one of the first persons to run steamboats on the Indian River in the 1880s, Paddison arrived in West Palm Beach in 1911 to take over his brother's interest in the Dade Lumber Company.[1]

Members of numerous business and civic organizations in fourteen eastern and central Florida counties (Nassau, Duval, St. Johns, Clay, Putnam, Volusia, Orange, Brevard, Osceola, St. Lucie, Palm Beach, Broward, Dade and Monroe) comprised this new chamber group. Dues were set at four dollars a year for each county, with each county entitled to cast one vote on all matters before the organization. In addition to a committee on inland

---

[1]George W. Piper (Boston & Florida company) to Hall and Ritchie, in trust, 22 June 1915, HGP. "Florida East Coast Chamber Commerce," *Fort Lauderdale Sentinel*, 23 July 1915.

waterways, members created committees on agriculture, publicity, roads, drainage and transportation.[2]

In December, another group competing with the Florida East Coast Canal Association dispatched members throughout the lower east coast to whip up public support for an alternate route to the old Florida East Coast Canal. On December 9, C. R. Walker, first vice president of the Florida Inland Waterway Association, along with E. T. Woodruff, secretary of the Inland Waterway Committee of the Sanford Commercial Club, visited Fort Lauderdale seeking the support of the Board of Trade there for a route following the St. Johns River south to Lake Harney, then by a proposed artificial canal to Titusville on the Indian River. Walker asked his audience to "carefully weigh the project now being furthered by the East Coast Canal Company thru the agency or efforts of the East Coast Canal Association to unload what they have proven to be an impossible proposition upon the general government and to have incorporated in the Rivers and Harbors Appropriation Bill provisions to take over the East Coast canal by the United States Government." In support of his plan, Walker argued that the St. Johns River route for the northern portion of waterway would save the government approximately two million dollars over the northern section of the East Coast Canal and create a waterway as distant as twenty-five miles from the ocean, making it immune from attack by a foreign foe at sea.[3]

In the middle of December, the Langfitt Board, a special board of three army engineers headed by Colonel William C. Langfitt, conducted a hearing at Jacksonville on the feasibility of the federal government taking over the old East Coast Canal versus constructing a parallel route using the St. Johns River. Both St. Johns River and East Coast Canal advocates presented arguments on the merits of their proposals. Among the supporters of the East Coast Canal route were delegates from St. Augustine, Ormond, Holly Hill, Daytona, Daytona Beach, Seabreeze and New Smyrna.[4]

In January 1916, just six months after their first meeting at West Palm Beach, delegates to the Florida East Coast Canal Association assembled in Miami, with Sam Drake presiding in the absence of Paddison. Members elected John D. Baker of Jacksonville to represent Duval County and T. E. Fitzgerald to represent Volusia County. Pioneer Stuart resident Stanley

[2]Florida East Coast Chamber, *Constitution*.

[3]"Florida Inland Waterway," *Fort Lauderdale Sentinel*, 10 December 1915.

[4]Hearing on Canal Purchase Held by Engineers Monday," 17 December 1915, *New Smyrna News*.

Kitching, later a member of the first board of commissioners of the Florida Inland Navigation District, urged the group to support the federal government's ownership of the East Coast Canal, but pushed for the adoption of the St. Johns River route for the northern part of the waterway instead of the existing coastal route. But Baker believed the measure might be controversial and cause friction among the east coast counties. No record of any action taken on Kitching's proposal is known to exist.[5]

During the middle of June, Boston & Florida stockholders learned rather disappointing news about suddenly decreasing Florida real estate sales. Although directors had declared a cash dividend of ten percent, a distribution of ten dollars for each share of preferred stock, the payout to investors dropped almost twenty percent from the year before. During the meeting of directors held at Boston, Sandford H. Fleming proposed pushing land sales and the others agreed, but all of them thought nothing more could be done. Company expenses now amounted to more than what had been received from land sales. It appeared that it would be a very long time indeed before the common stock would be of any value. Common stockholders had never received a dividend and couldn't until the promised dividends on the preferred stock had been paid.[6]

In August 1916, the Langfitt Board issued a decidedly unfavorable report on the East Coast Canal considering the relatively small east coast population to be served, declining to support improvements in the Florida waterway. In October, Florida canal company directors received more bad news. The Ely Dredging Company sued the company for damages when poor waterway maintenance delayed a tugboat, a launch, a dredge, three lighters, and thirty-four pontoons bound for Palm Beach an astonishing twenty-one days. A few months later, the directors encountered additional legal difficulties potentially more damaging than the Ely suit. In February 1917, the state of Florida brought a lawsuit seeking cancellation of the company's charter for failing to maintain the waterway. Fortunately, the state's highest court sided with the company and denied the state's request. The court held that the State of Florida was first required to point out specific areas of filling-in before the company's charter could be revoked. Each time the state filed a lawsuit to require work at a designated location, however, the company quickly sent in a dredge and cleaned out the blockage before the

---

[5]"Chamber of Commerce Meet," *Fort Lauderdale Sentinel*, 14 January 1916.

[6]George W. Piper (Boston & Florida company) to Hall and Ritchie, in trust, 16 June 1916; S. H. Fleming to Hall, 20 June 1916; both in HGP.

court had time to act. In the meantime, new shoals developed. In Tallahassee, a few Florida legislators attempted to remedy the problem. Winter Park legislator P. A. Vans Agnews filed a bill in the house to force a turnover control of the inland waterway to the federal government, but America's entry into World War I prevented the legislature from taking any action on the proposal.[7]

While ADWA officials finalized plans for their annual meeting in Miami in November, the group's leader, Pennsylvania Congressman J. Hampton Moore, informed members that the House of Representatives had appropriated $1.3 million to purchase the privately owned Chesapeake and Delaware Canal. A Senate committee reported the bill out with an amendment that eliminated a fixed amount for the purchase and authorized the Corps of Engineers to use its condemnation powers if a satisfactory price could not be agreed upon. Moore praised this important Atlantic coast link as the "American Kiel Canal" and compared the waterway to Germany's important industrial waterway. He also reported that the Corps had considered two Florida east coast canal routes south of the mouth of the St. Johns River. But a supplemental report filed by the Langfitt board recommended against the purchase of the existing canal or the construction of another waterway along a parallel route. The board's report was now under review by the Board of Engineers for Rivers and Harbors meeting at the nation's capital.[8]

Moore also informed ADWA members that at the last annual meeting of the Florida East Coast Canal Association held in Fort Lauderdale on November 14 and 15, resolutions had been adopted asking the Board of Engineers to delay final action on the Langfitt report until residents could gather additional information to submit to the board. The group called on the state's Senators Fletcher and Bryan, as well as Congressman Sears, to support the delay.[9]

On June 29, 1917, Boston & Florida directors declared another disappointing dividend, a meager six percent on the preferred stock the company issued in 1892, the second straight year of diminishing dividends and still

---

[7]H. Doc. 1147, 65th Cong., 2d Session, August 26, 1916. Declaration, *Ely Dredging Company vs. Florida Coast Line Canal & Transportation Company*, (Damages) Case No. 5680, filed on October 2, 1916, Duval County Circuit Court. *State v. Florida Coast Line Canal & Transp. Co.*, 75 So. 582, 587 (Fla. 1917); "Must Deepen Costal [*sic*] Canal," *Fort Lauderdale Sentinel*, 2 February 1917. Burgman, *Florida East Coast Canal*, 15.

[8]ADWA, *Bulletin*, IX, 3 (February 1917): 1, 12-13.

[9]*Ibid.*, 13.

more evidence of declining land sales. In July, Moore traveled to Miami to check out arrangements for the ADWA convention in November. He found Miamians "doing big things in waterway improvements and they have much to show that cannot be seen in any other part of the United States." While boasting that "congratulations" were in order for many gains in improvements, the Atlantic waterway's biggest booster also reflected on the importance of inland canals in the nation's defense of its shores against the growing military threat abroad. "There will be occasion for serious work," Moore warned, "and for a continuance of our fight for preparedness along the Atlantic seaboard in consonance with true military preparedness which the country demands." But political support for waterway improvements throughout the country had also diminished. "We cannot afford," Moore warned, "to ignore the opposition that has manifested itself toward river and harbor improvement."[10]

Writing to ADWA members just before the Thanksgiving convention in Miami, Moore reported that delegates from Texas, now making plans for the Interstate Waterway League of Louisiana and Texas's meeting at Corpus Christi, had purposely scheduled the convention to precede the ADWA's convention. The "live wires" of Texas and Louisiana had invited the members of the entire House Rivers and Harbors committee as their guests, and Moore expected many of these Gulf delegates to join committee members in Miami, following the Corpus Christi meeting. After the Miami meeting, busy House members planned to return to the nation's capitol to attend the annual meeting of the National Rivers and Harbors Congress.[11]

In October, ADWA officials, including its president, Congressman J. Hampton Moore and Trenton Mayor Fred Donnelly, along with Charles Elmer Smith, chairman of the Miami Excursion Committee, headed south for a two-week scouting trip down the Atlantic coast along inland waterways from Charleston, past Miami and all the way down to Key West. The tour's purpose, according to Moore, was "to prove up the inland waterway system along the Florida east coast to the end of the Keys preparatory to the convention." At an enthusiastic meeting held at Charleston, R. G. Rhett, president of the U. S. Chamber of Commerce and a long-time ADWA director, began plans for a reception there for delegates traveling south to the Miami convention. At Savannah, Mayor Wallace J. Pierpont and other

---

[10]George W. Piper (Boston & Florida company) to Hall and Ritchie, in trust, 2 July 1917, HGP. ADWA, *Bulletin*, IX, 9 (August 1917): 1.

[11]ADWA, *Bulletin*, IX, 11-12 (October-November 1917): 1-2.

friends of the movement welcomed Moore's advance party. At Jacksonville, Moore's group boarded the houseboat *Pastime*, supplied by the canal company's past president George Miles, another long-time ADWA booster, and piloted by George Gleason, for a trip down the East Coast Canal. Along the way, Congressman W. J. Sears joined the party. The group made frequent stops traveling south down the Florida waterway, visiting St. Augustine, Matanzas, Ormond, Seabreeze, Daytona, New Smyrna, Titusville, Eau Gallie, St. Lucie, Fort Pierce, Palm Beach and Fort Lauderdale, ending their trip at the Magic City. The twelve-day tour focused not only on assessing the condition of the inland waterway but also evaluating the various inlets, harbors and basins along the way. ADWA member Charles Smith later told a Fort Lauderdale paper that of six natural inlets along the east coast (Jacksonville, Titusville, Stuart, Jupiter Inlet, Fort Lauderdale and Miami), Fort Lauderdale's Lake Mabel (now the Port Everglades turning basin) was the "best natural harbor."[12]

Upon returning to Philadelphia, Moore boasted that a vessel of small draft, "our vessel drew 3-1/2 feet," could easily make the trip from New England to Miami. While a six-foot channel had been assured from the St. Johns River to Miami, Moore found no more than three and a half feet of water in many places and noted that some steamboat lines deemed the Florida waterway inadequate to meet commercial needs. Military craft patrolling the Florida coast also had been hindered by insufficient water; and for that reason, the federal government would be "totally unprepared should any great emergency necessitate their immediate use for carrying provisions or engaging in strategic work." Turning to Florida's agricultural production, Moore found the existing network of railroads inadequate to transport the state's large farm crops. The result was a higher cost of living for people in the North and the same for Floridians. Floridians claimed that they could furnish the entire nation with fruits and vegetables, but Moore found residents there paying exorbitant prices for eggs and butter as well as for flour and cereal produced in other parts of the country.[13]

A few weeks later, more than 2,000 delegates to the 10th annual ADWA convention gathered for four days at Miami to consider a twelve-foot inland waterway along the entire Atlantic seaboard and the construction of a cross-

---

[12]"Ft. Lauderdale Has Best Natural Harbor on Coast," *Fort Lauderdale Sentinel,* 14 December 1917; ADWA, *Bulletin,* IX, 11-12 (Oct.-November 1917): 7-8, 10-11.

[13]"Ft. Lauderdale Has Best Natural Harbor on Coast," *Fort Lauderdale Sentinel,* 14 December 1917; ADWA, *Bulletin,* IX, 11-12 (Oct.-November 1917): 7-8, 10-11.

state Florida ship canal. Among the dignitaries attending were Governor Sidney J. Catts, two cabinet officers and two governors of northern states. Admiral Robert E. Byrd, discoverer of the North Pole, was the featured speaker at the meeting. So important was the gathering that the entire membership of the U. S. House of Representatives' rivers and harbors committee planned to travel from Corpus Christi, where an earlier waterway association meeting had been underway, to attend the Miami convention. The Miami arrangements committee selected the large and spacious Hotel Halcyon, with accommodations for 300 guests, as official ADWA convention headquarters. Room rates for the Halcyon started at four dollars a day. The Miami Chamber of Commerce, headed by one of the city's long-time waterway advocates, Everest Sewell, an ADWA state vice president representing Florida, made elaborate plans for entertainment. There were to be daily band concerts by Arthur Pryor's acclaimed band, airplane flying exhibitions, a beach party and a luncheon at Miami Beach, automobile trips to neighboring farms and groves, tours into the Everglades, as well as boat outings on Biscayne Bay and the Miami River. Thanksgiving evening, delegates were to celebrate the meeting's end with an impressive marine pageant held on Biscayne Bay. Several hundred gaily lighted yachts and boats led by naval vessels were to participate, with prizes awarded for the best-decorated boats, topped off by a spectacular fireworks display.[14]

Senator Duncan Fletcher, a long-time supporter of the Florida East Coast Canal, attended the association's annual meeting once again, along with another leading waterway supporter and long-time Moore associate, Congressman John Small, now chairman of the powerful House rivers and harbors committee. The Miami convention's program emphasized the usefulness of the Florida East Coast Canal, not only in economic importance in meeting transportation needs but also in aiding the country's naval defenses at time of war, with many supporters pressing for a channel at least twelve feet deep and some favoring a 25-foot channel from Jacksonville to Key West. Members considered the development of Florida's harbors, which attracted the attention of rival Miami boosters of the Biscayne Bay (now Port of Miami), Fort Lauderdale supporters of Lake Mabel (now Port Everglades), and West Palm Beach area promoters of the development of "Santa Lucia inlet harbor" (now Fort Pierce Inlet). Summarizing the delegates' mood, a Fort Lauderdale newspaper opined that whether or not the

---

[14]"Deeper Waterways Convention at Miami," *Fort Lauderdale Sentinel,* 23 November 1917.

convention took action on the need for improved sheltered harbors, there was "little doubt" that the association would ask Congress to take over and deepen the "Coastal canal." Although George Miles spoke at the convention on the Florida East Coast Canal, no record of his remarks survives. Wartime conditions appear to have prevented the publication of the official proceedings that year. Moore Haven Mayor Marian N. Horwitz O'Brien, a former Philadelphian, told delegates about Florida's efforts to reclaim the Everglades as well as her own efforts to manage her own farm near Lake Okeechobee with "her fascinating story of pluck and persistence," according to the ADWA *Bulletin*'s brief account of her remarks published shortly after the convention's end.[15]

Resolutions passed at the meeting reflected the impending war with Germany. One such resolution, recognizing Florida's more than 1,000 miles of coast line the Atlantic Ocean and Gulf of Mexico, urged Congress to pass legislation for the selection of a route or several routes across the peninsula to connect the Atlantic with the Gulf. Members espoused the important service an Atlantic intracoastal waterway could provide in defending "our great ports from attack." Pointing to Germany's Kiel Canal as a success in linking two coasts, delegates urged that much the same advantage in "doubling" the strength of U. S. naval forces could be gained if an intracoastal waterway was constructed. Wartime conditions, Moore pointed out, compelled President Wilson to announce the federal government's takeover and unification of the nation's railways and the inland waterways controlled by railway companies. These waterways included two New Jersey canals, the Delaware and Raritan leased by the Pennsylvania Railroad Company and the Morris leased by the Lehigh Valley railway, as well as a Pennsylvania waterway, the Schuykill Navigation Canal leased by the Reading Railroad Company.[16]

State-owned waterways such as the New York Barge Canal could not be taken over by the federal government. In addition, privately owned waterways not controlled by the railway lines, such as the Florida East Coast Canal, the Chesapeake and Delaware, the Chesapeake and Ohio, and the Cape Cod Canal, which had been built under private charters and operated as toll roads, could not be taken over. These circumstances bolstered the

---

[15]"Atlantic Deeper Waterways Association Favors Deepening Coastal Canal," Fort Lauderdale *Sentinel*, 30 November 1917. ADWA, *Bulletin*, X, 1 & 2 (December 1917-January 1918): 12

[16]ADWA, *Bulletin*, X, 1 & 2 (December 1917-January 1918): 4, 6, 8-9, 17. ADWA, *Defense Value of Waterways*.

ADWA's contention that federal control of Atlantic intracoastal waterways would prove crucial in time of war. In a letter to Secretary of War James McAdoo, then also director general of the railroads, Moore pointed out the necessity of federal control over the waterways and advocated the government's purchase of the Chesapeake and Delaware Canal, which was then moving about a million tons of cargo a year, including substantial quantities of munitions and explosives. Twenty-four years later, on November 12, 1941, association delegates, again meeting in Miami, would pass another series of resolutions emphasizing the defense value of inland waterways, just twenty-five days before the Japanese attack on Pearl Harbor.[17]

Meanwhile, in a lawsuit brought by the Rhode Island Hospital Trust Company against Helen Bradley to determine the meaning of various portions of George Bradley's will, the state's Supreme Court, on April 17, 1918, ruled that the will did not entitle Helen to any of the income from Bradley's various Florida holdings, such as his shares in the Boston & Florida land company and the three Bradley trusts (Lake Worth, New River and Walker). Since his death in 1906, sales of Boston & Florida land had added $37,000 to Bradley's estate and sales of trust lands in Florida contributed another $38,100. Although Helen's lawyers claimed the distributions as income due her under the will, the court declared the earnings part of the principal of Bradley's estate to which the Emma Pendleton Bradley Home (later, Hospital) was entitled.[18]

A few months after the court's decision, on Friday, January 10, 1919, Helen died, at the age of sixty-four, while staying at the Hotel Belmont in New York City. She left her entire estate, after a few minor bequests, to the Emma Pendleton Bradley Home, named in honor of her deceased daughter. Many of the Bradleys' magnificent Old Masters paintings, including works by Corot, Courbet, Daubigny, David, Delacroix and Andrea Del Sarto, became the property of the Corcoran Art Gallery at Washington. Within four months of Helen's death, the Corcoran displayed the Bradley's impressive collection from May 3 until May 25. The Bradleys' gathering of 2,054 prints, including significant works by Cranach, Durer, Hogarth, Mantegna, Rembrandt, Rubens and Van Dyck, became the property of the Library of Congress. Within three months of Helen's death, on April 1, Sam Maddox, the canal company's longtime secretary and legal counsel, died at his home

---

[17]*Ibid.*

[18]*Rhode Island Hospital Trust Co. v. Bradley*, 103 A. 486 (R. I. 1918).

in Washington at the age of sixty-eight. Like Walker and the Bradleys before him, Maddox left a portion of his estate to charity. After leaving a few gifts to friends and relatives, Maddox's will established a $10,000 endowment to support the Rector of St. Mark's Episcopal Church in Washington County, Maryland, a church Maddox's grandfather Dr. James Thomas Notley Maddox had helped found in 1849.[19]

By October, Sandford H. Fleming had been receiving monthly reports on the Boston & Florida's land sales. He hoped there would be no hitch in the pending sale of 14,000 acres to a former New Jersey restaurateur, Harry Seymour Kelsey, at nearly $16 an acre. Proceeds would pay off the land company's preferred stockholders, thus permitting the distribution of future profits to common stockholders who had been waiting since 1892 for a dividend on their investments. Fleming noted that there had been a strong demand for Florida lands, which he attributed to American soldiers returning home after the end of World War I. Boston & Florida stock now rose to $380 a share. Boston & Florida directors soon completed the sale of 14,025 acres of Boston & Florida land to Kelsey for $213,213, but with a cash down payment of only $6,845, more cash on approval of the sale of $24,509 and installment payments totaling $181,858. The company's cash assets totaled just $13,381. Company notes receivable zoomed to $62,078 and directors estimated the remaining 41,000 acres to be worth an average of $15 an acre or a total of $615,000. Assets now totaled $896,827 against liabilities of $194,000, resulting in a net value to stockholders of $702,827.[20]

In April 1920, delegates in St. Louis for the annual convention of the Mississippi Valley Waterways Association heard that the nation's transportation system suffered a shortage of 800,000 railroad cars. It would take the country's factories five years to supply the cars required to meet the demand. Delegates passed resolutions urging Congress to pass a bill allocating $65 million in federal funds for waterway improvements throughout the country to allow this deficit in transportation to be met by water traffic. On June 5, Congress passed a momentous rivers and harbors bill which

---

[19]Archives website information, 2002, and correspondence from Laura Coyle, Curator of European Art, 20 February 2004, Corcoran Gallery of Art, Washington, D. C. *Estate of Samuel Maddox*, File No. 1063, County Judge's Court, Broward County, Florida; Crawford, "Sam Maddox."

[20]S. H. Fleming to Hall, 9 (Miles valuation and B & F statement of condition as May 31 1919 enclosed), 11 October 1919; both in HGP.

Barge bridge spanning the Florida East Coast Canal (Intracoastal Waterway) at Holl-wood, Florida, ca. 1920, looking toward the beach. (Courtesy, Broward County Historical Commission, Fort Lauderdale, Florida)

authorized the Army Corps of Engineers to study the feasibility of a federal takeover of the Florida East Coast Canal.[21]

Meanwhile, by the first week in July 1920, Sanford H. Fleming had returned to his home in Canada from a disappointing Boston & Florida land company meeting held at Portland, Maine. News had turned sour in Florida with reports of declining real estate sales, despite the dividends that had been declared the past few years. There would be no dividend distributions at all this year. Florida taxes had been very high, in fact, $29,000 for the year instead of the usual $9,000 annual tax bill in the past. It took all the money from the smaller land sales to pay the taxes on the remaining company land. And more bad news. Harry Kelsey had gotten behind in his land payments. Sanford H. had met Kelsey, president of the East Coast Finance Company, whom he thought "an energetic young man." Kelsey exuded great confidence that he would be able to make his project successful, but he needed Boston & Florida directors to give him a little more time to make the remain-

---

[21]The river and harbor act was approved on June 5, 1920. H. Doc. 586, 1. "Want Water Help in Freight Glut," *New York Times*, 20 April 1920.

ing payments. Directors acceded to the request because they wanted Kelsey to make a success of the project, which would make the rest of the Boston & Florida's holdings more valuable.[22]

Kelsey had already invested approximately half a million dollars in his vast Palm Beach County venture and formed the East Coast Finance Corporation to purchase and develop a stunning expanse of raw acreage into town sites, winter resorts, sugar plantations, cattle farms, citrus groves, truck farms, and industrial sites. In addition to Kelsey, who served as president and director, company directors included Percy E. Woodward of Loudonville, New York, president of Edward Walker's family business, the T. M. Walker Company of Springfield, Mass.; J. B. McDonald, director of the Palm Beach Bank & Trust Company; Samuel L. Bickford, vice president of Waldorf Systems, Inc, and later, founder of Bickford's, Inc., owner of the numerous cafeterias, restaurants, and food service companies located in several northeastern states as well as the M & M Cafeteria chain in Florida; and Donald J. Ross, of Boston and Pinehurst, North Carolina, a prominent golf course architect. The Kelsey company purchased 120,000 acres of land in parcels extending from the south end of West Palm Beach north seventeen miles, a mile short of Jupiter, nine miles wide in a number of places. Company holdings also included sixteen miles of ocean frontage, beginning at Jupiter and running south, intermittently, to Fort Lauderdale and over eight miles of lake frontage. In addition, Kelsey owned an 800-acre town site for a planned community aptly named Kelsey City (known today as Lake Park), six and half miles north of West Palm Beach along the Dixie Highway and the Florida East Coast Railway, bordering on Lake Worth.[23]

In October, erstwhile Brooklyn resident Commodore Avylen Harcourt Brook, a 53-year-old retiree to Fort Lauderdale, attended the ADWA's annual convention at Atlantic City as a Florida delegate. A long-time promoter of the Cape Cod Canal, Brook voted against a resolution supporting the St. Lawrence Seaway. To Fort Lauderdale city council members he later recommended that the town refuse to send delegates to future conventions until the ADWA addressed Florida's need for improvements in the East Coast Canal. Seven years later, in 1927, Brook would become a member of the first board of commissioners of the Florida Inland Navigation District,

---

[22]S. H. Fleming to Hall, 6 July 1920 (Prospectus of East Coast Finance Corporation enclosed in letter), HGP.

[23]*Ibid.*

the special taxing district charged with the responsibility of purchasing the Florida east coast canal and turning it over to the federal government.[24]

By the early 1920s, despite the lack of routine maintenance, the Florida canal company had accomplished much in the development of its inland waterway. Between Jacksonville and Miami the company had dredged six large and difficult artificial cuts. From Pablo Beach to the Tolomato (North) River, the company had constructed eighteen miles of canals, fifty feet wide at the bottom and five-and-a-half feet deep. South of Pellicer's Creek, the company had built a second canal, twenty-four miles long, through the Matanzas Basin to the Halifax River at Ormond, generally five feet deep and 60 to 100 feet wide. The company had also dredged a third canal, three-eights of a mile long and eleven feet deep, near the old Haulover canal. At the south end of the 103-mile-long Indian River at Jupiter Inlet, the company had constructed a fourth canal eight miles long to Juno. From Lake Worth south from Boynton, the company had built a 14-mile waterway through Lake Wyman and Lake Boca Raton, down the Hillsboro River to the Hillsboro Inlet, with an average depth of five feet. Below the inlet, a narrow canal extended south ten miles to the New River Inlet at Fort Lauderdale. From that inlet, the company had built a waterway about ten miles south, through Lake Mabel (today's Port Everglades turning basin at Fort Lauderdale and Hollywood), which continued down through Dumfoundling Bay and into Biscayne Bay at Miami.[25]

To maintain the waterway, the company stretched chains across the waterway at locations along six cuts to collect tolls from vessels plying the waterway: (1) from Pablo Creek down through dredged canals to the North River; (2) three miles north of Mount Oswald in Smith's or Halifax Creek; (3) south from the Mosquito Lagoon to a short canal three-eighths of a mile long leading to the Indian River, known then as the Haulover; (4) at Juno, at the southern entrance of a canal leading from Lake Worth; (5) at the draw bridge opposite Boynton along the canal leading south from Lake Worth; and finally, (6) in Broward County, south of the Dania cut-off canal one-fourth of a mile east of a lagoon to Hallandale beach Chain No. 6. Stretched taut just below the surface of the water, the chains prevented passage until the required tolls were paid. Published toll rates for passage along the

---

[24]"Chamber of Commerce Holds First Meeting Wednesday Night In New Headquarters," *Fort Lauderdale Herald*, 15 October 1920. Typewritten minutes of the Committee of Time and Place can be found at ADWA, Proceedings, October 4-8, 1920, JHMP, vol. 1 (unpaginated).

[25]Read, *Waterways of Florida*, 237-40.

waterway compared favorably with those initially approved by the state improvement fund trustees in 1913:

> "Barges and Lighters in tow, 8 cents per foot through each chain and 5% on freight; 8 cents per foot on tug through each chain. Total 16c per foot and 5% on freight through each chain. Empty, 5c through each chain. Tugs towing empty lighters 5c per foot through each chain. Total empty: 10c per foot through each chain.
> "Freight and passenger boats: 5c per foot through each chain and 5% on Gross Rates from freight and passengers.
> "Pleasure Boats and House Boats: 10c per foot through each chain. 8c per foot through each chain. Launches (40) foot and under not engaged in business.
> "Fish Boats, 3c per foot through each chain."[26]

During 1920, tolls generated revenue totaling $8,173 for the North River Chain alone; $1,151 for the Smith's Creek Chain; $1,174 at the Haulover Chain; $2,027 from the Juno Chain; $2,021 at the Boynton Chain; and $4,367 for the Hallandale Beach Chain. Altogether the chains produced a gross income of $19,016, against operating costs of $15,159, but the cost of constantly dredging the waterway to maintain the state-required depth produced a deficit in operations of $19,000 a year.

The next year, the Florida legislature created the Florida State Canal Commission to oversee the construction of a cross-state barge canal linking the Mississippi River's commerce to trade along the Atlantic coast across the northern part of the Florida peninsula, but the waterway would never be completed. The legislature promoted waterway improvements in the ensuing decades and created the Canal Authority of the State of Florida in the early 1960s to push the development of another Cross-Florida Barge Canal as well as other inland waterways throughout the state, including what would become Florida's Atlantic Intracoastal Waterway.[27]

During the latter part of May 1921, a West Palm Beach paper reported that negotiations were underway for the sale of the Florida waterway for $3 million to a group of western bankers. Florida canal company officials told Florida legislators that the group planned to spend as much as $1 million improving the waterway and providing transportation along the entire

---

[26]*Ibid.*

[27]*Ibid.* Ruge (Florida State Canal Commission) to Taylor, 4 May 1927, TP. Florida. Canal Authority, *passim.*

route. One state representative, however, filed a bill that, among other things, proposed to impose a fine of $500 or imprisonment if company officials failed to maintain the waterway. In addition to the proposed legislation, George Miles complained that a lawsuit the state filed in 1917 to force the canal company to maintain the waterway had been languishing in the courts without resolution, which further hindered the sale to the western bankers. The bill never became law and the western bankers never invested in the waterway while the lawsuit that had plagued the company since 1917 continued to wend its way though the Florida courts until 1933 when the Florida Supreme Court finally dismissed it for lack of prosecution.[28]

Along the East Coast Canal, freight business in 1922, including the fees charged for an oil company's boat, totaled a mere $34,744 and passenger fares adding a meager $2,643. Among the vessels passing through the various canals of the waterway during the year were 1,514 yachts, 2,190 launches, 1,061 freight and passenger boats, 123 tugs, 12 dredges, 1,586 fishing boats, and 237 barges, totaling 6,723 water craft. The sparse marine traffic proved a 'hard sell' for those advocating a federal takeover of the waterway. Nevertheless, waterway enthusiasts gathered at four important meetings called by the Corps of Engineers in May and June to hear public comment on the proposed takeover. Those who did attend the meetings differed as to which of the two routes proposed by the Corps they would back as a new federal waterway. But the Corps would recommend only one.[29]

---

[28]"Sale of Canal for $1,200,000 Is Now Pending," *Palm Beach Post*, 27 May 1921; Miles, "East Coast Canal." *State ex rel. Swearingen v. Florida Coast Line Canal & Transp. Co.*, 150 So. 137 (Fla. 1933)

[29]Read, *Waterways of Florida*, 235-36.

Chapter 18

A Lively Bunch Of Boys

While east coast chamber groups rallied for government ownership of the Florida waterway with increasing effectiveness, the Army Corps of Engineers conducted four meetings in 1922 to assess a possible federal takeover of the Florida East Coast Canal. The first took place at Titusville on May 16, with another the next day at West Palm Beach. A month later, the Corps conducted a meeting at Daytona on June 26, followed the next day by one at Sanford. Major William C. Lemen, the Army's chief engineer in Florida, held the hearings to gather information for a report to Congress on the proposed takeover. If Lemen's report advocated federal intervention, supporters expected Congress to spend $10 million to improve the waterway. The key issue in the study was whether the route of the new waterway would follow the line of the old Florida East Coast Canal or the more westerly St. Johns River route south to Sanford, then by artificial canal to Titusville, continuing south down the old East Coast Canal to Miami.[1]

The Titusville Hearing

During the first hearing held at Titusville on May 16, prominent Brevard County citrus grower J. J. Parrish espoused the benefits of a deep-water canal link such as the St. Johns River route, believing that he could ship sixty percent of the 600 carloads of fruit he shipped each year using such a waterway. W. F. Allen argued that Brevard County alone would "save $625,000 a year in freight if the Federal Government will build a 10-foot deep canal from Titusville to Sanford and down the St. Johns, over which freight steamers can carry the products of the Florida East Coast to Jacksonville, and thence on to the Eastern markets by the Atlantic Ocean." A local newspaper account described a large delegation from Orlando as "all 33rd degree boosters" for a deep-water canal from Jacksonville to Miami via the St.

---

[1]U. S. Congress H. Doc. 586, 16.

Johns River to Sanford; a ten-foot deep canal from Sanford to Titusville; and a 10-foot deep channel from Titusville to Miami.[2]

Sanford Delegation

The federal government's choice for the route of the proposed intracoastal waterway was critically important to the people of Sanford. In fact, whether the recommended federal waterway connected Jacksonville and Miami by way of the St. Johns River route or followed the route of the old East Coast Canal would essentially mean economic life or death for Sanford and other towns and cities dependent on the St. Johns River. The question was of such vital importance that nearly a hundred of Sanford's business leaders joined a hundred of Orlando's prominent citizens at the Titusville hearing on May 16 to advocate the construction of a waterway to connect the St. Johns River with the Indian River at Titusville. Sanford area information had been collected by the Chamber of Commerce and data on other sections compiled and forwarded to the Central Florida Water Traffic League, which assembled a brief on the St. Johns-Indian River alternate route on behalf of the twelve counties dependent on the proposed route. The construction of the waterway for these counties would mean a savings of millions of dollars in freight to farmers and growers and reclaim hundreds of thousands of acres of the most fertile land, supporters contended. The *Sanford Daily Herald* proudly announced the departure of the town's St. Johns River boosters by automobile caravan for the Titusville meeting:

"The St. Johns River Inland Waterways boosters left this morning promptly at 6:30 and they were very nearly 100 strong as there were about 25 cars in the Sanford delegation and they were a lively bunch of boys. They were lined at the Seminole Hotel and motored to the Osteen ferry where they met the Orlando bunch with fully 100 more live wire members of the Chamber of Commerce and Water Traffic League and they waited for all the South Florida cars from many cities that had come up from all points and then journeyed together to Titusville where today the U. S. Engineers will listen to the delegates and read the papers that have been prepared upon this important subject."[3]

---

[2]"Attend Meeting," Titusville *Star Advocate*, 12 May 1922; "Deepwater Canal From Titusville," (Titusville) *Star Advocate*, 19 May 1922.

[3]"Public Hearing at Titusville on Tuesday, May 16," *Sanford Daily Herald*, 15 May 1922; "One Hundred Boosters Left Sanford Early Today for Titusville," *Sanford Daily Herald*, 16 May 1922.

The Sanford paper couldn't restrain its exuberance in describing central Florida's interest in a possible St. Johns River inland waterway and called the gathering at Titusville "[o]ne of the greatest gatherings in south central Florida." Delegates included members of the Central Florida Water Traffic League, local chambers of commerce, and Rotary, Kiwanis and other clubs from Sanford, Orlando, Titusville, Cocoa, Winter Park, Osteen, Enterprise, De Land, Mims and Oak Hill.[4]

Orlando Judge W. T. Bland spoke for the Central Florida Water Traffic League, presenting a mass of evidence that, in the words of the *Sanford Daily Herald*, "staggered the hearers and which when given in the aggregate would have astonished the world should it be given publicity." Representative Sanford businessmen such as W. A. Leffler of Chase & Company, one of the state's largest citrus growing and packing businesses, spoke on the production of fruits and vegetables; Joe Cameron articulated the interests of cattle producers, while L. A. Brumley presented information on farming concerns.[5]

Describing the Daytona delegation's efforts to discredit the St. Johns River route at the Titusville meeting, the *Sanford Daily Herald*, while conceding that the delegation "had some figures," insisted nonetheless that Dave Sholtz's Triple Cities group "could not show and never will be able to show the tonnage that Central Florida can show and their chief asset, 'tourists' seemed about all they [Daytona] had to offer." The Central Water Traffic League's brief cited annual agricultural production for Central Florida of more than three million tons, comprised of vegetables, citrus, livestock, hogs, cattle, horses, mules, naval stores and fish. The territory of the study included the counties of Clay, St. Johns, Putnam, Flagler, Volusia, Lake, Seminole, Orange, Brevard, St. Lucie, Okeechobee, Osceola and Glades, with a total population of 131,294 — an increase in number of more than 100 percent over the census for 1900 of 63,707. Urging readers to back the St. Johns River route, the *Sanford Daily Herald* espoused "If all the people of this part of Florida would pull for the great St. John [sic] river they would be benefited to a greater degree than by any other route regardless of the claims of the east coast people and all the folks who cannot see anything but that little ditch that is filled up with sand now and will be until the end of time."[6]

---

[4]"St. Johns River Project Exploited Yesterday as Inland Waterway," Sanford *Daily Herald*, 17 May 1922.

[5]*Ibid.*

[6]*Ibid.*

The West Palm Beach Meeting

A notable group of fifty persons attended the second session held at West Palm Beach, including Fred C. Elliott, the state's Everglades drainage engineer, and a Fort Lauderdale delegation that included chamber secretary P. H. Thomson, Captain George J. Pilkington of the Pilkington Yacht Basin (reputedly Florida's largest covered yacht basin), W. C. Kyle, D. T. Hart, and Commodore Avylen Harcourt Brook. A former New York outdoor advertising executive, the British-born Brook had come to Fort Lauderdale just a few years before to become the city's biggest promoter. Short in stature and displaying a large blonde mustache, Commodore Brook would become a dominate force in the creation of the Florida Inland Navigation District, established in 1927 to turn the privately owned Florida East Coast Canal over to the federal government. After the death of Charles Burgman in 1932, Brook would serve as the district's chairman until his resignation in 1945. In addition to his work on Florida's Atlantic Intracoastal Waterway, Brook served as a vice president of the Waterway League of America, a director of the Atlantic Deeper Waterways Association, and as a member of the National Rivers and Harbors Congress. An avid yachtsman, he received the title of Commodore from Long Island's Jamaica Bay Yacht Club; he was also Commodore of the Canarsie Bay Yacht Club.[7]

Florida canal company officials conceded that waterway tolls were insufficient to maintain the canal and that the company had no other resources to pay for maintenance. Congressman Joe Sears promoted the advantages of a federal takeover in further developing and maintaining the waterway:

"When we have a canal that will handle goods, garden stuff and lumber as well as stone, direct from south of St. Lucie County to Miami and then have it transported directly to the north, millions of dollars will be saved and thousands of people will migrate to the Southern part of Florida to not only go into business, but to start into farming!

"I want to see a canal at least 150 feet wide and 8 feet deep so that we can handle every dollar's worth of business that can be produced."[8]

---

[7]"Lower East Coast Unites in Urging Government to Take Over Canal at Hearing before Major Lemen," *Palm Beach Post*, 18 May 1922. Burghard, *Half a Century*, 211-14; "A. H. Brook Dies Sunday," *Fort Lauderdale Daily News*, 15 April 1946; "Commodore A. H. Brook," *New York Times*, 16 April 1946, p. 25, Colonel 4; "Brook Head of E.C. Canal Body," *Fort Lauderdale Daily News*, 27 June 1932; Cutler, *History of Florida*, II, 248.

[8]"East Coast Citizens Show Engineers the Need for the Canal," *Fort Lauderdale Herald*, 19 May 1922.

Commodore Brook also favored nationalizing the waterway. He pointed out the almost ridiculous fact that it cost more to send goods by rail from Jacksonville to Fort Lauderdale than to transfer freight the greater distance to Miami. The first-class rate from Jacksonville to Fort Lauderdale, he noted, was $1.49 per hundredweight versus $1.04 per hundredweight for shipping goods another twenty miles south to Miami. Brook asked the waterway gathering, "Is it any wonder that we want a canal?"[9]

By far the largest delegation from the Florida east coast at the West Palm Beach hearing was the group representing St. Lucie County. Vero alone sent six delegates, including Anthony W. Young who, like Commodore Brook of Fort Lauderdale, would in a few short years become a member of the first board of commissioners of the Florida Inland Navigation District. North county delegates were Albert Schuman, T. B. Hicks and R. G. Hardee of Sebastian. J. B. McDonald, secretary of the Fort Pierce Chamber of Commerce, spoke on behalf of the St. Lucie County delegation. According to McDonald, in 1921, 1,500 railroad carloads of citrus, five hundred carloads each of vegetables, fish, naval stores, lumber, livestock and fresh meat, and one hundred cars of pineapple had been shipped out of the St. Lucie River region. McDonald argued that a considerable amount of the area's production could be shipped by water if water transportation were made available and further pointed out that existing water rates had been running twenty-five percent below rail charges.[10]

The Daytona Meeting

Two days before the U. S. engineers' meeting on June 26 at Daytona, fifty leading local businessmen spent a Saturday morning at the Casino Burgoyne getting ready for the hearing. Daytona attorney Dave Sholtz, later to serve as Florida's governor, focused the meeting on presenting the facts necessary to demonstrate Daytona's need for an inland waterway. Sholtz was to present a written brief and speak on behalf of the Triple Cities (Daytona, Daytona Beach, and Seabreeze). Other planning session speakers argued that the cutting off of the Florida East Coast Canal as a deep waterway would seriously wound the Triple Cities' economy, how serious "only those who were present at the meeting Saturday morning and who have studied

[9]*Ibid.*; "Canal Wrangle Often in Court," *Palm Beach Post*, 18 May 1922.
[10]"Strong Showing Made by St. Lucie County," *Vero* (St. Lucie County) *Press*, 25 May 1922.

the matter could realize." Cecil McDonald of the McDonald Boat Yards told of paying $335 in railway freight charges on a shipment of oak that cost only $235 wholesale in Philadelphia. Captain Dupont of the Jacksonville-Daytona boat line emphasized the heavy losses the Daytona port had sustained through the accumulation of debris in the channel and because of low water. To emphasize the importance of the hearing, Daytona Mayor George W. Marks issued a proclamation declaring Monday afternoon, June 26, a public holiday in the city between the hours of two and five o'clock in the afternoon, urging all citizens to attend the meeting at the Casino Burgoyne.[11]

According to a local paper, every chair in the Casino Burgoyne was filled for the hearing before Major William Lemen and many others stood "while the doors and windows were filled with those anxious to hear every word of the evidence presented." Seabreeze Mayor P. D. Gold presided at the meeting, with delegates from St. Augustine, Ormond, Seabreeze, Daytona Beach, Daytona, Port Orange, Wilbur, New Smyrna and Oak Hill. Judge D. R. Dunham presented St. Augustine's position on the proposed route of the waterway, calling attention to the fact that the East Coast Canal route was seventy-seven miles shorter, "all salt water," and that "when you get water transportation you have the railroad company where you want it."[12]

St. Augustine's city manager, Eugene Masters, noted the superiority of the Florida East Coast Canal for military defense and supported a canal 100 feet wide and ten feet deep. The *Daytona Morning Journal* reported that Jacksonville's George W. Parkhill "boomed the All-Florida spirit." Quoting Kipling, Parkhill commended "the everlasting team work of every blooming soul" in supporting the East Coast Canal. George N. Rigby, a prominent lawyer and Ormond's mayor since 1915, supported a federal takeover of the

---

[11]"Men of Daytona Must Move Fast for Canal Meet," Daytona *Morning Journal*, 24 June 1922; "Triple Cities Leading Men in Session on Saturday to Plan Meeting Major Lemen," *Daytona Morning Journal*, 25 June 1922; "Proclamation Issued by Mayor Marks," Daytona *Morning Journal*, 25 June 1922; "East Coast Canal Hearing Is Largely Attended," *Daytona Morning Journal*, 27 June 1922.

[12]"Men of Daytona Must Move Fast for Canal Meet," *Daytona Morning Journal*, 24 June 1922; "Triple Cities Leading Men in Session on Saturday to Plan Meeting Major Lemen," Daytona *Morning Journal*, 25 June 1922; "Proclamation Issued by Mayor Marks," *Daytona Morning Journal*, 25 June 1922; "East Coast Canal Hearing Is Largely Attended," *Daytona Morning Journal*, 27 June 1922.

Florida East Coast Canal and was "especially keen on the canal being kept open for the yachting tourist, who was a big asset of the Halifax Country."[13]

As expected, Dave Sholtz presented his brief in the afternoon for the Daytona Chamber of Commerce. In it, he compared railroad freight charges paid by residents of two cities equidistant from Jacksonville. In Daytona, first-class freight was charged $1.03 per hundredweight, in the other city, 58 cents. "The discrimination on the part of the railroad was possible because of the lack of opposition," Sholtz argued. Captain Dupont said that he could "increase his fleet as long as there was enough business to do so if the water depth was stabilized and the channel increased in width." Walt Snead told how Fuquay & Gheen could build houses more cheaply by as much as ten percent if the canal opened up transportation facilities large enough to carry the 649 carloads of construction materials the company required. Just five years later, in 1927, Florida Governor John Martin would appoint Dana F. Fuquay, president of Fuquay & Gheen, Inc., one of the state's largest builders, as Flagler County's representative on the Board of Commissioners of the Florida Inland Navigation District.[14]

The Sanford Meeting

By the time of the June 27 meeting, Sanford's "lively bunch of boys" and the central Florida cities supporting the St. Johns River route had compiled an entirely different brief to present to the Army engineers, contending that seventy-five percent of the commercial tonnage transported in Florida originated in the St. Johns River region. The *Sanford Daily Herald* described the hearing as "probably the most important meeting that has ever been held in the history of Sanford." Palatka's Wilson Cypress Company assured the attendees that the majority of its annual production of 94,000 tons of cypress could be shipped by water if proper transportation facilities were in place.

---

[13]"Men of Daytona Must Move Fast for Canal Meet," *Daytona Morning Journal*, 24 June 1922; "Triple Cities Leading Men in Session on Saturday to Plan Meeting Major Lemen," *Daytona Morning Journal*, 25 June 1922; "Proclamation Issued by Mayor Marks," *Daytona Morning Journal*, 25 June 1922; "East Coast Canal Hearing Is Largely Attended," *Daytona Morning Journal*, 27 June 1922.

[14]"Men of Daytona Must Move Fast for Canal Meet," *Daytona Morning Journal*, 24 June 1922; "Triple Cities Leading Men in Session on Saturday to Plan Meeting Major Lemen," *Daytona Morning Journal*, 25 June 1922; "Proclamation Issued by Mayor Marks," *Daytona Morning Journal*, 25 June 1922; "East Coast Canal Hearing Is Largely Attended," *Daytona Morning Journal*, 27 June 1922.

Other speakers supporting the St. Johns River route included S. O. Chase of Chase & Company, Sanford; M. M. Dickson of the Dickson-Ives Company, Orlando; H. E. McCuller, lumber manufacturer, Orlando; J. G. Dreka of the Dreka Company, one of the oldest businesses in DeLand; Charles E. Rowton, Palatka and P. J. Feitner of the Osceola Cypress Company, Osceola. George P. Parkhill of the Jacksonville Chamber of Commerce stressed the importance of cooperation among advocates of different projects and assured the Sanford group that it could count on Jacksonville's support in advocating the development of the St. Johns River route. The meeting adjourned at 3:30 p.m., with Sanford's St. Johns River supporters confident that they had advanced irrefutable data in support of their river route.[15]

Canal Company Attempts to Sell Waterway to U. S.

Just two weeks before the Sanford hearing, the Florida canal company had attempted once again to sell the private waterway to the federal government. In a June 14, 1922 letter to Major Lemen, canal company attorney Frank Swan — also the Bradley trust's lawyer — proposed the sale of the waterway to the United States for $1.2 million, $800,000 less than the price presented to a special board of Army engineers six years earlier, even though company's records reflected that the firm had expended more than $3.5 million for the excavation of almost thirteen million cubic yards of material in constructing the waterway over a 40-year period. A director of the Rhode Island Hospital Trust Company, Swan would later become the first president of the Emma Pendleton Bradley Home in 1931. Although the Corps of Engineers spurned Swan's offer, just three months later, the Corps would appoint an individual to replace Major Lemen as head of the engineers in Florida, a man who for the next thirty-six years would play a major role in the private waterway's turnover to the federal government and its conversion into Florida's modern Atlantic Intracoastal Waterway.[16]

---

[15]"Public Hearing Called for Inter-Costal [sic] Canal To Be Held in this City," *Sanford Daily Herald*, 24 May 1922; "Big Meeting Tomorrow Inter-Coastal [sic] Waterways Before U. S. Engineers, *Sanford Daily Herald*, 26 June 1922; "Waterway's Hearing Being Held Here Today Before Major Lehman," *Sanford Daily Herald*, 27 June 1922; "Great Report Submitted to Government Engineers Regarding St. Johns River," *Sanford Daily Herald*, 28 June 1922.

[16]U. S. H. Doc. 586, 10,15. *National Cyclopaedia*, 43:282-83; *Who Was Who*, 3:836.

The Colonel and the Union Leader

In August 1922, the Army named Colonel Gilbert Albin Youngberg to succeed Major Lemen as engineer of the Florida district of the Corps of Engineers. Born on February 12, 1875 in Minnesota of Swedish immigrant parents, Youngberg was graduated from the U. S. Military Academy in 1900 and joined the Corps of Engineers. Twenty-seven years later, after his retirement from the Army, Youngberg would serve for more than thirty years as the Florida Inland Navigation District's first chief engineer and director of right-of-way procurement for the Florida waterway, marking the beginning of a long tradition of employing former Army engineers in leadership positions at the waterway district.[17]

After his graduation from the Army War College, Youngberg was appointed head of the Department of Practical Military Engineering at West Point with the title of instructor. Spurred on by his lobbying efforts, Congress later elevated Youngberg's title to professor. In 1914, he served as engineer in charge of fortifications and river and harbor improvements in the Charleston District, in South Carolina and western North Carolina. During World War I, he became an executive officer for the chief engineer at the headquarters of the American Expeditionary Forces in France and later served as deputy assistant chief of staff in the supply section of the general staff. A founder of the Society of American Military Engineers in 1920, Youngberg served as its president when he became district engineer of the Florida peninsula. As district engineer, he supervised numerous projects, including major improvements in the St. Johns River, Tampa Harbor and Miami Harbor, and directed other less extensive waterway improvements throughout the state.[18]

Although the waterway hearings conducted by Youngberg's predecessor had been well attended, few hard statistics on the amount of freight expected to be transported had been collected to support the proposed Florida waterway. While Youngberg favored the project in a report sent to Washington in April 1923, a special engineers' board declined to accept Youngberg's recommendation and ordered Florida's new chief engineer to gather more information on the economic benefits of the proposed federal

---

[17]Downs editor, *Who's Who in Engineering*, 1481.

[18]"Colonel Youngberg Retires," *Florida Engineer and Contractor* (March 1926):253; *National Cyclopaedia of American Biography* A:272-73; *Who Was Who*, volume 5, p. 805; Moyer, editor, *Who's Who*, 287-88.

waterway. While Youngberg assembled more statistics, members of the state's east coast chambers of commerce compiled the massive of amounts of information necessary to justify the federal government's intervention.[19]

Bradley Estate Forecloses On Florida Waterway

Just as Youngberg began settling into his new post, the Rhode Island Hospital Trust Company began foreclosure proceedings on behalf of the Bradley estate against the Florida canal company for failing to pay anything on the bonds issued in 1907 to finish the waterway. The unpaid debt amounted to $500,000. With accrued interest of $437,423, the canal company's indebtedness rose to almost $1 million. The trust company held 492 of Bradley's bonds worth $492,000; as trustee under Helen Bradley's will, the company controlled the remaining eight bonds worth $8,000. Canal company property subject to the 1923 foreclosure suit embraced not only the Florida waterway itself but also the state lands granted the canal company for canal improvements.[20]

Named as defendants in the St. Augustine foreclosure action were a variety of prominent investors who collectively owned only a small number of the unsecured bonds issued by the canal company thirty years before. The majority of these unsecured bonds had been owned by Bradley and his wife.[21]

Defendants who held the remaining unsecured bonds, were the company's former president, John W. Denny (Boston); the company's current president, Frederic Amory (Boston); Frederic's brother, Harcourt Amory (Boston); Thomas J. C. Williams (Baltimore), brother-in-law and executor under the will of Samuel Maddox, now deceased, secretary of the Florida canal company; Jane Bradley (Providence), George Bradley's sister; William G. McKechnie (Springfield), executor under the will of Edward M. Walker; the Trustees of Tufts College; Henry D. Cooke (Washington); Helen C.

[19]Youngberg, "East Coast Canal," 28; "Report of Intercoast [sic] Waterway Exam. Favorable," Fort Lauderdale *Herald*, 27 April 1923; "McDonald Explains Move," *Fort Lauderdale Herald*, 20 July 1923.

[20]Bill of Complaint, and, Report of Special Master, *Rhode Island Hospital Trust Company, etc. vs. Florida Coast Line Canal and Transportation Company, et. al.*, Chancery Case No. 1408, St. Johns County Circuit Court, filed June 28, 1923 (hereinafter referred to as "Rhode Island Trust foreclosure"). Decree of Foreclosure, July 2, 1923, Rhode Island Trust foreclosure.

[21]Order for Publication As To Certain Defendants, February 27, 1923, and Decree of Foreclosure and Sale, July 2, 1923, Rhode Island Trust foreclosure.

Blackwell (Washington), a relative of Henry D. Cooke; John D. Maclennan's wife, Georgia Maclennan (Washington), daughter of Julia Harkness (Mary Harkness Flagler's youngest sister) and Barney York, a partner with Flagler in an early salt manufacturing venture; Sir Sandford Fleming's son, Sandford Hall Fleming (Ontario); Albert P. Sawyer's wife, Sarah R. Sawyer; Sawyer's son, Albert H. Sawyer (Newburyport); and Arthur M. Merriam (Manchester).[22]

Most of these investors had been officers, directors or stockholders of the canal and Boston land companies; others had been simply investors in the land trusts formed by Bradley and his associates in the 1890s. Still others had been involved with Miles in the Indian River and Bay Biscayne Navigation Company in the 1890s. Why these bond holders who held no mortgage encumbering the waterway were named in the litigation remains an unresolved question. Perhaps the rationale lies in the Florida canal company's practice of granting company lands in cancellation of company debt, as had been the case with Horace Cummings, Julia Tuttle and Henry Flagler during the 1890s, or permitting unsecured bond holders to redeem their investments in company land.[23]

The litigation appeared amicable, obviously designed to vest clear title to the waterway in Bradley's trustee. In fact, the suit was filed against the Florida canal company and on behalf of the Bradley trust by Charles M. Cooper, the Florida canal company's long-time Jacksonville lawyers.[24]

In the trust's foreclosure suit, unsurprisingly, neither the Florida canal company nor any of the other investors responded, prompting the St. Augustine court to enter defaults against all of them. In July 1923, the St. Johns County Circuit Court ordered a sale of the Florida canal company's waterway and other property to satisfy the money owed the Bradley trust.

---

[22]*Ibid.*, Exemplified copy of Will of SM, File No. 1063, Broward County, Florida, probate records; exemplified copy of Will of APS, File No. 1064, Broward County, Florida, probate records. Green, *Chief Engineer*, 16, 151. Helen Blackwell's address is that of Pitt Cooke, another brother of Jay Cooke, according to Oberholtzer, *Jay Cooke*, II, 18.

[23]Perkins to GAY, May 4, 1928, YP Box 4, File 9, quoting Frank Swan, the trust company's Rhode Island attorney. Transcript of Minutes of Canal Company, December 20, 1900, and filed February 19, 1901, Miscellaneous Book "B," at page 202, of the Public Records of Dade County, Florida. Satisfaction of Mortgage, executed on June 13, 1893, by Edward M. Cleary, Substituted Trustee, in favor of Canal Company, and filed June 21, 1893, in Satisfaction-of-Mortgages Book 1, at page 119, of the Public Records of St. Johns County.

[24]Transcript of Hearing before Special Master, June 13, 1923, Rhode Island Trust foreclosure; *Florida Coast Line Canal & Transportation Co. vs. Ellsworth Trust Co. et al.*, 144 F. 972 (5th Cir. 1906); *State ex. rel. Townsend vs. Florida Coast Line Canal & Transportation Co.*, 74 So. 816 (Fla. 1917); *State ex. rel. West vs. Florida Coast Line Canal & Transportation Co.*, 75 So. 582 (Fla. 1917).

Two months later, the waterway was sold to the trust company and the trust company, in turn, transferred ownership to the Florida Canal and Transportation Company, a new company whose stock was owned entirely by the Bradley trust. The trust also retained ownership of some of the state lands granted the company for dredging the east coast waterway as well as the dredge *Prickly Heat* and the launch *Three Sisters*, both of which had been used in the company's work. Meanwhile, joint real estate agents for the Flagler interests, the Boston & Florida company and the Bradley trusts continued to manage the sale of the firms' Florida land holdings acquired over a period of almost thirty years.

In December 1923, Albert Hayden Sawyer (son of Albert P. Sawyer), president of the Boston & Florida land company and trustee of the Bradley trusts, wrote one of their real estate agents, Frank J. Pepper, of the Miami firm of Pepper and Potter, seeking information on why properties in the Lake Worth Drainage District in the area of West Palm Beach had not been selling well. Pepper reported that there were four main reasons for the lackluster performance: (1) the drainage system there had not been working as well as expected; (2) the Lake Worth Trust could not demonstrate adequate agricultural yields from the land; (3) there existed no hard-surfaced roads to serve the area; and (4) the imposition of a confiscatory drainage tax of $2.50 per acre, as compared to list prices for the land of no more than $10 per acre; all of which made sales impossible. In sum, Pepper told Sawyer that "someone has got to spend more money for development" to sell the land.[25]

Burgman Rejuvenates Chamber Group

Deteriorating conditions along the poorly maintained Florida East Coast Canal soon drew national attention to the difficulties encountered in cruising down the waterway. On March 12, 1923, the houseboat *Pioneer*, transporting President Warren Harding and his golfing party, became stuck on a sandbar near Hillsboro Lighthouse north of today's Pompano Beach. Using the delay for a round of golf, Harding disembarked to play at the Lauderdale golf club. Just two years before, Fort Lauderdale's Commodore Brook rescued Harding after a stuck dredge blocked his vessel cruising down the

---

[25]Decree of Foreclosure, July 2, 1923, Rhode Island Trust foreclosure, p. 2; "East Coast Canals and Holding To Be Sold at Auction September 3rd," *Tallahassee Daily Democrat*, 16 July 1923; Decree of Confirmation of Special Master's Report of Sale, March 25, 1924, Rhode Island Trust foreclosure, p. 4. Pepper to AHS, 28 December 1923, MLC, Box 37, Folder 865 (Special File 1172).

Commodore Avylen Harcourt Brook (far right) aboard his yacht *Klyo* with President-elect Warren Harding (man standing in the middle with white pants) in the New River Sound, Fort Lauderdale, Florida, 1921. In 1927, Brook became a founding member of the board of commissioners of the Florida Inland Navigation District, and later served as chairman from 1932 until 1945. (Courtesy, Fort Lauderdale (Fla.) Historical Society Collections, Accession No. 5-8557)

waterway, allowing Harding his first day of golf at the Lauderdale links. The day after the president's extraction near the Hillsboro Lighthouse in 1923, Harding's boat became stuck once again, this time farther south, in New River Sound at Fort Lauderdale. One more time, Harding played golf, but in this instance, at the Hollywood golf club south of Fort Lauderdale.[26]

---

[26]"C. Of C. Sends Boat To Pilot Harding Thru Lake Mabel," *Fort Lauderdale Herald*, 28 January 1921; Harding Boat Sticks On Florida Mud," *New York Times*, 3 February 1921; "Spent 17 Hours in Fort Lauderdale Friday—Says He Likes the New Golf Links There," *Fort Lauderdale Herald*, 11 February 1921; "President-Elect Harding at Fort Lauderdale," *Fort Lauderdale Herald*, 4 February 1921; "President's Party Off to Ft. Lauderdale; To Reach Here Tomorrow," *Miami Herald*, 12 March 1923; "President and Party Encounter Delays in Getting by Sandbars," *Miami Herald*, 13 March 1923; " "Presidential Party Pays Visit to Fort Lauderdale and President Plays Golf," *Fort Lauderdale Herald*, 16 March 1923.

Seven months after the Harding incident, on October 11, 1923, Charles F. Burgman, president of the Daytona Chamber of Commerce, convened an important meeting of the Florida East Coast Chamber of Commerce at Daytona. The meeting focused on important issues affecting the east coast, particularly the deteriorating conditions along the East Coast Canal. Burgman's efforts quickly made him the acknowledged leader of chamber efforts to spur a federal takeover of the privately owned Florida East Coast Canal.

Charles F. Burgman

Florida's 70-year-old leader of the inland waterway movement, Charles F. Burgman, was born in Muenden, Hanover, Germany, on July 21, 1853. At the age of nineteen, Burgman fled to London to evade German military service. There he came in contact with Karl Marx, became interested in Internationalism and attended socialist meetings. A year later, Burgman emigrated to the United States, arriving in New York City in September 1873. After five years' service in the United States Army in Kansas and Arizona, Burgman built a home in Arizona. Later, Burgman relocated to San Francisco, where he became a tailor and represented the Tailors Union in the Tailors Assembly.

Elected to the Labor Congress of 1881 which met in Pittsburgh, Burgman helped found the American Federation of Labor and was one of the five members of the first executive board. [27]

In 1898, Burgman visited Florida and remained at Seabreeze, near Daytona, until 1903. There, he published *Freedom*, a paper devoted to mental science. Sometime later, Burgman formed Peninsula Publishing Company with his two sons. After 1909, Burgman engaged in a real estate and insurance business at Daytona. In May 1923, he was elected to the presidency of the Daytona Chamber of Commerce and served in that capacity until 1925. As early as 1910, Burgman advocated federal ownership of the East Coast Canal. As a driving force in the old Florida East Coast chamber association, he soon became chairman of the newly reorganized Florida association's Committee on Inland Waterway Transportation. [28]

---

[27]Gold, *History of Volusia County*, 306, 309; Cutler, *History of Florida*, II, 5-6; Lorwin, *American Federation of Labor*, 13, fn. 7; American Federation, iii, 65.

[28]*Ibid.*

In August 1923, Burgman, joined by Brevard County citrus grower J. J. Parrish, attended a meeting held in Orlando at the San Juan Hotel, along with two hundred representatives from around the state. Only seven represented the east coast and none of the speakers during the day-long meeting addressed a single issue of importance to that section of the state. The dearth of east coast concern prodded the two to travel up and down the coast during the next month to visit officials of every chamber organization then in existence. The two men also formulated five principal issues on which a new chamber group was to be organized. Of the five issues, four concerned east coast transportation issues, while the fifth question focused on the creation of a joint advertising fund to promote the Florida east coast. Three of the four transportation issues centered on the building of a state highway from Jacksonville to Miami, the need for double tracking the Florida East Coast Railway system and the construction of a cross-state highway from the Atlantic coast to the Gulf of Mexico. The fifth issue became the Daytona developer's greatest legacy: in the "Organized public demand for government ownership and improvement of the East Coast Canal."[29]

As a result of the efforts of Burgman and Parrish, fifty delegates representing ten east coast chambers of commerce assembled at Daytona a month later. From that small collection of representatives emerged a new group that would lead to the formation of the Association of Chambers of Commerce of the Florida East Coast. Miami pioneer and local chamber president Everest G. Sewell became the first president of a nucleus of five east coast chambers of commerce making up the new association. The next month, the association convened in Miami, but now with representatives of ten chambers attending.[30]

Born on September 17, 1874, in Elbert County, Georgia, Everest G. Sewell arrived in Miami at age twenty-two with his brother John to open a men's clothing store. At the turn of the century, he organized the local merchant's association and served as its first president. From 1915 until 1925, Sewell headed the Miami Chamber of Commerce and would serve as mayor from 1927 until 1929 and an additional three terms, on and off, until his death in office in April 1940. In addition to helping to develop the inland waterway, he assisted in bringing the federal highway down the east coast and improving the Miami harbor.[31]

---

[29]Burgman, *Florida East Coast Canal*, 8.

[30]Burgman, *Florida East Coast Canal*, 5-6.

[31]Dovell, *Florida*, IV, 785-86.

A leader also in the regional Atlantic Intracoastal Waterway movement, Sewell would be elected a vice-president-at-large at the annual convention of the Atlantic Deeper Waterways Association held at Richmond, Virginia, in 1926. Two years later, at the convention held at Cape May, New Jersey, he was re-elected as a vice-president-at-large. In 1928, Sewell served as a director of the American Shore and Beach Preservation Association, an organization formed to recognize that "our coasts and the shores of our lakes and rivers constitute important assets for promoting the health and physical well-being of the people of this nation."[32]

A hundred and fifty delegates from twenty chambers attended the newly reorganized Florida chamber association's quarterly meeting held at Melbourne in October 1924. Colonel Youngberg presented an important paper entitled, "Water Transportation and an Intracoastal Waterway from Jacksonville to Miami." The gathering voted to print 1,000 copies of the document for distribution along the east coast. Youngberg's paper, almost twenty pages long, described the development of transportation in Florida, detailed the relative costs of different kinds of transportation, compared rail and water transportation and specifically described a project he called an "Intracoastal Waterway from Jacksonville to Miami." Youngberg went on to urge the competing groups pushing for the two different routes under consideration to join forces in collecting the sizeable amount of statistics needed to provide an economic justification for a federal takeover. Delegates voted to hire former Army engineers Jacquelin Marshall Braxton of Jacksonville (Florida's chief engineer from 1918 until 1919) and Earl Wheeler to make an economic study of the waterway at a cost of $8,000. Braxton's and Wheeler's report of the study later became an important part of an historic Atlantic Intracoastal Waterway document used to justify the federal takeover.[33]

Meanwhile, Army engineers continued to study the feasibility of a takeover of the Florida waterway. In January 1925, the United States Board of Engineers, considering the two routes down the Florida coast, conducted a public hearing on the waterway at Fort Pierce and then traveled to Daytona to inspect the Halifax River,. At a dinner hosted for the engineers at the

---

[32]ADWA, Richmond, Va., 14-17 September 1926:161. American Shore and Beach Preservation Association ("ASBPA"), *Proceedings*, Jacksonville, Florida, 5-6 December 1927:3. ASBPA, *Report*, Washington, D. C., 8 December 1926:5.

[33]Burgman, *Florida East Coast Canal*, 6. Youngberg, "Water Transportation." One of the thousand printed copies of Youngberg's paper may be found in the Florida Collection, Jacksonville (Fla.) Public Library.

Arroyo Gardens Hotel, Colonel Youngberg predicted that the federal government would eventually become interested in the development of East Coast Canal and the St. Johns River. But there was still no indication what recommendation the board would make on the takeover question. Traveling from his home at Pomfret, George Miles conferred with Burgman in Florida about the chamber's plans for the waterway and announced his intention of establishing a third transportation company once the federal government's decision was known. Miles floated his scheme of a thrice-weekly boat and barge service between Jacksonville and Fort Pierce.[34]

The next month, Burgman's revitalized east coast association announced plans to ask the Florida legislature to create a special taxing district comprised of eight east coast counties, from St. Johns County in the north to Dade County in the south, authorized to construct or acquire and maintain a navigable waterway along the east coast. The body was to be known as the "Florida East Coast Navigation District." At the same time, the Baltimore-based trade paper *Manufacturers' Record* commented on the Army board's recent visit to Florida to survey two proposed routes for the southernmost link in a proposed Intracoastal Waterway from Boston to Miami. The old East Coast Canal, with a minimum of five feet of water, was said to be the most suitable route for freight motorboat traffic; the St. Johns River route, with eight feet of water, more useful for larger barges with greater cargoes. Commenting on the rivalry between the two routes' supporters, the *Record* praised the objectivity of the Army Corps of Engineers, writing that "the [Army] engineers will not be moved by strictly local considerations or wishes, but will try to determine what may be best for the Florida portion of the great project and for the intercoastal [*sic*] project as a whole." While the Army engineers deliberated over the alternative routes, a New York steel magnate and a New Jersey-born restaurateur vied to buy the privately owned Florida waterway from the Rhode Island Hospital Trust Company.[35]

[34]"Plans Are Made for Boat Service," *New Smyrna News*, 23 January 1925.

[35]"Notice," by Chas. F. Burgman, Chairman of the Special Legislative Committee of the Association of Chambers of Commerce of the East Coast of Florida, *New Smyrna News*, 24 April 1925. "Engineers Studying Florida Waterways," *Manufacturers' Record*, 12 February 1925.

Chapter 19

The Boston Restaurateur

While Florida chamber groups pressured state legislators to seek a forfeiture of the Florida waterway for the canal company's failure to maintain it, in January 1925, New York steel magnate Jacob Leonard Replogle paid $50,000 cash to the Rhode Island Hospital Trust Company, George Bradley's trustee, for an option to buy the Florida East Coast Canal. President of the Replogle Steel Company, the 47-year-old Pennsylvania native wintered in Palm Beach, where his card-playing ability among fellow elites was regarded as less than stellar, according to writer Cleveland Amory. The *Manufacturers' Record* predicted that Replogle's plans for development of the waterway would be "almost as important to a large section of Florida as the building of a new railroad from one end of the state to the other." It would create waterway transportation facilities," the publication expounded, "for freight up and down the east coast, the effect of which would be instantly felt for the good of the entire section."[1]

Replogle Loses Option

However wonderful the prospects might have been, Replogle failed to complete the purchase and allowed the option to expire. Recounting the events that led to the option's end, George Miles wrote that when Governor John Martin declined to assure Replogle that if he made the waterway navigable, the state wouldn't seek the waterway's forfeiture, Replogle declined to exercise his option and the trust company kept his $50,000.[2]

Sometime later, in November 1925, former New England restaurant chain operator Harry Seymour Kelsey bought the Florida waterway for $550,000.

---

[1] "Glimpses Along Inland Waterway in Florida Sale of which Will Provide Funds for Establishment of Hospital for Crippled Children," *Providence Journal*, 17 January 1925; "Prominent Steel Operator Buys Option On Florida East Coast Canal Company," *Manufacturers' Record*, 23 April 1925. "J. L. Replogle, 72, Steel Man, Is Dead," *New York Times*, 26 November 1948, p. 23, Col. 1. Amory, *Last Resorts*, 395. *Who Was Who*, vol. 2, "Replogle, J(acob) Leonard."

[2] GFM to Watson, 15 February 1927, YP Box 4, File 20.

For several years a Palm Beach County real estate developer, the 46-year-old Kelsey made significant improvements in the waterway, spending a considerable sum in the process. His plan initially was to use the waterway to transport building materials to West Palm Beach and one of his real estate developments, Kelsey City, one of Florida's early planned cities.

Born in Claremont, New Jersey, on March 26, 1879, Kelsey founded the Waldorf Restaurant Systems, a national chain of as many as 112 restaurants, bakeries and commissaries based in Boston. At the time Kelsey disposed of his restaurant interests, he controlled eighty-nine restaurants located in twenty-seven cities east of the Mississippi River. Shortly after his arrival in Palm Beach County in 1919, the New Jersey native purchased over 100,000 acres of land from the estate of Jacksonville attorney John M. Barrs and a large tract of land fronting the Atlantic Ocean at Lake Worth, along Dixie Highway, on Federal Highway and facing the eastern banks of the Florida East Coast Canal. The purchase included a section of land that for a time had been owned by Bradley's Lake Worth Land Trust as well as a large tract of Boston & Florida land. Kelsey engaged the Olmsted Brothers, a nationally acclaimed planning firm, to design a new city named Kelsey City to be built on a portion of the property. Kelsey also founded one of the largest nurseries in the state to provide trees, shrubbery and other landscaping materials for the city's avenues and parks and made town plans setting aside land for hotels, a public library, and churches. During 1925 and 1926, Kelsey expected building construction in the new town to cost no less than $2 million.[3]

In buying and improving the Florida East Coast Canal, Kelsey spent $844,713 and made ambitious plans for the waterway. He hoped to buy the boat *Cocoa* and six barges, build 100 more barges, and develop numerous floating hotels along the waterway. In addition to a cash down payment of $50,000, Kelsey gave a $500,000 note to the Rhode Island Hospital Trust Company to pay for the waterway.[4]

---

[3]"Kelsey Gets Millions To Finance Projects," *Palm Beach Post*, 14 June 1921; "Great Development Project Launched at West Palm Beach," *Fort Lauderdale Herald*, 26 October 1923; McKay, editor, *Book of Florida*, 220, 570; Gooding, compiler, *Tucked Between the Pages*, 5, 7, app. I; Lake Park, *Town of Lake Park Preservation Study*, 3. "Harry S. Kelsey," *New York Times*, obit.,1 December 1957.

[4]Earl Wheeler, "Investigation & Report of the Florida East Coast Canal for the Canal Committee of the Association of East Coast Chambers of Commerce," 3 March 1927, TP. Mucklow & Ford, "Report—Florida Canal & Transportation Company, 31 December 1926," Jacksonville, Florida, TP.

At first, Kelsey's investment in the waterway appeared sound and looked to be immensely profitable. For the year 1925 alone, Kelsey collected tolls from vessels plying the waterway amounting to an astounding $55,952. A year later, toll collections slipped slightly to $53,796. The collapse of the Florida land boom in 1926, however, completely destroyed his dreams for the waterway and Kelsey City. Toll figures for 1927 dropped dramatically to $27,560. The following year, for the nine-month period ending September 30, toll collections were a meager $12,409. With Florida waterway conditions continuing to deteriorate, state legislators pushed forward with efforts to seek a forfeiture of the Kelsey waterway. Adding to the legislature's demands, Burgman's east coast chamber group issued a statewide call to end the canal's private ownership because of poor waterway conditions.[5]

A first-hand account of a sailboat trip down the Florida waterway in the fall of 1925 confirmed the lack of maintenance that made stretches of the waterway nearly impassable. Traveling down from Jacksonville with five aboard, the yacht *Alice* encountered numerous patches of shallow water. In the 21-mile canal from St. Augustine to Daytona, crew members could not "relax for a moment," while nearly "the whole way through the canal a large wave followed the boat, showing that she had little water to spare beneath her." Particularly annoying on the trip were the ubiquitous sand flies, so small that even mosquito netting smeared with motor oil couldn't keep them away. Passengers were thrilled, however, with the sightings of white cranes, buzzards and the ever-present kingfisher, along with the large palm trees overhanging the water's edge against a backdrop of tall palmettos. Nearing Daytona and a widening in the river, travelers saw so many hundreds of ducks swimming together, they "appeared in the distance to be just a black patch on the water." Stopping next at Orchid, near present-day Vero Beach, the *Alice* took on a bag of oranges and grapefruit.[6]

Cruising farther south down the Indian River, crewmembers encountered numerous narrow channels and stretches of shallow water. To take soundings in the water that lay ahead, the crew launched a small dinghy with two men aboard. Soon the *Alice* was underway again; but alas, for only a short while. Stranded a third time, crewmembers spotted a dredge working in

---

[5]Perkins to GAY, 9 October 1928, with schedule of amount of tolls collected for the period 1925-28, YP Box 4, File 29. Gardner to GAY, August 26, 1927, YP Box 4, File 2; Youngberg, "East Coast Canal," 24; "Harry S. Kelsey," *New York Times*, 1 December 1957, p. 88, col. 8.

[6]Howard, *Yacht Alice*, 172-88.

the waterway ahead. The captain rowed over to the men working on the dredge. Dredge workers warned him that traveling farther south would require the *Alice* to motor through the Fort Pierce Inlet and take the outside route down the coast for the remainder of the trip. After dinner, the dredge crew used a tug to tow the vessel with great difficulty against a strong wind pushing the dredge to the side of the channel, where the crew tied the vessel to a second, larger dredge farther out to await a change in tide before going outside through the inlet. During the wait for the tow, the *Alice's* passengers learned that a boy working on the dredge had been eaten by sharks when he went overboard to pump out the dredge's pontoons.[7]

In April 1926 at Vero Beach, members of Burgman's Association of Chambers of Commerce of the East Coast of Florida meeting voted on a resolution asking Governor Martin to seek a forfeiture of the canal from the Kelsey company for failure to maintain the waterway. The next month, Association president Dave Sholtz urged members to fight for waterway improvements and called on local members of Congress to support the effort. On June 24, Burgman's association met at Eau Gallie and passed a resolution favoring adoption of a $50,000 advertising campaign to publicize the East Coast of Florida throughout the North and the Midwest, with expenses to be prorated among member cities in proportion to the number of members in each chamber of commerce. Members planned to spend $40,000 on advertising the Florida east coast in major metropolitan papers, beginning around September or October. Those in attendance also recommended that the east coast counties buy the waterway and form a "canal district," dispatching a committee of five to Tallahassee to pursue the proposal.[8]

In November, the group held an important meeting at the Hollywood Beach Hotel, located in Joseph Young's once burgeoning town of Hollywood-by-the-Sea. Only two months before, a fierce hurricane had slammed into Florida's Gold Coast, devastating towns in its path and thoroughly destroying the south Florida economy. Nevertheless, 250 delegates representing thirty-three east coast chambers with a combined membership of over 15,000 gathered for the meeting. Delegates re-elected Daytona Beach Chamber of Commerce President Dave Sholtz as president. One of the major issues to be debated at the conference was the question, "Shall the

---

[7]Howard, *Yacht Alice*, 172-88.

[8]"Seizure Asked in Waterway on East Coast," Fort Lauderdale *Daily News*, 22 April 1926; "Inland Route To Be Pushed," *Fort Lauderdale Daily News*, 29 May 1926; "Advertising Campaign for East Coast Urged," *Fort Lauderdale Daily News*, 24 June 1926.

agitation for government ownership of the Florida East Coast Canal be abandoned?"[9]

Brevard County Judge John Shares of the Eau Gallie chamber, later a member of the first board of commissioners of the Florida Inland Navigation District, delivered a compelling speech favoring government ownership of the canal. Born on October 2, 1867, Shares had been both a state legislator and a county judge. In 1927, he served as president of both the Brevard County Chamber of Commerce and the Association of Chambers of Commerce of the Florida East Coast; nine years later, he led the nascent Florida Hotel and Motel Association as president from 1936 until 1937.[10]

Shares argued that Governor Martin ignored the Florida canal company's failure to maintain the waterway. Amazed at what he perceived as Martin's indifference, Shares urged the breaking of the "voters trust" existing throughout the state so that public officials would heed east coast demands. There were fewer boats on the inland waterway than there had been twenty-five years before, he claimed, and "the rich men of the world and the commerce of the section should be using the canal instead of having it lay idle, choked so that no boat not equipped with 'balloon tires' could come through." Corroborating the deplorable state into which the private canal had fallen, the *Fort Lauderdale Daily News* observed that the southern part of the waterway had been "practically impassable in many places for boats drawing more than two feet of water because of the caving in of the shoulders and the filling in of many sections, especially the northern end of Biscayne Bay and in sections of Lake Worth entrances and exits and in the canal proper between Fort Lauderdale and Miami."[11]

Charles Burgman argued that the "canal owners have forfeited their right of ownership" in the Florida East Coast Canal. The association should require the state to take over the canal, he urged, so that the state can turn it over to the federal government for adequate maintenance. He even suggested that the association file lawsuits, if necessary, "but by all means to bring about public ownership of the waterway." However, Palm Beach attorney Mark Wilcox, Harry Kelsey's legal representative, asked that the Palm Beach County developer be given more time to do what he could to maintain the canal. Putting off Wilcox, the chamber group decided to

---

[9]Burgman, *Florida East Coast Canal*, 9.

[10]*Ibid.*, 15. Hughes, *Florida's Lodging Industry*, 208, 230.

[11]"Daytona Beach Man Re-Elected by Civic Group," Fort Lauderdale *Daily News*, 30 November 1926.

appoint a committee to confer with Kelsey about the canal work and make a report at the January meeting to be held at Flagler City. At the conclusion of the meeting, association members unanimously demanded the turnover of the canal to federal authorities.[12]

While the chamber group grew increasingly more discontented, Colonel Youngberg added new information to his report on the Florida waterway to the Army's chief of engineers at Washington, reporting that the *Cocoa*, a boat running on the waterway between Jacksonville and West Palm Beach, spent a staggering twelve days in making a round trip. The actual time for the trip had been nearly five days; the remainder of the time had been spent waiting for high tides at various bars and shoals. Still, the *Cocoa*'s freight rates stood about thirty percent lower than the existing rail rates. On the development of Broward County, Youngberg related that the town of Fort Lauderdale "with several large beach developments, is growing very fast, and is a popular winter residential community." With a slowdown in rail transportation, however, it was almost impossible to get satisfactory deliveries of building materials by rail. The Pilkington yacht storage basin, located on the New River, stored ninety-nine pleasure yachts which drew up to six feet of water during the 1923-24 season. The basin's owner estimated that during 1924 approximately 350 yachts used his basin there and reported his company had been building two dry docks.[13]

In the southern part of Broward County, Youngberg described the "[n]ew development of Hollywood." Begun by a private development company in 1920, the town had started with a tract of 2,500 acres and now embraced 10,000 acres, with over five miles of oceanfront. Youngberg estimated the permanent population of Hollywood in 1922 at 68; in 1923 at 400; and in 1924 at 768, with a winter population for the 1923-24 season of approximately 2,500. He also reported the Hollywood development company's intention to develop a private commercial harbor at Lake Mabel, between Fort Lauderdale and Hollywood, known today as Port Everglades.[14]

To the north of Broward County in Volusia County, within ten miles of the East Coast Canal, five million board feet of timber per mile of waterway straddled the fifty-mile stretch through the county. Mostly consisting of pine, oak, cypress, gum, magnolia, and hickory, the reserve was home to the Volco Cypress Company, which began operations in 1923 cutting 4.5 mil-

[12]*Ibid.*; Burgman, *Florida East Coast Canal*, 11.
[13]U. S. Congress H. Doc. 586, 68, 83.
[14]*Ibid.*

lion board feet of cypress during the year. The Jacksonville-based E. W. Grove Company, which made the new Climax wallboard out of the palmetto plant, had just opened a factory ten miles south of New Smyrna. There, palmetto branches were shaved into quarter-inch strips, then kiln-dried, bundled and shipped to the Jacksonville plant for manufacturing into the final product. The new palmetto wallboard reportedly was sound, heat and cold-proof. About three miles from the East Coast Canal, the New Smyrna plant was expected to ship a railroad car of finished wallboard a day in 1925.[15]

The proposed improvements in the East Coast Canal were also expected to aid the East Coast Preserving Company at Daytona in shipping about 500 tons of citrus and jelly preserve products annually. Rates for the Jacksonville-Daytona Boatline's service on the East Coast Canal averaged about 20 percent below railroad rates. Comprised of the boats *Indian*, *Osceola*, *Daytona* and *Oklawaha*, the line maintained regular freight service between Jacksonville, Daytona, and New Smyrna.[16]

East Coast Canal Route Chosen

In December 1926, Secretary of War Dwight W. Davis sent Youngberg's long-awaited Florida waterway report to Congress along with the chief of engineers' recommendations. To the dismay of Sanford and St. Johns River supporters, Youngberg's study rejected the Sanford route, recommending instead the route of the Florida East Coast Canal, conditioned only on the turnover of the waterway and necessary right-of-way to the federal government free of charge. Rejecting Youngberg's recommendation that the waterway be widened to 100 feet, the chief of engineers endorsed construction of a continuous Florida intracoastal waterway eight feet deep and seventy-five feet wide. Army engineers projected the cost of waterway improvements at $4,221,000, with annual maintenance expenses totaling $125,000.[17]

On January 1, 1927, Congress appropriated funds to enlarge the Florida East Coast Canal to a width of seventy-five feet and a depth of eight feet,

[15]*Ibid.*, 77-78.

[16]*Ibid.*, 78.

[17]River and Harbor Act, approved January 1, 1927; Ruge (Florida State Canal Commission) to Taylor, 4 May 1927,TP; Burgman, *Florida East Coast Canal*,12.

along with funds for annual maintenance. For the first time since the creation of the Florida State Canal Commission, at the urging of both the Florida and Georgia delegations, Congress authorized funds for a preliminary examination and survey by the Corps of Engineers of a long-anticipated Atlantic-Mississippi Barge Canal across the northern part of the Florida peninsula. Congress also funded three other Atlantic Intracoastal Waterway projects: (1) the purchase of the Cape Cod Canal, built by August Belmont, for $11.5 million; (2) the construction of a channel 12 feet deep and 90 feet wide from Beaufort, N. C., to the Cape Fear River, a distance of 93 miles; and (3) the modification of the old Chesapeake and Delaware Canal. Interestingly, of all the Atlantic seaboard states which had privately owned waterways, Florida was the only state required to buy its own waterway for turnover to the federal government. Nevertheless, all three Atlantic coast projects would later become crucial links in the future Atlantic Intracoastal Waterway system.[18]

With appropriations for the Florida waterway assured, Daytona lawyer Dave Sholtz began drafting the paperwork to create the Florida Inland Navigation District, the governmental body that would purchase the Kelsey-owned waterway for turnover to the federal government.

The Price Of A Cheap Cigar

The Florida east coast chamber association—led by Sholtz—pressed the Florida Legislature to buy the Florida East Coast Canal. Four years before, in 1923, Sholtz had submitted a bill patterned after Van Agnews' 1917 proposal to secure the waterway's purchase, but the measure died in the 1925 session. But now, in 1927, with federal funding assured, Sholtz returned to work on the old bill that would create what was to become the Florida Inland Navigation District. After the East Coast chamber group reviewed Sholtz's initial proposal, and following comments by east coast members of the state House and Senate, Florida's attorney general, the U. S. attorney general and New York bond counsel, a revised bill passed both houses of the Florida Legislature and was promptly signed into law by Governor John Martin on May 25, 1927.[19]

---

[18]River and Harbor Act, approved January 1, 1927; Ruge (Florida State Canal Commission) to Taylor, 4 May 1927,TP; Burgman, *Florida East Coast Canal*,12.

[19]Burgman, *Florida East Coast Canal*, 5, 20; Chapter 12026, *Laws of Florida* (1927).

Even before passage of the law, the chamber association's Canal Committee — headed by Charles Burgman — had begun preparations for the waterway's purchase. So resolute was Burgman's committee that all three members — Burgman, Judge Shares, and Colonel Earl Wheeler — signed an option on March 16, 1927, on the chamber group's behalf to buy the Kelsey-owned waterway for $844,713.[20]

To arrive at the option price, Burgman's committee hired Colonel Wheeler — author of the chamber group's East Coast Canal economic study that Youngberg incorporated in his report to Congress — to investigate Kelsey's company and report his findings. In turn, Wheeler retained the Jacksonville accounting firm of Mucklow & Ford to scrutinize Kelsey's books for the thirteen-month period beginning December 1, 1925, and ending on December 31, 1926. In its March 1927 report, the firm concluded that Kelsey had spent $844,713 in purchasing and improving the waterway. The study detailed the Palm Beach developer's ambitious plans to buy the boat *Cocoa* and six barges, build 100 more barges and put numerous floating hotels on the waterway. Of Kelsey's investment in the waterway, a cash investment of $50,000 as a down payment represented the developer's only outlay of cash toward the purchase of the canal from the Bradley estate. Kelsey gave a note for the balance of $500,000, which remained unpaid at the close of 1926.[21]

To more accurately reflect Kelsey's actual investment, Wheeler downwardly adjusted the auditor's figures to reflect savings totaling $48,443 — mostly in the salvaging of equipment, reporting that Kelsey's net cost for the waterway had been $796,270. Wheeler also pointed out that of the 222 miles of waterway controlled by the Kelsey company, nearly 144 miles ran through swamp lands and waterways already owned by the state.[22]

Local chamber group donations helped to defray canal committee members' expenses in traveling around the state on waterway business and in

---

[20]Memorandum of Agreement between Florida Canal & Transportation Co. and East Coast Canal Committee of the Association of Chambers of Commerce of the East Coast of Florida, 15 March 1927; Supplemental Memorandum of Agreement between Florida Canal & Transportation Company and East Coast Canal Committee of the Association of Chambers of Commerce of the East Coast of Florida, 2 April 1917; both in FIND LAN Box 89.13.

[21]Earl Wheeler, "Investigation & Report of the Florida East Coast Canal for the Canal Committee of the Association of East Coast Chambers of Commerce," 3 March 1927, TP. Mucklow & Ford, "Report — Florida Canal & Transportation Company, 31 December 1926," Jacksonville, Florida, TP.

[22]Earl Wheeler, "Investigation & Report of the Florida East Coast Canal for the Canal Committee of the Association of East Coast Chambers of Commerce," 3 March 1927, TP.

the hiring of Wheeler and the Jacksonville auditors. Still, by March, Burg-man's committee needed $9,000 for expenses, but only $2,300 had been raised. Jacksonville's local chamber group contributed the largest amount—$1,000; Hollywood's assembly gave $350; the St. Augustine, the Eau Gallie and the Miami Beach associations each donated $250; while the Ormond and New Smyrna chambers each sent in $100. In a letter to Sena-tor Anthony W. Young, later a member of the first board of commissioners of the Florida Inland Navigation District, Burgman asked for help in solicit-ing funds, informing the senator that he had spent his own money to help pay committee expenses. Sometime after the district's organization, the new public body paid back various local chamber groups and the estate of deceased engineer Jacquelin Marshall Braxton of Jacksonville (who per-formed an early economic study of the waterway) a total of $8,000 for appraisals and the cost of securing an option to purchase the waterway. In April, meanwhile, Burgman urged Brevard County residents at Cocoa to lobby their representatives to support a proposal to sell bonds by the pro-posed district, arguing that the projected tax of a half a mil for each $1,000 of assessed property would only amount to the price of "a cheap cigar" for the 10-year bond issue.[23]

While Burgman's committee lobbied for public support for the proposed bond issue, Governor John Martin considered a number of prominent men for appointment as commissioners to represent the eleven east coast coun-ties comprising the new waterway district. By the first of July, representa-tives of nine of the counties had recommended appointments; Duval and Broward counties still lacked firm suggestions—although it was rumored that a group of Fort Lauderdale citizens had circulated a petition endorsing Commodore Brook. Two weeks later, Governor Martin announced his selections. Burgman, the governor's Volusia County appointee, immedi-ately circulated telegrams to the other commissioners, calling a preliminary meeting for July 20, at Eau Gallie's Harbor City Hotel; at the same time, another appointed commissioner, Fort Pierce businessman Fred McMullen, lobbied Abram Taylor, St. Augustine's representative, for the selection of Fort Pierce as the district's first meeting place.[24]

---

[23]Burgman to Young, 31 March 1927, YP Box 4, File 1. FIND Auditor's report, [1931?], TP; "Cost of Bonding East Coast Canal Will Not Be Much," *Cocoa Tribune*, 27 April 1927.

[24]Burgman to Taylor, 1 July 1927, TP; Burgman to Taylor (Telegram), 14 July 1927,.TP; Kessler (Assoc. of Chambers of Commerce of the East Coast of Florida) to Taylor, 14 July 1927, TP; "Canal Body To Meet Wednesday at Eau Gallie," *St. Augustine Evening Record*, July 18, 1927.

A month later, on Monday, August 29, 1927, an impressive array of important east coast newspaper publishers, real estate developers, hotel operators, yacht club commodores and state senators assembled for the first formal meeting of the board of commissioners of the Florida Inland Navigation District at Eau Gallie. After some dispute over voting procedures, commissioners selected Burgman to serve as chairman. Other officers chosen were Colonel Frank B. Shutts, an attorney and owner and editor of the *Miami Herald*, as vice-chairman; Donald Herbert Conkling, owner and editor of the *Palm Beach Post* and Commodore of the Palm Beach Yacht Club, as secretary; and Frank Hoke Owen, chairman of the Jacksonville public utilities commission, as treasurer. Shutts replaced long-time waterway advocate Everest G. Sewell as Dade County's first representative when Sewell was elected mayor of the city of Miami.[25]

The Commissioners

Miami Herald Publisher Colonel Shutts

The district's vice-chairman, Frank Shutts, founded the *Miami Herald* in 1910, after moving from Aurora, Indiana, to Florida at the age of forty. The son of a cobbler, Shutts worked his way through DePauw University Law School, graduating in 1892. When the 1907 recession swept the country and scores of banks failed, including Miami's Fort Dallas National Bank, Shutts, an experienced bankruptcy lawyer, was appointed to serve as the bank's receiver in 1909. A year later, Shutts convinced Flagler to buy one of Miami's two newspapers, the *News Record* and agreed to be publisher; later Shutts reorganized it under the name *The Miami Herald* and began publishing the paper on December 1, 1910. Eventually Flagler sold the paper to Shutts for what he had in it — $29,000.[26]

---

[25]"Inland Canal Men To Meet on Wednesday," *Florida Times-Union*, 13 August 1927; Burgman, *Florida East Coast Canal*, 15; FIND minutes, 20 August 1927. ADWA, 4-8 September 1928:79

[26]"The Indiana Lawyer Who Built the Herald," *Miami Herald*, 16 December 1985; *Bench and Bar*, I, 58.

Commodore Conkling—*Palm Beach Post* Publisher

Like Shutts, the board's secretary, Donald Herbert Conkling, was a newspaper publisher. Owner and publisher of the *Palm Beach Post*, which he founded in 1910, Conkling was also Commodore of the Palm Beach Yacht Club. Born on July 11, 1879, in Denton County, Texas, Conkling had been educated first in Texas's schools and later in Florida's schools. Conkling's father, R.A. Conkling, relocated the family from Texas to an area near Melbourne, where the senior Conkling became known as a pioneer horticulturist, conducting large citrus grove operations in the region. After working as a printer for a number of years along the east coast, the younger Conkling came to West Palm Beach in 1909. There, he established a print shop, operating two presses until 1910 when he founded his weekly newspaper. Well-connected to the banking community, Conkling served as vice president and director of the Commercial & Savings Bank, as vice president and director of the Commercial Loan & Mortgage Company, and as a director of the Morris Plan Bank at West Palm Beach.[27]

Jacksonville Utilities Executive Frank Owen

The waterway board's treasurer, Frank Hoke Owen, was born in Anderson, South Carolina, on August 25, 1871. In 1882, Owen's father moved the family to Florida, where the elder Owen engaged in orange growing at Floral Bluff in Duval County; four years later, the family moved to Jacksonville. In 1903, Frank Owen began working for the Merrill-Stevens Engineering Company in the shipbuilding plant, where he became superintendent in 1915, building naval vessels for the federal government until his departure in 1920. Owen was also elected to serve on the Jacksonville City Council for a number of terms at different times until 1918 when he became president of the council. In 1918, Owen also helped to form the Dekle Lumber Company, which he later headed as president. In 1920, Owen was made chairman of the Jacksonville city board under a new form of municipal government. At the time of his appointment to the navigation district board, Owen was also chairman of the Jacksonville public utilities commission. In addition, Owen served as president of the Pinellas Water Company, which installed the water system for the city of St. Petersburg, and

---

[27]McKay, editor, *Book of Florida*, 182, 187, 570.

headed several utility companies in Alabama, Georgia and South Carolina, where he built the electric line to Myrtle Beach.[28]

Other board members appointed by the governor to the first commission were Abram Morris Taylor, a state senator from St. Johns County and president of the Peoples Bank in St. Augustine; Dana F. Fuquay, a Flagler County architect and real estate developer; Judge John O. Shares, a former Brevard County jurist, president of the Brevard County Chamber of Commerce, and president of the Association of Chambers of Commerce of the Florida East Coast; Anthony W. Young, an Indian River County state senator, real estate developer and executive secretary of the Everglades Drainage and Control Boards; Fred G. McMullen, president of the St. Lucie County Bank and chairman of the Fort Pierce Inlet Commission; Stanley Kitching, Martin County pioneer and Stuart Yacht Club founder; and Broward County's Commodore Avylen Harcourt Brook, a promoter of the Cape Cod Canal and a leader in the waterway improvement movement for many years. Of the eleven commissioners, Kitching and Brook had been born in England and were long-time supporters of the Atlantic Deeper Waterways Association; Taylor, Kitching, Conkling, and Brook were all associated with local yacht clubs and known as commodores.[29]

St. Augustine's Senator A. M. Taylor

Born on September 1, 1862, in Morris County, New Jersey, St. Johns County's representative on the district — 64-year-old Abram Morris Taylor — was state senator for St. Augustine and also president of the Peoples Bank. As a member of the Florida senate, Taylor sponsored the legislation creating the Florida Inland Navigation District. A graduate of the College of the City of New York and an actor for a time, Taylor performed civil engineering services when he first came to Florida. Taylor was also Commodore of the St. Augustine Yacht Club and known as the Dean of Past Presidents among Florida Elks because of his service as president for the first three years of the state organization's existence (1906-1908). Just as Commodore Brook was a charter member of the Fort Lauderdale Rotary Club, Taylor was also a charter member of the St. Augustine Rotary Club. Taylor made

---

[28]Cutler, *History of Florida*, II, 67-68; Williamson, interview, 13-14; "F.H. Owen Elected Member of Council," *Florida Times-Union*, 8 January 1910.

[29]Burgman, *Florida East Coast Canal*, 15.

St. Augustine his home in 1889 and became manager of the Hotel Alcazar's Casino; he was also the first manager of the Jefferson Theater. In 1927, along with fellow navigation district commissioner Stanley Kitching, Taylor attended the 20th annual convention of the Atlantic Deeper Waterways Association at Baltimore. Taylor retained his seat on the navigation board for fifteen years until his death in 1942.[30]

Flagler Beach Architect Dana Fuquay

Forty-six-year-old Dana F. Fuquay, Flagler County's representative on the waterway board, was a prominent real estate developer in both Flagler and Volusia counties and one of Florida's first registered architects. Born near St. Augustine on August 5, 1881, Fuquay became a contractor in 1902 and built a thousand homes in the Daytona Beach area. In 1914, Fuquay formed a general contracting partnership, later incorporated as Fuquay & Gheen, Inc., one of the largest and most important builders in the state. In the 1920s, the firm owned more than five million board feet of timber near Daytona Beach. In 1915, Fuquay became the thirteenth person to become registered as an architect by the state Board of Architecture. Also in 1915, Fuquay purchased land in Flagler Beach, and later built the Flagler Beach Hotel during the boom of 1924. In 1922, while interested in the development of Flagler Beach, Fuquay started a project to build an ocean shore boulevard from the Matanzas Inlet south to Ormond. Fuquay's residence in Flagler Beach, built in 1926, is said to have been the largest home in the new town, built at a cost of $50,000.[31]

Vero Beach Senator Tony Young

Indian River County's representative on the waterway district was 62-year-old Anthony W. Young, a state senator from Vero Beach and first

---

[30]"Casino Opening," *Tatler* (St. Augustine, Fla.), 22 January 1898; "A. M. Taylor Passes Away; Was Former State Senator and Beloved Local Citizen," *St. Augustine Record*, 21 May 1942; "Senator Taylor Started Coming Here in 1884," St. Augustine *Record*, 21 October 1954; Florida, House, Clerk, (A. M. Taylor). FIND resolution, 28 May 1942; ADWA, 9-15 September 1928:185.

[31]Moyer, *Who's Who*, 112; Clegg, *History of Flagler County*, 34-35; State of Florida, Board of Architecture, *Record of Applications*, Book 1, at page 5; Hebel, editor, *Centennial History*, 15. See, also, Nance, editor, *East Coast of Florida*, I, 219-20; Cutler, *History of Florida*, III, 222.

mayor of the city in 1919. Born on July 27, 1865, in Godfrey, Illinois, he served as mayor of Alton, before moving to Vero in 1912. He served several terms in both the Florida house and senate. Young planted several hundred acres of citrus and reportedly was the first person to grow Sea Island cotton in the area; he also championed sugar cane growing. While in the legislature, Young promoted the creation of Indian River and Martin counties from parts of St. Lucie County in 1925.[32]

Fort Pierce Entrepreneur Fred McMullen

Although relatively little is known about St. Lucie County's representative compared to other commissioners, Fred G. McMullen distinguished himself as a prominent Fort Pierce business leader. President of the St. Lucie County Bank and Trust Company and chairman of the St. Lucie Inlet Commission, McMullen also served as a member of the board of governors of the Fort Pierce Chamber of Commerce and as president of the Fort Pierce Finance and Construction Company, which built the New Fort Pierce Hotel. He formed the Fort Pierce Finance and Construction Company in 1919 to develop a port at Fort Pierce. Incorporated two years later in 1921, the company joined the Fort Pierce Inlet District to build the port. On May 9, a company dredge completed the cut to open up the Indian River to the Atlantic Ocean. Unfortunately, the collapse of the Florida land boom in 1927 wiped out many of the company's investors in the project. It was not until 1957 that stockholders in the venture would receive $33 a share for holdings long before written off as worthless.[33]

Stuart Pioneer Stanley Kitching

Unlike McMullen, much is known about Martin County's 53-year-old waterway district representative, Commodore Stanley Kitching. Born in Warrington, near Liverpool, England, in 1874, Kitching arrived in America with his parents at the age of eight in 1882. The family settled at Sebastian, then known as New Haven, where Kitching's father, Sylvanus, supplied cord wood for the Florida canal company's steam dredges in the early years.

---

[32]"Death Claims Senator Young Here Saturday," *Vero Beach Press Journal*, 18 June 1948.

[33]*Fort Pierce City Directory*, 20, 150, 231-32. Nance, editor, East Coast of Florida, I, 296-97.; *Miami Herald*, editor, Florida: The East Coast, "New Fort Pierce Hotel Company," 215.

In 1902, Kitching moved to Stuart where he erected the first store there, ran the first automobile agency, and helped to incorporate the town in 1914. In 1912, Kitching helped to organize the Bank of Stuart. He also helped to form the Board of Trade—the forerunner of the Chamber of Commerce. Known as the "Grand Old Man of the Waterways," Kitching organized the St. Lucie Yacht Club in 1916. For twenty years Kitching served as vice chairman and chairman of the waterway district and he encouraged the construction of the St. Lucie Canal and the Okeechobee Waterway, as well as the deepening of St. Lucie Inlet. In 1919, Kitching met with Florida's governor to launch a cross-state canal. Kitching served as mayor of Stuart from 1920 to 1922. In 1925, he helped carve Martin County out of portions of St. Lucie and Palm Beach counties. A leader in establishing an electric power company, he also promoted the building of bridges across the St. Lucie River. Like Commodore Brook, Kitching was also involved in lobbying for federal intervention in the movement to create the Atlantic Intracoastal Waterway. In 1926, he was elected a director of the Atlantic Deeper Waterways Association at the 19th annual convention held at Richmond, the Stuart pioneer would be re-elected to serve in that position at the conventions held at Baltimore in 1927 and at Cape May in 1928.[34]

Burgman By The 'Flip Of A Coin'

By an odd coincidence, Daytona's Charles Burgman became the waterway district's first chairman literally by a flip of a coin. With Jacksonville utilities executive Frank Owen absent, ten commissioners assembled at the Eau Gallie meeting to elect officers and appoint an engineer for the district. Election of officers was the first order of business. Fort Lauderdale's Commodore Brook nominated *Miami Herald* publisher Frank Shutts for chairman; Brevard County Judge Shares put forward the name of Charles Burgman. Apparently conciliatory, Burgman asked that his nomination be withdrawn in favor of the Miami newspaperman, but Shutts declined and requested that both names be voted on. The commissioners then agreed that the nominee receiving the highest number of votes should be considered elected chairman, with the candidate garnering the second highest vote automatically declared vice-chairman. Surprisingly, both candidates declined to cast their own votes in the election. With only eight commis-

---

[34]Cutler, *History of Florida*, III, 81. Ziemba, *Martin County*, 174-76, 221; ADWA, 1926-1928.

Florida Inland Navigation District Board of Commissioners, Fort Pierce, Florida, January 1928. Seated (left to right): John O. Shares (Brevard), Frank H. Owen (Duval), Chas. F. Burgman (Volusia, Chairman), Anthony W. Young (Indian River), Harry S. Kelsey (Owner, Florida East Coast Canal), Abram M. Taylor (St. Johns). Standing (left to right): Fred G. McMullen (St. Lucie), Bert Winters (Kelsey attorney), Donald H. Conkling (Palm Beach), Frank B. Shutts (Dade), Dana F. Fuquay (Flagler) Avylen H. Brook (Broward), Alfred A. Green (FIND attorney), Stanley Kitching (Martin). (Courtesy, Florida Inland Navigation District, Jupiter, Florida)

sioners casting votes, the vote for the office of chairman was a tie, with four commissioners supporting Burgman and an equal number favoring Shutts. A second ballot failed to break the tie. Finally, Colonel Shutts suggested that the question be decided by a toss of a coin. Winning the coin toss, Burgman became, by chance, the waterway district's first chairman; Miami's Frank Shutts, vice-chairman. For the remaining offices, commissioners chose *Palm Beach Post* publisher Donald Conkling over Judge Shares to serve as secretary and the absent Frank Hoke of Jacksonville over Fort Pierce banker Fred McMullen as district treasurer.[35]

---

[35]FIND minutes, 20 August 1927.

Immediately after the election of officers, commissioners unanimously chose former Army engineer Colonel Gilbert Youngberg to supervise an appraisal of the Florida East Coast Canal at a salary of $600 a month plus expenses. The board also authorized Burgman and Youngberg to appoint a committee of appraisers to work with Youngberg in arriving at a fair price for the waterway's purchase. Appraisal board members appointed by Burgman and Youngberg were Colonel C. S. Coe, a consulting engineer from St. Augustine and formerly a division engineer on the Key West extension of the Florida East Coast Railway; Colonel Earl Wheeler, a Daytona Beach consulting industrial engineer who had worked on the economic study of the canal for the Florida chamber association and appraised the waterway for acquisition and E. L. Price, chairman of the Fort Pierce Inlet Commission. Two months later, in October, the appraisal board reported to district commissioners that it had assessed the value of the Kelsey company's property at $1,151,500, with approximately $1 million assigned to the waterway itself and another $120,000 to obtain right-of-way.[36]

To arrive at those prices, committee appraisers examined the value of the waterway alone, the lands making up the right-of way on either side of the waterway, the toll collection rights and the value of any buildings, toll-houses and dredging equipment owned by Kelsey's company. To come to a fair price for the waterway, the committee decided first that the canal's value to the public was only the usable value of the excavation already completed from 1883 until 1923. After gathering information on a wide range of prices for dredging soft materials and rock as well as for cutting both natural and artificial waterways, appraisers applied the figures to the 8.8 million cubic yards of dredged material the committee considered usable to arrive at a tentative valuation of the already-performed dredging work. The committee assessed right-of-way lands by first determining to what extent Kelsey's company held title to the lands and by interviewing land owners along the waterway from Jacksonville to Miami to estimate the value of land on either side of the canal. In determining the worth of the Kelsey company's right to collect tolls, the committee set the value at zero because of the federal government's longstanding policy of not charging tolls on federally maintained waterways. Assessing the waterway's toll chains as essen-

[36]*Ibid.*, FIND resolution, 20 August 1927. Youngberg, "East Coast Canal," 29; Minutes of Board of Appraisers, FIND, 29 August 1927, YP Box 4, File 2; Burgman, *Florida East Coast Canal*, 18; "Appraisers Make Inventory of the East Coast Canal," *Vero Beach Press Journal*, 13 September 1927.

tially junk and finding little value in the toll houses and docks along the waterway, appraisers determined the company's two dredge excavators worth a total of $12,500 and the tugboat *Three Sisters*, three hundred dollars.[37]

The St. Johns-Indian River Canal

While district commissioners quickly moved forward with plans to buy the East Coast Canal, St. Johns River supporters got more bad news. Disappointed with the Army engineers' preference of the East Coast Canal over the St. Johns River route, Sanford and Titusville-area supporters asked state legislators to form their own special taxing district to construct a St. Johns-Indian River Canal. The Legislature answered the call. In 1925, special legislation created the Upper St. Johns River Navigation District. The newly formed district hired Colonel Gilbert Youngberg to devise a plan to link the St. Johns River to the Indian River through a series of existing lakes and streams, a proposed artificial canal and two canal locks. Youngberg engaged J. Marshall Braxton to help prepare the plan. But on August 19, 1927, just as Florida Inland Navigation District commissioners started planning their first meeting at Eau Gallie, Brevard and Seminole County voters soundly defeated the St. Johns River bond issue to fund the project by a two-to-one vote. The district would nonetheless persist in pushing for improvements well into the 1960s with assistance from the Canal Authority of the State of Florida but the project as originally conceived would never be completed.[38]

On November 12, 1927, a special committee of the Florida Inland Navigation District assembled at Fort Pierce to meet with Harry Kelsey to negotiate the purchase of the East Coast Canal. At the first meeting's end, Fort Lauderdale's Commodore Brook announced that the committee had rejected Kelsey's offer. Brook flatly stated that it was not the committee's intention "to make Mr. Kelsey a millionaire" by purchasing the canal from him. A week later, the entire board conferred an entire day at the New Fort Pierce

---

[37]TP, "Report of Value of The Florida Canal and Transportation Company Properties," 21 October 1927.

[38]"J. Marshall Braxton, Noted Civil Engineer, Dies at Jacksonville," *Tampa Morning Tribune*, 29 January 1927; "Engineers Report on St. Johns Indian River Canal Is Printed," *Cocoa Tribune*, 12 August 1927; "St. Johns-Indian River Canal Measure Defeated At the Polls By Taxpayers Tuesday," *Cocoa Tribune*, 19 August 1927; Florida, *Canal Authority*.

Hotel with Kelsey and his West Palm Beach attorney, Bert Winters. The next month, Judge John Shares, Brevard County's representative on the Florida waterway board and chairman of the negotiating committee, traveled with Youngberg and Alfred Green, the waterway district's attorney, to Washington to put together a contract with Kelsey.[39]

On January 4, 1928, an Army Corps of Engineers telegram from Washington brought district commissioners encouraging news — the Corps no longer required the district to turn over all of the right-of-way needed for widening the waterway to 75 feet before it accepted the waterway and started making improvements. The next day, after two days of negotiation, commissioners agreed to purchase the waterway from Kelsey's company for $725,000. To finance the purchase and obtain the necessary right-of-way, commissioners called an election to be held on June 26 in the eleven east coast counties comprising the district for approval of a $1,887,000 bond issue. From his home Pomfret, George Miles, one of the principal forces behind the waterway in the early years and an owner of land in four counties within the district, vehemently objected to the district's formation and the purchase of the waterway. He complained that owners of property within the district would be taxed but that no improvements would be made without commissioners first securing the required right-of-way. And he further claimed that the Florida canal company did not own large stretches of the right-of-way needed for widening the waterway. A year later, still not persuaded that the district would be able to obtain the necessary right-of-way, Miles wrote an open letter to the editor of the Titusville *Star Advocate* calling upon commissioners to "publish a full report of the progress made to date towards securing the right of way, etc. necessary to meet the conditions under which the government will consent to undertake the enlargement of the canals, and the opening of new stretches of natural waterway."[40]

---

[39]"Canal Cost Said Too High," *Florida Times-Union*, 13 November 1927; "East Coast Canal Purchase Subject," *Miami Herald*, 19 November 1927. Burgman to Green, 9 December 1927, and Green's transportation and hotel receipts, FIND LAN Box 89.13. See, GAY to Fletcher, 19 December 1927, (unsigned copy), YP Box 4, Folder 10.

[40]Jadwin to GAY, 4 January 1928, copy of telegram, YP Box 4, File 2. Burgman, *Florida East Coast Canal*, 18-19; FIND resolution, 5 January 1928; Articles of Agreement between Florida Canal & Transportation Co. and FIND, 5 January 1928, FIND LAN Box 89.13; "Canal Purchase Is Approved," *Florida Times-Union*, January 5, 1928; "Board Signs for Purchase of Waterway," *Florida Times-Union*, January 6, 1928. GFM to GAY, 14 April 1927; GFM to Burgman, 7 April 1927 (copy); GFM to GAY, 31 March 1927; GFM to GAY, 24 March 1927; GFM to Butler, 5 March 1927 (copy); all in YP Box 4, File 20.

Despite Miles's criticisms, on January 28, 1928, just weeks after they had agreed to purchase the waterway, commissioners announced the appointment of engineers to complete the survey work required for federal turnover. Youngberg, the district's chief engineer, organized the complex undertaking for surveying and right-of-way procurement into two major divisions: a northern division comprised of the stretch of the waterway extending south from the St. Johns River to the Haulover Canal opposite Titusville, to be directed by Colonel C. S. Coe (a former member of the appraisal committee); and a southern division encompassing the length of waterway from the St. Lucie Inlet to the Biscayne Bay, to be headed by A. L. Brunson of Kelsey City. The segment of the waterway between Titusville and the St. Lucie Inlet remained exclusively under federal control as it had been for the most part since 1893. Three days later, the commissioners unanimously agreed to borrow $100,000 to pay for the surveys and right-of-way. Board members also ordered Colonel Youngberg to prepare a handbook on the waterway's history and its economic benefits to be used during an intensive and widely conducted public-speaking campaign to persuade voters to pass the bond issue. Would Florida east coast voters approve the $1,887,000 bond issue with the collapse of the Florida real estate boom and a looming nationwide depression? Only time would tell.[41]

---

[41]"Survey of East Coast Canal Improvement Starts Soon," *Florida Times-Union*, 29 January 1928.

Chapter 20

A Crowning Achievement

On June 28, 1928, waterway commissioners held elections in the eleven east coast counties comprising the district for approval of the bonds needed to purchase the Florida East Coast Canal. The measure passed in all the counties by a resounding four-to-one margin following a hard-fought public relations campaign. In the southern part of the state, Broward County freeholders voted seventeen-to-one in favor of the issue. In the town of Hollywood, the vote was unanimous. To the north, in Duval County, the proposition passed by a considerably smaller margin, with 1,515 votes cast in favor of the bonds and 989 votes against.[1]

A few weeks later, commissioners met in the offices of Commodore Conkling at *Palm Beach Post* headquarters to map out a plan for acquiring the necessary right-of-way for waterway widening. Board members authorized Chairman Charles Burgman to ask Harry Kelsey to furnish an abstract of title to the waterway as well as copies of various legislative acts, maps and other legal documents showing his company's title to the waterway so that the materials could be forwarded to Army engineers for early approval of title by the federal government. The board also authorized commissioners representing Duval, St. Johns, Flagler and Volusia counties to secure rights-of-way in their areas at prices not to exceed ten dollars an acre, but they expected much of the land bordering the waterway in those counties to be donated in recognition of the anticipated benefits to be derived from an improved waterway. Appreciating that the waterway ran through land considerably more valuable in the four southern counties, the board empowered commissioners representing Martin, Palm Beach, Broward, and Dade counties to hire appraisers to assess the cost of securing right-of-way in those areas.[2]

---

[1] "Canal Bond Issue Passes Election on East Coast," *Fort Lauderdale Daily News*, 27 June 1928; Burgman, *Florida East Coast Canal*, 19.

[2] "Believe Work on East Coast Canal Be Well Under Way by Next Fall," *St. Augustine Evening Record*, 22 July 1928.

An unfortunate appeal by a Dade County prosecutor challenging the constitutionality of the bond issue delayed purchase of the East Coast Canal for fifteen months and held up surveying, appraisals, and the northern commissioners' right-of-way procurement work. Vernon Hawthorne, state attorney for Dade County, appealed the Volusia County Circuit Court's decision approving the bond issue to the Supreme Court of Florida. At a meeting with Charles Burgman, Hawthorne later admitted that he had never even read House Document No. 586, Colonel Youngberg's comprehensive and detailed report to Washington on the need for acquiring and improving the Florida waterway. Hawthorne's appeal forced the district to suspend surveying and spend $4,000 for legal counsel, a large sum at the time. Interest on the deferred payment to Kelsey required payment of another $25,000, while the district forfeited toll collections of $30,000 during the court proceedings. Even more damaging was a year's delay in federal appropriations for improvements. Bond election results profoundly changed George Miles's stubborn mind on the bond question. Conceding that the bond issue had received "the approval of a large majority of the people of the District," the former canal company president and general manager now found it unfair that "a few non-progressive citizens" might jeopardize plans for the waterway's improvements, obviously referring to Hawthorne's appeal. In May 1929, the Florida Supreme Court denied Hawthorne's appeal, which was quickly followed by the legislature's approval of the bonds. But the window of opportunity to sell the offering at a low four-percent interest rate had already closed, forcing the district to borrow funds at much higher rates.[3]

Despite the delay in the Florida East Coast Canal's improvements, civic groups pressed on with other inland waterway projects, including the ill-fated Atlantic-to-Mississippi or Cross-Florida Barge Canal. On January 4, 1929, 114 representatives representing thirty-one towns in fifteen counties, including delegates from Tampa, Ocala and Jacksonville, assembled at Leesburg to form the Florida Inland and Coastal Waterways Association. This new group lobbied for improvements in drainage, flood control and naviga-

---

[3]Burgman, *Florida East Coast Canal*, 20-21. "Notice of Sale," p. 2 ("General Information"), FIND ADM Box 68.12. Final Decree Validating Bonds, *FIND vs. State of Florida*, Case No. 1438, Volusia County, Florida, Circuit Court entered August 18, 1928 (copy), FIND LAN Box 89.13; *State v. Florida Inland Nav. Dist.*, 122 So. 249 (Fla. 1929); *Laws of Florida*, ch. 13638 (1929); GAY to GFM (copy), 11 September 1928, and GFM to GAY, 15 September 1928, YP Box 4, File 20.

tion in the Okeechobee-Caloosahatchee section of the state and for several cross-state waterway surveys, just as Hawthorne's appeal finally came to an end.

In August, Fred McMullen, Fort Pierce's representative on the FIND board, resigned his seat to become the district's first business manager at a salary of $500 a month. Judge Shares also resigned to accept the position of assistant manager at $400 a month. Shares would supervise right-of-way purchases along the waterway in the Northern Division, consisting of Duval, St. Johns, Flagler and Volusia counties. McMullen undertook oversight in acquisitions in the remaining seven counties comprising the Southern Division.[4]

Toll Chains Dropped

With an administration in place and bonds ready for sale, FIND commissioners began the process of closing on the purchase of Kelsey's Florida East Coast Canal. On December 3, 1929, the Corps of Engineers notified commissioners that the attorney general had certified that title to the waterway had been properly vested in the United States. Commissioners paid Kelsey $725,000, together with interest for the closing delay and some adjustments, using the district's newly issued bonds and some cash.[5]

Senator Duncan Fletcher, who almost forty years before had purchased 1,300 acres of land in what was to become Broward County from the old canal company for his ill-fated Florida Fiber Company venture, turned his attention once again to the waterway, easing the federal government's takeover of the canal as a member of the Senate's Committee on Rivers and Harbors. One of the more important steps Fletcher took was to persuade the Corps of Engineers to take control of the waterway and make improvements before the waterway district was able to turn over all of the spoil areas and right-of-way necessary for the corps' dredging work. Forty-seven years after the old Florida canal company first began work on the waterway,

---

[4]Thomas (Florida Inland and Coastal Waterways Association) to Taylor, 2 April 1929, TP. Auditor's Report, FIND, [1931?], TP, Box 3, Folder 5.

[5]Burgman, *Florida East Coast Canal*, 4; U. S. Army Corps of Engineers, *Annual Report*, 1930, 768. See, also, (Quitclaim) Deed executed by Florida Canal & Transportation Company in favor of the United States of America, 15 October 1929, recorded in each of the eleven east coast counties comprising the District, and found in FIND LAN Box 89.13. Owen to FIND board, 25 April 1930, FIND ADM Box 70.06.

the toll chains disappeared. The Florida East Coast Canal had finally become a free, public waterway of the United States. By an act of Congress the official name for the waterway became the "Intracoastal Waterway from Jacksonville, Florida, to Miami, Florida."[6]

Less than a year after the federal takeover, on July 3, 1930, Congress authorized the widening of the waterway from 75 feet to 100 feet. A month later, Commodore Brook wrote New York yachtsman Otto Schmidt, president of the Waterway League of America, that the Florida waterway district had eleven dredges working "night and day" in the Intracoastal Waterway. "Tell the boys," Brook gushed, "not to put their boats away, not to lay them up for the winter. Tell them that anyone with any kind of a cruiser can come to Miami this winter in perfect safety through this waterway." "Any boat drawing up to five feet can come through without touching bottom anywhere," Brook further assured Schmidt, "there are no tolls to pay, the bridges are all free, water, ice, supplies and repairs can be obtained every few miles along the way" and "no gouging or overcharging will be permitted."[7]

The Emma Pendleton Bradley Hospital

Twenty-five years after George Lothrop Bradley's death on April 8, 1931, the Bradleys' dream of a hospital devoted exclusively to the treatment of children with psychiatric illnesses finally became a reality. Bradley's trustees opened the Emma Pendleton Bradley Home, now known as the Bradley Hospital—the nation's first psychiatric hospital for children—in East Providence, Rhode Island. The couple's wills had poignantly stated their motivation in establishing the home as "arising particularly from our special sympathy with those who suffer from disease, because our child whose name said Home is to bear has been so afflicted through life. Out of this misfortune of our only child has grown the purpose and the hope that from the affliction of this one life may come comfort and blessing to many suffering in like manner." Unfortunately, the NIMBY ('Not in my backyard') syndrome almost killed construction of the three-story colonial-style building before it even started in the spring of 1929. When trustees let the first con-

---

[6]Burgman, *Florida East Coast Canal*, 13. See, also, FIND resolution, 29 June 1936.

[7]House Document No. 71, 71st Cong., 2nd session, submitted January 16, 1930; River and Harbor Act of July 3, 1930. "Information on Fla. Inland Waterway Is Given by Brook," *Fort Lauderdale Herald*, 29 August 1930.

struction contract for excavation work, local building officials held up the building permit because of neighborhood concerns over the ages and types of residents to be housed. After assurances that the hospital would serve only children and that no "insane cases" would be accepted, the town's zoning board and the Metropolitan Park Commission issued approvals following a public hearing. During the first two years of the home's existence, income from Bradley's endowment provided an astounding $196,238 to meet operating expenses of $209,623. By the end of the first decade, the Bradley charity provided service to a third of the 678 children admitted to the Home, at no cost, and the families of another 297 children paid less than five dollars toward the forty dollars a week cost for each resident. During the first eighteen years of the home's existence, Bradley's 1880s investment in the iron-rich Gogebic Range alone contributed $48,000 annually to the Rhode Island charity. In 1957, the home would become a full-fledged hospital.[8]

A year after the Home's opening, Commodore Brook became the Florida waterway district's chairman upon the untimely death of Daytona Beach's Charles F. Burgman. Burgman, who had spearheaded the Florida movement that led to the waterway's takeover, passed away suddenly the evening of June 6, the night before a primary vote on Burgman's re-election as a commissioner of the district representing Volusia County. The next day, the Daytona real estate entrepreneur and former American Federation of Labor leader lost the election posthumously.[9]

In 1933, while work progressed on the Atlantic Intracoastal Waterway, the Florida legislature created the Ship Canal Authority of the State of Florida to acquire the land and equipment necessary to build and operate a ship canal across the peninsula of Florida, a dream of Army engineers since 1824. Construction would actually start in February 1964, but growing concerns over the potential adverse impact on the environment forced Congress to ask the

[8]"Permission Given To Build Hospital," *Providence Journal*, 7 August 1929; "Bradley Home Is Unique," *Providence Sunday Journal*, 5 April 1931; Inventory of Estate of GLB, January 15, 1907, volume 26, pp. 592-95; Accounting of Estate of GLB, April 5, 1934, volume 32, pp. 201-18; Last Will and Testament of GLB and codicils, vol. 20, pp. 520-548; all in Pomfret (Conn.) probate records. Last Will and Testament of Helen McHenry Bradley and codicils, Pomfret (Conn.) probate records, volume 29, pp. 50-59. Johnston, *Out of Sorrow*, 15-19. Simister, *First Hundred Years*, 60. Emma Pendleton Bradley, *Annual Report*, 21; Gardner, "The 18th Anniversary."

[9]FIND, *Story*, 2. "Charles F. Burgman," pol. adv., YP Box 4, File 1; "Brook Head of E.C. Canal Body," *Fort Lauderdale Daily News*, 27 June 1932.

Corps of Engineers to re-examine the project. In 1977, the Corps recommended against continuing the project. Following de-authorization bills passed by both Congress and the state legislature, the Governor and other Cabinet members killed the project in January 1991. The Canal Authority, however, still administers management plans for the land acquired for the ill-fated venture.[10]

By 1934, state and federal taxpayers had spent more than $9 million improving the Atlantic Intracoastal Waterway since the purchase of the old Florida East Coast Canal. In November of that year, on their first inspection tour, waterway commissioners traveled the length of the 370-mile waterway from Jacksonville to Miami in just twenty-four hours over a three-day period—considerably less time than the six weeks the trip often required before the federal takeover. Now calling for a channel one hundred feet wide by eight feet deep, Army engineers completed the main channel in 1935. The following year Congress authorized extending the Florida portion of the Atlantic Intracoastal Waterway to Key West, but these improvements were never completed beyond Cross Bank in the Florida Bay. Except for a 5.6-mile stretch of the waterway between Cape Fear and Winyah Bay, South Carolina, a protected Atlantic Intracoastal Waterway extended 1,435 miles from Trenton on the Delaware River to Miami on the Biscayne Bay. In March 1937, commissioners of the Okeechobee Flood Control District invited Senator Abram M. Taylor and fellow FIND commissioners to join them on a tour through the new Caloosahatchee-Okeechobee Cross-State Waterway beginning at Stuart and ending the following day at Fort Myers on the Gulf of Mexico. By 1940, dimensions for the Atlantic Intracoastal Waterway of 100 feet wide by eight feet deep existed for a distance of 372 miles from Jacksonville to Biscayne Bay. Fifty-one bridges crossed the waterway from Jacksonville to Miami, excluding the bridges crossing the St. Johns River at Jacksonville.[11]

In December 1940, George Miles, the canal company's engineer for more than twenty years, passed away at the age of seventy-seven. Miles's wife,

---

[10]Chapter 16175, *Laws of Florida* (1933); Florida, State Archives, *Canal Authority of the State of Florida*, project files (1930-1990).

[11]U. S. Army Corps of Engineers, *The Intracoastal Waterway, Boston, Massachusetts to the Rio Grande*; "Jax-Miami Canal Is About Completed," *Jacksonville Journal*, 21 November 1934; Parkman, *History*, 110; E. M. Markham, "Progress Along the Coast," ADWA, Boston, Mass., 7 October 1935; E. M. Markham, "A Big Achievement." Official Invitation, Caloosahatchee-Okeechobee Cross-State Waterway," Okeechobee Flood Control District, TP (FIND 1928-1940).

Helen, who predeceased her husband by a year, had left half of her estate to the Bradley Home founded by their Pomfret neighbors.

In 1945, the district's long-time chairman, Fort Lauderdale's Commodore Brook, resigned after more than eighteen years' service as Broward County's commissioner and thirteen years as chairman at the waterway district; he was succeeded as district chairman by Martin County pioneer Stanley Kitching, another of the district's original commissioners.[12]

A new federal Rivers and Harbors Act authorized the enlargement of the Florida waterway to a depth of twelve feet and a width of 125 feet. The act also required local interests to modify certain standards and make improvements in connection with the waterway's use. To comply with the act, district commissioners began to change old draw-spans in antiquated bridges and modify pipelines, cables and other structures in the right-of-way of the waterway's channel for improved navigation and to meet new standards. In 1948, commissioners paid off the last of $850,000 worth of bonds sold in 1927 to buy the canal and pay for right-of-way.[13]

Even though plans for a waterway channel twelve feet deep had been approved as early as 1945, Congress didn't begin funding the project until President Harry Truman's yacht went aground near Vero Beach in the spring of 1950. On May 3, 1950, J. Hampton Moore, the heart and soul of the Atlantic Intracoastal Waterway movement, died at the age of eighty-six, four years after his retirement as president of the Atlantic Deeper Waterways Association, a post he had held since founding the organization in 1907.[14]

With federal funding assured, the district began the construction of a deeper and wider channel at the St. Johns River. The project would be completed to the new dimensions as far south as Fort Pierce by 1960, providing a completed channel from Trenton to Fort Pierce. In May 1958, after more than thirty years' service in his third career, Colonel Gilbert Albin Youngberg, the district's first and only chief engineer and director of procurement,

---

[12]Will of George F. Miles, Pomfret (Connecticut) probate records, volume 34, at pages 457-59; Will of Helen McHenry Miles, Pomfret (Connectictu) probate records, vol. 34, at pages 117-19.

[13]FIND, *Story*, 2; Parkman, *History*, 111. "Hit Truman on Rivers," *New York Times*, 23 November 1946, p. 32, col. 7. GAY, "Notes on the Intracoastal Waterway, Jacksonville, Florida to Miami, Florida," compiled 1 March 1945, p. 2, YP Box 4, File 10.

[14]"Senate Candidates Favor Waterway," and "President Truman Does 'Groundwork' for 12-ft. Channel," *F.I.N.D. Newsletter* (spring 1950). "J. H. Moore Dead; Political Leader," *New York Times*, 3 May 1950, p. 29.

resigned to re-enter private practice as a consultant at the age of eighty-three. Waterway district commissioners appointed Colonel Herman Schull to serve as chief engineer and director of procurement. Like his predecessor, Schull headed the Army Corps of Engineers for the Florida peninsula before his appointment to the district's post.[15]

In 1965, the Corps of Engineers completed dredging the channel from Fort Pierce to Miami to a 10-foot depth and a width of 125 feet. Reacting to charges of mismanagement at the navigation district, members of the state legislature initially moved to abolish the agency entirely, but ultimately decided instead to change the district's charter to prohibit the district from selling waterway spoil areas to pay operating expenses.[16]

In November 2004, Nassau County voters narrowly approved—by a margin of ninety-seven votes out of 29,735 votes cast—joining the waterway district as its twelfth member. District commissioners still serve without salary and receive only a state-prescribed per-diem allowance to reimburse the expense of attending district board meetings conducted in each of the twelve counties comprising the district. Unlike the original commissioners, many of today's commissioners possess backgrounds in the environmental sciences, land planning, engineering and other technical areas of expertise needed in managing the waterway in the 21st century. Today, the district's primary mission is to acquire and manage the dredge material sites required by the Corps of Engineers to maintain the waterway's project dimensions. The dredging work is supervised by Corps engineers who prescribe the sites necessary for the deposit of spoil created by dredging operations. Since the mid-1980s the district has been planning the acquisition of additional sites for spoil deposit to meet dredging needs for the next 50 years or more. One of the more perplexing problems confronting the district at the close of the 20th century was the filling up of the St. Lucie Inlet dredge site and the lack of an alternative spoil disposal area.[17]

The uneasy relationship between federal and state interests remains. The Corps of Engineers still plays a dominant role in the maintenance of the waterway, carrying on in the tradition of early Army engineers such as

---

[15]FIND, *Story*, 2. Buker, *Sun*, appendix A.

[16]FIND, *Story*, 2. Crawford, "Capone Island," 28.

[17]"Voters OK County Joining Inland Navigation District," *Florida Times-Union*, 13 November 2004. The referendum was conducted pursuant to a bill passed by the Florida legislature and approved by the Governor on April 14, 2004, authorizing the addition of Nassau County to the district. Ch. 2004-15, *Laws of Florida*.

Gadsden, Wright and Gillmore, who spearheaded the early surveying and dredging before the era of private ownership began in 1881. After Colonel Schull's retirement, former Army engineers continued to serve at the district in leadership roles until 1988 when Colonel Stirling "Butch" Eisiminger retired from his post as general manager at the age of seventy-two and Arthur Wilde, the first non-Army engineer at the district, became executive director. Even today, though, an Army engineer attends each meeting of the Florida Inland Navigation District's board of commissioners, continuing a tradition of Army involvement in the waterway more than a hundred and fifty years old.[18]

---

[18]Roach, Interview.

Epilogue

Given the limited funding available for development of Florida's east coast during the early 1880s, construction of what would become Florida's Atlantic Intracoastal Waterway proved nothing short of a miracle. From 1882 until the old Florida East Coast Canal's completion in 1912, dredged material excavated between Saint Augustine and Biscayne Bay totaled almost ten million (9,720,771) cubic yards for dredging waterways extending altogether nearly 268 miles. In the northern extension between Saint Augustine and the Saint Johns River, excavation work amounted to 3,194,960 cubic yards for a mere twenty-one-mile waterway, demonstrating just how difficult the work had been in that stretch alone. Material dredged over the thirty-year period totaled 12,915,731 cubic yards at a cost of $3,541,216.

By comparison, the Panama Canal, built from 1904 until 1914 with U. S. Government funds, dwarfs Florida's Big Dig in both material removed and cost. The Panama Canal required the excavation of more than 232 million cubic yards at a cost to federal taxpayers of $352 million, a hundred times the cost of the Florida waterway, but for a waterway only fifty miles long. On a per-cubic yard basis, the Panama Canal cost $1.51 a cubic yard. The Florida waterway cost a mere twenty-seven cents a cubic yard, entirely at private expense, and it extends the length of the Florida peninsula, almost 400 miles. The Panama Canal's construction claimed 5,609 lives from disease and accidents. Although there were scattered reports of a few Florida waterway workers afflicted with malaria and yellow fever, there do not survive reports of deaths during construction of the Florida waterway. Moreover, despite Florida canal company protestations over the waterway's cost, Florida canal investors reaped an enormous expanse of Florida land–over a million acres of prime east coast land stretching from Saint Augustine to Miami–that in turn generated enormous returns when Florida canal investors sold the lands as late as the boom years of the 1920s.[1]

Both the Florida canal company and the Flagler railway and their related enterprises competed for the right to transport freight and passenger traffic along the coast. Both competed for the limited amount of public land along

---

[1]On the cost of the Panama Canal, see, McCullough, *Path,* 610-11.

the coast available for distribution by state trustees to further waterway and railway development. Both competed for the sale of land to hundreds of settlers arriving along the coast beginning in the 1890s. At times, the companies became fiercely competitive, even squaring off against each other in litigation over the land grants in 1910 and again in 1912. At other times, the canal and railway enterprises worked together to develop and market jointly their immense land holdings along the Florida coast, particularly in the southern portion of the state.[2]

Today, over a million acres of Florida east coast land stretching from Saint Augustine to Miami originate in grants made to the Flagler railway and the Florida canal company for developing Florida's east coast transportation infrastructure, beginning in the early 1880s. Crucial to the development of the Florida east coast were the State's large reserves of public land and its willingness to grant land for railway and inland waterway development. Such grants led to the construction of Flagler's Florida East Coast Railway and what would become Florida's modern-day Atlantic Intracoastal Waterway. Flagler received public land not only from the State of Florida but also from private entities such as the Florida canal company and the Boston and Florida Atlantic Coast Land Company as well as from private individuals such as Julia Tuttle and William and Mary Brickell of Miami for extending the Florida East Coast Railway into the southern reaches of the Florida peninsula. Both Flagler and the Boston & Florida land company cooperated in developing settlements along the lower east coast such as White City (near Fort Pierce), Linton (Delray Beach), Boynton (Boynton Beach), Modelo (Dania Beach), and Halland (Hallandale Beach). In the final analysis, competition between the two enterprises lowered land prices and transportation charges for newly arriving settlers all along the Florida east coast.[3]

Seventy-four years after its founding, George and Helen Bradley's Emma Pendleton Bradley Hospital, now an affiliate of Brown University's School of Medicine, is today recognized as a national resource for the treatment of troubled children, providing a full array of services to the young from infancy to age eighteen. Located on forty acres in East Providence, Rhode Island, the Bradley Hospital also operates a special education school at Portsmouth and a residential program at East Greenwich. During the 1997-98 fiscal year, the Bradley charity provided hospital services to 792 children,

---

[2]Crawford, "Papers of Albert Sawyer."
[3]*Ibid.*

as well as 8,185 home health visits, 16,087 outpatient visits, and 25,140 residence days for suffering children, with uncompensated free care amounting to $5.4 million for that year alone. By the end of the decade, George and Helen Bradley's hospital endowment fund established more than eighty years before had grown to more than $40 million. In 1937, Dr. Charles Bradley, grand-nephew of George Bradley and medical director of what was then the Emma Pendleton Bradley Home (it became a full-fledged hospital in 1957), discovered the therapeutic effect of stimulant medication on children with hyperactivity (ADHD); the Bradley charity later led the way in the use of the electroencephalogram in diagnosing neurological disorders in children with epilepsy and promoted using least restrictive treatment environments in helping troubled children. Since 1982, the Hospital's health care professionals have contributed more than a thousand scholarly papers and articles on children's mental health. George and Helen Bradley would indeed be proud of the legacy they left the nation, a happy byproduct of the sale of the Florida waterway by George Bradley's estate in 1925.[4]

A few years ago, following in the footsteps of Moore's Atlantic Deeper Waterways Association, fifty commercial and trade association groups interested in the maintenance of the Atlantic Intracoastal Waterway banded together to form the Atlantic Intracoastal Waterways Association. In November 1999, Association members gathered at Savannah, Georgia, for the group's first meeting. The purposes of this new organization are to promote the use of that portion of the waterway stretching from Norfolk to Miami, document the waterway's benefits, and secure funding for proper maintenance. This section alone moves almost five million tons of commerce annually, including large volumes of forest products, petroleum, and chemicals. But by the turn of the millennium, federal funding for waterway improvements and maintenance throughout the country had diminished considerably under pressure from groups asserting the limited economic benefits of some waterways and the adverse environmental consequences of dredging others. In Florida, the decline in federal funding for Atlantic Intracoastal Waterway maintenance has pressured the Florida Inland Navigation District to take up the slack.[5]

---

[4]Bradley Hospital website, 11 January 1999, http://www.lifespan.org/about/bradley; Brown University School of Medicine website, 11 January 1999, http://www.brown.edu/Departments/Psychiatry/hosp.shtml#brown.

[5]Harry N. Cook, president of the National Waterways Conference, Inc., open letter, 18 November 1999, Washington, D. C.

Today the Florida waterway produces a staggering $7.9 billion impact on the state's economy. Commercial barges deliver 504,000 gallons of fuel daily to the Florida Power & Light Company's Turkey Point plant in Miami-Dade County. In 2002, commercial barge traffic on the waterway totaled 213,000 ton miles. Megayachts — yachts eighty feet long or longer–make up the fastest growing category of users of the Florida waterway. But in assessing the waterway's usefulness for federal funding purposes, the Army Corps of Engineers is permitted by law to count only commercial barge traffic, not recreational vessels like the thousands of pleasure boats and yachts that use the waterway each year. Commercial traffic on the waterway declined from 4.7 million tons in 1991 to 1.8 million in 2001, further eroding the case for federal funding. While $15 million is needed for today's waterway maintenance, the proposed 2007 President's budget for maintenance along the Florida stretch alone allocates just $2,350,000.[6]

Whether or not present supporters will succeed in their efforts to persuade Congress to maintain the Atlantic Intracoastal Waterway remains an open question. Perhaps the Atlantic Intracoastal Waterway Association, along with other business, trade, and civic groups along the Atlantic seaboard, will band together to 'sound the alarm' and advance the waterway's cause, much like the dozens of inland waterway groups across the nation that joined together to promote America's inland waterways during the early 1900s. The English politician John Elliott Burns once wrote, "I have seen the Mississippi. That is muddy water. I have seen the St. Lawrence. That is crystal water. But the Thames is liquid history."[7] As with the Thames, the same can be said about Florida's Atlantic Intracoastal Waterway: It is liquid history indeed."

---

[6]"For Intracoastal, A Bumpy Ride," *Miami Herald*, 15 August 2003; Interview with David Roach, FIND, 31 May 2006.

[7]Partington, ed., *Oxford Dictionary*, 160: 22; *Concise Dictionary of National Biography*, 99.

ABBREVIATIONS

The following abbreviations appear in the notes at the bottom of each page of text.

ACE	Army Corps of Engineers
AGBP	Alexander Graham Bell Papers (Library of Congress)
ADWA	Atlantic Deeper Waterways Association
APS	Albert P. Sawyer
AHS	Albert H. Sawyer
ELCP	Elmer Lawrence Corthell Papers (Brown University)
FA	Frederic Amory
EW	Edward M. Walker
FECR	Florida East Coast Railway Company
FIND	Florida Inland Navigation District
GAY	Gilbert A. Youngberg
GLB	George Lothrop Bradley
GFM	George F. Miles
HGP	Hall, Gillespie Papers (Trent University, Canada)
JHMP	James Hampton Moore Papers (Historical Society of Pennsylvania)
MIIF	Minutes of the Trustees of the Internal Improvement Fund
MLC	Model Land Company Papers (University of Miami)
NRHC	National Rivers and Harbors Congress (Proceedings)
SM	Samuel Maddox
SP	Sawyer Papers (State Library of Florida)
TP	Abram Morris Taylor Papers (Library of Florida History)
TIIF	Trustees of the Internal Improvement Fund
YP	Youngberg Papers (Rollins College)

Bibliography

Akin, Edward N. Flagler: *Rockefeller Partner and Florida Baron*. Gainesville: University Press of Florida, 1991 paper.

_____. "The Sly Foxes: Henry Flagler, George Miles, and Florida's Public Domain," *Florida Historical Quarterly* 58, No. 1 (July 1979): 22-36.

American Book Prices Current. Vol. 104. 1997-1998. New York: R. R. Bowker, 1998.

American Federation of Labor and Congress of Industrial Organizations. *American Federation of Labor: History, Encyclopedia and Reference Book*. Vol. 3, Part 1. Washington, D.C.: 1960.

American Shore and Beach Preservation Association (ASBPA). *Proceedings*. Trenton, N.J.: MacCrellish & Quigley Co. Printers, 1928.

American Shore and Beach Preservation Association (ASBPA). *Report*. Trenton, N.J.: [1927?]

Amory, Cleveland. *The Last Resorts*. New York: Harper & Brothers, Publishers, 1952.

Appleton's Cyclopaedia of American Biography, see, Wilson, et al., ed.

Armstrong, G. K. *The Hallowes Genealogy*. Internet source: (http://ourworld.compuserve.com/homepages/gkarmstrong), n.d.

Association of American Railroads. Bureau of Railway Economics. *An Economic Survey of Inland Waterway Transportation in the United States*. Washington, D.C., 1930.

Atlantic and Gulf Coast Canal and Okeechobee Land Company (Florida). *Lands of the Atlantic and Gulf Coast Canal and Okeechobee Land Company*. [Philadelphia, Pa.: s.n., 1881].

Atlantic Deeper Waterways Association (ADWA). *Annual Convention of the Atlantic Deeper Waterways Association: Report of the Proceedings (Proceedings)*. Philadelphia: Atlantic Deeper Waterways Association, 1909-1926.

_____. *Atlantic Intra-Coastal Waterway: The Project Advocated by the Atlantic Deeper Waterways Association, Official Survey Lines and Present Status of the Work in Its Various Sections*. [Philadelphia? 1914]

_____. *Bulletin of the Atlantic Deeper Waterways Association*.

_____. *Defense Value of Waterways*; Resolutions of the Thirty-fourth Annual Convention, Atlantic Deeper Waterways Association, Miami, Florida, November 12, 1941. [Miami?, 1941?]

Bar Association of the District of Columbia. *Annual Banquet Program*. 5 December 1998.

Bathe, Greville. *The St. Johns Railroad, 1858-1895: A Commemorative History of a Pioneer Railroad*. Saint Augustine: 1958.

Bayles, Richard M., ed. *History of Providence County, Rhode Island*. Vol. I. New York: W. W. Preston & Co., 1891.

_____. *History of Windham County, Connecticut.* Part II. New York: W. W. Preston & Co., 1889.

Bell, Alexander Graham Papers (AGBP). National Archives, Washington, D.C.

Bench and Bar of Florida. Vol. 1. Tallahassee, Fla.: Horace Evans, 1935.

Berton, Pierre. *The Impossible Way: The Building of the Canadian Pacific.* New York: Alfred A. Knopf, 1972.

_____. *The National Dream: The Great Railway, 1871-1881.* Toronto: McLelland and Stewart Limited, 1979.

Bicknell, Thomas W. *History of the State of Rhode Island and Providence Plantations: Biographical.* New York: The American Historical Society,1920.

Biographical Directory of the American Congress, 1774-1949. Washington, D. C.: GPO, 1950.

Biographical Directory of the American Congress, 1774-1996. CQ Staff Directories, Inc., Alexandria, Va., compiled 30 September 1996.

Blake, Nelson M. *Land into Water – Water into Land: A History of Water Management in Florida.* Gainesville: University Presses of Florida, 1980.

Boston Directory. Boston: Sampson, Murdock & Company, 1890.

Brooks, John. *Telephone: The First Hundred Years.* New York: Harper & Row, Publishers, 1976.

Broward, County of. Corporations Books. Fort Lauderdale, Florida.

_____. Plat Books. Fort Lauderdale, Florida.

_____. Probate Records. Fort Lauderdale, Florida.

Broward, Napoleon B. "The Florida View of an Intracoastal Waterway Connecting New England with the South." ADWA Proceedings, 8 August-3 September 1910: 209-216.

Brown University. School of Medicine. "The Emma Pendleton Bradley Hospital." Internet source:
(http://www.brown.edu/Departments/Psychiatry/hosp.shtml#brown).

Brown, William E. Jr. and Karen Hudson. "Henry Flagler and the Model Land Company." *Tequesta* LVI (1996):46-78.

Buckman, Henry H. "Defense Coordination of the Panama and Florida Canals: A Preliminary Study," U. S. Senate Document No. 198, 76th Congress, 3d Session.

Buker, George E. *Sun, Sand and Water: A History of the Jacksonville District, U. S. Army Corps of Engineers, 1821-1975.* Fort Belvoir, Va.: U.S. Army Corps of Engineers, GPO, 1981.

Burghard, August. *Half a Century in Florida: Land of Matters Unforgot.* Fort Lauderdale: Manatee Books, 1982.

Burgman, Charles F. *The Florida East Coast Canal: A Federal Waterway.* Daytona Beach: Burgman, 1930.

Business Directory Guide and History of Dade County, Fla. for 1896-97. C. M. Gardner and C. F. Kennedy, Publishers, West Palm Beach, Florida (Tropical Sun Print).

Bibliography

Caemmerer, H. Paul, ed. *Records of the Columbia Historical Society of Washington, D. C., 1946-1947.* Vols. 48-49. Washington, D.C.: Columbia Historical Society, 1949.

Casson, Herbert N. *The History of the Telephone.* Chicago: A. C. McClurg & Co. & Co., 1910.

Centennial History of the United States Military Academy at West Point, New York: 1802-1902. Washington, D. C.: Government Printing Office: 1904. Vol. 1.

Carter, Clarence E., ed., *Territorial Papers of the United States.* Vols. 22-26: Florida Territory. Washington, D. C.: 1956-1962.

Chapin, George M. *Florida, 1513-1913: Past, Present and Future.* Chicago: The S. J. Clarke Publishing Company, 1914.

Champlin, Peggy. *Raphael Pumpelly: Gentleman Geologist of the Gilded Age.* Tuscaloosa: The University of Alabama Press, 1994.

Chandler, David Leon. *Henry Flagler.* New York: Macmillan Publishing Company, 1986.

Charlick, Carl. *The Metropolitan Club of Washington: The Story of Its Men and of Its Place in City and County.* Washington, D. C.: Metropolitan Club of Washington, D. C., 1965.

Clarke, Mary Stetson. *The Old Middlesex Canal.* Easton, Pa.: Center for Canal History and Technology, 1974.

Clegg, John. *History of Flagler County.* John Clegg, 1976. Flagler Beach Public Library, Flagler Beach, Florida.

Cocoa Tribune (Cocoa, Fla.). Various dates.

Compilation of the Messages and Papers of the Presidents, 1789-1897. Edited by J. D. Richardson. Vol. 2. Washington, D. C.: Government Printing Office, 1907.

Coon, Horace. *American Tel & Tel: The Story of a Great Monopoly.* Plainview, N.Y.: Books for Libraries Press, 1939, reprinted, 1976.

Corning, Charles R. *Horace S. Cummings: July 1, 1840 - Dec. 7, 1911.* [S.l.]: [s.n.], [1911]. New Hampshire Historical Society, Concord, New Hampshire.

Corthell, Elmer Lawrence. Papers. John Hay Library. Brown University, Providence, Rhode Island.

Cosmos Club. *Cosmos Club Bulletin.* Washington, D.C. (September 1972).

Crawford, William G. Jr. "A History of Florida's East Coast Canal: The Atlantic Intracoastal Waterway from Jacksonville to Miami." *Broward Legacy* 20, nos. 3-4 (summer/fall 1997):2-31.

_____. "Capone Island: From Swampland to Broward County's Deerfield Island Park, 150 Years of History." *Broward Legacy* 19, nos. 3-4 (summer/fall 1996).

_____. "Sam Maddox and the Florida Waterway," *Hearsay.* Bar Association of the District of Columbia, vol. V, no. 3 (Nov.-Dec. 2001).

_____. "The Papers of Albert Sawyer and the Development of the Florida East Coast, 1892 to 1912." *Tequesta* LXII (2002): 5-39.

Cummings, Horace S. *Dartmouth College, Sketches of the Class of 1862*. Washington, D. C.: Geo. E. Howard Press, 1909.

Cutler, Harry G. *History of Florida, Past and Present*. 3 Vols. Chicago: The Lewis Publishing Company, 1923.

Dade, County of. Deed Books. Miami, Florida.

_____. Circuit Court. Minute Books 1 and 2. Miami, Florida.

_____. Plat Book B. Miami, Florida.

Daily Florida Citizen (Jacksonville, Fla.). Various dates.

Daily Times (Maryville, Tenn.). 14 August 2005.

Dau, Frederic W. *Florida Old and New*. New York: G. P. Putnam's Sons, 1934.

Davis, Elise Dancy. "Notes on Miller Hallowes," *Florida Historical Quarterly* 41, no. 4 (April 1963):405-07.

Davis, T. Frederick. *History of Jacksonville, Florida and Vicinity, 1513 to 1924*. Facs. repr. of 1925 ed. Gainesville, Fla.: University of Florida Press, 1964.

Davis, William Watson. *The Civil War and Reconstruction*. Facs. repr. of 1913 ed. Gainesville: University of Florida Press, 1964.

Daytona Daily News (Daytona Beach, Fla.). Various dates

Daytona Gazette-News (Daytona Beach, Fla.). Various dates

Daytona Morning Journal (Daytona Beach, Fla.). Various dates.

Dickinson, Donald C. *Dictionary of American Book Collectors*. Westport, Conn.: Greenwood Press, 1986.

Dillon, Jr., Rodney E. and Knetsch, Joe. "The Florida Fiber Company, Duncan U. Fletcher and the Middle River Enterprise." *Broward Legacy* 21, nos. 3-4 (summer/fall 1998): 34-45.

Dixie (Jacksonville, Fla.). Various dates.

Dodge, Laurence P. "Sea Water Gold." MSS. February 23, 1954. Newburyport (Mass.) Public Library.

Dovell, Junius E. *Florida, Historic, Dramatic, Contemporary*. 3 Vols. New York: Lewis Historical Publishing Company, Inc., 1952.

_____. *History of Banking in Florida, 1828-1954*. Orlando, Fla.: Florida Bankers Association, [c. 1954].

Downs, Winfield Scott, ed., *Who's Who in Engineering*. New York: Lewis Historical Publishing Co., Inc., 1931.

DuBois, Bessie Wilson. *A History of Juno Beach and Juno, Florida*. Palm Beach County Library: West Palm Beach, 1978.

Duval, County of. Circuit Court Civil Cases, 1913, 1916. Jacksonville, Florida.

Eads Concession Company. President's Report to Stockholders, July 31, 1886. S.l.: S.N., N.D. Tulane University, Special Collections. New Orleans, Louisiana.

East Coast Advocate (Titusville, Fla.). Various dates.

Electrolytic Marine Salts Company. *A Sketch of the Discovery of a Commercially Profitable Process for the Extraction of Gold and Silver from Sea Water*, Series One. Boston: Robinson Press, 1897-98.

_____. *Gold from Sea Water at a Profit, The Facts*, Series Two. Boston: Robinson Press, 1897-98.

Elliott, E. J. *Florida Encyclopedia*. Jacksonville: E. J. Elliott, 1889.

Elliott, F. C. "Report of Florida Coast Line Canal to Trustees of the Internal Improvement Fund and the Directors of the Florida Coast Line Canal and Transportation Co.," 4 January 1915. Florida State Archives. Tallahassee, Fla.

Eminent and Representative Men of Virginia and the District of Columbia of the Nineteenth Century. Brant & Fuller, 1891. Library of Congress, Washington, D.C.

Emma Pendleton Bradley Home. *Annual Report, 1931-1932*. Providence, Rhode Island: Emma Pendleton Bradley Home, 1932.

Everglade Magazine. Various dates. Microfilm. Library of Congress, Washington, D. C.

Fagen, M. D., ed. *A History of Engineering and Science in the Bell System: The Early Years (1875–1925)*. Bell Telephone Laboratories, Incorporated, 1975.

Farrar, Cecil W. and Margoann Farrar, *Incomparable Delray Beach–Its Early Life and Lore*. Boynton Beach, Fla.: Star Publishing Company, Inc., 1974.

Farson, Robert H. *The Cape Cod Canal*. Middletown, N. Y.: Wesleyan University Press, 1977.

Fleming, Sandford. *The Intercolonial*. Montreal: Dawson Brothers Publishers, 1876.

Florida. Acts *of the Legislative Council of the Territory of Florida*. 7th and 8th sessions (1828 and 1831).

_____. Board of Architecture. *Record of Applications (Form 1) and Certificates Issued Without Examination to Practice Architecture in the State of Florida*, 1.

_____. Canal Authority of the State of Florida, Project Files (1930-1990), Florida State Archives; *Annual Report*. October, 1964.

_____. Department of Environmental Protection. Division of State Lands. Land Records and Title Section. "Old Railroad Bonds, etc."

_____. House of Representatives. Office of the Clerk. *People of Lawmaking in Florida*. Tallahassee: The Office, 1975-.

_____. Internal Improvement Fund. *Minutes of the Trustees*. 1-9 (1855-1872 to 1911-1912).

Laws of Florida. Chapter 1987. 1874.

Laws of Florida. Chapter 3166. 1879.

Laws of Florida. Chapter 3327. 1881.

Laws of Florida. Chapter 12026. 1927.

Laws of Florida. Chapter 13638. 1929.

Department of State, Division of Archives and Records Service, Series 755, Carton 2.

Office of Secretary of State. Mortgage Records, 19 January 1866 to 4 March 1891.

_____. Railroad Maps, 1853 to 1958, Florida State Archives

_____. Supreme Court Reports. Cases Argued.

Florida Coast Line Canal and Transportation Company. *Prospectus of the Florida Coast Line Canal and Transportation Company.* [Washington, D. C. ?] 1882. Library of Congress, Washington, D. C.

Florida East Coast Chamber of Commerce. *Constitution and By-Laws of the Florida East Coast Chamber of Commerce, 1915.* University of Miami, Richter Library, Miami, Florida.

Florida East Coast Railway. Correspondence, 1898. Saint Augustine, Florida.

_____. *Announcement: Key West Extension of the Florida East Coast Railway Opened January 22, 1912.* Florida East Coast Railway, 1912

Florida Inland Navigation District. Minutes and Resolutions. 1927, 1928, 1942.

_____. Records (actual and CD-ROM).

_____. *The Florida Intracoastal Waterway From the St. Johns River to Miami, Florida.* Jacksonville: H & W.B. Drew Co., [1935?].

_____. *The Story of F.I.N.D.: Fernandina Beach to Miami, Florida. Florida Inland Navigation District, 1967.*

_____. *Newsletter,* 1948-1950.

Florida Engineer and Contractor, 1926.

Florida Star (Titusville, Fla.). Various dates.

Florida Times-Union (Jacksonville, Fla.). Various dates.

Folger Shakespeare Library. "An Exhibition of Some Books of the Cosmos Club held at the Folger Shakespeare Library, November - December, 1947." Washington, D.C., 1947.

_____. "The Cosmos Club Collection in the Folger Library, October 14 - November 18, 1972." Washington, D.C., 1972.

Fort Lauderdale Daily News (Ft. Lauderdale, Fla.). Various dates.

Fort Lauderdale Herald (Ft. Lauderdale, Fla.). Various dates.

Fort Lauderdale Sentinel (Ft. Lauderdale, Fla.). Various dates.

Fort Pierce City Directory and St. Lucie County Gazetteer. Asheville, N.C.: Florida Piedmont Directory Company, 1927-28.

Fort Pierce Herald (Ft. Pierce, Fla.). Various dates.

Fulton, Robert. *Report on the practicality of navigating with steam boats, on the southern waters of the United States.* Philadelphia: Printed by Thomas Town, 1828.

Gaillard, Edward McCrady. "A Brief Outline of My Family Background." *Transactions of the Huguenot Society of South Carolina.* No. 82 (1977): 85-109.

Gamewell Fire Alarm Telegraph Company. *Emergency Signaling.* New York: The Gamewell Fire Alarm Telegraphy Co., 1916.

Gardner, Preston H. "The 18th Anniversary of the Emma Pendleton Bradley Home." Speech at annual meeting on April 9, 1949. Typed manuscript copy. Bradley Hospital Collection. Rhode Island Historical Society, Providence, Rhode Island.

Garvey, Eleanor M. and W. H. Bond. *Tenniel's Alice: Drawings by Sir John Tenniel for Alice's Adventures in Wonderland and Through the Looking Glass.* Cambridge, Mass.: The Houghton Library, Harvard University, 1978.

Bibliography

Glades County (Fla.) Board of Commissioners, comp. *Glades County, Florida History*. Moore Haven, Fla.: Rainbow Books, 1985.

Glick, Juneanne Wescoat. *Waistcote, Westcoatt, Wastcote, Westcot, Wescoat, Westcott, Wescott, Wescote, Westcoat, Wasgatt, Wesket, Yescut, Wisgitt, Etc.*. Clayton, N.J.: Juneanne Wescoat Glick, 1991.

Gold, Pleasant Daniel. *History of Duval County, Florida*. Saint Augustine, Fla.: The Record Company, 1928.

_____. *History of Volusia County, Florida*. Deland, Fla.: Painter Printing Co., 1927.

Gooding, Dorothy Borden, comp. *Tucked Between the Pages of Time: a History of Lake Park and Environs*. Dorothy Borden Gooding, 1990.

Grant, G. M. "Time-Reckoning for the Twentieth Century," *The Century* 33, no.1 (November 1886): 155-56.

Green, Lorne. *Chief Engineer: Life of a Nation Builder, Sandford Fleming*. Toronto: Dundurn Press, 1993.

Hall, Gillespie Law Firm (HGP). Papers. Trent University Archives, Bata Library, Peterborough, Ontario, Canada. 94-001, Box 13, Case No. Folder 80, 18.

Hallet, Richard. "The Great Quoddy Gold Hoax: One of the Greatest Swindles of the Age." *Down East*. 1 (Winter, 1955):18-20.

Hammond, E. Ashby. *Medical Profession in 19th Century Florida*. Gainesville, Fla.: George A. Smathers Libraries, University of Florida, 1996.

Hampden, County of. Register of Probate. Springfield, Massachusetts.

Hartman, David W., comp. *Biographical Rosters of Florida's Confederate and Union Soldiers 1861 - 1865*. Vol. 2. Wilmington, N.C.: Broadfoot Publishing Company, 1995.

Haupt, Lewis M. "A Policy and Not a Project." *Manufacturers' Record*. 31 August 1911.

_____. "The Intercoastal Waterway." *Manufacturers' Record*. 24 June; 22 July; 5, 12, 19 August 1892.

Hebel, Ianthe Bond, ed. *Centennial History of Volusia County, Florida 1854 - 1954*. Daytona Beach: College Publishing Company, 1955.

Hellier, Walter R. *Indian River: Florida's Treasure Coast*. Coconut Grove, Fla.: Hurricane House Publishers, Inc., 1965.

Hibbard, Benjamin Horace. *A History of the Public Land Policies*. New York: The MacMillan Company, 1924.

Hill, Forest G. *Roads, Rails & Waterways: The Army Engineers and Early Transportation*. Westport: Greenwood Press, 1957.

Hodges, Charles E. *The First American Liability Insurance Company*. New York: The Newcomen Society in North America, 1957.

Howard, Henry. *The Yacht Alice: Planning and Building*. Boston: C. E. Lauriat Co., [1926?].

Hughes, Kaylene. *Florida's Lodging Industry: The First 75 Years: An Official History of the Florida Hotel & Motel Association, Inc.* Tallahassee: Florida Hotel & Motel Association, Inc., 1987.

Hull, William J. and Robert W. Hull. *The Origin and Development of the Waterways Policy of the United States.* Washington, D.C.: National Waterways Conference, Inc., 1967.

Jacksonville Metropolis (Jacksonville, Fla.). Various dates.

Johnson, Emory R., Grover G. Huebner, and Arnold K. Henry. *Transportation by Water.* New York: D. Appleton-Century Company, Inc., 1935.

Johnson, Miriam. *Clermont, Gem of the Hills: A History of Clermont, Florida, and Neighboring Communities.* Clermont, Fla.: M. W. Johnson, 1984.

Johnson, Rossiter, ed.. *Twentieth Century Biographical Dictionary of Notable Americans.* Vols. I-X. Boston, Mass.: The Biographical Society, 1904.

Johnston, Michelle Dally. *Out of Sorrow and into Hope: The History of the Emma Pendleton Bradley Hospital.* Riverside, R.I.: Emma Pendleton Bradley Hospital, [1991?].

Kerber, "Florida and the World's Columbian Exposition of 1893," *Florida Historical Quarterly,* 66, No.1 (July 1987): 25-49.

Ketcham, Ralph. *James Madison: A Biography.* Charlottesville: University Press of Virginia, 1990 Paper.

Knetsch, Joe. "A Finder of Many Paths: John Westcott and the Internal Development of Florida." In *Florida Pathfinders,* Wynne, Lewis N. and James J. Horgan, editors. Saint Leo, Fla.: Saint Leo College Press, 1994.

_____. "Inventive John Westcott: Surveyor, Surveyor General and Renaissance Man." *The Florida Surveyor* 2, No. 8 (May 1994):5-17.

_____. "John Darling, Indian Removal, and Internal Improvements in South Florida, 1848-1856." *Tampa Bay History* (fall/winter 1995):6-19.

_____. "One of Flagler's Men: William W. Dewhurst." *El Scribano* 30 (1993):16-32.

_____. "Steps Toward the Intracoastal Waterway: The Blake Surveys of 1843 and 1845." *Tequesta* 54 (1994): 27-40.

Lake Park, Town of. *Town of Lake Park Historic Resources Report* (Draft). Saint Petersburg, Fla.: Janus Research, June 1998. Lake Park (Fla.) Public Library.

_____. *Town of Lake Park Preservation Study* (Florida Master Site File Forms Draft). Saint Petersburg, Fla.: Janus Research, 1998, Lake Park (Fla.) Public Library.

Lakes-To-The-Gulf Deep Waterway Association. *Report of the Annual Convention of the Lakes-To-The-Gulf Deep Waterway Association.* Saint Louis: The Lakes-To-The-Gulf Deep Waterway Association, 1907.

Larson, Henrietta M. *Jay Cooke: Private Banker.* Cambridge, Mass.: Harvard University Press, 1936.

Library of Congress. *Report of the Librarian of Congress and Report of the Superintendent of the Library Building and Grounds.* Washington, D. C.: Government Printing Office, 1919.

Lifespan. Providence, Rhode Island. "About Bradley Hospital." Internet source: http://www.lifespan.org/about/bradley.

Lodge, Henry Cabot, ed. *The Federalist.* New York: G. P. Putnam's sons, 1888.

Lorwin, Lewis L. *The American Federation of Labor: History, Policies, and Prospects.* Washington, D.C.: The Brookings Institution, 1933.

MacKenzie, George Norbury, ed. *Colonial Families of the United States of America.* Vol. 5. Baltimore: Genealogical Publishing Company, 1966.

Maclean, Hugh. *Man of Steel: The Story of Sir Sandford Fleming.* Toronto: The Ryerson Press, 1969.

Manufacturers' Record. Various dates.

Markham, Edward M. *A Big Achievement: Address by Major-General E. M. Markham at Celebration of "Completion of a Protected Inner Route along the Atlantic Coast extending from the Delaware River to Miami..." at Socastee Bridge, South Carolina, April 11, 1936.* [Philadelphia]: Atlantic Deeper Waterways Association, 1936.

Marquis, Albert Nelson, ed. *Who's Who in New England.* 2nd ed. Chicago: A. N. Marquis & Company, 1916.

Martin, Sidney Walter. *Florida During the Territorial Days.* Athens, Ga.: The University of Georgia Press, 1944.

_____. *Florida's Flagler.* Athens, Ga.: University of Georgia Press, 1949.

Mason, John. "The Great Sea-water Swindle." *Yankee.* 29 (February, 1965): 38-60.

Massachusetts soldiers, sailors and marines in the Civil War. Boston: Mass.: Adjutant General, 1937.

Mather, Irvine. "Inland Water-Ways of Florida." *Florida Magazine* 6, no. 1 (January 1903):5-15.

Maver, William Jr. *American Telegraphy: Systems, Apparatus, Operation.* New York: J. H. Bunnell & Company, 1892.

McCullough, David. *The Path Between the Seas: The Creation of the Panama Canal, 1870-1914.* New York: Simon and Schuster, 1977 ppr.

McGoun, William E. *South Florida Pioneers: The Palm & Treasure Coasts.* Sarasota, Fla.: Pineapple Press, Inc., 1998.

McKay, D. B., et al., ed. *The Book of Florida: An Illustrated Description of the Advantages and Opportunities of the State of Florida.* N.P.: Published by Florida Editors Association, 1925.

Meredith, Gertrude E. *The Descendants of Hugh Amory, 1605-1805.* London: privately printed, Chiswick Press, 1901.

Metropolitan Club. A Brief History of the Metropolitan Club of the City of Washington. Washington, D.C.: Metropolitan Club, 1909.

Miami Herald (Miami, Fla.). Various dates.

Miami Herald, ed. *Florida: The East Coast, Its Builder Resources, Industries, Town and City Developments*. Miami, Fla.: The Miami Herald, [1926?].

Miami Metropolis (Miami, Fla.). Various dates.

MIIF. See, Florida, Internal Improvement Fund, *Minutes of the Trustees*

Miles, George F. "East Coast Canal Important Route," *Palm Beach Post*, 11 June 1921.

_____. "The Florida Coast Line Waterway and Its Tremendous Possibilities." *Manufacturers' Record*, 6 July 1922.

_____. "Florida's Inland Waterways and Harbors," ADWA *Proceedings*, 4-6 September 1912: 307-315.

_____. "History of the Florida Coast Line Canal and Transportation Company." mss. n.d., transmitted to Gilbert A. Youngberg by letter dated 30 September 1928. Youngberg Papers, infra, Box 4, Folder 1.

_____. "The Inland Waterways of Eastern Florida," ADWA *Proceedings*, 17-20 November 1909: 86-91.

_____. "The Waterway of the Florida Coast Line Canal and Transportation Co." *Engineering News* 52, No. 8 (August 25, 1904): 163-165.

Mississippi to Atlantic Waterway Association. *Bulletin*. Apalachicola, Florida, 1911.

Model Land Company Papers ("MLC"). University of Miami, Miami, Florida.

Mooney, Ralph E. "Robert Devonshire's Letterbook." *Bell Telephone Magazine* 28, No. 2 (summer 1949):118.

Moore, James Hampton. Papers (JHMP). Historical Society of Pennsylvania, Philadelphia, Pennsylvania.

Morris, Richard B., ed. *Encyclopedia of American History*. New York: Harper & Row, 1965.

Moulton, Harold G. *Waterways Versus Railways*. Boston: Houghton Mifflin Company, 1912.

Moyer, Homer E., ed. *Who's Who and What's What to See in Florida*. Saint Petersburg, Florida: Current Historical Company of Florida, Incorporated, [1935?].

Munroe, Ralph Middleton, and Vincent Gilpin. *The Commodore's Story*. Miami: Historical Association of Southern Florida. 1930.

Nance, Elwood C. ed. *The East Coast of Florida: a History*. Delray Beach, Fla.: The Southern Publishing Company, 1962). Vol. I.

National Cyclopaedia of American Biography. Vols. 12, 14, 43, J. New York: James T. White & Company, 1904.

National Rivers and Harbors Congress (NHRC). *Proceedings*. v.p. 1906-28.

Nelson, Liz. *Newburyport: Stories from the Waterside*. Beverly, Mass.: Commonwealth Editions, 2000.

Newburyport and Amesbury Directory. Boston: Sampson, Murdock & Company, 1891, 1892-3.

New-England Historical and Genealogical Register 39, No. 1 (January 1885).

New-England Historical and Genealogical Register 45, No. 180 (October 1891).

Bibliography

New-England Historical and Genealogical Register 64, No. 253 (January 1910).

New-England Historical and Genealogical Register 66, No. 264 (October 1912).

New York Times. Various dates.

Nielsen, George R. *The Danish Americans.* Boston: G. K. Hall & Co., 1981.

Oberholtzer, Ellis Paxson. *Jay Cooke: Financier of the Civil War.* Vol. 1. Philadelphia: George W. Jacobs & Co., 1907.

O'Brien, Robert E. *Florida Coast Line Canal and Transportation Co.: Report on its Property and Prospects.* 9 February 1885. Copy, Fort Lauderdale Historical Society, Ft. Lauderdale, Fla.

Official Program: 1851, City of Newburyport Fiftieth Anniversary. Newburyport, Mass.: Newburyport Daily News, [1901?]

Paddison, O. H. "A History of the Steamboats in Operation on the Indian River as I Remember Them from 1888 to 1895." Richard Porson Paddison Papers, Collection No. 327. East Carolina Manuscript Collection, J. Y. Joyner Library, East Carolina University, Greenville, N.C.

Paine, Albert Bigelow. *In One Man's Life.* New York: Harper & Brothers, 1921.

Palm Beach, County of. Deed Books. West Palm Beach, Fla.

_____. Circuit Court Cases (Chancery), 1910, 1919.

_____. Clerk of Circuit Court.

Palm Beach Post (Palm Beach, Fla.). Various dates.

Parkman, Aubrey. *History of the Waterways of the Atlantic Coast of the United States.* Fort Belvoir, Va.: National Waterways Study, U.S. Army Engineer Water Resources Support Center, Institute for Water Resources; [Washington, D.C.: Supt. of Docs., U.S. GPO, distributor] 1983.

Parsons, John D. *Newburyport: Its Industries, Business Interests and Attractions.* Newburyport, Mass.: William H. Huse & Co., 1887.

Payne, Albert Bigelow. *In One Man's Life: Being Chapters from the Personal & Business Career of Theodore N. Vail.* New York: Harper & Brothers, 1921.

Peters, Eleanor Bradley, comp. *Bradley of Essex County.* New York: The Knickerbocker Press, 1915.

Pomfret, Town of. Probate Records. Pomfret, Connecticut.

Poore, Henry V. *Manual of Railroads of the United States for 1879.* New York: H.V. & H.W. Poor, 1879.

_____. *Manual of Railroads of the United States for 1881.* New York: H.V. & H.W. Poor, 1881.

_____. *Poore's Manual of Railroads, 1885.* New York: H.V. & H.W. Poor, 1885.

Porter, John Addison. "Picturesque Pomfret." *The Connecticut Quarterly*, II, 1 (Jan.-March 1896): 3-24.

Pozzetta, George E. "Foreign Colonies in South Florida, 1865-1910." *Tequesta* 34 (1974): 45-56.

Prince, Richard E. *Atlantic Coast Line Railroad: Steam Locomotives, Ships, and History.* Green River, Wyo.: Richard E. Prince, 1966.

Proctor, Samuel. *Napoleon Bonaparte Broward: Florida's Fighting Democrat.* Gainesville: University of Florida Press, 1950.

Providence (R.I.) Journal. Various dates.

Pumpelly, Raphael. *My Reminiscences.* Vols. 2. New York: Henry Holt and Company, 1918.

Putnam, County of. Clerk of Circuit Court. Palatka, Florida.

Putnam Patriot (Putnam, Conn.). December 19, 1940.

Rae, John Bell. "Federal Land Grants in Aid of Canals." *Journal of Economic History* 4:167-77.

"Railroads and Railroad Construction" [author is identified as "B. F. W."], *DeBow's Review* 19 (Sept. 1855): 316-23.

Read, Henry H. *The Waterways of Florida, Illustrated.* New York: The Read Press, 1921.

Remini, Robert V. *Daniel Webster: The Man and His Time.* New York: W. W. Norton & Company, Inc., 1997.

Rerick, Rowland H. *Memoirs of Florida.* Vol. 1. ed. Francis P. Fleming. Atlanta: The Southern Historical Association, 1902.

Rivers and Harbors Convention. *Proceedings of the Harbor and River Convention: Held at Chicago, July Fifth, 1847.* Chicago: Printed by R. L. Wilson, Daily Journal Office, 1847.

Roach, David. Telephone interviews by author with FIND director (various).

Saint Augustine City Directory (St. Augustine, Fla.), 1885.

Saint Augustine Evening Record (St. Augustine, Fla.). Various dates.

_____. "Saint Augustine, Saint Johns County, Florida, Illustrated." Pictorial ed., 1908.

Saint Augustine Record (St. Augustine, Fla.). Various dates.

St. Johns, County of. Circuit Court Civil Cases. Saint Augustine, Florida.

St. Johns, County of. County Records. Saint Augustine, Florida.

St. Johns, County of. Mortgage Books. Saint Augustine, Florida.

St. Johns, County of. Miscellaneous Books. Saint Augustine, Florida.

St. Johns, County of. Satisfaction of Mortgage Books. Saint Augustine, Florida.

Sanford Daily Herald (Sanford, Fla.) . Various dates.

Saunders, William H. "The Wreck of Houseboat No. 4, October 1906." *Tequesta* 19 (1959):15-21.

Sawyer, Albert P. Papers (SP). State Library of Florida, Tallahassee, Florida.

Sawyer, Eleanor Grace. *Sawyer Families of New England, 1636-1900.* Strafford, N.H.: Eleanor G. Sawyer, 1995.

Scott, Patrick, ed. with notes. "The Hunt in Florida: The Senie Douthit Letter." *Broward Legacy* 21, nos. 1-2 (winter/spring 1998):2-18.

Shallat, Todd. *Structures in the Stream: Water, Science and the Rise of the U. S. Army Corps of Engineers.* Austin: University of Texas Press, 1994.

Bibliography

Shappee, Nathan D. "The Celestial Railroad to Juno." *Florida Historical Quarterly* 40, no. 4 (April 1962): 329-49.

Shaw, Ronald E. *Canals for a Nation: the Canal Era in the United States, 1790-1860.* Lexington: The University Press of Kentucky, 1990.

Shofner, Jerrell H. *Nor Is It Over Yet: Florida in the Era of Reconstruction, 1863-1877.* The University Presses of Florida, Gainesville: 1974.

Simister, Florence Parker. *The First Hundred Years.* Providence: Rhode Island Hospital Trust Company, 1967.

Skillman, Harry B., ed. *Compiled General Laws of Florida,* 1929. Atlanta: The Harrison Company, 1929, compact ed.

Smith, E. V. et al. *Souvenir Edition of The Philomusian: The Historical Background of Guzman Hall.* Providence: Providence College, n.d.

Social Index of Winter Residents and Visitors to Palm Beach - Miami Beach and Other Florida Resorts, 1937. Palm Beach: Social Index Association, Inc., 1937.

Springfield (Mass.) *Daily Republican.* Various dates.

Springfield Today. New York Industrial Recorder, comp., 1898. Connecticut Valley Historical Museum (Springfield, Mass.).

State Street Trust Company. *Some Industries of New England.* Boston, 1923.

Stevens, Wallace B. *The Log of the Alton.* Saint Louis: Printed by the Voyagers, 1909. Tulane University Library, New Orleans, Louisiana.

Stiber, Linda S., Eusman, Elmer, and Albro, Sylvia, "The Triumphal Arch and the Large Triumphal Carriage of Maximilian I: Two oversized, multi-block, 16th-century Woodcuts from the Studio of Albrecht Durer." *The Book and Paper Group Annual.* The American Institute of Conservation. 14 (1995) (online).

"Sunset Colonies: Fair Oaks and Olive Park in the heart of California." Chicago: Howard & Wilson Publishing Co., ca. 1895 [pamphlet].

Tallahassee Democrat (Tallahassee, Fla.). Various dates. See, also *Weekly True Democrat.*

Tatler (St. Augustine, Fla.). Various dates

Taylor, Abram Morris. Papers (TP). Alma Clyde Field Library of Florida History, Florida Historical Society, Cocoa, Florida.

Thomas, Alan G. *Great Books and Collectors.* New York: G. P Putnam's Sons, 1975.

Thompson, S. A. "The Ups and Downs of Waterways," *National Waterways* 8 (September 1929).

Titusville, Fla. *Florida Star.* Various dates.

Titusville, Fla. *Advocate.* Various dates.

Titusville, Fla. *Star Advocate.* Various dates.

Twentieth Century Biographical Dictionary of Notable Americans. See, Johnson, Rossiter, ed.

Tropical Sun (Juno, Fla.). Various dates.

Tropical Sun (West Palm Beach, Fla.). Various dates.

U. S. Army. *Army Register for January, 1881.*

Army Register for January, 1884.

Corp of Engineers. *The Intracoastal Waterway, Boston, Massachusetts to the Rio Grande.* October 1936.

The Intracoastal Waterway: Part I - Atlantic Section. November 1940.

Annual Report of the Chief of Engineers, 1900 (Part 3), 1930 (Part I).

U. S. *Census of Agriculture.* 1880.

Congress. House. *Intracoastal Waterway, Beaufort, N.C., to Key West, Fla., Section,* 63rd Congress, 1st session, House Document 229 ("H. Doc. 229").

Congress. House. *Intracoastal Waterway from Jacksonville, Fla. to Miami, Florida.* 69th Congress, 2d session, 1926. House Document 586 ("H. Doc. 586").

Congress. Senate. *Letter from the Secretary of War transmitting copy of report from Lieut. Col. Q. A. Gillmore, Corps of Engineers, upon a survey of Indian River, Florida, with a view to opening a passage to the Mosquito Lagoon, by way of the Haulover, January 4, 1882,* 47th Cong., 1st Session, Senate Ex. Doc. No. 33.

Department of Commerce. U. S. Coast and Geodetic Survey. *Inside Route Pilot: New York to Key West.* 3rd ed. Washington D.C.: GPO, 1916.

Inland Waterways Commission. *Preliminary Report of the Inland Waterways Commission.* Washington, D.C.: GPO, 1908.

Military Academy. *Cadet Application Papers,* 1805-1866. Archives Microfilm Publication 688.

The Centennial of the United States Military Academy at West Point. Vol. 1. Washington, D.C.: GPO, 1904.

Van Orsdel, Ralph A. "History of the Telephone System in the District of Columbia." In *Records of the Columbia Historical Society of Washington, D. C., 1946-1947,* Vols. 48-49, edited by H. Paul Caemerrer. Washington, D. C.: Columbia Historical Society, 1949.

Vero Press (Vero Beach, Fla.). Various dates.

Vero Beach Press-Journal (Vero Beach, Fla.). Various dates.

Volkmer, Roland. E-mail (in German) from senior clerk in charge of Freiberg University (Mining Academy) archives to author, 22 June 2000.

Volusia, County of. Circuit Court Civil Cases. 1928.

Wallace, John F., J. A. Ockerman, and W. J. Karner. "Elmer Lawrence Corthell, President, Am. Soc. C. E." *Transactions of the American Society of Civil Engineers* 81 (1917): 1658-63.

Wallace, W. Stewart. *The MacMillan Dictionary of Canadian Biography.* 3rd ed. New York: MacMillan, 1963.

Walsh, J. Leigh. *Connecticut Pioneers in Telephony: The Origin and Growth of the Telephone Industry in Connecticut.* New Haven, Conn.: Morris F. Tyler Chapter, Telephone Pioneers of America, 1950.

Warner, Ezra J. *Generals in Blue: Lives of the Union Commanders.* Louisiana State University Press, 1964.

Washburn, Wilcomb E. *The Cosmos Club of Washington: A Centennial History, 1878-1978.* Washington, D.C.: The Cosmos Club of Washington, 1978.

Bibliography

Washington Star (Washington, D.C.). Various dates.

Washington Times (Washington, D.C.). Various dates.

Watson, Phyllis A. "John Humphrey Small and the Development of the Atlantic Intracoastal Waterway, 1899-1921." Unpublished master's thesis, East Carolina University, 1971.

Weekly True Democrat (Tallahassee, Fla.). Various dates. See, also *Tallahassee Democrat.*

Wheat, Max. "Florida Waterways Offer Cruise of Enchantment." *F. I. N. D. Newsletter* 3, no. 2 (April 1949).

Whitman, Alice. "Transportation in Territorial Florida." *Florida Historical Quarterly* 17, No. 1 (July 1938): 25-

Who Was Who in America. Vols. 2, 3, and 5 (1943-1950; 1951-1960; 1969-1973). Chicago: The A. N. Marquis Company, 1963.

Wiggins, Larry. "The Birth of the City of Miami," *Tequesta* 55 (1995):5-38.

Williamson, Virginia S. interview by Rose Shepherd, 27 February 1940. *Manuscripts from the Federal Writers' Project, 1936-1940.* Library of Congress, Washington, D.C.

Wilson, James Grant Wilson and John Fiske, ed. *Appleton's Cyclopaedia of American Biography.* New York: Appleton, 1888.

Windham County (Conn.) *Observer*, 15 January 1919.

Work, Henry H. "George Lathrop [sic] Bradley and the War over Ritalin." *Cosmos Club Journal.* Washington, D.C.: Cosmos Club, 2001

Yorke, Dane. *Able Men of Boston.* Boston: Boston Manufacturers Mutual Fire Insurance Company, 1950.

Youngberg, Gilbert A. Papers (YP). Manuscript Collection. Rollins College, Winter Park, Florida.

_____. "The East Coast Canal." *Florida Banker* 7 (September 1931):5-30.

_____. "Water Transportation and an Intracoastal Waterway from Jacksonville to Miami." [1925?]. Copy, Florida Collection, Jacksonville (Fla.) Public Library.

Ziemba, Caroline Pomeroy. *Martin County, Our Heritage: A Historiography.* Stuart: Stuart Heritage, Inc., 1997

INDEX

INDEX

V

Vero Beach, Fla., 181, 250, 295, 311-312, 323, 337

Volco Cypress Co., 315

W

Walker, Edward M. (ca. 1845-1905) (Springfield, Mass., Florida canal co. investor), 66, 70, 71- 72, 80-81, 85, 87, 90, 103, 106-08, 111, 112, 113, 115, 120-122, 125-127, 133, 135-136, 142, 143, 146-147, 153-156, 159, 173, 184, 284, 286

Walker Land Trust, 105-106, 119

Waterways, U. S., 'free waterways' policy, xiii, xix, xx-xxi; early conventions assemble, at Memphis, Tenn., xxii-xxiii, at Chicago, Ill., xxiii; Roosevelt appoints Inland Waterways Commission, 194

Waterway, Florida, construction begins, 16; O'Brien survey, 21; Corthell survey, 29-33; Indian River stretch abandoned to U.S. government, 58; completed, 257; sold to Kelsey, 309; Kelsey sells to FIND, 333

Webster, Daniel (1782-1852) (U. S. senator), xxiii

Westcott, James Diament, Jr., 8-9

Westcott, John Diament (1807-1889), life of, 10-12 (12); 15, 18, 21, 27

West Palm Beach, Fla., 62, 66, 79, 106-110, 129, 134, 139, 148-150, 154-155, 164-165, 170, 172, 175, 186, 236-237, 250-251, 261, 266, 269, 272, 275, 286, 291, 294-295, 302, 310, 314, 320

Wheeler, (Col.) Earl, 306, 317-318, 326

White City, Fla., 60-62, 70, 84, 99, 102, 127, 139, 342

White, Pleasants W. (1820-1919), 9, 18, 34, 60

Wilde, Arthur, 339

Williams, Hiram Smith (1833-1921), 129-131, 269

Wilson and Howard Publishing Co., 114, 137

Wombwell, Lucius B., (Fla. commissioner of agriculture, 1897-1901), 34-35

Wright, (Gen.) Horatio Governeur (1820-1899), 3, 4, 6-8, 23, 338

Wright, James O. (Florida engineer), 243, 245

Wrotnowski, Arthur Fancis (1839-1911), 28-30, 32

X

Y

Young, Anthony ("Tony") W. (1865-1948) (Indian River County FIND commissioner and state senator), 318, 321, 323, 325

Youngberg, (Col.) Gilbert Albin (1875-1962), 298-300, 306, 314-315, 317, 326-329, 332, 337

Z